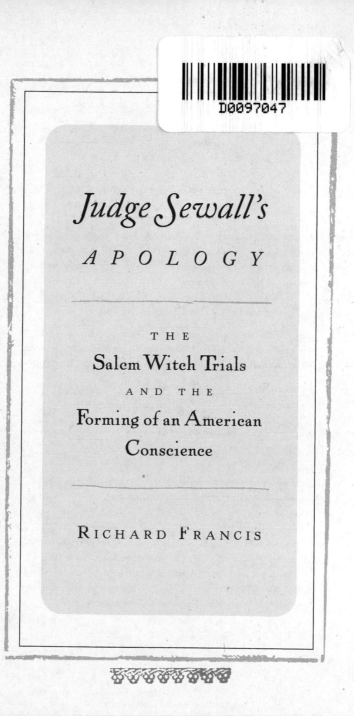

Judge Sewall's
APOLOGY

THE

Salem Witch Trials

AND THE

Forming of an American Conscience

RICHARD FRANCIS

HARPER ● PERENNIAL

A hardcover edition of this book was published in 2005
by Fourth Estate, an imprint of HarperCollins Publishers.

HarperCollins books may be purchased for educational, business, or sales
promotional use. For information please write: Special Markets Department,
HarperCollins Publishers, 10 East 53rd Street, New York, NY 10022.

FIRST HARPER PERENNIAL EDITION PUBLISHED 2006.

Book design by Barbara M. Bachman

THE LIBRARY OF CONGRESS HAS CATALOGUED
THE HARDCOVER EDITION AS FOLLOWS:

Francis, Richard.
  Judge Sewall's apology : the Salem witch trials and the forming of an American
conscience / Richard Francis.
    p. cm.
  ISBN 0-00-716362-2
  1. Sewall, Samuel, 1652–1730.   2. Sewall, Samuel, 1652–1730—Ethics.
3. Puritans—Massachusetts—Biography.   4. Judges—Massachusetts—Biography.
5. Merchants—Massachusetts—Biography.   6. Massachusetts—History—Colonial
period, ca. 1600–1775.   7. Trials (Witchcraft)—Massachusetts—Salem—History—
17th century.   8. Salem (Mass.)—History—Colonial period, ca. 1600–1775.
        I. Title.

        F67.S525   2005
        974.4'02'092—dc22
        [B]   2004065353

    ISBN-10: 0-00-716363-0 (pbk.)
    ISBN-13: 978-0-00-716363-2 (pbk.)

06 07 08 09 10 ❖ / RRD 10 9 8 7 6 5 4 3 2 1

To Jo

"Francis is a guide we quickly come to trust. . . . He enriches the religious and political context of the trials, and gives the suspects faces and voices."
—*Providence Journal*

"Before the eighteenth-century Founding Fathers came the seventeenth-century New England Puritans. They were a strange and wonderful tribe, bewitched or otherwise. In this superb study, Francis brings them back to life."
—James Grant, author of
John Adams, Party of One

"A sensitive and scholarly rendering with far-reaching perspectives that bring Sewall off the page. . . . [A] fresh, insightfully written examination of how colonial Puritanism's core beliefs and ragged edges produced its most ungodly legacy."
—*Kirkus Reviews* (starred review)

"A timely and disturbing book. Francis draws no contemporary parallels but it is hard to ignore the implications of the early ingrained vision he explores here with such lucidity: a threat of nameless, invisible, omnipresent terror so menacing that it overrides the rule of law and legitimizes extremes of violence or torture in the name of the invincibly righteous, pure, and innocent American people."
—*Daily Telegraph*

Claire McName

About the Author

RICHARD FRANCIS is a biographer, historian
of American culture, and novelist. He was an
American Studies Research Fellow at Harvard,
and taught American literature at the universities
of Missouri and Manchester. He is now Professor
of Creative Writing at Bath Spa University in
England.

HARPER PERENNIAL

NEW YORK • LONDON • TORONTO • SYDNEY

Contents

LIST OF ILLUSTRATIONS   xi

INTRODUCTION   xiii

Part One
AMERICAN TRAGEDY

Part Two
AMERICAN COMEDY

LIST OF ILLUSTRATIONS

Introduction

✿✿✿

SAMUEL SEWALL WAS ONE OF THE NINE JUDGES APPOINTED to hear the Salem witch trials in 1692; five years later he stood up in church in front of fellow members of the congregation while the minister read out his apology. None of his colleagues on the bench followed suit.

For all of us, it's difficult to say we're sorry. An apology means repudiating an aspect of our past selves; in that way it's like a little suicide. And those in public life find it almost impossible ever to admit they have made mistakes and errors of judgment. They fear doing so will suggest weakness and unreliability, a poor capacity for decision making, ultimately a fatal crack in the facade of leadership. There's particular poignancy in the case of a judge. A person whose job it is to supervise the passing of a verdict on other people switches that responsibility clear around, like a soldier suddenly pointing his rifle at himself.

But there is another way of looking at it. Apology can be a creative act. It can liberate both an individual and his or her society. Apology frees you from the past and gives access to the future. It allows a person to evolve in response to the shifting demands of life. It requires an ability to inspect and evaluate your actions as if from the outside, and demands a high degree of courage and honesty. Apology can be heroic.

Though Sewall's apology was an act of individual courage and integrity, I believe it also marks one of those moments when something shifts in the status quo, when you can catch a culture in the act of rethinking itself, when you feel you are present at one of the birth pangs of the modern world. The witchcraft crisis went out of control so quickly and became so harrowing precisely because those concerned thought it represented a major threat to the very existence of their society, and in a sense they were right. Their belief in a homogeneous Puritan community, "saints in light" supporting each other in a dark and fallen world, was about to be proved untenable. The terrible events that began in the Parris parsonage in Salem Village were ultimately brought about by anxiety that the whole of the Christian adventure in the New England wilderness had been based on a superannuated dream; ironically, the outcome of the crisis confirmed that diagnosis. The witch trials represented a last-ditch attempt to continue to see the world as a simple allegorical struggle between the forces of good and evil, God and Satan. But a more relativistic and psychological way of assessing and accounting for the drama of human life was becoming necessary. In following Sewall's story, we can see how he learned that lesson. At the same time, his own vision of the millennial future of America, one that rested on the ultimate reconciliation of whites and Native Americans, was, if anything, actually strengthened by the trauma of the witchcraft crisis.

Sewall's story is richer and more detailed than that of any other colonial American. The diary he left behind provides sufficient material to re-create the most rounded human being (in more senses than one) of all the New England Puritans. It teems with the detail of daily experience. We are given access to a man whose life is public and private, comic and tragic—someone with a finger in every pie. We can get to know his hopes and fears, even his dreams. He cries in sympathy with his children, chases pirates along the New England coast, tucks into large meals (lots of these), and enjoys the sights and sounds of England as the first American tourist (at least, the first to leave behind a record of his experiences). Sewall gives us a warm human alternative to our general impression of beetle-browed Puritans fiercely disapproving of all and sundry. Three hundred years ago he was schooling a Native American boy in his own house for entry to Harvard. He penned one of the first attacks on the institution of slavery ever written in English. He was a loving husband and father, a diplomat, a politician, a poet, an anti-slavery agitator, an advocate for Indian land rights, a utopian theorist, a merchant, a judge, a campaigner against the wearing of periwigs, a friend and confidant of people from every section of colonial New England society—and, finally, a gallant wooer of respectable Boston widows. We can observe in wonderful close-up the four courtships (and two marriages) he undertook in the last years of his life, experiences that are sad, funny, and rich. Here are the most subtle and significant of all the consequences of the witchcraft crisis.

As Sewall captures the unpredictability of the women he woos, trying to interpret their words and gestures, the way they tend the fire and arrange their furniture, the significance of the snacks and drinks they offer, he shows how he has learned the lesson of the trials, and developed a respect for the hidden mysteries of the heart and the psychological intricacy underlying human actions. Somehow, by the end of his life, the former witchcraft judge had made himself into a recognizably modern man. His life had a coherent development, with all its varied and dramatic elements contributing to a single, moving story.

I have not modernized spelling and punctuation in my quotations. On the rare occasions where the meaning is obscure or ambiguous, I have glossed it in square brackets. The "y" in such words as "y^e" is the Old English letter thorn, and is pronounced as "th." I normally refer to Native Americans as Indians because it seems more important to be reminded of a past perspective than to superimpose a later one. I have, however, used the modern calendar in giving dates, in order to avoid muddle. In Great Britain and its colonies, it didn't officially supplant the Julian one (which began the year on 25 March) until 1752, long after Sewall's death, though people of his time contrived to inhabit both systems at once. They celebrated the New Year as we do, on 1 January; and in giving dates between then and late March, Sewall would express the year as $\frac{1702}{1703}$.

The English colonists in North America used the currency of their mother country—pounds, shillings, and pence—though a shortage of specie developed because of England's unwillingness to allow precious metals to leave its shores, and for some years Massachusetts produced its own silver coinage (the mint master being John Hull, Sewall's father-in-law). Spanish pieces of eight (that is, silver coins worth eight reals) were also in circulation, worth around six English shillings. The buying power of a pound in Sewall's day was perhaps a hundred times greater than that of one pound sterling today.

It's worth mentioning some slightly different uses of honorifics in Sewall's lifetime. Men and women of the artisan class were often referred to as goodman and goodwife (or goody). As it happens, Sewall himself makes little use of those terms, but they are very common in the documentation of the Salem witch trials. Middle-class women, whether married or not, were referred to as mistress (often abbreviated to Mrs.) and women of high social status were called madam. Clergymen were usually known as master or mister (they normally had the degree of master of arts), abbreviated to Mr. Only in the last twenty years of his life did Sewall get into the habit of calling them reverend.

I am grateful to the following for helping me to tell this story: the Arts and Humanities Research Council for an award under their Research Leave Scheme; Bath Spa University College for matching it and for providing travel funds; Arts Council England for giving me one of their Writer's Awards of 2003, which I used in part to help fund my research in the United States; Peter Drummey, Kimberly Nusco, Megan Milford, and the rest of the staff of the Massachusetts Historical Society for all their help and kindness to me and my wife while we consulted the Sewall Papers and other resources in that marvelous collection; Bath Spa University College Library; the Boston Public Library, and particularly Eric P. Frazier of the Rare Books and Manuscripts Department; the British Library; the Essex Institute in Salem, Massachusetts; the Harvard University Libraries; the Massachusetts Archives; the John Rylands University Library of Manchester; and Yale University Library. In 2002, I had the opportunity to try out my interpretation of the Salem witch crisis when I gave the Les Arnold Memorial Lecture at Bath Spa University College, and presented papers at the Oxford University American Studies Research Seminar and the Bath Royal Literary and Scientific Institution. I am grateful to the Massachusetts

Historical Society, the Massachusetts Archives, the Boston Public Library, and the Baker Library of Harvard University for allowing me to quote from unpublished manuscripts in their collections.

The following people gave me various kinds of advice, support, and hospitality: Gareth Davies, Philip Davies, Jean Day, Barry Day, Jeffrey Denton, Will Francis, Helen Francis, Ian Gadd, Victor Gray, Tessa Hadley, Richard Kerridge, Peter Marshall, Paul Meyer, Tim Middleton, H. Vern Noyes (descendant of a family Sewall knew well and proprietor of a gas station next to the old Sewall property in what is now Newburyport), Anthea Reilly, Gene Reilly, David Shepherd, David Timms, and Ian Walker. I am particularly indebted to my friend Boyd Schlenther, who read and annotated a draft of this book with great care. He is not, however, responsible for errors and infelicities that remain—nor indeed are any of those who have given me help and advice. I'm hugely grateful to my agent, Caroline Dawnay, to Alex Elam, and to my editors, Christopher Potter, Mitzi Angel, and Courtney Hodell. My wife, Jo, has worked full-time on the project with me, acting as researcher and adviser at every stage. The book is dedicated to her, with my love.

Part One

AMERICAN TRAGEDY

...

*A*ND I LOOKED, and behold a pale horse:
and his name that sat on him was Death,
and Hell followed with him...

—REVELATION 6:8

*T*HERE IS NO OTHER Verse in the Bible that doth so
pathetically, and with so much amplitude & Variety,
foretell the Destruction of Mankind. And yet nothing
less would have made an Adequat Representation of the
Blood & Slaughter of America.

—SAMUEL SEWALL, MARGINAL COMMENT
ON REVELATION 6:8 IN *Annotations Upon All
the Books of the Old and New Testament*,
BY MÉRIC CASAUBON ET AL.

CHAPTER ONE

The Shaggy Dog

DURING HIS ADULT LIFE, SAMUEL SEWALL WOULD BE HAUNTED by an image in the book of Revelation: an angel, with a rainbow on his head, is standing with an open book in his hand. The angel plants one foot on the sea and the other on the earth. Sewall came to interpret that stance as meaning that the angel was straddling Europe (the earth) and America (the land discovered in the middle of the sea), and from that reading he derived a glorious vision of America's destiny. Perhaps one of the reasons why the picture had such imaginative power for him was that it seemed to sum up his own condition, from the moment of his birth, as someone with a foothold in both the Old World and the New.

Samuel Sewall was born on 28 March 1652, in the Hampshire village of Bishop Stoke, a little north of Southampton, before dawn on a Sunday. It gave him pleasure to reflect later that Sabbath light was the first to enter his eyes, as if it provided a spiritual basis to everything he subsequently saw.

North America, as a European settlement, was less than half a century old, New England not much more than a quarter of a century, but already this child born in Hampshire had roots there. The Pilgrim Fathers had crossed the Atlantic on the *Mayflower* in 1620 and settled in Plymouth, just to the west of Cape Cod; ten years later, a fleet of ships led by the *Arbella* brought a company of Puritans under the leadership of John Winthrop to build a community in a natural harbor that they called Boston, and establish the Massachusetts Bay colony. Only five years after that, Sewall's father, Henry Sewall, arrived. He brought "English servants . . . Cattel and Provisions sutable for a new Plantation" across the Atlantic with him, and took a grant of five hundred acres in the settlement of Newbury, on the northern edge of Massachusetts Bay.

The immigrants had come across the ocean for reasons of conscience: the desire to practice their faith without harassment from authorities wanting them to conform to orthodox Anglicanism. But they also had to make a living, and those who'd invested in their adventure wanted to make a profit—mixed motives from the start, though both elements reinforced community values and the need to make order out of chaos. John Winthrop gave a sermon as the *Arbella* made its way over the ocean toward the New World. He didn't evoke the vast wilderness to which he and his party were heading but instead pictured the future result of their efforts, an exemplary city on a hill, which others would look up to as an example of spirituality and civic harmony: "wee must be knit together in this worke as one man . . . always haveing before our eyes our Commission and Community in this worke, our Community as members of the same body." As John Eliot, the great minister to the Indians, would put it, "for as hell is a place of confusion, so heaven of order."

However, despite this need for cooperation on both spiritual and material planes, certain other settlers were less orderly. It was a raw, challenging environment, attracting its share of adventurers and misfits. As early as 1627, one colonist had attempted to set up an alternative community at Merry Mount, where members got drunk, danced round a maypole, and hobnobbed with the Indians.

Henry Sewall was only twenty when he arrived in America, and the cattle and provisions represented a family investment. He'd been sent by his father, Henry Sewall Sr., who joined him a year later. The latter's motive in organizing this family upheaval seems to have been the standard blend of practical and spiritual reasons: farming on the one hand, a "dislike to the English Hierarchy" (that is, of the existence of bishops in the Anglican church), on the other. But though the Sewalls were descended from a long line of successful merchants and community leaders (several of them were mayors of Coventry), and though the prevailing culture among fellow Puritans in the early settlement was of sobriety and austerity, Henry Sewall Sr. was immune to the civic respectability that these combined traditions brought with them.

He was a rough, individualistic, cantankerous sort of settler, with an undercurrent of violence. His father left a will asking him to admit his misbehavior toward his mother; his mother left one forgiving him but cutting him off with only a shilling. Almost as soon as he arrived in Newbury, he arranged a legal separation from his second wife, Ellen (Samuel Sewall was the grandson of her predecessor, Anne), and three years later he appeared before a grand jury on a charge of beating her. He got into trouble with the law for other reasons too, including contemptuous speech and carriage to Richard Saltonstall, one of the leaders of the colony, and was bound over in the sum of £66 13s. 8d. He seemed to have a problem with hierarchy in general, not just that of the English church. After a row about whether the Newbury meetinghouse should be moved from its site (conveniently near to his own house on Newbury's Lower Green), he moved out in high dudgeon, went across the river, and settled in Rowley, where in due course he was in trouble again, for disturbing worship and arguing with the pastor at the Rowley meetinghouse. Rumor had it that he was slightly deranged. He was a brooding, difficult man of the frontier, while order was being asserted around him in the face of the wilderness.

No such problems are evident with respect to Henry Sewall Jr., though he was once fined a shilling for missing a town meeting. His cattle farming went well, and he accepted new grants of land as pasture over the years. In 1646, he was married to Jane Dummer by Richard Saltonstall, the man Henry Sr. had insulted six years earlier (for the Puritans, marriage was a secular state, not a sacramental one, and therefore weddings in those early days were conducted by magistrates, rather than ministers).

Jane's parents had had enough of the climactic extremes of New England, and decided to return to England the following winter; the newlyweds went with them. Charles I had surrendered to the New Model Army, and under Cromwell's protectorate there was no longer any pressing reason for dissenters to go to, or remain on, the other side of the Atlantic. Indeed, many Puritan pastors were appointed in England at short notice, and Henry Sewall Jr. became one of them, despite the fact that he hadn't received the education normally required for the ministry.

During his childhood in the late 1650s, Samuel Sewall might have picked up some sense from his parents of a cultural identity that no one in history could have experienced before: being an American exile in England. What he actually remembered about this period of his life was the way his mother looked after him—"she lavish'd away many Thousands of Words upon me, before I could return one word in Answer"—and the beginnings of his education at Romsey Grammar School. But detail is sparse: he left for America when he was nine. Of course, we can go in search of what we don't remember as well as for what we do; in 1688, when he was thirty-six, Sewall set out to spend a year in England, and during that time he would engage in two contrasting occupations—rediscovering his mother country, and trying to free his colony from her clutches as far as was possible.

Irascible Henry Sr. died in 1657, and Sewall's father went back to America to claim the estate. Henry Jr. was a man of some importance by then as he carried with him a letter from Richard Cromwell, who had succeeded his father as lord protector of England, asking the governor and magistrates of Massachusetts Bay to enable him to settle his affairs speedily so that he could return to his ministry at North Baddesley. Shortly afterward, however, the Commonwealth collapsed, and Henry Jr. decided to remain in Massachusetts, resume his farming and business pursuits, and call his family over to him.

The middle-aged Sewall vividly remembered his nine-year-old self setting out on his great journey to the New World. The weather was dramatic and the moment portentous: ". . . being at Bishop Stoke and Baddesly, April 23, 1661, the day of the Coronation of K. Charles the 2^d, the Thunder and Lightening of it." Sewall's journals are rich in weather—porridges of snow, drisky rain; he was a man who scanned the sky for rainbows, those bridges between the old dispensation and the one to come, between earth and heaven, signs of God's blessing. On this early occasion, the storm—at least as he evoked it retrospectively—

marked the end of Puritan hopes in Britain and provided a dramatic fanfare for his long journey to America, a pilgrim son following in the footsteps of the fathers: "Quickly after[,] my Mother went to Winchester with 5 small Children, Hannah, Samuel, John, Stephen and Jane; there to be in readiness for the Pool Waggons."

He recalled the details of parting, one uncle in tears, another giving the children raisins and almonds (a snack Sewall loved all his life). Then the voyage: "We were about Eight Weeks at Sea, where we had nothing to see but Water and the Sky: so that I began to fear I should never get to Shoar again." The nervous boy contrived a shrewd antidote to panic: if there wasn't a good chance of a safe arrival, he told himself, then the captain and crew, grown-ups who could make their own decisions, would never have agreed to come on the voyage in the first place.

The *Prudent Mary* arrived in Boston harbor on 6 July 1661, a Saturday evening—the beginning of the Sabbath as far as Puritans were concerned—and therefore the ship's company decided not to fire cannon to announce their arrival. To their annoyance, the Castle, a protective fortress built on an island in the harbor, boomed out its greeting anyway, wrong-footing them. The family found lodgings while they waited for Sewall's father to make his way down from Newbury to collect them. Then they traveled up the coast by boat and Sewall was brought ashore in a canoe, his American initiation.

Years later, as he tried to recover from the greatest crisis of his life, the Salem witchcraft trials, and find again his confidence in and love for the world, he would evoke his boyhood haunts in Newbury and its surroundings in the most lyrical prose achieved by any colonial American: Plum Island being pounded by the Atlantic Ocean; seabirds patrolling the coast; the fish-rich Merrimack River; cattle grazing on the sloping meadows by Turkey Hill; Old Town Hill beyond, dotted with sheep and looking down on the Parker River and the fertile marshland that bordered it, with its corn and barley and white oak trees. This was home, because his parents had been married there and his grandfather was buried nearby, but it was also a promised land, achieved after a frightening ocean voyage.

For those Puritans crossing the Atlantic from the Old World to the

New, a spiritual journey across real geography, there would have been some analogy with the journey of the soul itself, from the material world to the heavenly. For Sewall, Newbury was at least a village, if not a city, on a hill, bathed in that Sabbath radiance his eyes had been born to see, a place from which the saints could be translated into light. He would one day be the first American publisher of *The Pilgrim's Progress*, and in his own journey, like those of the previous generation, he recapitulated that giant stride of the angel in Revelation toward a millennial destiny.

Newbury was a town of fewer than fifty households, each of which stood on its own four-acre site so that the community as a whole could not be overwhelmed in a sudden Indian attack. Relations between settlers and Indians were relatively peaceful during the early years of the European colonization of New England—indeed, Indians had taught the whites some of their farming methods and established alliances with them, even while their own rights and titles to land were being undermined. There had been small-scale skirmishes and acts of aggression on both sides, but only one major explosion of hostilities, the Pequot War of 1636–37.

That conflict was triggered by the killing of a number of English traders and adventurers: in retaliation, the Massachusetts Bay military leader, John Endecott, led a raid on Pequot territory; the tribe hit back in turn, killing and capturing some of the settlers; and a short, brutal war ensued, with the result that the Pequots were decimated, more than seven hundred men, women, and children being killed. About four hundred of these were massacred when a force composed of troops from the Massachusetts Bay and Plymouth colonies, along with Narragansett Indians who had allied themselves with the English, set fire to one of their villages, trapping the inhabitants. The Plymouth governor, William Bradford, described the carnage: "It was a fearfull sight to see them thus frying in ye fyer, and ye streams of blood quenching ye same, and horrible was ye stink & sente there of."

No further major conflict took place until the outbreak of King Philip's War, when Sewall was in his twenties. But all the settlers were aware that beyond their fields and houses, the forests contained people whose culture and values seemed to threaten the very basis of Puritan belief. When the Pequot War had broken out, the settlers assumed two things: that they were being punished for their own loss of faith, and that the Indians were the servants of Satan, determined to thwart the Christian community. This cross-reference from guilt to blame would reappear in a potent and disastrous form during the Salem witchcraft trials later in the century.

There were wolves in the forest too, and their heads were nailed as trophies to the door of the Newbury meetinghouse, for a bounty of 10s. apiece. The township was dwarfed by the scale of the wilderness stretching away on one side of it, and of the ocean on the other. Surrounded by a threatening landscape, putting their faith in a sometimes fierce and always relentless God, the inhabitants of Newbury must have been subject to stress, anxiety, and emotional turbulence, even if (unlike Sewall's grandfather) they hadn't actually brought such baggage to America with them. But one can overstate the extent of conflict and tension. Only seven years after the Pequot War, a certain Native American by the name of John Indian owned property in the town. Certainly, the grown-up Sewall looked back on a spiritual community, a nurturing environment ("In Peace profound our River Run / ... Herbs, Trees, Fowls, Fishes, Beasts, and Men, / Refresh'd were by this goodly Stream"), and a stimulating education.

Newbury was too small to merit a proper grammar school, but the village pastor, Thomas Parker, took responsibility for the education of the village boys anyway. He was formidably well qualified for the task of preparing children for Harvard, having studied at Oxford, Dublin, and Leyden Universities, and taken the degree of master of philosophy at the Franeker University in Holland. Parker was very much the community's father figure, and had given the settlers their first sermon on the banks of that profoundly peaceful river that would, in due course, be named after him. The town itself was too, indirectly at least, because its name commemorated the fact that Parker's first ministry had been in England's Newbury.

He was Sewall's "dear master" and gave him a lifelong taste for writing Latin and English verse, and for singing the psalms. Parker was famed for the sweetness of his voice as well as of his temperament, though that sweetness didn't extend to his own sister, who'd published a little book in London called *Scripture-Prophecies Opened*, predicting the Second Coming on lines rejected by her brother: "Your printing of a Book, beyond the custom of your Sex, doth rankly smell, but the exultation of your self in the way of your opinions, is above all." Theology was definitely not women's work as far as most seventeenth-century Puritans were concerned; in any case there's nothing more vitriolic than a paper battle between utopians. Only the year before, Parker had developed his own millennial history of mankind based on interpretations of the prophecies of Daniel, an image of an imminent spiritual destiny that would have a profound influence on his pupil.

Sewall was a diligent student but enjoyed less austere pleasures too, fishing for pickerel and eyeing the schoolgirls in their "hanging sleeves" as they made their way home from their own lessons. Even on the colonial frontier there were the perennial rites of passage to go through.

In 1667, when he was fifteen, he was able to show he had sufficient Latin and Greek to be accepted by Harvard, and traveled the forty miles down to Cambridge, a separate township on the other side of the Charles River from Boston, to begin seven years of study there.

It was a small, intense community. There were only eleven students in Sewall's class, one of whom was a certain Edward Taylor, who joined the following year, on his arrival from England, but received a year's course remission because he was a twenty-six-year-old former teacher. He and Sewall were "Chamber fellows and bed-fellows" for two years of their studies, an intimacy that lingered on for the rest of their lives, though Sewall settled in Boston while Taylor became pastor at Westfield, very much a frontier community. It was a friendship of opposites who, as it turned out, would become two of colonial America's most important writers: Sewall the social being, utterly at home in his burgeoning town, recording in his diary the rich details of his daily experience in a bold, rounded, transparently readable script; Taylor, passionate introvert in his remote village, meditating on his relationship with the Lord and scribbling crabbed, muscular verse in a crabbed, muscular, almost illegible hand throughout his long ministry (he died in 1729, shortly before Sewall himself). It would be more than a century after Sewall's death before his diary, begun during his Harvard days, would see the light of publication. It would be more than two centuries after Taylor's death that his manuscripts would be discovered in the Yale University Library, and he was retrospectively established as the key poet of the American colonial period.

The Harvard regime promoted a highly regulated life, more aimed at Sewall's age group than Taylor's, with classes at hourly intervals from eight until eleven in the morning, and from two to five in the afternoons. Sewall received his first degree in 1671, and then began studying for his MA. A letter he wrote to a classmate, Daniel Gookin, in 1672, when Sewall was just coming up to his twentieth birthday, gives some idea of American student banter three centuries ago. He was temporarily back home in Newbury because of illness, and replying to news of the college from his friend: "You (I thank you) acted the part of a Comedian in writing to me. But I must return such as the Country affords, . . . ; viz. Tragedies." It's a playful point, and he handles it facetiously, though in fact some of the raw material he communicates is tragic enough. The local midwife had to use an obstetric hook to draw a baby down the birth canal, just like the one "we were wont to lend Pickerill, when we intended to give them a lift towards resigning their watery plain near the West-field." Two local men had died. A friend who had longed for a son for a long time finally had a dead one, "or at least one disputably alive." A witness in a court case had proved to be mentally disturbed: "Here was one, who be[i]ng call'd to give in a Testimony, answered nothing but Ra Ra Ra with great deliberation: which expressions though very pathetical, and figurative; yet to a Civil Judge provd insignificant." His final anecdote is of "Reinord, a base thief" who broke into two of their "houses" and robbed them of "the fellow which should daily mind us in the beginning of the day"; in other words, a fox had made off with the cockerel. This cozy realm of nursery fable seems a long way from those wolves' heads on the meetinghouse door—"Pray enquire," Sewall asks his friend, "of some in the College who have studied Law, whether (if ever we have oportunity to bring him to Trial) We cannot make it Burglary: If we can; He will hardly escape with his Life."

Sewall is straining to amuse a fellow student, but the distinction he makes between his rather haphazard catalog of rural tragedies, and the comedy of a more sophisticated social environment, is a prophetic one. The climax of the first half of his life would be the witch crisis that originated in Salem Village in 1692, twenty years after his letter to Gookin: a rural tragedy indeed. Tragedy implies that individuals are preyed upon by forces more powerful than themselves. This was very much the view of existence Sewall shared with his contemporaries in the 1670s and 1680s, and that would culminate in the trials. Comedy, meanwhile, tends to focus on the interplay of characters in a social context, their misunderstandings, their attempts to learn what makes others tick, their ultimate development. As Sewall moves into middle age we will see a switch of emphasis from the first perspective to the second, from the elemental spiritual drama of the witchcraft to a comedy of manners, of observation and of psychological nuance, while he conducts his late courtships. It's a process that coincides with the growth of the social infrastructure of colonial New England and the increasing secularization of its culture—with a shift from rural to urban values, in fact, and from traditional, almost medieval, ways of thinking to characteristically modern ones. Connecting the two acts of this drama is an overarching apocalyptic vision, in which a bloody and terrible struggle will culminate in the inauguration of the millennium in America.

Sewall was chosen, along with Daniel Gookin, to be one of the three residential fellows of the college for the last year of his studies there—less of an honor than it might have been in more buoyant times because Harvard was in serious decline, with only three men graduating in 1673 and four the following year, by which time just three students remained in residence. In 1674, he presented himself for his MA examination before the president of the college, Leonard Hoar. This was a public occasion, with the candidates giving an oral reply in Latin to a question put to them before invited guests. There was, it turned out, an important member of Sewall's audience on that day: a sixteen-year-old relative of the Harvard president by the name of Hannah Hull. Sewall's question was *An Peccatum Originale sit & Peccatum & Pœna?* (Is original sin both sin and punishment?) He made his case for the affirmative.

Sewall was a devout Puritan for the whole of his life, and this was an issue that takes us to the very heart of his faith. The concept of original sin was seen not merely as referring to the act of Adam and Eve, but as a punishment carrying on through the generations. The Puritans followed Calvin in believing that human beings were innately depraved and unredeemable, save through the intervention of God. From this lowly position we cannot earn God's favor or preempt his will. God is outside history, and therefore has always known whom he has saved or, to use the Puritan verb, elected. When Sewall was at school in Newbury he had recited a catechism that stated this doctrine with uncompromising lucidity:

Q. What is Election?
A. An eternal act of God, whereby he did determine to glorifie
   himself in saving a certain number of persons through Faith
   in Christ.
Q. What is reprobation?
A. An eternal act of God, whereby he did determine to glorifie
   himself in condemning a certain number of persons for their
   sins.

Though salvation coincides with faith and condemnation with sin, God's decisions are made prior to the evidence, so to speak. If this belief is taken to its extreme, it becomes a form of predestinarianism, the antinomian heresy, in which the impossibility of actually *earning* salvation leaves a person no incentive to live a virtuous life.

While we don't know the gist of Sewall's argument, it no doubt followed Puritan orthodoxy. The trick was to reverse the most obvious (but for them blasphemous) system of moral cause and effect: virtue leads to salvation. If salvation comes first, you cannot actually do anything to bring it about. What you can do, however, is to assert that the salvation is appropriate because grace has entered your soul. This process is known as justification. Puritanism was a stressful faith both intellectually and emotionally. At its heart there was the need to run in order to stay put, to prove you have qualified for a dispensation that has already been awarded.

This assertion had to be made in the meetinghouse before the congregation: as God was listening too, a lie would be utterly self-destructive, though a conscientious individual might subsequently be plagued by doubts as to whether he or she had told the truth. Sewall himself would suffer this exact spiritual crisis when he made his own declaration of grace a few years later.

It's an odd arena to modern eyes, the Latin theological polemic, but Sewall obviously shone in it, because he not only achieved his MA but won the heart of his future wife as well. We don't know how he looked as he took the stage, first for his examination, and then for his degree. The only images of him that survive are two very similar portraits painted at the same time as each other, a few months before his death more than half a century later, as if his family had suddenly realized they needed to catch his image before it was too late. It's a fairly hopeless task trying to extrapolate a twenty-two-year-old's face from images of a man of seventy-seven, but he had dark, lustrous eyes (and presumably dark hair), with well-shaped brows and a large, downward-thrusting beak of a nose. His mouth in old age is slightly collapsed through loss of teeth, but he retains a big, strong-looking chin. Sewall was a firm, principled man, with a gentle nature, sensitive to the feelings of others. He was confident for much of the time but could be gauche and awkward too, both socially and physically. He was devout in his faith but loved the good things in life, especially music, food, and drink. By his latter years he had become heavy, but even in middle age he carried a fair amount of weight, yet was fit and active for the whole of his adult life, which suggests he was big-framed, perhaps quite tall.

Some, or all, of these qualities were visible to Hannah, only daughter of the wealthy Boston merchant John Hull, and she immediately "set her Affection" on Sewall, though he himself had no idea of the impact he had made until after they were married, a year and a half later.

After gaining his MA, Sewall went back to live with his parents in Newbury. He had to decide on a profession, and the obvious one in view of his education, and indeed his intellectual and spiritual inclinations, was as a minister of religion. Clearly, it was public knowledge he was

Judge Samuel Sewall (1729), by John Smibert.
Photograph copyright © Museum of Fine Arts, Boston.

leaning in that direction, because on 24 November 1674, his father received a letter from a Captain Pike, of Woodbridge in East Jersey, asking him to persuade his son to become that town's minister. (The Puritans rejected the hierarchical organization of the Church of England in favor of allowing the members of individual meetinghouses to elect their own ministers, which is why they called themselves Congregationalists.) Pike himself, and many of Woodbridge's inhabitants, had moved there from Newbury, so the Sewalls were known to them.

That particular offer didn't appeal, but the possibility remained in Sewall's mind throughout the winter, and was finally put to the test the following April. Thomas Parker, his old teacher, blind and ailing, invited his protégé to help out by giving the afternoon sermon at the Newbury meetinghouse. It wasn't a success. Like many a novice public speaker, Sewall was terrified of drying up too early, and therefore didn't dare look at the clock while he spoke. As a result, "ignorantly and unwittingly," he kept at it for two and a half hours. The Puritans expected substantial sermons, and were prepared to sit through two on Sundays and another during the week on Lecture Day, but this was excessive even by their standards, and Sewall never tried again. Significantly, he made no record of the text he expounded.

The summer of 1675 was an uneasy one for Sewall as he cast about for what to do, now his long years at Harvard were over. It was an uneasy summer generally, full of rumors of imminent hostilities. The consolidation of the settlements, and the pressure westward in search of new agricultural land, demoralized the Indians and threatened the integrity of the tribes and the status of their leaders, the sachems. Inevitably, there was cultural colonialism as well as the political and economic variety.

The Puritans took it for granted that the laws and customs of the Indians were inferior, that their animistic religion was mere superstition and should be replaced by Christianity, if at all possible. Obviously, this could be used as a convenient justification of mercenary forms of exploitation. Sewall marked the following sentence in one of the books in his library, though it was by no means a view he shared himself: "We may with more comfort expect and enjoy the externalls of the Indians, when wee pay them our Spiritualls, for their temporalls, an easie and yet most glorious exchange" (in other words, they get our God, and we get their goods). But it's pointless to demand some kind of anthropological relativism of seventeenth-century Puritans. To assume that their behavior toward Native Americans was simply motivated by hypocrisy, cynicism, and greed is to fail to take on board the historical and cultural context, the structure of belief, which they inhabited—in other words, to be as blinkered in relation to them as they in turn were in relation to the Native Americans.

As far as they were concerned, the biggest favor they could do the Indians, indeed anybody, was to convert them to Christianity, to their own Puritan doctrines. That project had its own kind of idealism, and carried with it an acknowledgment that the Indians were fully human. One of the most revered members of the first generation of Puritans was the "apostle" John Eliot, minister of Roxbury, who devoted his life to missionary work with the Indians. Eliot believed they were descended from the lost tribes of Israel, so that converting them would chime in with the general conversion of the Jews, which in turn would trigger the millennium. This belief would become one of the central preoccupations of Sewall's own life (he visited the eighty-six-year-old Eliot just before he died and was proud to record that the old apostle embraced him and called him "brother"). Most Puritans believed the Second Coming of Christ was imminent. It would take place when the scattered tribes of Jews were reunited and converted to Christianity. A place would be made for them in the glittering New Jerusalem that would then come into being, according to Revelation 21. If the American Indians should prove to be the lost tribes of Israel, then it might well follow that the New World, in geographical and historical terms, might prove to be the New World in redemptive terms as well, the culmination of both earthly and spiritual history, the site of the New Jerusalem. For Eliot, this made the task of converting the Indians one of the utmost urgency: the destination of Christendom might depend on it. As Sewall explained, "Mr.Eliot believ'd the Americans [i.e., the Native Americans] to be of the Ten Tribes; if so, He that shall come will come and will not tarry—here will be a very beauteous Bride, and they will be extream happy who have been any way imployd in wooing Her for Christ."

Eliot had done what he could to further the Second Coming by translating the Bible into Algonquian, the language of the northeastern

Indians, a task he completed in 1658; it was published in 1663, one of the most extraordinary cultural achievements of colonial America. Eliot himself was by no means impervious to the danger of colonial complacency. In one of his books, he has a converted Indian named Piambohou explaining to members of his tribe that "When we exhort you to pray, and to serve the God of the English, we call you to imitate the virtues and good wayes of the English, wherein you shall be acceptable to the Lord: We do not call you to imitate their sins, whereby they and you shall provoke the anger and displeasure of the Lord."

When Harvard's original charter was drafted in 1650, it contained a specific commitment to provide education for Indians as well as whites, offering "All other necessary provisions that may conduce to the education of the English and Indian youth of this Country in knowledge: and godliness." A brick building was erected at Harvard in 1654–55 where the races could learn each other's languages (Eliot produced an Algonquian grammar to facilitate the task). It was a substantial structure, large enough to provide lodgings and study space for twenty students, and Sewall himself lived in it for part of his time at Harvard, as well as attending tutorials there in the chamber of one of his tutors. However, the building was becoming dilapidated during Sewall's day— a symptom of the general decline of the college—and by the end of the century only four Indians had actually been entered for their BA. Nevertheless, it's striking to think that a handful of Native Americans attended Harvard in the seventeenth century. Its first president declared his intention of making the college "the Indian Oxford as well as the New England Cambridge." Sewall would take an active part in encouraging Indians to prepare for a Harvard education, including having an Indian boy living at his house.

In 1641, Thomas Mayhew bought Martha's Vineyard, the island off the Massachusetts coast to the south of Cape Cod, and began teaching and preaching to the Indians who lived there and on the nearby islands; his son and grandson followed him in this work. Elsewhere, Christian Indians were organized into little townships of their own. Daniel Gookin, superintendent of Indian affairs and father of Sewall's classmate at Harvard, reported in 1674 that there were fourteen of these townships of "praying Indians," numbering eleven hundred individuals in all. Most of them would disappear in the devastation that was about to come.

King Philip, originally called Metacomet, was the sachem or chief of the Wampanoags, who lived on Mount Hope Peninsula and the Narragansett Bay islands southwest of Cape Cod. He and his brother had been given English names at their own request, but nevertheless he'd been treated heavy-handedly by the white authorities in Plymouth Colony over the years, accused of plotting against them with European enemies and rivals, the French and Dutch, as well as with hostile Indian tribes, and on one occasion being forced to surrender weapons belonging to himself and his tribe, a humiliation before his own people and his enemies alike. Philip's Wampanoags were rivals of other tribes such as the Narragansetts, Mohegans, and Niantics, and any loss of prestige affected a complex web of enmity and alliance. Matters came to a head with an incident that illustrates the volatile interplay of European and Native American cultures.

John Sassamon was a "praying Indian" selected by John Eliot to act as Philip's secretary, writing letters to the colonial authorities on his behalf, and teaching him to read and write English, with a view to converting him. In the late 1660s, Philip decided against conversion and Sassamon left him, to act as an Indian minister in the Plymouth Colony. He returned in 1674, perhaps to try again to convert Philip. Here he heard rumors that the Wampanoags were allying themselves with other tribes, in particular with their rivals, the Narragansetts, in order to attack the settlers. He communicated this information to the Plymouth leadership and then, in January 1675, was found dead from a head wound, lying on the ice of Assawomset Pond—an inevitable end, perhaps, for someone who had been shuttling so dangerously between two worlds. Three men were in due course arrested for Sassamon's murder, one of them Philip's adviser. In order to allay suspicion of prejudice, Indians as well as whites were included on the jury. The men were nevertheless found guilty, and were executed on 8 June. Soon after this, the authorities received news that the Wampanoags were preparing for war. It's likely that this incident had confirmed Philip's feeling that the Indians were always going to come off worse in transactions between the two cultures, and that a prompt confrontation was the only hope of arresting a long decline. Twelve days later, his men attacked several houses in Swansea, the colonies assembled a united force to retaliate, and one of the most savage conflicts ever to take place on American soil had begun.

A month later, Sewall had a dream.

That day there had been a tragedy—one of those country tragedies—in the nearby village of Rowley, the place where his grandfather had settled after arguing about the location of the Newbury meetinghouse. The house of a carpenter called Thomas Wood caught fire; his ten-year-old daughter shepherded her brother to safety, but then died herself, "consumed to ashes." "*Væ malum*," Sewall wrote; woe, evil.

When he went to bed he dreamed that he had a neighbor's child in his arms, the mother following him, as they climbed up a staircase that led to heaven. They were all weeping. The dream stairs went up and up until he almost stopped believing there was any such place as *sedes beatorum*, the seats of the blessed. He rebuked himself for this moment of doubt. It was easy to lose faith in the existence of somewhere you had only heard of and never seen, especially if it was difficult to get there (perhaps he was remembering those weeks on the ocean with only sea and sky in sight, and America itself no more substantial than a story told to him by his mother). But at last he came to a "fair chamber with goodly lodgings."

"Is this all?" he asked.

What had happened was a play on the very nature of metaphor: the image of the seats of the blessed to which he'd aspired had been converted into literal furniture in an actual room—literal and actual at least as far as the dream world was concerned.

Sewall began to wonder how the furniture had ever been brought up the steps. The room seemed to him to be in the new building at Harvard, then in another building, Goff's, that was joined on to it (the decaying Indian College was part of this structure). Because the setting was now the college, a scholar popped usefully into the dream to explain that the furniture had been winched up on a pulley and passed in through a decrepit window like the one over the fellows' chamber. At this point everything seemed to become vile, and Sewall woke up.

Obviously, the dream had been triggered by the thought of the little girl trapped in her house, and Sewall's desire to help her escape to heaven. It was also a dream about loss of faith, an issue that would trouble him acutely over the next few years. Above all, it reflected deep insecurity brought about by the outbreak of a war in which the Christian community was under attack by pagan forces. The notion of hoisting furniture through the "ranshacled window," as Sewall calls it (the *Oxford English Dictionary* suggests the adjective is an older form of *ramshackle* and means "wrecked or destroyed by plundering"), made him feel everything had become vile, despite his initial impression of a "goodly" (though disappointing) chamber. Presumably, the window acted as an image of the plight of Harvard in general, the place where Sewall had explored Puritan theology, but where infrastructure, students, and administration were currently all in decline, and where the mission of converting the Indians had failed. The previous October he'd been asked to give evidence to an official inquiry into this collapse, and had done what he could to defend President Hoar, asserting that "the causes of the lowness of the Colledge were external as well as internal." Nevertheless, Hoar had resigned in March, and would shortly die, crushed by his failure.

The fact that "ranshacled" carried with it the notion of plundering hints at that tendency to toggle from guilt to blame, and back again, that had also been apparent in relation to the Pequot War forty years previously. Harvard itself might in turn stand for the Puritan commonwealth of New England, that city on a hill; neglect and spiritual decline had allowed pagan forces to penetrate it and threaten its integrity, indeed its very existence. Spiritual furnishings were missing from the edifice; the earthly sort had been forced in to take its place. A Puritan history, written in the immediate aftermath of the war, makes the connection between guilt and blame quite explicit. The Indians are "vile enemies . . . yea *the worst of the heathen*," but their attacks, however blameworthy they might appear, are actually a punishment for Puritan guilt, for spiritual backsliding (though this would, no doubt, have been news to Philip and his allies, who must have felt the Puritans were only too full of belief in their own rectitude); "that should be an affecting humbling consideration to us, that our heavenly Father should be provoked to set *vile Indians* upon the backs of his Children to scourge them so severely, because of the provoking of his sons and daughters." The calamity of the war happened at this point in time because the first generation of settlers, who had kept the faith, had given way to the second: "Nor were our sins ripe for so dreadfull a judgement, *until the Body of the first Generation* was removed, and another Generation risen up which hath not so pursued, as ought to have been, the blessed design of their Fathers." Sewall's dream reflected his disillusion and guilt at the current failure of the Harvard project, the loss of hope of rapport between the races, and the consequent deferral of the possibility of spiritual harmony. Six months later, Indian forces would be within ten miles of Harvard.

The war rapidly became a bloody series of attacks and counterattacks, with no mercy to women and children on either side. In September 1675, Sewall recorded "that lamentable fight, when Capt. Latrop with sixty-four killed." Lathrop had been escorting evacuees from the town of Deerfield (many vulnerable frontier towns were emptied in this way) when he was ambushed near a river that was promptly rechristened Bloody Brook.

As the autumn went on, preparations were made for a major campaign against the Narragansett Indians, who were believed to be allying themselves with their rivals, the Wampanoags, and an army of a thousand men was assembled for that purpose. In this foreboding atmosphere, Sewall described strange meteorological conditions on 11 November. It was mild but menacing: ". . . the wether exceedingly benign, but (to me) metaphoric, dismal, dark and portentous, some prodigie appearing in every corner of the skies." Despite this suggestion of disturbing events about to happen, there was an eerie stillness: "Nothing moves, at which Mother was exceedingly troubled."

A month after Sewall's climatic premonition, the crucial battle against the Narragansetts took place, the Great Swamp Fight of 19 December.

The army of the United Colonies marched through deep snow to attack an Indian fort, breached the palisade on the second attempt, and set fire to the wigwams within. Six hundred Narragansetts died that day, half of them women and children, along with eighty of the colonists' forces.

Over the next few months, the war continued savagely, and soon began to threaten Boston. Sewall did not take an active part in the fighting; indeed, during this period he was courting Hannah Hull, whom he married on 28 February 1676, oddly making no reference to the event in his diary, momentous as it must have been for this most family orientated of men. The wedding took place at Hannah's parents' house, which was situated on the main street, later christened Newbury Street in honor of Sewall's childhood home (later still Washington Street), in Boston's south end. It's now the site of a Macy's department store.

The great nineteenth-century American writer, Nathaniel Hawthorne, was obsessed with colonial history, and retold many incidents from the first two centuries of the European settlement of New England in a children's book called *The Whole History of Grandfather's Chair*, including the legend that Hannah's dowry was her own weight in shillings. Her father, John Hull, was a leading merchant with an interest in fourteen ships, a landowner, and—particularly relevant to the story—the colony's mint master, a position he'd held since 1652, when specie had become chronically short. As far as the mother country was concerned, Massachusetts's use of its own coinage to supplement the supply from England was one example among many of a dangerous and provocative leaning toward independence. But it made Hull wealthy, since he was allowed to keep one of the pine tree shillings, as they were known (they had the image of a pine tree stamped on them), out of each batch of twenty he minted, and during King Philip's War he actually helped to bale out the colony with his own money. He gave the happy couple a total of £500, 10,000 shillings in all, which would weigh 125 pounds, probably not far off the weight of an eighteen-year-old girl; but in fact he couldn't have balanced out his daughter and the dowry in a gigantic pair of scales, as Hawthorne alleged, since Sewall, in his meticulous way, recorded in his ledger that payment had been made in several installments.

Tantalizingly, we know little about Hannah's character and nothing about her appearance. For Hawthorne, she was "as round and plump as a pudding," having consumed too many of the same, and no doubt would have brought with her a dowry of well over the 125 pounds actually recorded, but his description is fanciful—indeed, he calls her Betsey throughout his tale, perhaps a more suitable name for his greedy, and edible, creation. Hannah, assertive enough to make the opening maneuver in her relationship with her future husband, nevertheless remains a shadowy figure for the duration of her long and happy marriage, preoccupied with that demanding and often terrible responsibility of the age to produce babies year after year.

Sewall moved into Hannah's parents' home, a substantial building reflecting the wealth of the family, and known as the Mansion House. He remained there for the rest of his life. He rapidly became devoted to his in-laws and was introduced to the world of the merchants by John Hull. The war came close to home, to this new home, during the early part of 1676.

In February, there was a successful Indian attack on Lancaster, with the defenders being killed or captured, and the town burned to the ground. Mary Rowlandson, wife of the minister, wrote a famous account of the massacre and her subsequent captivity: "It is a solemn sight to see so many Christians lying in their blood . . . like a company of Sheep torn by Wolves . . . all of them stript naked by . . . hell-hounds, roaring, singing, ranting, and insulting, as if they would have torn our very hearts out." Less than two weeks later, Medfield—twenty miles from Boston—was burned, despite a substantial body of troops defending it, and within two more days the Indians were a couple of hours march from the city. The following month, plans were drawn up for a palisade to surround Boston, leaving the nearby towns, many of which had been destroyed or evacuated already, outside it. The praying Indians were removed from their townships and interned on Deer Island; some were beaten or lynched. At the end of the war, only four of their communities would be resettled.

As spring came on, Sewall reported many of the grim events that occurred: the burning of the town of Sudbury (a Pyrrhic Indian victory, since they lost huge numbers in their onslaught); the slaughter of two hundred Indians (later believed to be three hundred) near the upper falls of the Connecticut River; the death of a Mr. Hezekiah Willett, who was decapitated by Narragansett Indians—much to the disapproval of Philip's Wampanoags, who had known him, and who expressed their grief by combing the hair on his severed head and hanging peag from it (peag was the Algonquian word for wampum, ornamental strings of beads used as currency by North American Indians).

The tide was turning in favor of the colonial forces. A Narragansett chief, Canonchet, was captured and executed, and the celebrated Indian fighter Benjamin Church succeeded in his diplomatic endeavor to persuade the female leader Awashonks, and her Sogkonate people, to switch sides. Another squaw-sachem in Philip's alliance, Weetawoo, was defeated near Taunton and drowned while fleeing the battlefield. On 12 August, Philip himself was ambushed by Church and shot by an Indian in the service of the colonists.

Many captured Indians were put to death; others were made slaves, and some of those were sent to work in the West Indies, in the harshest of conditions. The war was shattering for both sides. As far as the colonists were concerned, it killed one man in sixteen of military age, while great numbers of men, women, and children perished too, or were captured, or rendered homeless. About half of the ninety towns in New England had been attacked; seventeen settlements were completely destroyed, and another twenty-five badly damaged. The war was even more devastating for the Indians. The Wampanoag, Narragansett, Nipmuc, and Mohegan tribes were effectively crushed, and the Native American population of the whole region had begun its long and irreversible decline.

In September, there were some executions in Boston. Stephen Goble was hanged for killing three allied Indians. Three Indians were executed at the same time for burning Thomas Eames's house in Sherborn and killing his wife and some of their children. The hangings were not an edifying spectacle. Four members of the audience, "two men and two impudent Women," sat on the gallows, and one of the women laughed. The following day, a Dr. Brackenbury dissected the body of one of the executed Indians for the benefit of several invited onlookers,

Sewall included. This was probably only the second public dissection ever performed in America, and it's interesting to speculate on the motives of those present. Perhaps Sewall, son-in-law of an influential man and insulated from the heat of battle, needed to feel he was at last making a physical confrontation, coming to grips with the heart of the matter (Richard Hooper, a physician and surgeon from Watertown, did his professional credentials no good at all by holding up the dead Indian's heart and claiming it was the stomach). Drink eased the tension of the occasion: Sewall spent six pence on ale and the same on Madeira.

It was a harsh world, but there was room for frivolity and whimsy. A woman visitor to Boston at this time had never before "seen such an array of fashion and splendour," the women wearing "silken hoods, scarlet petticoats with silver lace, white sarsenet plaited gowns, bone lace and silken scarfs," while the men displayed "fancy ruffles and ribbons." On the "small but pleasant Common," another English visitor claimed, the "Gallants a little before Sun-set walk with their Marmalet-Madams . . . till the Nine-a-Clock Bell rings them home." Sewall was not a man to go in for ruffles and ribbons but he did find room for polite literature. In October, he went down to Cape Cod, charged with gathering together a herd of horses owned by his father-in-law that had been allowed to roam free. It was an exhausting task, but he loved it. He saw the Herring River, "exceeding Pleasant by reason that it runs pretty broad, shallow, of an equal depth, and upon white sand," and encountered running oak for the first time, "Acorns upon bushes about a foot high . . . ; it is content with that stature." The trip moved him to write a poem.

> *The Humble Springs of stately Sandwich Beach*
> *To all Inferiours may observance teach,*
> *They (without Complement) do all concur,*
> *Praying the Sea, Accept our Duty, Sir,*
> *He mild severe, I've (now) no need: and when—*
> *As you are come: go back and come agen.*

This witty piece seems a world away from the savagery of war, and the dissection of an executed Indian. Its very subject is politeness, from inferior to superior, though it seems to have an ironic undercurrent, as the paternalistic tide, calm but massively inexorable, takes no notice of the streams' overtures but insists on sending them back to their starting point so that when it recedes, they will have to undertake the journey all over again (Sewall, living with a rich and powerful father-in-law, must have felt some sympathy for their plight). The nicest moment in the poem is when the sea breaks off its train of thought to deliver the stern instruction in the last line, the dash at the end of the line above catching the moment of tide turn, as the ocean begins its journey back up the shore.

Sewall, would-be merchant, could be careful with his stock. He kept this poem for forty-seven years, and then published it in the *Boston News-Letter*, having dropped "Sandwich," a settlement on Cape Cod, and substituted the more resonant "Plimouth," a few miles up the coast.

Sewall made room for whimsy, but postwar Boston could still be an alarming place. People's nerves were on edge. In nearby Salem, a lad going duck shooting saw a black-haired man near the pond. He thought it must be an Indian, so fired his gun and fled home, terrified that more would come springing out of the bushes. The next day, it was established that an Englishman had been shot dead, and the youth found himself in prison. Hannah and her mother had just recovered from severe flux (diarrhea), with Sewall acting as a kind of bowel-movement bookkeeper, monitoring their every stool. Then fire broke out in Boston, destroying much of the north end of the town—forty-six dwellings and a meetinghouse.

A couple of weeks later, nine-year-old Seth Shove came to live in the Hull/Sewall household, a common arrangement in colonial New England—children of both sexes were sent to other families to do domestic chores, learn a trade, or complete their education, while becoming independent of their own families. Nor was this option confined to poorer parents. A month after Seth's arrival, Sewall's seventeen-year-old sister Jane traveled down from Newbury to Cambridge to act as a maid to Mrs. Bridget Usher, though because of a misunderstanding, Mrs. Usher had already given the job to someone else. As it happened, the Sewalls and Hulls needed a maid themselves, so Jane worked for them for some months, serving her own brother with beer when he entertained guests.

In the case of Seth Shove, though (as in a number of others), Sewall took his responsibilities to an impressive level. Seth was the son of a clergyman who had recently remarried, and as there wasn't a niche for him at home any more he became a permanent member of his new household. Sewall sent him to Harvard, paid for him to get his MA, helped him obtain his first post as a teacher in Newbury, and for the rest of his life sent him letters and books, while Seth pursued a career as a minister and schoolmaster.

On the evening of Seth's arrival, Sewall discovered a shaggy dog had found its way into the kitchen. "I am afraid we shall be troubled with that ugly dogge," he told John Alcock, a nineteen-year-old apprentice who was also living in the household. John asked where it had gone. "Out at the Street door," Sewall told him. John then went after the animal with a piece of piping.

Streets were of course dark on winter nights in seventeenth-century Boston. John came across something that he took to be the dog and gave it a mighty blow—so much so that Sewall felt sorry for it, ugly or not. But the victim turned out to be little Seth, who had gone out of the door just before John. His head swelled up "almost from the forehead to the crown," and he went to bed that night, his first in a new house, wearing a cap. "'Twas God's mercy the stick and manner of the blow was not such as to have spilled his Brains on the Ground," commented Sewall. He then went on to make a reflection that is illuminating in respect of later events: "The Devil, (I think) seemed to be angry at the child's coming to dwell here."

This is not a throwaway line or a figure of speech, but characteristic of the mode of thinking of his place and time. The Devil resented the fact that Seth had landed in a Christian house, where his spiritual health would be taken care of. He therefore sent in an agent, or familiar, in the form of a shaggy dog, to trick John Alcock into killing the child on his behalf. To modern eyes this seems tortured logic, a shaggy dog story in quite another sense, but it was exactly how the operations of evil would be perceived during the Salem witch trials.

CHAPTER TWO

"Our Hithertos of Mercy"

ONE DAY EARLY IN 1677, AN UNPLEASANT SCENE TOOK PLACE between Sewall and his father-in-law. John Hull was sitting in his great hall fuming because, as collector of taxes for the colony, he'd just received a payment in oats rather than money. Sewall put a larger log on the fire than his father-in-law deemed necessary, and got the full force of his rage: if he was going to be so stupid, he, Hull, could have no confidence in him; it showed he was an intellectual weathercock, shifting with the wind.

Hull was anxious because the family business would eventually pass to Hannah, his only child, and he desperately needed Sewall on board to continue the dynasty. Behind his outburst was the fear that Sewall could not be relied on to take up this task. Sewall was so upset he began singing Psalm 37: "Fret not thy self because of them / that evil workers bee . . ." (New England Congregationalists used their own translation of the Psalms, popularly known as *The Bay Psalm Book*, because it was rendered into regularly rhymed verses suitable for singing). Religion was so near the surface of daily life; it could be popped out like a jack-in-the-box. He had a good voice, and this was a neat way of stopping the old man in mid-rant and reminding him of the priority of religious concerns, whatever career choice he decided to make.

Sewall, at age twenty-four, was being buffeted by conflicting winds, sure enough. One visitor—with John Hull sitting in and lending his weight to the argument—told him to get to know the merchants of the town (start networking, as we'd say) and invited him "(courteously) to their Caballs." Another said he believed Sewall should be a minister, and not give up his studies to become a merchant, implying that Hull was seducing him from a life of the spirit into materialism. Meanwhile, Sewall himself was worried about whether he could even agree to join his in-laws as a member of the South Church, one of Boston's three Congregational meetinghouses. He questioned his own worthiness on the grounds of his "continuance in Sin, wandering in prayer," and also felt uneasy about the caliber of the spiritual community he would be joining, "by reason of the weakness, or some such undesirableness in many of its members."

During this period, he was attending prayer and discussion meetings at individual houses, and these may have made him wonder about the whole institution of formal Congregationalism, because on 3 March he had a conversation with a certain John Norton, who suggested "that one might be of the Church (i.e., Mystical) though not joined to a particular Congregation." This was a most subversive suggestion, since the congregation was at the very heart of Puritan faith, acting as spiritual witness and community support to each of its members. However, Sewall came to the conclusion that his unwillingness to enter "into strict Bonds with God" was caused by his own "sinfullness and hypochrisy." He was eventually admitted into the South Church of Boston on 30 March 1677.

It was hardly a straightforward rite of passage. He and Hannah were expecting their first baby at any moment, and he worried he'd fooled himself out of a desire to have the child baptized. He wrote out his case for joining the church on a piece of paper, but intended to supplement it with a full confession of his sins. In the heat of the moment, while he was reading out his reasons to the congregation, this plan for an unscripted exploration of the darker reaches of his soul went right out of his head. The result was that his worries about the worthiness of the church evaporated clean away, but instead "I began to be more afraid of myself." The following Saturday, he met Goodman Walker, one of the founding members of the South Church, who knew him well and had been acquainted with his father and grandfather back in

England. Walker made no comment about Sewall's admission to membership of the congregation, and failed to wish him a blessing, which convinced Sewall he must be visibly unworthy, and terrified him so much he "could hardly sit down to the Lord's Table."

His spiritual fright trapped him in a paradox. "I never experienced more unbelief," he said. He'd lost faith in the existence of his redeemer, yet at the same time was afraid of being struck dead for his sin. At the meetinghouse, he peered forlornly about for a sight of Christ. He imagined catching just a glimpse of him leaving the building, some tiny flicker of divinity going round the corner. But he saw nothing. The day after he was admitted to the South Church, he wrote about his spiritual terror to the new president of Harvard, Urian Oakes: "Those words, *If your own hearts condemn you, God is greater*, and *knoweth all things*, have often affrighted me."

That night he woke up at two in the morning to find his wife in pain. He lit a candle in the hall fire and used it to get the fire going in the bedroom. When the family awoke at five, his mother-in-law sent him for the midwife. That evening, Sewall was sitting with his father-in-law in the great hall when they heard the baby's first cry. It was a boy, to be called John after his maternal grandfather. By two in the morning, Goody Weeden, the midwife, was ready to go home, and Sewall escorted her. She had her own portable stool for use in bedside attendance, which was taken apart and put in a bag he carried for her. On the way, they were spotted by the watchmen, who made them stand still and asked what they were up to. When Sewall explained, they gave their blessing and let them go on their way.

The baby went to a wet nurse at first (people believed colostrum was bad for infants, which maybe helps explain their high death rate), but within a week Hannah was ready to try feeding him herself. The baby played up but eventually sucked her right nipple, the longer of the two. Two days later, he was coping with her short left nipple as well.

Fatherhood wasn't a cure for spiritual crisis—indeed, it only increased one's anxiety. As settlers in the wilderness, Puritans were very concerned about keeping themselves going through the generations, maintaining their hard-won achievements (which explains why John

Hull was giving Sewall such a hard time), consolidating and developing their community. This applied to their religious life in particular: they needed to reproduce themselves not just physically, but spiritually as well. Individuals became full (or "inward") members of the church when they felt able to testify to an experience of grace before the fellow members of their congregation; their children were considered partial (or "outward") members of the congregation from birth, and accordingly baptized during infancy. When the children grew up, they were expected to have the spiritual experience that would allow them, in turn, to become full members.

The problem was that many second-generation church members in Massachusetts Bay were unwilling, or unable, to make the necessary public declaration. They couldn't convince themselves, let alone other members of the congregation, that they had experienced grace. The penalty for faking such testimony was spiritual self-destruction, since God would know they were lying—poor Sewall had wobbled badly enough, but plenty of his fellow citizens dodged the risk altogether. This meant that future recruitment to the congregation, in the form of their offspring, was also threatened. In 1662, a ministerial synod established the Half-Way Covenant to counter this. It permitted children of church members who had not themselves had the full conversion experience to be baptized. Many Puritans were uneasy about this concession, however. Certainly, it was easier to accept the notion of Christian inheritance if the parents acknowledged themselves to be of the elect, so that their grace could in due course bathe their sons and daughters in its afterglow.

This issue was much on Sewall's mind when baby John was baptized, just a week after Sewall's own botched admission. He prayed that the Lord would ensure "the Father and Son may be convinced of and washed from Sin in the blood of Christ." Three weeks later, he visited Urian Oakes, and discussed his panic with him. He must have mentioned hoping in vain for a glimpse of Christ, because Oakes put him right in no uncertain terms: "Told me 'twas not safe to conceive a resemblance of Xt. [Christ] in ones mind any more than to picture him [i.e. paint pictures of him]." Nevertheless, Oakes tried to allay his fears by reading him a passage from a sermon he'd delivered the day before, "wherein he amply proved the confirmation and gathering together in a head the elect Angels in Xt."

Sewall's diary record for the period from midsummer 1677 until the beginning of 1685 is missing, so we can't follow the progress of his religious crisis, though he kept a notebook of his discussions on spiritual topics at the informal meetings he attended, which runs to several hundred meticulously indexed pages. On the subject of election, he found comfort quoting a generous and inclusive definition by the theologian John Owen: "No man ought, no man can justly Question his own Election, doubt of it, or disbelieve it, until he be in such a condition as wherein it is impossible that the Effects of Election should ever be wrought in him; *if such a condition there be in this world.*" By the time his diary resumes, Sewall comes across as secure in his faith and in his membership of the congregation of the South Church of Boston, though like other Puritans he questioned himself and his assumptions energetically throughout his life.

During the lost interval, children were born and died. Little John was suffering convulsions by the time the record breaks off, and died in 1678. By then, however, another child had come along, Samuel Jr., who was to live to adulthood (and cause his loving father a large amount of worry and heartache). Years later, Sewall explained to him how to count one's blessings in an age of great infant mortality: "So that by the undeserved Goodness of GOD your Mother and I never were without a child after the 2^d of April 1677." They were to have fourteen children (if one includes a stillborn son), of whom six lived to adulthood, but the point was that at any given moment, at least one was alive.

With the resolution of Sewall's religious crisis came acceptance of a secular career, as if he was now able to achieve a balance between the sacred and secular demands of life. He joined the ranks of the merchants and helped his father-in-law in his extensive business interests. At the same time—and this was perhaps his way of creating a synthesis out of the conflict between idealism and materialism—he set about his civic responsibilities. In May 1678, he became a freeman of Boston, which meant he had the right to vote for candidates for membership of the

House of Deputies. The following year, he became one of a team of eight constables appointed to undertake patrols and watches, and in particular to deal with public house disorders and to prevent Sabbath breaking. Because the Sabbath began at nightfall on Saturday, drinking in ordinaries, as taverns were usually known, was banned on Saturday evenings as well as on Sundays. Special cages for Sabbath breakers were set up in the Boston marketplace.

An important responsibility came Sewall's way when he was appointed the colony's official publisher in 1681. He obtained a press and type and employed a printer, Samuel Green, whose premises, at the sign of the Dove, were close to his own home. He learned to set type himself, and composed two of the books issued by the press during his tenure (in later life he enjoyed setting his own works in type). He published *The Pilgrim's Progress* soon after taking up his responsibilities, and during his three years in the post he compensated for rejecting a life in the ministry by putting out the writings of some of New England's most distinguished clerics. These included the extraordinary father-and-son team of Mathers, Increase and Cotton. Hugely learned, egotistic, spiritual, vain, and energetic, this pair would be Sewall's friends and—occasionally—enemies, for the rest of their lives. Increase Mather was minister at the North Church of Boston, where his son would soon join him (the Congregational meetinghouses of Boston were normally run by teams of two pastors, one senior and the other junior). If Congregationalists could have had bishops (and the whole point was that they couldn't), the Mathers would have been such—archbishops indeed, at least in the case of Increase (Cotton had a raw, vulnerable, strident side and took offense too easily). Certainly, they regarded themselves, and were regarded by others, as spiritual leaders of their community. At the same time, they were amazingly prolific (Cotton has a claim to have put more words on paper than anyone who has ever lived) and interested in a gargantuan range of topics, so Sewall published not just their sermons but a book on comets by Increase, and an almanac for the year 1683 by Cotton. Almost as accomplished and fertile was Samuel Willard, Sewall's own pastor and another close friend (though again their relationship would have at least one rocky moment). Among the last works published by Sewall was Willard's sermon on the death of John Hull.

Sewall's father-in-law died in 1683. In his sermon, Willard dealt lucidly with the vexed question of why people elected to salvation from the time before they were ever born, from the time beyond time itself, nevertheless clearly have flaws and commit sins (he must have known this was a problem that troubled Sewall, both in relation to himself and to his generous but overbearing father-in-law). The saints are perfect when they reach heaven, but while on earth their perfection is still evolving. Grace is not a fixed state but a vocation, giving them a motive for the struggle. The concept of partial perfection allows the absolute and eternal to coexist with the temporary and relative. Sewall kept a copy of this sermon in his library for the rest of his life.

The Hull estate duly passed to Hannah, except the house itself, which became the property of her mother, Judith. Sewall took over complete responsibility for Hull's business interests, and many of his civic offices as well. He became a nonresident deputy for the town of Westfield. The government of Massachusetts was divided into two houses, the Deputies (representing the townships) and the Council (consisting of the governor and his assistants); when they met as a bicameral legislature, they were known as the General Court. John Hull had represented the same community (and, of course, Sewall's friend, the poet Edward Taylor, was minister there). Six months later, Sewall was elected to the Council (his father-in-law had been an assistant from 1680 until his death), a post carrying with it responsibility as a magistrate or judge (the terms tended to be interchangeable). Though he continued business activities throughout his life, from this point on his center of interest shifted toward the law. He also became a member of the Board of Overseers of Harvard College, another responsibility close to his heart.

Less congenial were military duties. The uncertainties of frontier life and the ferocity of the recent war made it essential for the colony's males to develop and maintain martial skills. John Dunton, a London bookseller and publisher who visited Boston in 1686, was astonished to find that he was required to report for militia training himself, even though he was just a visitor, "*knew not how to shoot off a Musquet*," and "was as unacquainted with the *Terms of Military Discipline*, as a *wild Irishman*." He was also startled when the captain led prayers both before and after the exercises.

Sewall was not a born soldier, either. One day in May 1677, he had gone out on to the common to train all by himself, hoping to avoid other soldiers on account of his nervous horse, but the animal spotted a company in the far distance and bolted, with Sewall clinging on and having to hold his hat under his arm, the result being that he succumbed first to earache, and then to a sore throat, which grew so bad Increase Mather had to come around and pray for him. Nevertheless, after John Hull's death, he became captain of his militia company (one can hear him clicking gently into the vacant slots, one after the other), and in 1685 took charge of the South Company of Boston, leading drills every month or six weeks on Boston Common.

Despite his conscientiousness, a major problem soon arose. Orders came through that the cross of Saint George should be inserted into military flags. The colonists had removed it years previously on the grounds that it was an idolatrous image. Sewall felt strongly on the subject: "But the Cross in ye Banner is ye Image of an Idol: to wit of the Cross whereon Christ was crucified, wch is the greatest Idol y^t [that] ye Papists go Whoring after, to this day." This was an issue that rapidly escalated into a crisis of ultimate magnitude for him: "I was and am in great exercise about the Cross to be put into the Colours, and afraid if I should have a hand in 't whether it may not hinder my Entrance into the Holy Land."

He went to ask Increase Mather's advice. Mather agreed that inserting the cross into the flag was a sin, but said orders were orders. Not good enough for Sewall: "I could hardly understand how the Command of others could wholly excuse them." Shortly afterward, he resigned his commission, though that wasn't the end of his military adventures.

Despite the catastrophe of King Philip's War, Sewall believed passionately in American destiny, and the role of the Indians in bringing it about. On Christmas Day of 1684—and Christmas was emphatically not a festival to be celebrated by a good Puritan—he wrote an antifrivolous missive to Cotton Mather (perhaps the least frivolous person ever): "Please also, instead of some Recreation, when you can spare the time, to give me your Reasons why the Heart of America may not be the seat of the New-Jerusalem," the arguments to be laid out under appropriate headings. Sewall's belief that the establishment of the New Jerusalem in America depended on the conversion of the Indians to Christianity was hardly shared by most of his fellow colonists. It was the custom in New England to put notes on the meetinghouse door asking for prayers on behalf of relatives who were sick, or for their souls when they'd died. Sewall put one on the door of the South Church on behalf of the Indians, but got exactly nowhere. He gave this setback the best gloss he could: the congregation didn't have time to get around to it. "I put up a Note to pray for the Indians that Light might be communicated to them by the Candlestick, but my Note was with the latest, and so not professedly prayed for at all."

Sewall's mind was very much on new beginnings. In February 1686, his baby son, Hull, said his first word: "Little Hull speaks Apple plainly in the hearing of his Grand-Mother." The next day Sewall wrote to his uncle Stephen Dummer about the death of another of his children, Henry (Hull himself wouldn't progress much beyond "apple": he died that summer), but then went on to welcome the new edition of Eliot's Indian Bible, and to embark on an intriguing train of thought about the relationship of man to God in bringing the millennial outcome to pass: "I am persuaded twould be a most acceptable sacrifice to God, importunatly to beseech Him to put his Hand to that work, and not in a great measure as it were to stand and look on." Even if one takes his words to mean that it's humankind who are standing and looking on when they should be importunately praying to the Almighty, there's still an implicit notion that God himself needs a bit of a push in the direction of the Indians. He went on to talk of Dr. Thomas Thorowgood's analysis, thirty years previously, that showed the "Americans [i.e., the Native Americans] to be of Abraham's Posterity." Sewall found the argument compelling, though not certain. In his copy of the book, he marked a passage in which Thorowgood compared Jewish menstruation ritual with the Indian custom of segregating women "in a little Wigwam by themselves in their feminine seasons." Other evidence included similarities in dress, a love of dancing, the hatred of pork, and the practice of circumcision. However, even if the Indians weren't the lost tribes of Jews, the outcome might well be the same: their conversion could establish America as a promised land and new Zion. "Should God but open this Morning-Womb, as Rachel's of old, the Converted would become numerous like the Drops of Dew, and God would settle his Abode, and no Longer content Himself with a movable Tabernacle; but we should see the divine illustrious Temple mentioned Rev. 11. 19." That temple contains the ark of the covenant, and is surrounded by all the meteorology even Sewall, as a weather collector, could want, "lightnings, and voices, and thunderings, and an earthquake, and great hail."

One evening the previous summer, there'd been thunder and lightning when he went to bed. That night he dreamed he was away at Newbury, while Hannah had gone to Roxbury or Dorchester and had died there. He was crushed by the news and kept calling out her name. He asked where his father-in-law was (John Hull had actually been dead for two years at this point) and was told that now that his daughter had died he was free to go where he wanted, so he had set off for England. Sewall's own four-year-old daughter, Elizabeth (one of the children who would survive to adulthood), whispered to him that her mother's death had been caused in part by Sewall's neglect of her and failure to show her enough love. When he woke up, he embraced his wife with joy, as if they were newly married.

He recorded this experience in Latin, so that Hannah wouldn't be able to read it and become upset if she chanced to look at his diary. A couple of weeks later, he took her out on a jaunt to Dorchester, one of the two towns in which, in his dream, she could have died. He needed to exorcise that ghost, though ostensibly the trip was "to eat Cherries and Rasberries, chiefly to ride and take the Air." They called at the house of a friend, Josiah Flint. Hannah sat in the orchard with Esther Flint, while Sewall, incorrigibly seeking out some masculine religious space, read Calvin on the subject of the Psalms in Josiah's study.

It was an earnest outing, triggered by anxiety, but at least it demonstrated Boston existence wasn't completely sunk in gloom. The visiting bookseller, John Dunton, made thumbnail sketches of local characters doing their utmost to achieve joie de vivre. Mr. King was able to sing *"All Hail to the Mirtle Shades*—with a Matchless Grace, and might be call'd an accomplish'd Person," but unfortunately had a beloved whose heart was made of stone. Mr. York similarly was able to treat "the Fair Sex with so much Courtship and Address, as if LOVEING had been all his trade," while Mr. Gouge, whose brain was a *"Quiver of smart Jests,"* made a pretense of living as a bachelor "but is no Enemy to a Pretty Woman." Nevertheless, despite these examples of gallantry, the fate of Francis Stepney tells another story altogether.

One of life's heroic losers, Stepney arrived in Boston in the autumn of 1685 with the intention of setting up classes in mixed dancing. He entered the fray leading with his chin, and announced that his classes would be every Thursday, Boston's Lecture Day, when the midweek sermon was preached. Not abashed in the slightest by the outrage this caused, Stepney claimed that a single one of his dancing lessons could teach more divinity than either Mr. Willard, pastor of the South Church, or the whole of the Old Testament.

Stepney managed to secure the backing of one of Boston's leading citizens, Samuel Shrimpton, but this failed to shield him from the wrath of the community. Indeed, both Stepney and Shrimpton were brought to court in December. They insisted on trial by jury, were bound over in the sum of £50 to the next session, and Stepney was forbidden to keep a dancing school in the meantime. Sewall was on the bench, and reported Shrimpton's sarcastic response: "Mr. Shrimpton muttered, saying he took it as a great favour that the Court would take his Bond for £50." In February, Stepney was fined £100, of which he was required to pay £10 down. This gave him the opportunity of skipping away rather than settling the rest, an option that the court obviously hoped he would take. He decided to brave it out, however, and announced his intention to appeal, with Shrimpton and another reputable Boston citizen, Humphrey Luscomb, acting as his sureties. Meanwhile, Increase Mather was moved to publish a swingeing attack entitled *An Arrow against Profane and Promiscuous Dancing*: "It is spoken of as the great sin of the Daughters of *Sion*, that they did walk with stretched-out necks, and with wanton eyes, walking and mincing as they go, and making a tinkling with their feet."

. Clearly, it was an uphill task persuading the people of Boston to stretch out their necks and tinkle with their feet, and Stepney's nerve finally failed in July, when he fled town to avoid his debts (it was another twenty-eight years before the selectmen approved Boston's first legitimate dancing and music master).

But Stepney's shenanigans were just an irritant: Boston, and New England as a whole, had more formidable threats to face.

ON 30 MARCH 1687, Increase Mather, learned divine, Puritan of Puritans, put on a wig and a long white cloak, and crept out of his house under cover of darkness. An agent of the government was waiting outside to arrest him, but the sight of this spindly spectral figure proved too much, and Mather got away.

This odd episode occurred at a late stage of a long period of tension between the colony and the English Crown. Massachusetts was administered under the terms of a charter drawn up before it was even settled. This document gave the colonists a considerable degree of autonomy in handling their affairs. From the beginning, New Englanders had the sense that they were a special case, a providential community based on a coherent and all-embracing religious creed. The Crown found it difficult to monitor the administration of a land on the other side of a three-thousand-mile-wide ocean that took months to cross and was sometimes too dangerous in winter to navigate at all. There were other causes of friction too, chief among which—perhaps the most resonant of them all, considering the long-term future—was a tendency on the part of the colonists to avoid paying taxes on trade.

With the fall of the Protectorate, these developments were exposed to close and unsympathetic scrutiny. In 1676, Charles II sent Edward Randolph to Massachusetts as his special messenger, and he was to spend the next dozen years shuttling back and forth as the monarchy's spy and fixer, reporting somewhat unreliably on the behavior and opinions of the colonists, and representing the royal will to an increasingly

resentful population. He was given the specific responsibility of enforc-
ing the trading laws when in 1679 he was appointed collector, surveyor,
and searcher for all the New England colonies, the title carrying a premonition of some sort of officious and humorless Dickensian beadle,
snooping about and poking into private corners, paid to be exactly
where he wasn't wanted. He had with him a letter from the king demanding that the Massachusetts Bay colonists should toe the line: that
members of the Church of England should be eligible for the franchise
and civil equality, that the colony should pass over the administration of
Maine and New Hampshire to the king, and that it should increase the
number of assistants in accordance with the original charter.

The Massachusetts General Court did its best to stall the king's
wishes, conceding an item here, delaying a decision there, ignoring certain issues altogether. Randolph was in no doubt of their perfidy, writing to the king that the "Bostoneers" had no legal title "either to land or
government in any part of New England, but are usurpers" (an issue
that would in due course bear directly on Sewall), that they had illegally
formed themselves into a commonwealth, coined their own money, put
people to death for religious reasons, removed the royal commissioners
from New Hampshire by force, imposed their own oath of fidelity, and
violated the acts covering trade and navigation to the tune of a massive
£100,000 yearly.

Randolph brought no diplomacy to bear; it was never part of his
agenda to look for the basis of accommodation. To be fair, neither of
the parties involved seemed much interested in rapprochement. When
Randolph set off for the colonies from Whitehall two years later with
another letter from the king, his superior, William Blathwayt, surveyor
and auditor general of revenues arising in America, wrote to him with
some advice. He mustn't allow the dangerous and delinquent Bostonians to slip through his guard (as if somehow Randolph was in danger
of being naively genial and conciliatory): "At Boston you have but one
rock to avoid, which you ought to be aware of; I mean, the letting them
come within you, after which they will easily give you the Cornish hug."
The latter is an apparently affectionate squeeze that leads to the prompt
collapse of the victim.

As it happened, Randolph's temper meant that he was quite as likely to threaten violence as be threatened by it. One day on the Boston exchange, he bumped into Elisha Hutchinson, a prominent figure on the local scene and shortly to be elected an assistant, and the two men had an argument about the fact that—ironically—Randolph felt he was paying too much in local taxes.

"Seven men may cut a man's purse on the highway," Randolph declared.

"Such a knave as you," Hutchinson replied, "may cheat twenty men."

"Who are you?" Randolph asked sarcastically.

"A man."

"When you have your buff coat on."

"As good as you with your sword on," Hutchinson told him.

"You are no commissioner here." (The inevitable pulling of rank.)

"I have as good a commission as you; my staff is as good a commission as your sword."

"Would I had you in a place where I could try it."

Eyeball to eyeball: "Try now."

Randolph backed off: "He went away and left me," wrote Hutchinson, with obvious satisfaction. John Dunton reckoned that Hutchinson was the tallest man he'd ever seen, so Randolph was tactically correct.

Given this atmosphere, it's easy to picture Randolph's agents being "very much beaten" as they searched a warehouse for smuggled goods, or Randolph himself being threatened with a knock on the head when he tried to seize a ship. Prophetically, he reported: "I expect hourly to have my person seized and cast into prison."

The colony made some attempt to avoid the inevitable. In 1683, Sewall was appointed by the town of Boston to a committee entrusted with pressuring the General Court to move toward reconciliation: "That there be an order made that yᵉ whole body of lawes be revised & all such lawes that are repugnant to the lawes of England (if there be any such) . . . may be left out." But matters finally came to a head the following year, when through a legal instrument called a quo warranto the colony's charter was cancelled. This removed at a stroke the basis for the legal and administrative infrastructure of Massachusetts Bay. Of course, a replacement couldn't simply be imposed by the wave of a wand: there was a sort of phony peace after the decision was made, during which de facto arrangements continued much as they had before. This lasted for two years, because Charles II died shortly after the termination of the charter, and the new king, James II, needed time to formulate his plans for New England.

During this oppressive interval, at least one "Bostoneer" was able to preserve his sense of a special American status and destiny. Sewall spent 1 January 1686 reading a commentator on the book of Revelation, that book of all the books in the Bible that seemed to him to tell of a great religious destiny for his country. That night he had "a very unusual Dream." He dreamed that during his time on earth, Christ had actually come to Boston for a while, living, like Sewall himself, at Father Hull's house. Still within his dream, Sewall pondered on the significance of this fact. It struck him that Boston had so much more to be proud of than Rome, which could only boast of Peter's being there (Sewall refused to use the title "saint"; it was unbiblical and idolatrous). The competitive nature of that dreamy thought itself reflects the imperial wistfulness of a colony that was in the process of being put firmly in its place. He ought to have shown Father Hull great respect, since he was the man whose dwelling Christ had chosen to share (some guilt about his own sharing, through Hannah's inheritance, of his father-in-law's property, shows here). Christ's decision to spend some of his short life in the town revealed both his goodness and wisdom (and justified the utopian aspirations Sewall kept to for the rest of his long life). The chronological absurdity of the event, he declared, never entered his head while he was in the dream.

But it wasn't Christ who turned out to be the next important visitor to town. At eight in the morning of 14 May 1686, the frigate *Rose* docked in Boston harbor with the inevitable Edward Randolph on board, bringing news that the New England colonies were to be lumped together under the interim presidency of Joseph Dudley. Dudley was the son of one of the early governors of the colony, a founding father, but proved a less heroic—and much less popular—figure altogether, a selfish, scheming man perpetually compromised in the public's eyes by his royalist affiliations. His fate and Sewall's would in due course become permanently entangled. The gulf between the settlers and the Crown was nicely revealed by the fact that two days previously, Dudley had failed to get himself elected to the Court of Assistants.

The change of government was formally instituted at a sitting of the General Court on 17 May. Dudley showed his seal of office, along with those for his seventeen council members—all directly appointed by the king (Randolph being one of them)—who would take the place of the elected assistants. When he and his council had left the room, a small group of citizens remained to discuss what, if anything, could be done. There was some talk of a protest. Sewall disagreed: ". . . the foundations being destroyed what can the Righteous do"? Four days later, he joined the former magistrates and deputies in prayers: "Thanked God for our hithertos of Mercy 56 years."

Dudley held the reins of power only till the end of the year, when Sir Edmund Andros took over as royal governor of the Dominion of New England. Andros knew exactly how to make his presence felt. Almost the first thing he did was speak to the ministers about doubling up services in one of the Boston meetinghouses, so that the Anglican community, which did not have a church of its own, could worship there. The ministers met with representatives of their congregations the following day and agreed they couldn't consent. Andros seemed to accept this verdict for the time being, Anglican services being held in the Town House.

Randolph, meanwhile, had been appointed secretary and registrar of the Dominion, with a responsibility close to his heart: to pursue the implications of the fact that with the vacating of the charter, all titles to land and property in New England technically became void—every acre belonged to the king.

As Easter approached, Andros made his move on the Boston meetinghouses. On 22 March 1687, he inspected all three of them and decided that Sewall's, the South, was the most suitable for his purposes. The following day, he sent Randolph over for the keys. A deputation, including Sewall, immediately went off to see Andros to explain that the meetinghouse was the property of its congregation. They showed him the deed for the original purchase of the plot, and explained how the building had been subscribed for, some people like Sewall's father-in-law paying £100 each.

It's impossible to overstate the symbolic power of this issue. The colonists were the proud children of people who had made a heroic journey over the ocean because they couldn't accept the hierarchical structure of the Church of England, and now that church was being shoehorned into a meetinghouse they had built for their own worship. Of course, their argument for ownership fell on deaf ears: nobody in New England could any longer prove they owned anything.

Two days later, on Good Friday, Andros had his way. "Smith and Hill, Joiner and Shoemaker" were sent to force the door ("being very busy about it," Sewall observed sourly), Goodman Needham, the sexton, was prevailed upon to toll the bell, despite an earlier refusal, and the cohabitation had begun. The following Sunday, the Anglican sermon went on and on: ". . . twas a sad Sight," Sewall wrote, "to see how full the Street was with people gazing and moving to and fro because they had not entrance into the House." A fearsome thought, in the seventeenth-century context: duration of sermons used as a political weapon.

A year later, Sewall and a fellow member of his congregation, Captain Theophilus Frary, had a meeting with Andros and his team in hopes of sorting the matter out. Andros cut to the chase: ". . . asked who the House belong'd to." They told him the title was on record. Andros turned to John Graham, his attorney general, and gave a sinister instruction: "Mr. Attorney we will have that look'd into."

Soon things turned ugly. He, Andros, "would defend the work [the cohabitation] with his company of soldiers." He became bitter about the congregation's failure, as he saw it, to subscribe for an Anglican church (though one might ask why the Anglicans weren't expected to subscribe for their own). People didn't want to give, he said, and that was unreasonable because —suddenly he lost his temper completely— "if any stinking filthy thing" were in their meetinghouse they would pay to have it removed, but they nevertheless refused to pay toward the cost of a new building (his rage creating an accidental equation between Anglicans and decaying rubbish).

Sewall and Frary pointed out the topsy-turvy nature of this complaint: "Said came from England to avoid such and such things, therefore could not give to set them up here." If the boot was on the other foot, "the Bishops would have thought strange to have been ask'd to contribute towards setting up the New-England Churches."

Andros's fury had spent itself for the time being: he told them the Anglicans would try to have their service over by nine in the morning. The air was cleared for one Sabbath at least. The following day, the Anglican services finished before nine, and then at about a quarter past one, "so we have a very convenient time." But the week after, the rot set in once more: the "Governour takes his old time again after our coming out."

Meanwhile, Sewall himself had managed to cross swords with the royal authorities on another front altogether.

IN THE EARLY months of 1687, the Sewalls made an ambitious purchase: they spent £2,000 on buying virtually the whole of Hogg Island, which was situated in Boston harbor. It had originally been designated for the use of the people of the town, but over the years had been sold off into private ownership. The island was west of Point Shirley— Pollen Point in Sewall's day—tucked quite closely into the shore of East Boston (it's now underneath Logan Airport). The estate comprised 498 acres, and included the whole of the landmass of the island with the exception of some small patches of marshland that Sewall subsequently set about acquiring. The deal included 7 oxen and steers, 8 cows, 160 sheep, 13 eponymous pigs—it begins to sound like "The Twelve Days of Christmas"—2 horses and a mare, 4 beehives, 3 hen turkeys and a cock, and 12 dunghill fowls, along with a boat complete with mast, sail, and oars. Goodman Belcher was the tenant farmer who went with the property.

It was, no doubt, an investment: it was also an ideal, a dream, a private domain, particularly valued at a time when the country as a whole seemed to be slipping from the colonists' grasp. Sewall and Hannah had gone there the previous September, and Sewall went again in April 1687 and gathered pussy willows. He took a number of Boston dignitaries with him the following month, and they walked in two columns to "witness my taking Livery and Seisin of the Iland by Turf and Twigg and the House." The first thing he did on claiming possession was plant some chestnut trees—all his life he loved tending trees (two days later he was at the Boston cemetery busily pushing caterpillars off the apple trees there).

Soon after this ceremonial beginning, the first sinister sign appeared. Sewall went to the island to work out the best place for a causeway for landing his boat, and picked a basketful of cherries to take home. Close by, on Noddles Island, he saw a surveyor, with two redcoats, taking measurements.

The bombshell came the following year, just a couple of weeks after Sewall and Frary had had their difficult meeting about cohabitation. Sewall was informed that he, along with several other landowners, was the subject of a writ in which they were all named as being "violent intruders into the Kings Possession," an insultingly reductive charge given the graceful formalities he'd gone through. The paper had been served on his tenant, Jeremiah Belcher, and the next day Sewall tried to get over to the island to see it for himself, but wind and tide were against him; they broke an oar and had to turn back. The following day, Goodman Belcher managed to get over to the mainland to tell him what had happened.

A week later, Sewall sent Andros a formal petition for confirmation of his possession of the property, agreeing to pay "such moderate Quit-Rent as your Excellency shall please to order." He was being forced to make a deal on a property for which he had paid a huge price the year before. Many New Englanders would regard his appeal as pandering to the oppressor (though most wouldn't have invested so much, so recently). As he put it in a letter to Increase Mather: "The generality of people are very adverse from complying with anything that may alter the Tenure of their Lands, and look upon me very sorrowfully that I have given way." It's easy to see how direct rule by the royal governor and his entourage could demoralize the colony.

This frustration didn't stop Sewall from giving the Indians a piece of the Hull estate in Sandwich and building them a meetinghouse upon it, a reflection of his deep conviction that the key to America's future lay in their conversion. As he put it in a letter, "if these springs Burst forth amonge the Natives too, twill make America more Renowned among her sisters Asia Africa and Europe for this new Gospell Heaven than for her Silver and Gold."

Domestic life had its own adventures. He went fishing for cod and lost his hat overboard; there was "great Uproar and Lewd rout" as a certain Gammar Flood staggered past the Sewall house in a "drunken raving" state, causing people to hurry to their windows to see if there was a fire anywhere; Sewall was at prayer in his kitchen when he was startled by an unusual noise, and when he went to investigate he discovered that two cows had run onto their porch, "the like to which never fell out before, that I know of." Ten days after that, his six-month-old son Stephen died: "Had two teeth cut, no Convulsions."

Despite endless bereavement, Sewall never lost his capacity for sympathy and sorrow. He wrote a lovely letter to his aunt Dorothy Rider, who had "some eating thing" in her face: "And seeing neither I, nor your sister, nor any of your Relations, can give any reason why God should measure out this suffering to you, and not to us: and why he hath not rather appointed this pain and affliction to us, and made you bear your part in sympathising with us; we are the more engaged to this Duty, which I pray God help us to exercise and that more and more, and pardon us wherein we fall short." The grave cadences and rhetorical balance only serve to enhance our sense of his sympathy and emotional engagement.

The day after Sewall sent this letter, political drama once more took center stage: Increase Mather donned a white cloak and wig, disguising himself as a sort of ghost, and made a remarkable escape from the confines of his own house. A trail of diplomacy and intrigue had led up to this surreal and melodramatic act.

ON 4 APRIL 1687, King James II had published his first Declaration of Indulgence, which, on the face of it, was a liberal and enlightened policy change, suspending the laws against nonconformists, allowing Catholics and dissenters to worship freely, and removing religious tests for civil and military appointments. The first reaction of New Englanders was to welcome this newfound tolerance, since both they and fellow Congregationalists in the mother country obviously stood to benefit from it, at least in theory. Soon, though, they began to suspect James's true intent, which was to begin to turn Britain into a Catholic country. A year later, when the king issued his second declaration (on very much the same lines as the first), leading nonconformists in England actually sided with the Anglican bishops in their repudiation of the initiative.

The Boston churches felt it was high time serious negotiations were begun with the English authorities about the grievances suffered by the colony, with a view to getting the charter reinstated. It was at this moment that Increase Mather stepped into the center of the fray. He suggested he should return cunning with cunning—go to the court to thank the king for his apparent liberality, and use the opportunity to put the Massachusetts case. This was agreed. Puritan minister in the role of diplomat: perhaps the final time the roles would be so fully intertwined, the last hurrah of New England's theocratic possibility. Looking at the tight sharp face of Increase Mather's portrait, eyes wary, mouth pursed and reticent, it's easy to see how this minister of religion might fancy mixing it with the power brokers in the old country.

Andros and Randolph clearly had every reason to want to prevent Mather going off and reporting behind their backs on the colonists' bitter resentment of their administration, and as luck, or scheming, would have it Randolph managed to get his hands on a letter purportedly written by Mather five years previously, in which he attacked the Anglican church and praised Lord Shaftesbury, Titus Oates, and others who were anathema to James II because of their opposition to the Catholic cause, a letter that established him as a "Bellows of Sedition & Treason." Mather vigorously denied ever having written it, claiming the forgery had been perpetrated by Randolph himself, or perhaps his brother: "It is reported that he has a notable art in imitating hands; that he can

Increase Mather (1639–1723).
Oil on canvas by John van der Spriett, 1688. MHS #1442.

do it so exactly that a man cannot easily discern the knavery." Nevertheless, he was arrested in December. The case came to trial in January 1688, and he was acquitted. Randolph ordered his rearrest, however, on an "action of scandal" (basically the original charge was being kept alive). Mather found himself effectively under house arrest, knowing that if he set foot outside his property, he was liable to have the warrant served on him by an agent waiting in the street.

After making his escape in disguise, Mather stole to a friend's house, where he remained hidden for several days while Randolph's men searched for him. Then he was smuggled by ketch and shallop to the ship *President*, the vessel he'd originally booked passage on, and was able to sail off on his mission to England, along with his thirteen-year-old son, Samuel. A few months later, Sewall followed him.

Sewall didn't specify his motives for this journey he embarked on late in 1688, but one can infer them from his actions when he arrived. He went to give support to Mather in his negotiations; he also needed to settle certain matters of business pertaining to land and property he'd inherited in England; and he passionately wanted to sightsee in the country he'd left as a small boy, and which he'd never visit again in the course of a long life. Despite the deep political antagonism between the colony and the mother country, and despite Sewall's own burgeoning sense of a great American destiny, he, like his fellow New Englanders, regarded himself as English, and was fascinated by, and even proud of, his inheritance. Nevertheless, he was about to pioneer a new cultural phenomenon, one of a number in a life that was remarkably innovative, given the conservative temperament of the man who lived it. He was about to become the first American tourist, or at least the first we know of, the first to leave behind a detailed record of his experiences.

CHAPTER THREE

The First American Tourist

𝕊EWALL DIDN'T HAVE TO SNEAK OUT OF NEW ENGLAND AS Mather had done. As far as the authorities were concerned, he was a respectable merchant off to settle some personal business, despite being referred to as a "violent intruder" on the warrant for Hogg Island. On 15 October 1688, he arranged to have a barrel of beer bottled for his journey. He was planning to be away for a full year and had to set his affairs in order. He rented out his warehouse and wharf in northeast Boston to Nathaniel Henchman for the whole twelve months and drew up a contract with a man called Jonathan Wales, who agreed that if war should break out, he would fight in Sewall's stead. Sewall would spend £5 on equipping him (though the arms were returnable at the end of the arrangement) and give the same amount to Wales's wife. There had recently been some outbreaks of trouble up in Maine from Indians allied to French forces in the nearby Canadian territories, isolated incidents in fact, but triggering fears of large-scale attacks.

As the time for departure approached, Sewall became nervous. Since his arrival in America as a small boy he'd never traveled far afield, and it would be a wrench leaving Hannah and the children, four of them by this point: Samuel Jr., now ten; Hannah Jr., eight; Elizabeth (or Betty), six; and baby Joseph, less than three months old. He felt particularly guilty at leaving his wife to deal with a suckling infant—they'd already lost four children in the first few months of life, so there was no more than an even chance that he would ever set eyes on Joseph again.

He was worried about his own safety too. The ship upholsterer told him that the *America*, on which he'd booked his passage, was laden too much by the head and sailed badly.

At eleven o'clock in the morning of the day he received this worrying verdict, he saw Goody Glover, an Irish washerwoman in the household of John Goodwin, going past in a cart on her way to be hanged, the full panoply of marshals, constables, and a judge in attendance. She'd been found guilty of bewitching the children of the Goodwin family, for whom she worked. The case that culminated in this grim procession had the unfortunate effect of bringing witchcraft to the foreground of people's consciousness, particularly as the following year Cotton Mather published a book about it, *Memorable Providences Relating to Witchcraft and Possessions*. He'd taken one of the tormented children into his own household and devoted months to curing her of her possession. He graphically described the physical distortions and seizures that her bewitchment had allegedly brought about, unintentionally providing a handbook for later use.

In the light of Goody Glover's execution, Samuel Willard chose Job 30:22 as his text for the midweek lecture that day: "For I know that thou wilt bring me to death, and to the house appointed for all living." That night, Sewall pondered on 2 Corinthians 1:9, a verse that had been worrying him recently: "But we had the sentence of death in ourselves, that we should not trust in ourselves, but in God which raiseth the dead." "Sentence of death," he glumly wrote in his diary. Sewall at thirty-six was as nervous of the ocean as he had been when he was nine. The following day, he went on board the ship, with his brother Stephen coming along to give him moral support. Stephen was five years younger, but the two were close throughout their lives. He had also attended Harvard, but wasn't suited to the regime of study and left without graduating. He apprenticed himself to a maltster at Salem instead and over the years established himself as a respected member of that community, a merchant and civic official, acting as county registrar and court clerk, and becoming a major in the militia. Stephen commended the vessel, which no doubt made Sewall feel more optimistic, and they had a glass of Madeira and dinner with the captain. On 22 November, the *America* sailed for England.

Five days out to sea, Sewall ate a pasty Hannah had baked for him, and the thought of his wife "cut me to the heart," the intimacy of cooking and eating made poignant by the stretch of ocean that now separated the two. He had the nervous landlubber's eye for detail, meticulously recording the wind direction, and noting down problems that arose: ". . . the Ship being under a hard Gale of wind, the whipstaf is somehow loosed from the Gooseneck, which puts us into great consternation: and the word is given, Turn out all hands. Several go into the Gunroom and steer there for awhile, and by God's blessing no great harm. Some of the men said if she had not been a stiff ship would have been overset." "Whipstaf," "gooseneck," "stiff ship": a wide-eyed Sewall pins his faith in technical language, hoping it was sufficiently watertight to keep him afloat on the high seas.

One night, a casement was left open and a wave washed through the cabin, "to our great startling and discomfort," especially Mrs. Baxter's, who "lay athwart ships at the bulkhead, the most wet." The two sexes slept together, dormitory style (this happened in roadside inns too). The water floated the binding from his copy of Erasmus. More gastronomic nostalgia: on 5 December, he ate one of Hannah's plum cakes for breakfast. Later he dreamed she gave him a piece of cake to take to a former servant of theirs, Hannah Hett. He also had a dream his wife was giving birth and he was stuck in a high gallery, unable to get down to her and help, the panic of being distanced from family responsibilities turning itself into a sort of vertigo.

On 21 December, Sewall laid a wager with a fellow passenger, Nathaniel Newgate, that they wouldn't be able to see any part of Great Britain by sunset a week on Saturday (it was a Friday), one of those bets where you back the unwanted possibility, so you win whether you win or lose. Newgate had been the owner of some of the marshland on Hogg Island; given they were now on gambling terms, that matter must have been settled amicably between them. The following day, the passengers all contributed to a purse to be given to whoever first spied land. Sewall provided a piece of eight, worth about 6s. (the colonists used Spanish as well as English money).

On 30 December (Sewall must have collected his winnings from Mr. Newgate), they spoke with a ship seven weeks out of Barbados. That ship had in turn spoken with an English vessel the previous Friday, and had heard momentous news: the king was dead, and the Prince of Orange had taken England, landing at Torbay six weeks previously. It was the first, garbled, inkling of the Glorious Revolution. James II had become increasingly unpopular and discredited because of his Catholic sympathies, and finally William, his Dutch son-in-law, had been moved to invade. Prophetically, Sewall had had a rather warlike dream the night before. He was in the Town House, the colony's equivalent of a parliament building, and was summoned out by Major Gookin, who wanted to have a word with him. The major was looking fresh and lively and was wearing a coat and breeches of bloodred silk. Two days later they met up with another ship and received more accurate though still out-of-date news. The Prince of Orange was marching on London.

The *America* sailed on in company with the ship from Barbados, its consort. On 8 January, the crew of the consort all gathered on their starboard side and "made a horrid outcry, Land! Land!" Sewall and his fellows looked toward larboard and saw "horrid, high, gaping rocks." One passenger thought it must be the French coast. They asked their consort, who replied (somewhat ambiguously), "Silly! Silly!" They were in the perennially dangerous vicinity of the Isles of Scilly. There were rocks ahead, and they had to trim sails rapidly to avoid running onto them, and then tack. They encountered more rocks on the evening of the following day, "some even with and some just above the water under our lee, very near us, but by the Grace of God we weathered them." Then another challenge: "In the next place we were interrogated by the Bishop and his Clerks," a huge rock with three smaller spired rocks beside it.

After this narrow squeak—this close interrogation, to borrow Sewall's lovely image—another sort of danger threatened the next day. They spied a man-of-war, not knowing if it had hostile intent (the seizure of power by the Protestant William was likely to lead to an outbreak of war with the French, who supported James). It put out the English ensign, however, and proved to be a London vessel homeward bound from the Canaries. It confirmed the landing of Prince William but informed them King James wasn't dead after all. Next day, they came upon the Isle of Wight, "a long space of Land, Hills and Valleys." On 12 January, they met up with a warship out of Liverpool, and got another update. The king and his son, the Prince of Wales, had gone to France "somewhat privatly." The little prince was "a chcat" (the popular belief was that James's sixth-month-old heir was an imposter, cunningly produced during a faked accouchement to ensure a Catholic succession). The warship transmitted some more alarming rumors: French men-of-war were flying English flags and ambushing ships, tying Englishmen up back-to-back and flinging them overboard to drown. On a more cheerful note, the ship sold them three cheeses and swapped some bottles of very good beer for one of Sewall's bottles of brandy. With help from his shipmates, he'd presumably disposed of his own barrel of beer by now.

On 13 January, the Sabbath, they landed at Dover after more than seven weeks at sea. Sewall and Nathaniel Newgate rushed off to find a dissenting service and ended up listening to a certain Mr. Goff "in a kind of Malt-House." Next day, Sewall did a spot of sightseeing ("The Harbour not altogether unlike Boston Dock but longer"), had a drink in the Antwerp Tavern, and then was off to Canterbury. The cathedral was "a very lofty and magnificent building, but of little usc [i.e., not used much]." Within a few days he was in London, taking in the sights with another Boston merchant, Thomas Brattle. Sewall enjoyed measuring public buildings with his joint-rule. The Gresham College library was sixteen yards wide; Guildhall, which he and Brattle measured together, was fifty yards by sixteen. Perhaps this compulsion was a seventeenth-century precursor of photography, a way of generating evidence that you've really been to such and such a place, and can take home some flavor of the actuality of the experience.

On 11 February, he and Brattle went to a concert at Covent Garden. Sewall loved music but none would be played in Boston at a professional level until after his death, so it must have been a revelation. The next day, Princess Mary of Orange arrived in London, and Sewall was there: "At the Star on the Bridge, Mr Ruck's, saw the Princess arrive in her Barge, Ancients [ensigns] and Streamers of Ships flying, Bells Ringing, Guns roaring." It was a strange and memorable historical moment—James II's daughter arriving to join her husband in taking over her own father's throne. She was being rowed to Whitehall; the next day she would be queen. Merchant as he was, Sewall had his eye open for other arrivals too: "Saw three Waggons full of Calves goe by together."

Sewall left London the following day, on a trip to the south and southwest. First he went to Winchester, county town of his home turf of Hampshire. He bought a bay horse for £4 at the fair, and clopped off to visit relatives. At the home of his cousin Jane Holt, he munched his way through "very good Bacon, Veal, and Parsnips, very good shoulder of Mutton and a Fowl rosted, good Currant suet Pudding and the fairest dish of Apples that I have eat in England." Throughout his diary, he makes a record of food and drink he has enjoyed, and does so with particular glee during his English trip, providing a sort of travelers' guide to English cuisine in the late seventeenth century. He went to the Hall at Winchester to watch the knights of the shire being chosen. As a Hampshire man, he was entitled to cast a vote himself, but was disqualified because he refused to put his hand on the Bible and kiss it, believing that use of the holy book to be idolatrous, just as it was to have a flag with a cross on it. He rather spoiled this principled gesture by his unheroic entrance into the Hall, breaking his rapier on the steps as he came down into it. He visited Winchester College and gave it a copy of John Eliot's Indian Bible, which is still there, with Sewall's signature in it.

Then he was off to Salisbury, where he persuaded the cathedral organist to play for him. He had dinner with the chancellor's clerk. Devout Congregationalist that he was, he never had any problem respecting Anglican ministers, officers, and edifices—and despite the battle over cohabitation, was even on friendly terms with Robert Ratcliffe, the Church of England rector in Boston, who had blessed him before his departure for England. The chancellor's clerk's wife couldn't dine with them because she had to go to a christening, but she gave Sewall a whirlwind tour of her house. He noticed that she took her four-month-old daughter out of her cradle and kissed her, "though asleep." The thought of six-month-old Joseph all those miles off in Boston must have given him a pang.

From Salisbury he rode through the local towns and villages— Wilton, Chilmark, Hendon, Barwick, Mere, Gillingham—until he arrived at Shaftesbury, where he noted there was a great market of "wheat, Barley, Beans, Beef, Mutton, Leather, Cloaths etc," and that the town drew some of Gillingham's water, for which they paid the consideration of a calf's head and a pair of fringed gloves. Even quainter— and an American could treasure folk traditions of the past even from what is now the long-ago vantage point of 1689—he recorded that "With Bread and Beer, a Duz. or two Come dancing down the Hill the Monday before ascension day; i.e., the two persons last married whom they call the Lord and Lady, but now generally there is a stated Dancer, a merry arch jocose Man, who procures a Lady."

New England itself took a dim view of such behavior, as its treatment of Francis Stepney, Boston's erstwhile dancing master, had proved only a couple of years previously. In May 1687, Sewall had recorded that the maypole in Charlestown, just north of Boston, had been cut down only to be replaced immediately by a bigger one, with a garland on top of it to emphasize the point. The next day he'd discussed the matter with Robert Walker, one of Boston's oldest settlers. He was the patriarch whose failure to acknowledge Sewall's entry into the congregation of the South Church of Boston had caused him spiritual terror, though the omission may simply have been caused by an incoming tide of slumber. Walker had suffered from narcolepsy for the past sixty years, and being a sort of Rip Van Winkle remembered all the more vividly a far-off Manchester where lavender grew in abundance (perhaps helped by the fact that he was currently taking lavender drops medicinally). Father Walker explained that the custom in that lavender-smelling England of his youth had been to dance about maypoles to the accompaniment of music, and he feared such customs might take hold in America. But now that he was in England himself, Sewall could afford to be relaxed about folk customs. The Atlantic offered a handy symbol of compartmentalization; in crossing it, he was able to make contact with and enjoy a part of himself that he suppressed in Boston, a merry, arch, jocose dimension that could be conveniently embodied in the myths and rituals of the old country.

Soon he was off to Yarborough Castle and then Stonehenge, where he rode between some of the standing stones, and noticed the tenon-and-mortise structure by means of which they had been capped. On 6 March, he went to Lee, a village below Romsey and near the Test River, to visit a property he'd inherited there, for which he was offered £400 by a certain Mr. Nowes. Then he traveled from Romsey to Redbridge to Southampton. While he was driving along with an acquaintance after hearing a sermon, he noticed a small boy running parallel with them. Sewall "lent" him half a crown to buy paper and quills and told him that if he learned to read and write well he could keep it; but if he didn't, Sewall said that he "must have it again with I know not how much interest."

Off he went again, to take formal possession of a property at Lee, and stay in his birthplace of Bishop Stoke. He wrote a short poem commemorating a kinswoman, Mrs. Mehetabel Holt, whose life had had the opposite trajectory from his—she'd been born in Newbury, New England, and died at Bishop Stoke, eleven years previously: "America *Afforded me my Birth / And Friendly* Europe *grants me whit'ning Earth*," that last telling adjective giving life to the formal exercise, with its simultaneous suggestion of decay and purification. Then he rode east to Tichfield and Gosport, and walked around the ramparts, and next over to Fareham and Portsmouth (where he saw plenty of shrimps). Back in Winchester, he had a pickled hog's cheek at a pub called the Checker, then sent for his cousins Gilbert Bear and John Dummer and treated them to ale and wine, though his uncle Richard came too and insisted on buying a round ("indeed Cous. Mercy Stork and he seem the most kind of all my Relations").

On his return to London, he went to the Jews' cemetery at Mile End, noting that the inscriptions were engraved in Hebrew, Latin, Spanish, and English, sometimes all on the same stone. Sewall's millennial beliefs centered on the conversion of the Jews, whose tribes would be reunited in the New Jerusalem. He had a great respect for Jewish tra-

ditions and spirituality, and, like most Puritans, was devoted to the Old
Testament, particularly the book of Psalms. Above all, despite his own
deep convictions, on a personal level he was habitually a tolerant and
open man. So we have a touching vignette of him conversing with the
cemetery keeper: "I told the keep[r] afterwards wisht might meet in
Heaven: He answered, and drink a Glass of Beer together, which we
were then doing."

He visited Saint Paul's, "a great and excellent piece of work," and out
came the ruler again: "The Stairs are five foot 1/2 long and four inches
deep." He watched the election of the mayor in Guildhall, and enjoyed
the ceremony of it all: "When the People cry'd, a Hall, a Hall, the Al-
dermen came up two by two, the Mace carried before them, came in at
the dore opposite to the Street dore out of another apartment. I stood
in the Clock-Gallery."

He had been on one jaunt, to the southwest and south; he undertook
two more, again very much those modern tourists might choose—one
to Oxford and nearby towns, the other to Cambridge. He set off on the
Oxford trip on 28 March, traveling with Increase Mather, who had
brought his thirteen-year-old son, Samuel, with him. At Colebrook,
Sewall dined alone on a bullock's cheek and in the evening had a supper
of two dunghill fowls with the Mathers. Forty years later, he wrote a
letter of reminiscence to Samuel Mather, who was then minister at
Witney, near Oxford, recalling "our leaving the Doctor your Father at
Maidenhead while you and I footed it along the meadow to Bray
Church," the phrasing nostalgically evoking life's prime from the stand-
point of old age ("I am still praying that God wou'd Mercifully rectify
the disorders of my Back, strengthen my weak Hands, and confirm my
feeble Knees").

Tourists could be rooked in 1689 just as efficiently as they are today:
the last five miles in the coach to Oxford—"little ones" at that—cost
the threesome 12s. He was impressed by the colleges; he enjoyed their
provender too. At New College, thanks to a letter of introduction to the
agreeably rhyming Mr. Benjamin Cutler, the butler, he was treated to
"Ale, wine, Lent cakes full of Currants, good Butter and Cheese."

He went to Abingdon on 1 April, a windy day, and diligently recycled all the visitor information he acquired there: pike and perch and eels were caught in the River Ock, running along the bottom of the gardens on one side of Ock Street before flowing into the Thames; the flatboats moored by the stone bridge carried seventy tons of malt, and needed flashes—sudden rushes of water discharged from a weir—to help them over the shallow places. Back in Oxford, he visited the Bodleian Library, and out came his ruler: "The galleries very magnificent about 44 of my Canes in length and near 8 in breadth." He enjoyed looking at a book "which in Cuts [engravings] sets forth the Glory of Old Rome."

Then he was off on a trip to Warwick and Coventry, where he saw his great-grandfather's name carved in the City Hall, and visited some relatives who had inherited land on which he himself had a claim. He offered to confirm their right to the property for a consideration, but got short shrift from his kinswoman's husband: "Lapworth said he would not give 3^d." Perhaps to cheer himself up, he had himself serenaded the next day: "Had 3 of the City Waits [watchmen] bid me good morrow with their wind Musick." Back at Warwick, he saw soldiers and townspeople getting themselves drunk on brandy punch while effigies of the pope were being carried about, and had his hair cut. Then, in Oxford, he attended three Anglican services on the same day, 14 April, all conducted by fellows of the colleges, and shortly after that returned to London. At this point, he started on diplomatic activity on behalf of New England.

Increase Mather had been having a frustrating time in his negotiations with the English court. Initially, he'd made some progress with James II, who, as his political position became more precarious, had become proportionately more willing to listen to New England's case. Though William was more in tune with the perspective of the colony, he had less reason to forgo his authority over their affairs. On 24 April, Sewall went to Whitehall hoping to have an interview with the Earl of Shrewsbury, the secretary of state, though this was postponed. Four days later, he wrote a letter to the member of Parliament for Dover, Thomas Papillon, who was descended from the Huguenots and who had relatives in Boston: "I, and several besides me, are here far removed from our Wives and Children, and have little heart to goe home before some comfortable settlement obtained, whereby we might be secured in the Possession of our Religion, Liberty and Property."

Sewall still enjoyed seeing the sights, including those visible through new optics demonstrated by the brilliant and cantankerous astronomer royal, John Flamsteed. Elisha Hutchinson, the Boston giant who had once had a standoff with Edward Randolph, took him on a visit to the Tower of London, where he saw very much what visitors see today: the crown and scepter, the armory, and the mint (they were not allowed in to witness the milling of the coins). On 9 May, he was back in harness on behalf of New England, going to Hampton Court with other lobbyists like the prominent Bostonian merchant Richard Wharton, to wait upon the king and his council—who failed to show up. Increase Mather didn't appear, either, sending a message that he was ill, though Sewall understood he'd been seen on the Exchange, which was where the New England faction congregated. Sewall's trip was obviously a red herring, and he was beginning to guess that Mather preferred to operate without him being privy to the negotiations. On his way to his lodgings, he was cheered up in Clapham with cider, ale, oysters, and ox tongue.

The situation grew more uncertain. On 11 May, war (King William's War, it would be called) was declared against France. French warships or privateers could now threaten English shipping and Sewall, on the wrong side of the Atlantic Ocean, felt trapped. "The dangers of the Passage are now multiplied," he wrote in a letter. Still, he continued to stockpile his London experiences. On 15 May, he went to a tavern called the Garden at Mile End, and drank currant-and-raspberry wine. Then he was off to the Dog and Partridge (where a soldier had been shot by his drunken companion the night before), and played ninepins. The following day, the future chief justice of Massachusetts went to the Old Bailey to watch some trials.

On Saturday, 18 May, Sewall was one of a whole party of New England representatives summoned by the attorney general to Hampton Court, and this time Increase Mather did turn up. Just as Sewall went about recording the dimensions of public buildings with his joint-rule, so here he noted the scale and gravity of the occasion by using a mercantile unit of measure: the party occupied two coaches that cost 21s. apiece, not counting the money paid to the drivers. Despite this expensive entrance and the fact that the New England contingent was represented by two counsel, the proceedings were an anticlimax: ". . . dismissed *sine Die.*"

Nevertheless, things were warming up. That same day, a pamphlet was published attacking New England for abusing the charter, and accusing it of making itself independent of the crown. Sewall attended a meeting on the Monday to formulate a reply to these accusations, only to discover another tract had come out, this time attacking "our repugnant Laws, full of Untruths almost as the former." When he got back to his lodgings after this depressing occasion, Sewall found a letter from his brother, telling him that Hannah and the children were all well, which was some consolation, "but New England [was] bleeding." A few days later, Mather published a reply to the pamphlets, *New-England Vindicated.*

New England was bleeding, and Sewall carried on with his campaigning letters, but old England continued to fascinate him too. The Dutch ambassadors made a ceremonial entrance to London: ". . . were about 50 Coaches, with Six Horses apiece, besides Pages on foot, and youths on Horsback." He was astonished at the crowds: "The main streets thwacked with people." He went to see a certain Elizabeth Nash, age twenty-five and only three feet tall, observant as always: "Her hands show Age more than anything else." The poor creature had no breasts, and "By reason of her thickness and weight can goe but sorrily." He heard the cries of London and translated them: "Green Hastings, i.e. Pease[,] are cry'd at 6^d a Peck, in little carts." That was on 4 June; on the eleventh, he noted that green hastings had gone down to fourpence. On 13 June, he signed a petition for leave to go home, in effect an application for an exit visa.

The next day, he had an odd and revealing experience. He was walking up and down in his room while his landlady was preparing dinner, and the need came over him to ask for a blessing. He thought about the fact that he'd just bought himself some clothes, and this made him decide to ask for the blessing to be directed at his physical self, "so I mentally pray'd God to bless my Flesh, Bones, Blood and Spirits, Meat, Drink and Apparel." A little later he was sitting at dinner and sawing the crust off his bread when the knife slipped and he cut his thumb. Looking at his spilled blood, he remembered that he'd been praying for his blood a short time before, and that he couldn't recall ever having used the word "blood" in prayer previously. It was one of those moments when he thought he could glimpse a pattern in his experience, some crossover between the inward spiritual word and the outward physical one.

It's when you have to begin preparations for the return that homesickness really sets in. A week after signing his petition to leave, Sewall had another dream of Hannah's death, "which made me very heavy." Nevertheless, a few days later, on 26 June, he set out on his jaunt to Cambridge, in company with Increase and Samuel Mather, and a relative, Edward Hull. His first impression of the place was not favorable, because of "the meanness of the Town-buildings, and most of the Colledges being of brick." However, he soon warmed to the magnificence of individual colleges, Trinity and Kings especially, though as always his eyes were open to the smaller sights too, like the sparrows in Trinity College's hall: "At meal-Times they feed of Crums, and will approach very near Men." He was also much taken with a petrified cheese that was displayed in St. John's College library. He plodded up Castle Hill, and enjoyed the view. The prison and courthouse were situated there, and he cast a professional eye over them. The courthouse wasn't anything special: indeed, it looked just like a cowshed. Lo and behold, it turned out cattle were inside, sharing with the justices the privilege of "free egress and regress there." So much for the dignity of the law—but at least the gallows were handy, situated "in a Dale, convenient for Spectators to stand all round on the rising Ground." At the university printing room ("60 foot long and 20 foot broad"), he, former printer for Massachusetts Bay, had his name printed by one of the six presses.

On 28 June, the party set out on the journey back to London. At about eleven the following morning, they arrived at a coffee house belonging to a Mr. Cropper. Here Sewall was handed a newsletter and when he set eyes on it, he was "surpris'd with joy." New England had had a revolution.

A YOUNG MAN called John Winslow had brought the news of William of Orange's landing to Boston on 4 April, five months after it had taken place. It's easy to forget the communication lag in a horse- and wind-powered age. Mather and Sewall were representing a community that had no idea what monarch they were actually trying to negotiate with. The royalist authorities in Boston must have been appalled on hearing of James's fall from power. He'd been their sponsor, the guarantor of the legitimacy of their authority in the hostile environment of Massachusetts. Governor Andros had Winslow jailed to stop him spreading the news, but it spread anyway. There was a fortnight's lull while the Bostonians digested the implications. They had no guarantee that William's invasion had been successful. Only three years previously the Duke of Monmouth had led an unsuccessful rebellion against James II on behalf of the Protestant cause. If that precedent was anything to go by, the whole thing might have turned into a blood-soaked disaster by now.

Nevertheless, hope worked away like yeast, and on 18 April a rising took place in Boston. Many of the leading citizens assembled in the Town House, and at noon, Cotton Mather stood on its gallery and read a declaration of the injustices Massachusetts had suffered under Andros's administration. While Increase Mather was plugging away at the English court, his son was in the thick of things in Boston: between them, they covered both ends of Massachusetts's revolution. Randolph and other officials were thrown into jail. Andros himself was a slightly trickier prospect, as he was sheltering in Boston's fort.

That afternoon, the frigate *Rose* leveled guns at the town and tried to rescue him. The ship had been commissioned into the service of Massachusetts three years before, as per an order signed by Samuel Pepys. A landing party was sent to the shore, but the sailors were promptly disarmed by militia, hardly the scenario envisaged during all that trooping about on the common, but the years of discipline came in useful anyway. The colonists then surrounded the fort and Andros surrendered to them. He spent the night under guard in a prominent citizen's house, and the following day was sent back to the fort as a prisoner. The sails of the *Rose* were removed to disable the ship, an elegant solution to the problem posed by the awkward symbolism implicit in capturing a vessel of His Majesty's navy. Andros made a picturesque attempt to escape, dressing himself up in women's clothing, rather as Toad would do in *The Wind in the Willows* two centuries later. He got past two sentries, but the third noticed that he was still wearing men's shoes. Chief Justice Joseph Dudley had been on his judicial rounds while these dramatic events unfolded, but he was also captured and placed under house arrest.

A provisional administration was set up, the "Council for the Safety of the People, and Conservation of the Peace," the title containing an odd premonition of revolutions a century later. On 22 May, a convention of delegates from the New England towns voted to establish an interim government according to the rules of the old charter. One of New England's founding fathers, Simon Bradstreet, now eighty-six, was appointed acting governor, and a court of Assistants was appointed (all interim posts, pending the outcome of the negotiations in London on the future of the charter). Four days later, a ship arrived from England with the news that William and Mary were indeed on the throne, and general rejoicing (and relief) prevailed.

News of the uprising was joyful indeed to the negotiators in England, but from a diplomatic point of view it was also a little tricky. The king had to be persuaded that the deposing of his royal governor reflected loyalty rather than sedition. When William had come to the throne, he originally ordered that Andros should continue in office, but Mather had managed to intercept the directive. In due course, he got William to agree that Andros should be returned to England to face charges of maladministration, so in that respect at least the colonists' actions received retrospective justification.

Sewall continued busily to write letters and attend meetings for the cause of New England and the permanent restoration of the charter. He was very much aware that his role was simply to provide support for Increase Mather, who was at the sharp edge of the negotiations: ". . . we that are here count it our Duty if we can assist Mr. Mather." He saw two men who had spoken out against the government getting "exceedingly pelted with dirt and Eggs" in the pillory outside the Royal Exchange, while another, who had committed fraud, had nothing thrown at him, an interesting lesson in relativity. That evening, "with a concern'd Countenance," Cousin Hull told him he had some bad news, and Sewall waited with bated breath. It turned out that his suit was getting moth-eaten. On 8 July, he and Brattle hired a wherry and went out on the Thames for a swim, Sewall taking the plunge in his drawers: "I think it hath been healthful and refreshing to me." A week later, he rode to Tyburn and watched eighteen people, sixteen men and two women, being hanged.

Some days later, he had a humiliating rebuff. Increase Mather told him he'd decided that two Boston representatives, Elisha Hutchinson and Samuel Appleton, should act as witnesses to the charge that Sir Edmund Andros was guilty of maladministration. He asked where Hutchinson could be found, and Sewall led him there. He was not invited to appear himself, however. He knew now for sure that he'd been sidelined. He must have wondered if this whole visit to England, this great upheaval in his life, had been worth it. He returned to his lodgings to think matters through, swallowed his pride, and went off to William Whiting, who was representing the legal interests of Connecticut in the battle against Andros (all the separate New England colonies, together with New York and New Jersey, had been lumped together as the Dominion of New England during Andros's presidency). Whiting was coordinating proceedings with Increase Mather, so Sewall thought there might be a chance of inveigling his way back into the action through him. He explained that he too was in a position to testify. Whiting took little notice. Sewall could attend the court if he wanted to, but he doubted if he could contribute. Whiting seemed to be offended with him. All Sewall could think of was a conversation he had had with Mather a month or two before. At that stage, Sewall had been unenthusiastic about leveling charges at Andros because the Corporation Bill was about to go through Parliament, a measure designed to restore the old charter of Massachusetts Bay. His fear was that any move against Andros while that was taking place would make his allies determined to block the bill. But the strategic caution he'd advocated then was irrelevant now. The bill was a hopeless cause anyway: ". . . the Bill is even despair'd of, and our friends in N.E. are in for Cakes and Ale, and we must doe all we may to sink or swim with them."

Because of Puritanism's antipathy toward the stage, Sewall's was a world without Shakespeare, so it's odd to see him use a phrase forever associated with Sir Toby Belch's rebuke to the puritanical Malvolio in *Twelfth Night*. Sewall was fond of cakes and ale himself (on 24 July, he enjoyed "a Dish of Bacon with Pidgeons, Sauce, Beans and Cabbage. Then roast Veal, Tarts") but here he is using the tag in a different sense entirely, to mean for better or worse. (A century later, in another revolution, Franklin would talk of the need to hang together to avoid being hanged separately.) Sure enough, on 3 August Sewall recorded that the "Corporation-Bill sticks in the Birth." Meanwhile, he had gone to Westminster with Hutchinson and Appleton, holding on to their coat-tails and hoping for his chance to testify against Andros, but "there was not an opportunity."

On 1 August, a ship arrived from America with the news that the towns and cities of New England had proclaimed William and Mary their rightful sovereigns, that all processes of law would run in their names, and that they were about to send two envoys over to "have their Liberties confirmed." Sewall's personal diplomacy had come to naught, but this felt like an upnote, a good moment to take leave. He'd seen to some family business, with mixed success, and had explored his mother country, paying his respects to his past. He'd agitated for the interests of his colony as best he could. America was where his current commitments, his family, business, and career, were waiting for him; it was where his future lay. On 13 August, Sewall went with Brattle, Hutchinson, and others from the Salutation Inn at Billingsgate to Woolwich, where they saw the King's Ropeyard (nine score paces long—Sewall was still addicted to measurement). Increase Mather was not invited to join the party. They went on to Gravesend, and boarded the *America* about ten that evening.

Sewall made one of his inglorious entrances, barking his shin on the end of a chest as he went into his cabin. The ship wouldn't sail for some time; his object at present was simply to make preparations for the journey, and to supervise the loading of his goods, which included barrels of cheese and peas, beer and ale, a box of biscuits, another small cheese wrapped in lead that he was taking as a present for friends (William Vaughan and his wife, Margaret), a cheese store (a bit of a theme emerging by now), three small trunks for his children with their initials and birthdates picked out in nails, another for his wife with the initials H.S. on it, four hats, a great deal of linen, and a fishing rod.

He spent the night in lodgings with Brattle, and when he woke the next day found his nightshirt was covered with blood from his graze. Increase Mather arrived, very angry with them for leaving him behind the day before. Sewall apologized, saying he'd come on ahead because he thought he might be more useful at Gravesend and Deal than in London. It was his way of pointing out that he'd been made to feel he was no use at all in London. Busy, important, bad-tempered Mather wasn't tuned into the subtleties of his sarcasm; as soon as he realized the ship wasn't about to sail, he turned on his heels and went back to his diplomatic machinations in the capital.

Over the next days, Sewall went sightseeing around Kent. At Sandwich, he noticed the little sand cliffs and inner sand hills were "something like Plum Island," a beautiful place of dunes and salt marshes tucked into the Massachusetts coast beside his home town of Newbury. The cause of the delay was that war with the French meant the *America* needed the escort of a naval vessel when it took to sea. On 3 August Sewall had written to Hannah, telling her that "Several of us are very desirous to come home; but judge not fit to venture without a Convoy." He was longing for his family by that stage, signing off with "My hearty Love to thee, & to our dear Quaternion Samuel, Hannah, Elizabeth and Joseph from thy affectionately loving Husband," and addressing the letter simply "To his dear Wife Mis. Hannah Sewall at Boston in New-England." Momentous events had taken place there, but Boston was still a small town. The escort vessel, the *Exeter*, duly arrived on 23 August, and the party, once again including the Mathers, was summoned on board four days later.

For the next two weeks, adverse weather prevented the *America* and its escort from sailing. During this period, young Samuel Mather came down with smallpox, and he and his father had to leave the ship. By the time he recovered, the *America* had long since departed, and it had become clear to Increase Mather that the tide was running against the New England interest and that reinstatement of the charter would be a long and complex task. As it turned out, the two remained in England for another three years. At the end of 1689, Mather and Sir Henry Ashurst were officially recognized as agents of the colony, and were joined by two other representatives, Elisha Cooke and Thomas Oakes. The following year, the agents were finally asked to formulate their case against Andros, and proceed with the very business that had caused Sewall such frustration. Mather wanted to press the charges, but the new agents thought it would create too adversarial a climate, rather as Sewall had feared the previous year. At this stage, however, caution was a mistake and seriously damaged the New England cause, making it appear their grievances were not well founded.

Early in 1691, Mather presented his proposal for a new charter. Not surprisingly, it was turned down, in favor of another version prepared by William Blathwayt, secretary of the Committee for Trade and Plantations. This charter was far more disadvantageous than the old one, but Mather managed to make some modifications and was pragmatic enough to realize it was the best deal he could get, so he signed it.

The charter related to Massachusetts, Maine, Plymouth, and Nova Scotia, and under its terms the governor would be appointed by the king, though just to sweeten the pill a little, Mather was allowed to make the first appointment, and chose a Massachusetts adventurer called Sir William Phips. He was also permitted to choose the first twenty-eight members of the Governor's Council, the upper house of government (one of them would be Sewall). Each year thereafter, they were to be elected by the General Court, consisting of the two houses of the legislature, subject to veto by the governor (Sewall retained his membership until 1725, when he retired, often achieving reelection with the highest number of votes). There were to be two representatives from every town in the lower house, elected by freeholders who no longer had to be church members. This was a very significant development. The governance of the province, as it was now called, was being secularized. The governor had the power to veto laws passed by the General Court (the Governor's Council and the House of Representatives together), and was in charge of the militia and appointed judges. Nevertheless, the General Court had the sole power to raise taxes, and land titles were confirmed. Nobody would be able to take Hogg Island away from the Sewalls.

It was a compromise deal, which maintained a degree of local control over the province's business, and one for which Mather could take credit and in which he felt justifiable pride. But like most political compromises, it was an uneasy one: over the next decades, the representatives expressed their disapproval of having governors thrust upon them by refusing to pay their salaries, and the wrangling between New Englanders and the mother country would be a constant theme for the next century.

THE *AMERICA* finally set sail on 15 September 1689. After a couple of days of strong winds, and the fright of losing touch with the *Exeter* in the night, Sewall confessed, "Am ready to wish myself with Mr Mather and my Namesake, recovering of the Small Pocks at Deal." The next day, the *America* had a skirmish with a privateer and lost its flagpole; one of the company by the name of Will Merry dislocated his thumb. Nevertheless, they landed safely at Plymouth. No naval vessels were currently available for escorting duties across the Atlantic, so they had to remain perched there for the time being.

While they waited for their voyage to resume, Sewall and Brattle obtained lodgings near the harbor with Mr. and Mrs. Jennings, a couple who would become friends. Sewall inspected Francis Drake's watercourse, and went for a meal at the lodgings of Mr. Bedford, a fellow passenger, where he "Had a dish of Fowls and Bacon with Livers: a Dish of Salt Fish, and a Piece of Mutton reaching from the neck a pretty way of the back, the ribs reaching equally from the back bone, Cheese and fruit: no Wine." The excursion into sheep anatomy testifies to Sewall's sincere enjoyment of the pleasures of the table, as does the sad concluding announcement.

Plymouth was awash with soldiers, some of whom lodged cheek by jowl with Sewall in the Jennings' household. An ensign who was stationed in the town died, and was buried on 5 October; Sewall witnessed the ceremony and recorded the tattoo performed by the drums of the watch. Looking at his attempt to reproduce the sound is a strangely evocative experience, very different from reading a musical score, which is only the blueprint for a rendition. Here we have something much more like a seventeenth-century tape recording, sounds beating through the air of long-ago Plymouth and caught by the pen (Latin: stylus) of a man who was there. Three sets of drums took it up, one after the other.

Samuel Sewall (1652–1730). Diary entry for 5 October 1689.
Samuel Sewall Diaries, MHS.

On 7 October, Sewall heard that a frigate had been taken by the French off the Isles of Scilly, and his courage nearly failed: ". . . am wavering as to my going." Captain Allen (one of the passengers) left the ship and he nearly left it too; but "he returning I returned." However, it was arranged that they would go in convoy with several vessels and escorted by a warship, and they finally set sail three days later. The next day, two rogue ships appeared to windward, but were sent packing by their man-of-war. However, the *America* lost touch with her fellow ships when they were only forty leagues beyond the Scillies, and never made contact with them again. To compound matters, a French Huguenot passenger called Captain Dumenee became ill on 19 October. There was always the danger of an epidemic breaking out on board, a claustrophobic possibility in a small vessel picking its solitary way across the Atlantic. But the next day, Sewall saw a "pleasant Rainbow," a comforting sign, and the day after he had the pleasure of discovering that in their haste to leave the ship, the Mathers had left a cake behind.

Dumenee was dangerously ill by 28 October; then Will Merry, he of the dislocated thumb, went down with measles. Just as Dumenee began to recover, Brattle started spitting blood and, on 10 November, another passenger, Captain Wilkinson, was taken ill. However, the weather turned unexpectedly mild and the passengers were able to take their meals at a table on the deck. After a few days of these picnics it became foggy, but by then they were over the Grand Banks, and another of the French Huguenot refugees among the passengers, Mr. Fannevol (a member of whose family would one day donate to Boston the famous market house known as Faneuil Hall), caught a large cod, "which had several small Fish in him, suppose to be Anchovas." It was a symbolic moment: ". . . now we have tasted afresh of American Fare."

Another alarm came on 20 November. Two ships approached, possibly rogues, at worst enemies. The small arms were loaded. The next day, however, the *America* put out its ensigns and the ships responded: ". . . find them to be Jersy-Men, our Friends." The Jerseymen informed them that as they must have suspected, the *America* was the hindmost of all the fleet. The incident had given Sewall another scare: ". . . there wanted not Some Probability of my being beholding to the sea ffor a buriing Place." He decided to make a will, leaving some books in memory of his old teacher, Thomas Parker, and of Charles Chauncy, the president of Harvard who had admitted him to the college. He left his "new Cloath-colour'd suit with the Chamlet Cloak" to his brother Stephen. His watch would go "to my dear wife . . . as a Token of my Love," and a loving token, a gesture, was exactly what it was, because, in fact, "as to the things mentioned on this and the other side of this Leaf, I leave them to the Discretion and good liking of my dear mother [i.e., mother-in-law] and Wife, to do them or leave them undone, because the Estate is theirs." The will was unnecessary, except to ease the panic of the moment. In any case, if the worst came to the worst, it would spiral down to the sea bottom with its maker. By the time of Sewall's death, it had long been discarded. But for now it gave Sewall the opportunity to remind himself of his debts to those who had made him what he was: the men who had given him an education, the family who had provided him with the wealth and status he now enjoyed, the people he loved.

As they approached the shore, a purse was once again established for first sighting, and Sewall contributed 5s. It was won by a seaman called Sauny, spying land from the topsail yard, at three o'clock on 28 November. Not only that, but the land in question included a glimpse of the scene of Sewall's boyhood: "The Mate Wallis and Gunner say 'tis Pigeon-Hill on Cape-Anne. Gunner, who is a Coaster, saith also that he sees Newbury Old-Town-Hills, and Rowly Hill. All see it plain on deck before sunset. Pleasant wether, clear skie, smooth sea . . . Blessed be God who has agen brought me to a sight of New-England."

They landed at the Great Island in the Piscataqua River the following day. The first thing Sewall did was to send Madam Vaughan the cheese he'd bought for her and her husband. The next day, he arrived at Newbury and "fell into the affectionate Embraces of family and friends." On 2 December, at between nine and ten at night, he arrived at home in Boston.

CHAPTER FOUR

The Yellow Bird

ยยย

$\mathcal{A}$ WEEK OR TWO AFTER ARRIVING HOME, SEWALL FACED A crisis at family devotions. Grown-ups and children took it in turns to read from the scriptures, and eight-year-old Elizabeth found herself assigned one of the most gloomy chapters in the whole Bible, Isaiah 24: "Behold, the Lord maketh the earth empty, and maketh it waste, and turneth it upside down, and scattereth abroad the inhabitants thereof." She hadn't been well, and the bleak prophecy proved too much.

This was the first of a number of episodes of spiritual despair that Betty experienced while growing up. Sewall, always the involved father, burst into tears as well, his emotions charged by "the Contents of the Chapter, and Sympathy with her." The contents of the chapter could be seen to be speaking directly to the state of New England in 1690, its political limbo while the charter was being renegotiated over in England, and its anxiety that the city on the hill was illusory or already in ruins, given the diminishment of spirituality and the falling off of covenanted members of the New England congregations. The sense of crisis had been heightened by the outbreak of war with the French, King William's War, which triggered savage raids by their Indian allies. To top it all, smallpox had broken out in the community: "The earth mourneth and fadeth away, the world languisheth and fadeth away, the haughty people of the earth do languish. The earth also is defiled under the inhabitants thereof; because they have transgressed the laws, changed the ordinance, broken the everlasting covenant" (Isaiah 24:4–5).

Two days later, Sewall told Sam Jr. about the death of a boy from smallpox, and warned that he too needed to prepare himself for death and make sure he really meant the words when he said the Lord's Prayer. Sam carried on munching his apple, apparently impervious, but when it came time for "Our Father" he suddenly gave out a bitter cry. Sewall asked him what the matter was, but at first he was too upset to speak. Then he cried again, and said he was afraid he was going to die. Sewall prayed with him and read him scriptural passages that gave reassurance about dying, such as "O death where is thy sting," a question that unfortunately seems to cut both ways, reminding the listener of death's sting even while claiming there's no such thing—especially, perhaps, when the listener is only eleven.

In the weeks following, one of Sewall's nieces died of smallpox and another contracted it. Then, in February, came news of a terrible massacre in Schenectady, a little above Albany, in the colony of New York: "60 Men, Women and Children murder'd. Women with Child rip'd up, Children had their Brains dash'd out." Meanwhile, Sewall had other worries closer to home. He was particularly disturbed by a judicial decision he'd had to make, concerning the death sentence passed on a pirate.

Piracy plagued the New England seaboard for the remainder of Sewall's lifetime. It was an area where the distinction between war and crime became blurred. In principle, freelance raiding of enemy ships for booty—privateering—was a perfectly legitimate business enterprise, though targeting neutral or allied vessels was, or should have been, a different matter altogether. But the enormous amorality of the ocean seemed to tempt its entrepreneurs to modulate from the first activity to the others, perhaps just a failure of anticipation, a sense that out of sight of land the machinery of justice couldn't or wouldn't operate, that the story would never get back. Boston in the late seventeenth and early eighteenth centuries was an outpost of civilization threatened by anarchic forces on all sides—hostile savages inland, freebooters out to sea— and fresh from his ocean terrors Sewall was particularly sensitive to the latter danger.

While he was in England, the pirates Thomas Pound and Thomas Hawkins had embarked on short but spectacular careers. Pound had been pilot of the frigate *Rose*, the ship prevented from rescuing Andros during the Massachusetts Revolution. It was a time when defining service to the colony was not a straightforward matter. Frustrated when the *Rose* was put into purdah, Pound sailed off in Hawkins's fishing boat, intending to take a larger vessel and use it to attack French ships in the West Indies. The ship they captured, however, was a Salem ketch, the *Mary*, and soon they were preying on other vessels along the New England coast.

Perhaps getting a close-up view of the transience of political power encouraged Pound's recklessness. His adventure ended with a bloody confrontation between his men and a ship commanded by a Captain Pease, who had been commissioned to pursue the pirates (Pease's vessel being the *Mary*, in point of fact, abandoned by the pirates in favor of subsequent captures, ships and men changing their colors as rapidly as the sea itself). Pease was killed, as were a number of the pirates, but the rest were captured.

Sewall had been installed as a member of the interim Court of Assistants as soon as he returned from his trip to England, and was on the bench for Hawkins's trial on 9 January 1690, and that of the other pirates on the seventeenth. They were found guilty, and five of them were due to be executed on 27 January. However, Wait Still Winthrop, another of the assistants and a close colleague of Sewall's over the next decades, lobbied earnestly for their reprieves (his brother had been married to one of Hawkins's sisters), and on the day scheduled for the executions, several judges—including Sewall—met at Acting Governor Bradstreet's house and reprieved two of them. Sewall then went home, and in his absence another pirate was pardoned. At the very last minute, Winthrop and two fellow judges rushed around to Sewall's house to ask him to sign a reprieve for Hawkins. This he did, though with great reluctance. Only one of the pirates, Thomas Johnson, actually hanged that day. Hawkins's reprieve arrived when he was on the gallows. The crowd was waiting for him to be turned off, and was naturally disappointed.

Sewall felt he'd been cajoled into an error of judgment, and feared his moment of weakness might offend the Almighty: "Let not God impute Sin," he wrote. A month after his own safe landfall, he seemed to have become infected by the waywardness and confusion of the high seas.

In April, he went off to New York with William Stoughton, the deputy acting governor, to attend a meeting convened to establish military cooperation between the colonies in the war against the French and Indians. Just before they set out came the doleful news that between eighty and a hundred lives had been lost in a French and Indian attack on Salmon Falls, New Hampshire. During the trip, Sewall was in a deep depression: "I have had great heaviness on my Spirit before, and in this journey; and I resolved that if it pleas'd God to bring me to my Family again, I would endeavour to serve Him better in Self-denial, Fruitfullness, Not pleasing Men, open Conversation, not being solicitous to seem in some indifferent things what I was not, or at least to conceal what I was . . ." One Sunday during this stay, Sewall read Psalm 25, one of the most guilt-ridden in the whole book: "For thy name's sake, Jehovah, I / do humbly Thee entreat: To pardon mine iniquitie, / for it is very great." It was, he said, "a Psalm extraordinarily fitted for me in my present Distresses."

Sewall was not a morbid Puritan; the overall picture the diary presents is of a buoyant, optimistic, and vital man. But at this time he seems particularly worried about the great pitfall of public life: being overeager to attract the good will of others by not being true to oneself. His guilt at allowing himself to be browbeaten into reprieving Hawkins had something to do with this melancholy and helps explain how he would soon be a member of a court that tried twenty-seven people for witchcraft and found them all guilty. It would be like him to confide his anxiety to Stoughton, a man unrelenting in his espousal of judicial severity, who would have rebuked him in no uncertain terms.

When he got home, he found his daughter Hannah had gone down with smallpox, though "very favourably" (she developed fifty or sixty pustules on her face, but rapidly recovered). In May, there was bad news from "the eastward"—or, as we would say it, the north—Casco Bay in Maine. "'Tis believed Casco garrisons and fort are burnt and the inhabitants destroyed: so that we do not understand that there is one escaped, or shut up, or left." Later that summer, another baby was born to the Sewalls. She was baptized Judith, Mr. Willard using plenty of water in the process, though she didn't cry at all. A month later she was dying, her father watching over her in the small hours and asking a clergyman to "give her a Lift towards heaven." On her coffin was "the year 1690, made with little nails." Another daughter, Mary, was born the following year. She had better luck, and lived to adulthood, or very nearly.

One day when little Joseph, just three years old, was being lifted into his cradle, he said, "News from Heaven, the French were come, and mention'd Canada." Sewall marveled at this precocity: "No body has been tampering with him as I could learn." The toddler was living in a saturated solution of war and danger. "The Lord help us to repent that we may not perish" was Sewall's response. His friend John Alden, adventurer and sea dog, was taken at sea by a French frigate a few weeks later, and Alden's son, along with Colonel Jonathan Tyng, was held for ransom in Canada while he returned to arrange terms for their release.

In early December 1691, stormy weather, with rain and snow, came to Boston. Sewall's sister Jane was visiting. "By the fire I speak earnestly to Sister, to make sure of an interest in Christ, being alone." On 4 January, a great snow fell, and Sewall had trouble going to one of the many burials he attended. On the twelfth, the weather eased; that day brought Sewall more scope for gloomy reflection, however. A middle-aged woman by the name of Hamlen had a row with her son, and beat him. The incident upset her so much that she wouldn't take supper with her husband and his visitor. She cleared the shoulder of mutton away when the two had finished, took it into another room, and then tore off a piece of gristly meat and popped it into her mouth, the sort of sad stressed-out lonely gobble you need in times of crisis. It stuck in her throat.

Goodwife Hamlen stamped her foot and pointed her finger at her mouth, but to no avail. Sewall quoted Ovid, expressing amazement that evil can occur with so little discrimination.

On 26 January 1692, news came of an Indian raid on York, just a few miles north of Sewall's home town of Newbury. Some days later, when he was up-to-date on the horrible details, Sewall wrote to an acquaintance about the destruction of the town. Fifty people had been killed, nearly ninety captured. "The Reverend Mr. Shabael Dummer, their godly learned pastor, was shot dead, off his horse . . . which is the more sorrowful to me, because my Mothers Cousin german [i.e., my mother's true cousin] and my very good friend." A couple of weeks later he took notes of a gloomy sermon by Mr. Willard: "This Land . . . hath been long weltering in blood ever now and y^n [then] our neighbours are barbourously murthered, and more barbourously captivated."

There were strong winds in the second half of February. On the twenty-seventh, Sewall heard the roaring of a beast he imagined to be an ox that had broken free from its butcher, but it turned out to be his own cow, bitten so badly by a dog they had to put her out of her misery, despite her copious yields of milk. "Happy are they," Sewall wrote, drawing the inevitable Puritan moral, "who have God for their Spring and Brest of Supplies."

During the course of the coming months, he would hear tales about a different, demonic kind of suckling.

A FEW MILES north of Boston, the inhabitants of Salem Village had similar reasons to feel demoralized and anxious, along with a few special ones of their own. Their community is not to be confused with Salem Town, though it's the latter that now rattles with Halloween junk in commemoration of the tragedy that was just about to strike. The village was an agricultural settlement, and had come into being as a kind of overspill, several miles to the west of Salem proper. Salem Town itself had been the site of one of the original points of entry for the white settlers of New England, a place known by the Indians as Naumkeag. John Endecott's ship, the *Abigail*, landed there on 6 September 1628. It was, according to Cotton Mather, "the Centre and First-Born of all the Towns in the Colony," and at one time had been in line to become the capital of New England. In 1692, it was still one of New England's most important ports, a plump and prosperous town where Sewall's brother Stephen was a leading light. Meanwhile, Salem Town's rural sibling was a straggling, out-of-focus community without the right to set its own taxes or arrange its own civic responsibilities.

Independence was denied the village right up until 1752, when it became the township of Danvers. In 1670, it had been granted permission to raise funds for a meetinghouse and the salary of a minister, but the church wasn't able to admit members of the congregation to the full covenant, or administer communion, until 1689, not long before the crisis began. As a result of the difficulties and tensions caused by this subordinate and impoverished status, the first three clergymen appointed in the period between 1672 and 1689 all left after troubled and foreshortened ministries. Two of them, George Burroughs and Deodat Lawson, both acquaintances of Sewall who had dined at his table, were to play their parts in the events of 1692—one a victim, the other an enabler, of the witch hunt. It was in the house of the fourth minister, Samuel Parris, that the story began.

In mid-January 1692, two little girls, Betty Parris, nine-year-old daughter of the minister, and her eleven-year-old cousin Abigail Williams began behaving strangely, going into paroxysms, wriggling and writhing with apparently involuntary movements that seemed more extreme to the people called in to witness them than epileptic fits. Cotton Mather claimed subsequently that the whole phenomenon started because a group of young people had been experimenting with the supernatural: they began with "little *Sorceries*" and "would often cure Hurts with *Spells*, and practise detestable Conjurations with *Sieves*, and *Keys*, and *Pease*, and *Nails*, and *Horse-shoes*, and other Implements." A local minister, John Hale of Beverly, who examined the children at this early stage later claimed that a victim of possession (possibly therefore one of the experimenters at the parsonage) had been trying her hand at fortune-telling, using a Venus glass to try to make out the form of her future husband. (A Venus glass was a homemade crystal ball: one poured egg white into a tumbler and tried to glimpse something in its shifting opalescence.) It's as likely a scenario as any other, a way of filling up the long winter afternoons and alleviating the restlessness of isolated rural existences, just as children and teenagers might now play with an Ouija board. Hale claims that instead of finding out her future husband's profession— "tinker, tailor, soldier, sailor"—the girl saw the shape of a coffin.

It's appropriate that the germ of the tragedy should be lost in obscurity, because the whole point is that an enormous malevolent threat came out of an insignificant context. The sorceries, as Cotton Mather described them, had been little ones; but the "*Devils* which had been so play'd withal . . . now broke in upon the Country, after as astonishing a manner as was ever heard of."

Mary Sibley, a woman from the village, had a recipe for a witch cake, an unappetizing mixture of rye or barley meal with urine from the afflicted children. She persuaded John Indian, one of a married slave couple belonging to Samuel Parris (perhaps acquired by him during a period spent in Barbados), to bake the cake and feed it to a dog, the idea being that if the dog became bewitched it proved the children were too. It must have worked, or seemed to have. Of course, the only way the experiment could have been a success was by making matters worse. During February, the contagion attacked two other young people, twelve-year-old Ann Putnam and seventeen-year-old Betty Hubbard, and later that month the girls began to attribute blame.

It was a logical enough development. One explanation for suffering, from a Puritan perspective, is that God is punishing you for your guilt, which would mean the girls themselves were to blame for what they were going through. That was the solution initially suggested by Samuel Parris (who appears at this stage not to have known about the witch cake), since it became the burden of a sermon he preached on 14 February: Jesus, he said, "governs his church, not only by his word & spirit, but also by his Rod, & afflictions: therefore we are to beware of fainting when we are chastened, or despising the Rod." Sewall's own children could experience spiritual despair when confronting their guilt and mortality; shifting the blame for their suffering from themselves would be an understandable psychological maneuver on the part of the afflicted girls in Salem Village. The witch cake diagnosis made that strategy possible, particularly when Parris called in the local physician, William Griggs (whose maidservant Betty Hubbard was one of the afflicted), to ask for his verdict on what was happening. Griggs concluded the children were bewitched and "under an Evil Hand."

The girls had to avoid jumping out of the frying pan into the fire. If Christ were causing the paroxysms, they must have behaved badly to deserve them. But if they were possessed by the Devil, the implications could be truly appalling. Twenty years before, Elizabeth Knapp, a maid-servant in the household of Samuel Sewall's pastor, Samuel Willard, had experienced thirty-four days of fits, and attributed them to Satan. Willard wondered if his servant had made a covenant with the Devil; luckily for her, he was unable to come to a firm conclusion. The Salem Village girls would have intuitively understood the importance of es-tablishing that they were *victims* of witchcraft rather than practitioners of it. If their behavior could be seen as being not symptomatic of God's disapproval or of possession by the Devil, but as a visible struggle against incursions by others who were themselves the agents of the De-vil, then they could expect praise rather than blame.

They began by naming three women, all of them vulnerable in vari-ous ways: Tituba, slave in the Parris household and wife of John Indian; Sarah Good, an impoverished village character known for her bad tem-per and habit of muttering to herself in a threatening manner; and Sarah Osborne, a propertied woman but involved in litigation, with a whiff of scandal about her. The Salem outbreak had become a legal matter, and therefore a concern of Samuel Sewall's. It was to prove the key event of his life.

The judicial procedure in Massachusetts fell into three parts: a pre-liminary examination in which the accusations were explored; a grand jury hearing, which assessed the case the preliminary examination had established and decided whether to lay formal charges; and the trial it-self. The colony was operating under provisional arrangements pending the arrival of Sir William Phips, the new governor, who was appointed in January and who would arrive to take up his duties in May. Before his arrival, only preliminary proceedings were heard, with two Salem Town members of the Court of Assistants, John Hathorne and Jonathan Cor-win, appointed to go over to the village and take charge of them. De-tailed records of these examinations were taken, and these, along with written depositions by witnesses, were sent along to the grand jury, when it had finally been convened by the trial court to rule on the specific cases that had been selected by the prosecutor for their decision. When the grand jury found there was a case to answer, the material went on to provide the basis of the trial itself, held before another jury. The official records of this final stage have been lost, though Cotton Mather wrote up five of the trials using them, and in any case the rich material that we have from the earlier stages gives us access to the developing narrative of the Salem witchcraft.

The record of the preliminary examinations has a very different status from normal. In almost every example, the charge at the subsequent trial was that the accused's specter had afflicted the victims while the preliminary examination was actually under way. To make a crude analogy: imagine being arrested on suspicion of being a murderer. The expectation would then be that at the preliminary examination you would commit another murder in open court, thus providing the basis for your later trial. The reason for this strange piece of stage management was the problematic invisibility of spectral crime. Two witnesses were necessary to establish guilt, and the public forum of the preliminary proceedings was the best place to get them.

There was, then, an unusual link between the preliminary examinations and the trials proper, since the latter were deliberating on crimes that had been committed in the former. The paperwork we have gives us not just the background and context, but the *content* of the witchcraft narrative that unfolded through the spring and summer of 1692. The preliminary examinations sometimes took many hours, and indeed days, over a single case (Hathorne, who took the lead in questioning the accused, worked formidably hard over the next six months, earning himself the enduring contempt of his great-great-grandson, Nathaniel Hawthorne). The trial sessions, however, for which Sewall was one of the judges, were much shorter, sometimes disposing of a number of cases in a single day, so it's clear that the later hearings built on the groundwork that had already been established, which is still available to us. Moreover, in many of the cases that hadn't made it to the second or third stage by the time Governor Phips brought matters to a halt in the autumn, there were developments in, and embellishments to, the witch-craft narrative that had a bearing on the cases that Sewall and his fellow judges actually did hear.

Sewall tells us little about the Salem witch trials while he was actively involved in them. In the months and years following, though, we can see him trying to come to terms with what had happened, and with the extent of his own responsibility for it, a process that was to culminate, a few years later, in the greatest crisis he ever faced. And as we track beyond that point, it becomes apparent that the events of 1692 marked the beginning of a profound shift in his perspective on himself, on people in general, and on the matter of good and evil.

Over the next few months, Sewall's biography becomes projected into the experiences of dozens of other people who were caught up in the crisis. Their story is in one sense or another his story, because he had access to all that happened and was of course a central player himself, though for the most part we lack a record of his contributions. "Story" is the word, because from the beginning it's clear that the authorities regarded everything that was taking place as part of a single evolving narrative. All the cases were connected with each other in a grand conspiracy, and as new themes were introduced at individual sessions they percolated through to all the other proceedings and enriched the totality of the narrative.

Sewall sat on two of the preliminary hearings himself, and in May was appointed a member of the Court of Oyer and Terminer that would hear the trials of the defendants. Though only five of the nine members of that court had to be in attendance at any one time, Sewall's record as a member of the Court of Assistants, and later his long career as a justice of the Superior Court of Judicature, shows him to be an indefatigably regular attender, and it is very unlikely that he missed any of the witchcraft trials. He was a friend or colleague of all the prominent citizens involved in the unfolding drama; moreover, his brother Stephen, to whom he was very close, was himself a friend of many of the principals, as well as looking after one of the afflicted girls in his home and becoming official clerk to the court for the trials of which Sewall himself was one of the judges.

Sewall was not, it's true, present at the first few examinations, but they provided the foundations of all that followed, introducing the themes and issues that characterized the tragedy overtaking the community. In the first of them, which took place on 1 March at the Salem Village meetinghouse, defendants and accusers introduced explanations and patterns of behavior that set the agenda for much that was to follow. As the accused women tried to answer questions, the accusing girls writhed and called out in torments, claiming that they were being tortured by invisible specters projected from the defendants.

Several important components of the witchcraft narrative were introduced straightaway. Goody Osborne claimed a "thing like an indian all black" had visited her one night in bed, and pulled her by the back of her head toward her door. She was trying to put herself in the same boat as the accusers, as the victim of strange visitations rather than the cause of them, but lacked their confidence, confessing it might just have been a dream. This was significant, a suggestion that spectral manifestations could be imaginary, though obviously a counterproductive point for Osborne to make about herself.

She also mentioned once saying at the meetinghouse that she would never be tied to "that lying spirit any more." The spirit, it turned out, had been a voice telling her not to go to church. She was trying a preemptive strike, knowing full well that someone would in due course bring this unwise remark to the attention of the court. So already there's the sort of connection between guilt and blame apparent in two earlier conflicts, the Pequot War and King Philip's War. Loss of faith is punished by hostility from a malignant force (perhaps resembling an Indian). The unfortunate Osborne had inadvertently set herself up as an embodiment of this issue. She defied the spirit, she claimed, and went to meeting the following Sabbath, but had to admit not having attended since: "Alas, I have been sike and not able to goe."

Tituba Indian took a different tack from her codefendants: she confessed. She probably felt it was impossible for a slave like herself even to begin to refute allegations put to her by figures in authority. Ironically, it turned out she had stumbled upon the best strategy for survival. It soon became clear that those who confessed wouldn't be brought to trial, but used, instead, as witnesses in other cases. Tituba began to give life and color to the witchcraft narrative. Despite being an Indian herself, the material she introduced came from the traditional Western stockpile of supernatural imagery, but its preoccupation with the animal world suggests a great deal about the attitude of her community to the natural forces all round them. There was agricultural land surrounding, and within, the village, but the presence of livestock wasn't necessarily reassuring. Horses got colic, cows dried up, pigs squealed and bolted, especially small black ones, and people jumped to conclusions (Sewall, as we have seen, concluded that the shaggy dog that came into his kitchen was an instrument of the Devil, sent with the purpose of getting Seth Shove's brains dashed out). And the other sort of countryside, that of the New England forests and wilderness, contained greater threats still: wild animals, and people who followed an animistic religion. The first pioneers had totted up the wild beasts seen in this terrain: bears, wolves, foxes, beavers, otters, great wild cats, a thing called "a molke as big as an ox [perhaps a moose]," and even lions, reported sighted at Cape Ann, just up the road from Salem.

The Devil asked Tituba to serve him; he was accompanied by four women—Good, Osborne, and two others she didn't know—along with a tall man from Boston (the cast of the drama has already begun to multiply). They hurt the children and made her do the same. As Tituba tries to keep Hathorne happy by telling him what he wants to hear, giving an answer to every question, conceding every allegation, dreamlike images begin to slide and shift through her testimony. A thing like a hog wanted her to kill the children. Sometimes (as though by the power of rhyme) it changed into a great black dog; then it would be a man with a yellow bird. There was a red rat and a black rat. When this motley crew—women, animals, the tall man—went off to attack the children, they rode upon sticks to get there. An important development in the imagery, or rather an important image of development: the yellow bird flew from the man to Sarah Good, and suckled her between her fingers.

As Tituba's examination drew to a conclusion the children fell into torments.

> H[athorne]: Doe you see who it is that torments these
> children now
> T[ituba]: yes it is goode good [Goody Good] she hurts them
> in her own shape.

At that moment, the children must have communicated that the source of their suffering had changed, looking in a new direction, choosing a different trajectory of recoil. The specters that projected themselves from the bodies of the accused, strode (or flew) across the courtroom, and tormented the girls and young women who made the allegations could only be seen by witches and those they persecuted. But the writhing and choking that resulted was taken as the outward and visible sign of demonic malevolence. The Puritans habitually looked at the world as the visible product of an unseen creative spirit; this was simply the same perspective as it involved the play of a malevolent power.

> H: & who is it that hurts them now.

The afflicted were inviting Tituba to expand the circle of blame, but she'd had enough: "I am blind noe I cannot see."

She was blind in a rather special sense, of course. What she meant was that she had lost her ability, for the time being, to see invisible specters.

Witchcraft charges had cropped up from time to time in New England, and occasionally, as in the case of Goody Glover, led to death; but normally the allegations were made by an individual, or a group of family members, and directed at another individual. There were inevitable limits within which the issue would be contained. But here a *group* had been accused, all of them outsiders, each an outsider in a different way. Moreover, the accusers themselves were a group, well known to each other but not limited to membership of the same family; each had her own allegiances and connections. This outbreak did not have self-limiting features built into it. Instead, sufficient permutations were available to ramify the crisis in many different directions.

In the middle of March, Parris invited Deodat Lawson, his predecessor as minister, to come over and see the state of the afflicted for himself. Lawson's old village had become a grotesque and alarming place. He counted ten people in a state of affliction; three children, three adolescents, and four women. On Saturday, 19 March, a warrant was sworn for the arrest of a woman called Martha Corey. Like the other accused witches, she was in some ways a vulnerable target—as in the cases of Osborne and Good, her own husband proved willing to testify against her. But she nevertheless demonstrated the growing ambition of the accusers, because she was a covenanted member of the Salem Village Church—where, the following day, Lawson acted as guest minister.

He was soon made to realize that the social and religious hierarchy was under threat, getting heckled during the morning service. In the afternoon, Martha Corey was brought into the meetinghouse, perhaps in shackles. While Lawson was giving his sermon, Abigail Williams suddenly cried out: "Look where Goodw[ife] C[orey] sits on the Beam suckling her Yellow bird between her fingers!" The little bird in Tituba's vision, which belonged to the mysterious man, had fluttered from the specter of Sarah Good to be suckled by that of Martha Corey, up in the rafters of the meetinghouse. It's not just that the net is widening: the inhabitants of Salem Village are being provided with a way of visualizing that very phenomenon at work, the start of a myth of growth and expansion that inexorably led to the naming of more and more alleged witches.

Before beginning to preach, Lawson had hung his broad-brimmed hat on the peg by the pulpit. Suddenly, Ann Putnam Jr. claimed that the yellow bird had settled on it.

All day long, Lawson's hold over the congregation had been tested out. The accusers were getting more ambitious. They already had their most elevated target yet in their sights, the elderly Rebecca Nurse, who unlike her predecessors was a respectable member of the community, dividing her church attendance between the Salem Village meetinghouse and the church in Salem Town, of which she was a covenanted member. A logical next step upward in the spiritual hierarchy would be to leap the gender divide, and accuse a clergyman. But Ann Putnam was hushed by her neighbors in the pews—targeting a male who was also a minister was wishful thinking at this stage. But given that Lawson had come to the village as a sort of expert observer, perhaps even an umpire, reminding him of his own vulnerability could be a fine guarantee that he wouldn't spring to the defense of Rebecca Nurse.

The next day, Martha Corey faced her examination in the meeting-house. A child called out that there was a man whispering in her ear. Corey claimed stoutly: "We must not beleive all that these distracted children say." The afflicted responded to this skepticism with "extream agony." Corey put up a brave defense, claiming that the magistrates' and ministers' eyes were blinded. "You say you would open our eyes we are blind," she was asked. "If you say I am a witch," she replied.

By becoming "blind," Tituba had meant that she could no longer see specters. Corey's meaning was that there were no specters to see. The proceedings were charged and at times chaotic. Sometimes she laughed out loud at the absurdity of it all.

Corey was remanded to Salem jail and then transferred to Boston, leaving attention to focus on the newest recruit to the ranks of the accused, Rebecca Nurse. Lawson visited the Parris household on the Wednesday, and watched while Ann Putnam's mother, Ann Sr., apparently struggled for her soul against Nurse's spectral presence. The day before, Nurse had allegedly appeared with the "little red book" of the Devil, and striven to persuade Ann Sr. to sign it; now, with Lawson in attendance, Ann cried out to Nurse's image: "Your Name is blotted out of Gods Book, and it shall never be put in Gods Book again." Two books of covenanted members, one for the saints and the other for the damned, side by side—an alternative, invisible congregation, symmetrically opposite to the visible one, is being set up.

At Rebecca Nurse's examination, Hathorne pointed out that it wasn't just children accusing her but "grown persons" also, including Ann Putnam Sr. who took the cue and cried out: "Did you not bring the Black man with you, did you not bid me tempt God and dyē How oft have you eat and drunk y'r own damnāōn [damnation]." She was alleging that Nurse participated in a devilish version of the Lord's Supper. Nurse replied, "Oh Lord help me," and spread out her hands. Throughout the examination, the afflicted imitated all her bodily movements. As Samuel Parris, who had been deputed to make a transcript of the proceedings, reported, "she held her Neck on one side, & accordingly so were the afflicted taken." Nothing could be better calculated to panic someone fighting for her life; and it let onlookers believe they were actually glimpsing the invisible structure of agency—Devil to Nurse, Nurse to the afflicted—that was allegedly at work. Hathorne reminded her that Tituba professed much love for Betty Parris, but her apparition, nonetheless, did the child mischief. This eventually forced Nurse to say, "I cannot help it, the Devil may appear in my shape."

The first clause is sadly ambiguous. Nurse obviously means that the Devil must have been using her form without her permission, but it could equally be taken as meaning that she'd surrendered her will to him. Presumably this is how Hathorne interpreted it, because the written record of the examination ends there, though we are told "by reason of great noyses by the afflicted & many speakers, many things are pretermitted."

Nurse's examination took place in the meetinghouse. When it was concluded, Lawson gave the midweek sermon, the lecture. The congregation, most if not all of whom had just witnessed the chaotic events of the hearing, were anxious and excited. He chose a text well calculated to address the danger that he, as a minister, had found himself in the previous Sunday, Zechariah 3:2. Joshua, the high priest, is standing before the angel of the Lord, with Satan at his right hand. In this verse, the Lord comes to his assistance, rebuking Satan and calling Joshua "a brand plucked out of the fire." Joshua is redeemed, and in subsequent verses the role of the priesthood is affirmed, the Lord declaring he "will remove the iniquity of that land in one day," and offering a vision of a community nourished and made neighborly through the church.

But the Salem Village community have just had a glimpse of a demonic alternative to that sacramental redemption, and the main thrust of Lawson's sermon gave ground and substance to that sighting, spelling out the implications of the accumulated imagery of the hearings: "You are therefore to be deeply humbled, and sit in the dust Considering. First, the signal hand of God, in singling out this place, this poor Village, for the first seat of Satans Tyranny, and to make it (as 'twere) the Rendezvous of Devils, where they Muster their infernal forces . . ."

Lawson removed, at a stroke, the great objection that could be offered to the accumulation and acceleration of sightings and afflictions taking place: that the sheer quantity seems unreasonable. The issue of scale was the central one of the whole episode, the question of how what is small can so rapidly become huge. During the centuries since 1692, the judicial, religious, and political authorities have been criticized for letting the situation they faced get out of hand. But what the authorities confronted, or rapidly came to believe they confronted, was a situation that was intrinsically structured so it *would* get out of hand. That wasn't a careless by-product of the crisis, but its very nature: this was Lawson's point. The yellow bird had been busily fluttering from one person to the next, even landing briefly on his own hat. What we are dealing with is not an event, but a process. The community had been singled out for an alternative settlement. Satan was making his headquarters here. This was the place where the devils rendezvous—and gather their armies.

Apocalypse was in the air. Even children could pick up the ominous atmosphere—and not just the accusers. Young Joseph Sewall believed he was getting information from heaven about military threats; his sister had burst into tears at those grim words in Isaiah about laying waste the land and scattering the inhabitants thereof.

Lawson established the credentials of Salem Town's less successful sibling as an—as *the*—important interface between the visible and invisible worlds. There is malevolent grandeur in this conception, a dark dignity in the very scale of the crisis he claimed was unfolding. He gave meaning and purpose to the fears and visions that were besetting the village, and laid the groundwork for a myth of negative colonization, an inverted recapitulation of those landfalls of only a lifetime ago, the Pilgrim Fathers, Winthrop's city on a hill, the arrival of the *Abigail* at

Naumkeag (later to become the bustling port of Salem Town). We are witnessing a new kind of landfall, made just to one side of one of the original points of entry, and leading to the creation of an alternative community, symmetrically balancing the original settlement, and devoted to the worship of Satan. It was an outcome anticipated in Sewall's dream nearly seventeen years previously, at the beginning of King Philip's War, when he ascended a staircase at Harvard College in search of the seats of the blessed, and instead found an apartment containing earthly furniture that had been winched through the "ranshacled" window: a spiritual institution violated by materialism as a result of internal decline and external attack—the failure of the Indian College, with its mission to bring Indians to Christian understanding, allowing the forces of paganism in. Ironically, the Salem Village meetinghouse, only twenty years old, was neglected and decrepit. Many of the windows were broken, with some open to the weather and others boarded up, so that, according to the villagers, the interior was "sometimes so dark that it is almost unuseful." A perfect setting, therefore, not just for Lawson's sermon, but for the examinations and the satanic manifestations that took place in them.

Lawson paid his dues for surviving the preliminary forays of the afflicted in church the previous Sunday. If the accusers were to do more than just make sporadic accusations, if they were going to be able to point to a whole community of witches, and establish, by means of the sheer frequency of their allegations, the existence of a coven, that coven would require spiritual leadership to achieve shape and cohesion, just as the village itself had needed a minister to give it identity. This need could have been the conscious or unconscious motivation behind the accusers' tentative attempt to incriminate Lawson. The outbreak had after all begun in a minister's household: from the very beginning, satanic and saintly had been in uneasy proximity.

Tituba's second examination demonstrated this vividly. She described meeting a man who claimed he was God, and who arranged to come again to see her at the minister's house the following Wednesday. Four apparitions appeared to her on the appointed day, while Mr. Parris was praying in the next room. They all trooped in, but "my master did nott See us, for they would nott lett my Master See." That issue of blindness again: Parris was tantalizingly close to hand but, as the leader of the Christian community, he was hardly available. Lawson made a more feasible target, as a minister who had left the community and was now back in it—a journey amenable to allegorization in terms of repudiating good and embracing evil. But as soon as he had become aware of this, he established for himself a different, safer, role: that of authenticating the evolving structure from the outside by means of his ministerial authority. He gave pastoral confirmation to the vision of the devilish commonwealth without having to participate in it. The internal appointment would lie vacant for another month, until George Burroughs was accused.

Over the next months, Ann Putnam Jr. alone was to claim to be bewitched by sixty-eight separate people. On some days, by her own evidence, there must have been a queue of witches waiting their turn to torment her. But the myth as it was evolving, from Tituba's sighting of the yellow bird to Lawson's account of Salem Village as Satan's port of entry, gave a rationale to such excess and prevented the authorities from showing skepticism. If invisible invading hordes had chosen the humble village of Salem as their gateway into New England, there was no need to be surprised that the first line of resistance should be composed of the humble forms of young Ann Putnam and her companions. And the very frequency of their complaints gave them a heroic role as defenders of their community.

In his sermon on Sunday, 27 March, on the text "Have not I chosen you twelve, and one of you is a Devil?" (John 6:70), Parris completed the work begun by Lawson, emphasizing that even covenanted members of the Christian community could be the Devil's agents, and therefore absolving himself of any responsibility to protect those to whom he ministered. The verse could have been targeted at Martha Corey, one of his own church members, or at Rebecca Nurse, who was covenanted to the Salem Town church though she frequently attended his, since she, like the disciples, seemed to be an unimpeachable member of the Christian community—yet was (allegedly) an evil interloper.

Parris explained that hypocrisy was the most heinous of all sins:

"Hypocrites are the very worst of men . . . the sons and heirs of the Devil, the free-holders of hell—whereas other sinners are but tenants." It was the ultimate sin, because it involved being an alien and inappropriate presence in a community in which you had no rightful place: "The Church consists of good: & bad; as a Garden that has weeds as well as flowers: & as a field that has Wheat as well as Tares." This imagery cut across the Congregationalist belief that the covenantal system established a body of divinely elected saints at the heart of their community (the Half-Way Covenant had already begun to erode that assumption). Hypocrisy was a sin that betrayed the possibility of America as a community of the saved. Hypocrites had permanent allegiance outside a theocratic society. They were freeholders of hell and interlopers in a Christian commonwealth, undermining it from within. They allowed the spiritual project of New England to go into reverse.

That same Sunday, Parris turned his attention to Mary Sibley's witch cake, the one that had been made with the urine of the afflicted girls and fed to a dog. A month had gone by since it was baked; whether he had only just found out about it, or whether he had deliberately waited for this moment to speak out on the subject, is impossible to tell. Nevertheless, his fierce public rebuke of Mary Sibley is illuminating. Witchcraft had got loose in the community—"the Devil hath been raised among us, and his rage is vehement and terrible, and, when he shall be silenced, the Lord only knows"—and it was all down to the baking of the cake: "Nay, it never brake forth in any considerable light, until Diabolical means were used, by the making of a Cake by my Indian man, who had his direction from this our sister, Mary Sibly."

This might have been an attempt to transfer the ultimate blame for the contagion that was sweeping the community away from events in which his own daughter—and his own household—was implicated (by this time, little Betty Parris had been squirreled off into the care of Sewall's brother Stephen and wife, Margaret). It was one thing for the Devil to sneak into the village through openings unintentionally made by children and young people; but if the means of resistance to him were in fact derived *from* him, then there may be no stopping his progress. What had happened was "a going to the Devil for help against the Devil," and this had turned a mere dabbling with the supernatural into an incremental process. When Sister Sibley (sister in the Christian sense: one of us) used the Devil's means to identify the Devil, that distinction between the Christian realm and the Devil's kingdom collapsed. There was an overlap of the two worlds, the cake itself acting as a kind of gateway between them. Internal guilt—loss of faith—and external blame—attack by dark forces—had been baked into a single entity.

On 31 March, the Salem Village congregation observed a fast day in an attempt to secure spiritual help for dealing with the terrible curse that had fallen upon the community. Four days later, on 4 April, a warrant was issued for the arrest of Sarah Cloyse, Rebecca Nurse's sister, and for Elizabeth Proctor, wife of a substantial property owner in the district.

It was at this point that Samuel Sewall became directly involved in the crisis.

CHAPTER FIVE

"Vae, Vae, Vae, Witchcraft"

THE HEARINGS HAD BEEN HELD IN THE SALEM VILLAGE MEETING-house, but now there was a switch. The examination of Sarah Cloyse and Elizabeth Proctor took place in the larger, longer-established, better-maintained meetinghouse in Salem Town on 11 April. To match the more imposing venue, there was an array of big guns. The local team of John Hathorne and Jonathan Corwin were joined by four out-of-town colleagues on the Court of Assistants—James Russell, Isaac Addington, Samuel Appleton, and Sewall himself—with the deputy governor, Thomas Danforth, presiding over the hearing. The crisis was escalating, and even by Massachusetts standards the authorities must have felt they were operating in an institutional vacuum. The new governor would just be setting out from England; when he arrived a new council would take charge, a new charter would come into force. In the awkward interim, it was politic to make a show of authority. We cannot tell how many people were expressing their distaste for what was going on. One was, at least.

The day after Rebecca Nurse's examination, John Proctor, Elizabeth's husband, gave his opinion on the events that were taking place. Proctor was a practical, assertive, aggressive man of sixty, successful at business (he ran the family farm while Elizabeth, his third wife, took charge of their tavern), the first example of a phenomenon that would be repeated a number of times over the next few months: a foursquare no-nonsense Yankee suddenly stumbling into the mystical fog of the witchcraft. Brisk modern pragmatism comes up against superannuated superstition. Proctor's maidservant, Mary Warren, had been having fits along with the other afflicted girls and women. His solution: keep her working hard and threaten to thrash her. This, he claimed, had done the trick, at least until he had been called away from home, when she had relapsed. Unless something was done, the afflicted would quickly establish everybody as "Devils & witches." He wanted to whip them, or even more drastically—and ironically, given his own subsequent fate—to "hang them, hang them." In the meantime, he was going to fetch home his "jade" and "thresh the Devil out of her."

Proctor reversed the equation between accusers and accused, transferring evil possession to the afflicted—naturally enough, since his own wife was going to be in the dock. If you were convinced that an accused person was innocent, then, of course, the accusers themselves looked demonic. This probably explains why the first women to be charged had husbands who wouldn't come to their defense. By now, aggrieved friends and relatives of the accused were beginning to accumulate; the community was becoming divided.

According to Sewall, "a very great Assembly" was present in the court. The two women were examined together. This reflects the attitude of men of affairs wanting to get a job done, but also shows that the authorities were thinking of witchcraft as an essentially collective endeavor. Mary Walcott testified that she'd been persecuted by Cloyse, Nurse, and Martha Corey, along with a great many others she didn't know. The constituency of evil was expanding again, and that fact provided a cue for the first question to the next witness, Abigail Williams: "Did you see a company at Mr Parris's house eat and drink?"

Williams had: about forty people had been sharing a satanic sacrament at the minister's house under the deaconship of Cloyse and Sarah Good. They were drinking the blood of the afflicted.

There was now an alternative congregation with its own religious hierarchy, holding a dark sacrament in the minister's house. It was an inverse reflection of the village's official worship, like the image of the haunted house Edgar Allan Poe would describe nearly a century and a half later in "The Fall of the House of Usher," the greatest portrayal in

American literature of the way the spectral universe can seem to provide a symmetrical reversal of reality: "I reined my horse to the precipitous brink of a black and lurid tarn that lay in unruffled lustre by the dwelling, and gazed down—but with a shudder even more thrilling than before—upon the remodelled and inverted images of the gray sedge, and the ghastly tree-stems, and the vacant and eye-like windows." A topsy-turvy Salem Village was coming into view. The hauntings were developing both scale and structure.

When Elizabeth Proctor was interrogated, the accusers as usual began going into fits. Abigail Williams and Ann Putnam Jr. recovered from attacks of dumbness sufficiently to cry out they could see her upon a beam, another hunched bird-woman among roof timbers, beadily eyeing the gathering. Then suddenly the specter of John, Elizabeth's husband, was sighted too.

At this point, a grotesque choreography began. The afflicted cried that John Proctor's specter was going to raise up the feet of one of the women present, Mrs. Bathshua Pope. Sure enough, her feet rose up. He protested his innocence, but as he did so Abigail Williams called out that Proctor's specter was approaching Mrs. Pope again, and she duly collapsed. Then Williams cried out that he was heading toward another woman, Goody Bibber, who also went into a fit. The cooperation of the afflicted in this spectacle must have been unnerving—and riveting—for the audience. Because of the Puritan proscription of the theater, the New England public had never had the opportunity to see actors performing on stage. Sewall wrote in his diary that " 'twas awful to see how the afflicted persons were agitated." In the margin he wrote, "Vae, Vae, Vae, [Woe, woe, woe,] Witchcraft."

John Proctor found himself remanded to jail at a hearing of which he wasn't even a subject. The following day, Samuel Parris, acting as court clerk, tried to paper over the procedural anomaly by drawing up a retrospective summary of the case against Proctor, with help from Abigail Williams, John Indian, and Mary Walcott. Perhaps it was the memory of cobbling together this paper that helped trigger Parris's later confession: ". . . in and through the throng of many things written by me, in the late confusions, there has not been a due exactness always used." Proctor had the bluff purposefulness and impatience of a power-ful member of the community, but he had shown himself to be an en-emy of the afflicted and they had reacted promptly, demonstrating to him and anyone else tempted to cross them that they had the upper hand.

The examinations returned to Salem Village, and the original team of Hathorne and Corwin. Ironically, one of the accused was Proctor's "jade," Mary Warren, thrashed out of the safe camp of self-professed witchcraft victims by her furious master and now floundering among the alleged practitioners. The crunch question was put: "You were a lit-tle while ago an Afflicted person, now you are an Afflicter: How comes this to pass?" Warren lapsed into a manic dialogue with herself.

> I shall not speak a word: but I will, I will speak Satan—She saith she will kill me: Oh! she saith, she owes me a spite, & will claw me off—
>   Avoid Satan, for the name of God avoid And then fell into fits again: & cryed will ye I will prevent ye in the Name of God.

It was hardly surprising she was so schizophrenic, given the fact that she'd been on both sides of the divide. A little later, in Salem jail, she admitted that while her head was distempered, she thought she saw the apparitions of a hundred people, but when "Shee was well Againe Shee could not Say that Shee saw any of the apparissons at the time Afore-said." Her remarks suggest a kind of contagious madness.

This was not an explanation that could be accepted at this stage by the authorities, and their failure ironically testifies to the very signifi-cance of the Salem phenomenon, the extent to which it marks a turning point in moral and psychological perception. The justices were still liv-ing in a universe of binary alternatives. The accused were liars; if not, their accusers were would-be killers. As Hathorne put it to Rebecca Nurse, "They accuse you of hurting them, & if you think it is not un-willingly but by designe, you must look upon them as murderers." The prosecutors were engaged in indefatigable pursuit of the either/or. They were incapable of using what we would regard as common sense, because they could not allow for inner conflict and contradiction. In short, they could not accept complex explanations, acknowledge confusion, live with ambiguity. They were inhabiting a myth in which good and evil were always separately embodied, like characters in an allegory. As Samuel Parris put it in a sermon, "We are either saints or Devils: the Scripture gives us no medium." Mary Warren could not remain both an accuser and an accused, even though a little probing of her mental anguish in having that double role might have yielded the real secrets of the terrible tragedy that was overtaking the community.

Mary Warren was left to resolve the contradiction for herself. She resumed her career as an accuser, incriminating not simply her employers but everyone else she could, those she knew and those she was merely told about, bearing witness against seven of those who were eventually executed. The choice she made in doing so liberated her from prison, and saved her from the rope.

From this point, the complaints and examinations flowed thick and fast, but the mythology expanded to keep up with the process. The single most important development was announced right at the beginning of the testimony of a girl called Abigail Hobbs, who claimed the Devil had visited her "at the Eastward, at Casko-bay." The Hobbses had lived in Casco Bay in Maine, some seventy miles north (and marginally east) of Salem Village, a few years before, when Abigail was a little girl (she was fourteen now). The clergyman there was George Burroughs, formerly of Salem Village, Deodat Lawson's predecessor. The yellow bird that had alighted tentatively on Lawson's hat was just about to land on its chosen minister.

Two days later, 21 April, Thomas Putnam, husband of Ann and father of Ann Jr., wrote a letter to the examining magistrates. He began by praising their efforts in fulsome tones, then gave a melodramatic warning of what was to come: ". . . and we, beholding continually the tremendous works of divine providence—not only every day but every hour—thought it our duty to inform your Honors of what we conceive you have not heard, which are high and dreadful: of a wheel within a wheel, at which our ears do tingle." News from the front line, from the very center of Salem witchcraft accusation. Events were unfolding at an urgent, exciting pace—"not only every day but every hour"—and there was a major revelation on hand, something that would take the examiners to the heart of the mystery with which they were dealing. In due course, his daughter Ann would claim to have had a vision of Burroughs on 20 April, the day before Putnam's letter, and he was obviously referring to this alleged sighting. It's hard to imagine a more blatant attempt to influence proceedings. Putnam puffed out a quantity of gothic miasma—"our ears do tingle"—so it could swirl around the hint provided by Abigail Hobbs's testimony, dramatize a convenient sighting by his own daughter the following day, then drift across the examinations that were to follow.

Abigail Hobbs claimed to have attended the Devil's sacrament described by Abigail Williams, though the location was now just outside the minister's house rather than in it: "She was at the great Meeting in Mr Parris's Pasture when they administered the Sacram'tt, and did Eat of the Red Bread and drink of the Red wine att the same Time." Parris had talked of the church as a garden with weeds and flowers, and as a field with wheat and tares. Now this imagery had been formally separated out, and the pasture adjoining the parsonage dedicated to the cultivation of spiritual weeds and tares. Just as devilish colonization took place at Salem Village, to one side of the original settlement of Salem Town, so his dark worship took place in a field to one side of the Christian minister's house. After Putnam had sent his letter, Abigail's stepmother, Deliverance, also described such a sacrament. It, too, was in the pasture by Parris's house, and John and Elizabeth Proctor, Rebecca Nurse, Martha Corey and her husband, Giles, and a woman called Bridget Bishop were present, along with Sarah Osborne, Sarah Good, and another Sarah, the elderly Sarah Wilds. But there was one major addition, that "wheel within a wheel" Putnam had written about. George Burroughs was there to preside over this alternative church.

A warrant was issued for Burroughs's arrest on 30 April. Meanwhile, the examinations continued, with everyone who appeared before the justices being remanded to prison, with the single exception of a young man called Nehemiah Abbott, whose identity the accusers couldn't agree on, and who therefore became the only named person to walk away from the witchcraft proceedings of 1692 completely unscathed. The story of the ceremony of the black sacrament continued to be elaborated. Susannah Sheldon described how Goody Bishop, Elizabeth English (wife of a prosperous merchant in Salem Town), and Giles Corey came to her in company with a black man who wore a high crowned hat. Mrs. English had the familiar yellow bird in her bosom, while Corey was suckling two hawks at his. "Then good man Care [Corey] and Goody oliver kneeled doune beefour the blak man and went to prayer." A defendant called Susannah Martin, a sixty-seven-year-old woman from Amesbury, north of Sewall's hometown of Newbury (the yellow bird was flying further afield by now), made the theologically sound case that the Devil had demonstrated his ability to take the form of innocent persons in the Old Testament, when the Witch of Endor fabricated a specter of Samuel to torment Saul (1 Samuel 28). This was a crucial precedent, because it cast doubt, or should have cast doubt, on the reliability of spectral evidence. It may have been that the accusers were seeing not projections of Susannah Martin and the others, but mirages contrived by Satan to cause chaos and injustice. In her consistently brave replies, Martin made it clear that she didn't believe the accusers were seeing anything at all:

> Do you not think they [the afflicted] are Bewitcht?
> No. I do not think they are.
> Tell me your thoughts about them.
> Why my thoughts are my own, when they are in, but when they are out they are anothers.

The Salem authorities assumed that people's innermost thoughts and feelings could be reliably inferred from their appearance, their expressions, and from what they said in the tense and confusing atmosphere of the court. The defendants, of course, knew they were being misinterpreted and misjudged. Martin was making a crucial distinction between her private self—"my thoughts are my own, when they are in"—and the public misrepresentation and appropriation of that self—"when they are out they are anothers."

A week after Martin's examination, the legal proceedings against Casco Bay's minister, George Burroughs, began.

The Burroughs case was pivotal. If a clergyman were to be convicted of witchcraft, it would prove to the hilt Parris's claim that the Devil could be found even in the most elevated of saintly circles, as Judas had been found among the disciples. A minister-wizard was an unprecedented phenomenon, and would cast a grave shadow over the whole nature of the American spiritual project. Burroughs would provide the leader figure necessary for a myth of negative colonization, for the establishment of a dark alternative to the bright city on a hill. His conviction would irrevocably establish the witchcraft outbreak as a social and political threat of the first magnitude. The day before the examination, Parris preached a sermon on a text that foregrounded the issue of the satanic sacrament: "Ye cannot drink the cup of the Lord, and the cup of Devils" (1 Corinthians 10:21).

As on 11 April, the decision was made to beef the proceedings up. Once again Sewall was brought in, along with a fellow judge, William Stoughton. Stoughton was about sixty-one, with a long history as a prominent member of the Court of Assistants. He was a touchy bachelor, full of his own rectitude, very much on his dignity, utterly sure of himself. His portrait shows a grim mouth and hard staring eyes with dark rings under them. On this occasion too, the hearing was transferred to Salem Town.

The first part of the examination took place behind closed doors. Burroughs was asked about his religious practice. He admitted he couldn't even remember when he'd last partaken of the Lord's Supper, and that only the oldest of his children had been baptized. Though it had no immediate bearing on the specific charge of witchcraft, this suggested he was a minister engaged in undermining the faith, just a small step away from being one who promoted an alternative, devilish system of belief.

Burroughs's Harvard training had overlapped with Sewall's, and then he had been a minister at Casco Bay in Maine. In 1676, his community was destroyed in an Indian raid, and thirty-two inhabitants were killed or captured. Burroughs and his family escaped by fleeing to a small island in the bay. Dark-haired and dark-complexioned, he arrived in Salem Village from a vortex of Indian trouble, being appointed minister in 1680.

Like his predecessor, James Bayley, and his successors Deodat Lawson and Samuel Parris, he had a difficult tenure in the new post, with constant problems arising from village factionalism and salary arrears. He was consistently sharp with his wife and tried to get her to sign a

William Stoughton (1631/2–1701), by an unidentified artist.
Courtesy of the Harvard University Portrait Collection, Gift of John Cooper
to Harvard College, 1810. Photo by Rick Stafford.

document promising never to reveal his secrets. When she died, he borrowed money for her funeral and ended up imprisoned for a night in the ordinary for debt. In 1683, he returned to Casco Bay, though he came back to Massachusetts from time to time. On Wednesday, 18 November

1685, Sewall spent a difficult day at the Court of Assistants, because of sharp exchanges between the governor and William Stoughton. Then he went home and entertained George Burroughs to dinner. They were Harvard alumni after all. His diary entry, nearly seven years before the witchcraft trials, preserves himself and Stoughton, who would both be appointed judges at the Salem court, and Burroughs, who would become the most prominent of the victims of that court, in permanent juxtaposition like flies in amber.

Back in Maine, Burroughs treated his second wife no better than the first. He censored her letter writing, and when he came back from a journey he would claim to know what she had said about him while he was away. She had the sensation of being breathed upon when lying in bed with her husband asleep beside her, a good metaphor for a claustrophobic marriage. The magistrates asked Burroughs if the house was haunted. He denied it, but "owned there were Toads."

Burroughs was a small man, but strong, and took pride in certain party tricks like lifting a barrel of molasses with just two fingers inserted in the bunghole. He comes across as a secretive show-off, not an attractive combination. Add to that the fact that he tried to covenant with two short-lived wives (by the time of his witchcraft arrest, he was married to a third) to ensure they kept his secrets, just as the Devil covenanted with the accused witches; that, though a minister, he had neglected religious observance and perhaps held heretical ideas; that he had survived an Indian attack that wrecked his community; and that he had made enemies in his unsuccessful stint at Salem Village—and he became the perfect candidate for leadership of the witches' coven. With his dark coloring and minister's hat, he might have been the Devil himself. True, the Black Man was sometimes described as tall, but more usually was perceived as small, as in the case of Mercy Lewis, who became afflicted during the course of the summer, and who claimed that "the Divel that visited her . . . was a wretch no taller than an ordinary walking-stick; hee was not of a Negro but of a Tawney, or an Indian colour; hee wore an high-crowned Hat, with strait hair; and had one Cloven-Foot." Often Satan or his agents were perceived as impish, animal-like creatures, like a phenomenon seen by a certain John

Louder, who on 2 June swore a deposition against Bridget Bishop. Having been tormented by her, he felt unwell and stayed at home one Sunday instead of going to church (shifting the blame for his failure of observance more successfully than Goody Osborne had). He was then haunted by a black pig, and subsequently "did see a black thing Jump into the window and came & stood Just before my face . . . the body of itt looked like a Munkiey only the feete ware like a Cocks feete w'th Claws and the face somewhat more like a mans than a Munkiey." Appropriately for the Lord's Day, the thing addressed him with messianic gravity: "I am a Messenger sent to you for I understand you are trobled in mind." This is evidence directed at Bishop, but it fits Burroughs's small stature, dark complexion, and animal muscularity well enough.

He was remanded in custody, to await trial. A day later, another male found himself accused of witchcraft, an old man called George Jacobs. Sixteen-year-old Margaret Jacobs, herself an accused witch, pointed the finger at both George Burroughs and her own grandfather.

Jacobs walked with the aid of two sticks—his specter too apparently made use of them, hobbling along to its task of terror. It was a man with two staves, said another of his accusers, Mary Walcott. One of the most common witch traits was mobility. One witness, for example, saw Bridget Bishop "goe Out under the End window at a little Creviss about so bigg as I Could thrust my hand into." And at the very beginning of the crisis, Tituba had introduced the magic of a flying stick. But Jacobs wasn't granted the gift of flight, nor of agility, nor of shapeshifting. He entered his accusers' fantasies with the aid of staffs, as he did the dock, and it's painful to imagine by what means, a few months later, he would mount the gallows themselves.

But in his examination, Jacobs gave some of the most robust and salty replies of any of the accused, showing a brave contempt for the whole proceeding from the moment he maneuvred himself into court:

Here are them that accuse you of acts of witchcraft.
Well, let us hear who are they, and what are they.
Abigail Williams—
Jacobs laught.

He directed his incredulity straight at the magistrates: "Your worships all of you do you think this is true?" "Here are three evidences," the justices tell him. The reply, from a decrepit old man headed inexorably for the rope, has a life-affirming toughness that provides one of the great moments of the tragedy: "You tax me for a wizard, you may as well tax me for a buzard I have done no harm." When his servant girl, Sarah Churchill, claimed in court to have been frightened by his specter, he replied, "Well: burn me, or hang me, I will stand in the truth of Christ, I know nothing of it." "Bitch witch," he called her.

Like Susannah Martin, Jacobs was more theologically sound than the justices themselves, even though he made a mess of reciting the Lord's Prayer. "The Devil can take any likeness," he told the court. "Not without their consent" was the reply from his examiner. This was the crux of the matter, because the magistrates' interpretation allowed guilt to be tracked back from the specter to the person it resembled. It was Jacobs's version that would be vindicated.

ON 14 MAY, the four years of diplomacy conducted by Increase Mather finally bore fruit. Sir William Phips, the new governor, arrived aboard the frigate *Nonsuch* bearing the new charter for the province. He was accompanied by Increase Mather, who had been instrumental in getting him the appointment. Candles were lit in honor of Phips's arrival at the Town House, and eight companies of militia accompanied him home. It was a grand spectacle in a small town, very different from the ceremonial of great arrivals in the city of London, as Sewall had witnessed them three years before: Princess Mary's Cleopatra-like progression on a barge, with the hurly-burly of traffic going over London Bridge and the sweep of the city all around, or the procession of Dutch ambassadors through streets "thwacked with people." Boston was a community of seven thousand inhabitants and one thousand buildings, a tiny settlement in relation to its political and cultural impact. Even on a geographical level, the city was much smaller than we can readily imagine now. In 1690, Sewall described the town's layout to an English correspondent: "Tis built on an Island & Peninsula extended in [length] from N. East to Southwest about a Mile & half, from the Ferry to the Fort[if]ication. The Buildings reach but little more than a Mile and quarter and more thinly at yᵉ South-end. My house stands just a mile from yᵉ Fe[rry]." In Sewall's day, the peninsula was 487 acres in area; now, it's more than double that size, with 500 acres of made land, the result of many years of infilling of the Charles estuary and the sea. After depositing Phips, the militia escorted Mather to his home. It was the last time the Massachusetts clergy could associate themselves so directly with the mainsprings of political power.

Boston Town House 1657–1711. Charles Lawrence drawing, 1930.

Courtesy of the Bostonian Society, #1014.

No volleys were fired in greeting because it was Saturday night, the start of the Puritan Sabbath. On the Monday, there was another military procession to escort Phips and his councillors back to the Town House, Sewall being one of them, also appointed on Mather's recommendation. When the procession arrived, however, Sewall's brother-in-law came up to him and said his father had fallen dangerously ill, so he slipped away before taking his oath. On his way to the bedside, he saw a rainbow, a sign of the Lord's favor that always cheered him up. It was an image of the covenant between God and his people, of the great underlying spiritual structure of the American colonies, one that seemed perpetually under threat as Indian wars, loss of faith, and institutional uncertainty challenged society, along with the current threat from witchcraft. When Sewall arrived at his father's, the good omen was fulfilled, the old man proving much better than expected.

The first General Court was held on 24 May, and Sewall took his oath then. The next day, Phips ordered the formation of a court of Oyer and Terminer (to hear and determine). The medieval phrase described an ad hoc court set up for a particular purpose, in this case obviously the witchcraft trials (there would be seventy people remanded for trial by 2 June), though its stated remit was vaguer than that: ". . . to enquire, hear and determine all manner of crimes and offences perpetrated within the counties of Suffolk, Essex and Middlesex." There were nine justices appointed to the court: William Stoughton (now deputy governor of the province, again at Mather's suggestion), presiding; and Jonathan Corwin, Bartholomew Gedney, John Hathorne, John Richards, Nathaniel Saltonstall, Peter Sergeant, Samuel Sewall, and Wait Still Winthrop on the bench, a quorum being any five of them under the leadership of either Stoughton, Gedney, or Richards. The next phase of the witchcraft crisis could now take place.

First, though, the newly reconstituted General Court proclaimed a fast to be held throughout the province, "to seek the Lord that he would rebuke Satan & be a light unto his people in this day of darkness." On the day of the fast, Sewall recorded the theme of Mr. Willard's sermon: "The great Sin of New-Eng: is unbelief," his diagnosis of the malaise that had brought about the witch crisis.

The arrival of a new administrative authority, legitimized by the crown, and the appointment by that authority of a court to deal with the witchcraft cases might have given a sense of perspective—even exerted a calming influence—over the developments in the Salem area that had been taking place during the previous three months. The political and social uncertainties brought about by the loss of the old charter, and the consequent executive and administrative limbo that the colony had inhabited for so long, had obviously caused demoralization and anxiety and contributed to the atmosphere in which the witchcraft narrative could germinate. But the underlying tendency of the crisis was precisely to formulate a claim that New England society as a whole was under threat, and the establishment of legal procedures to address the issue served to confirm the enormous scale of the threat, rather than to provide an instrument for cutting it down to size.

CHAPTER SIX

Oyer and Terminer

$\mathcal{W}$HILE SEWALL WAS TAKING HIS OATH AS A COUNCILLOR AT THE Town House in Boston, strange events (even by Salem Village standards) were taking place just up the coast. A woman called Elizabeth Cary heard she was being named as a witch, and decided to visit Salem Village to see what was going on. She and her sea-captain husband, Nathaniel, lived in Charlestown, across the river from Boston. They didn't know the one accuser they'd heard about, Abigail Williams, and wanted to find out if—and how—she could recognize Mrs. Cary.

They were startled to discover Abigail was just eleven or twelve. The accusing girls didn't recognize Mrs. Cary and kept demanding her name. The couple arranged to meet Abigail in the village tavern. While they were waiting, John Indian, Tituba's husband, came in, called for some cider, and started showing off some scars he claimed were caused by witchcraft, though they looked like old ones to the Carys. Then, in grotesque carnival, a whole group of girls trooped in, began to "tumble down like Swine" and to call out "Cary!" Immediately afterward a warrant for Elizabeth Cary was sent from the justices, who, said Nathaniel, "were sitting in a Chamber near by, waiting for this." As in the case of John Proctor, the court was actively seeking its prey.

In the meetinghouse that afternoon, Elizabeth was made to stand with her arms stretched out. Nathaniel asked if he could hold one of her hands, but was forbidden to do so. She asked him to wipe the tears and sweat from her face, which he did. Then she pleaded for permission to lean on him. "Justice Hathorn replied, she had strength enough to torment those persons, and she should have strength enough to stand"— Hathorne, as always, taking it for granted the accused was guilty. John Indian came into court to add his accusations to those already in place. In his torments, he fell down. Elizabeth Cary was told to touch him as a cure, but when she tried to do so "the Indian took hold on her hand, and pulled her down on the Floor, in a barbarous manner."

The setting is a New England Puritan church building; an Indian slave, whose own wife is in prison on suspicion of witchcraft, is rolling on the floor with the wife of an out-of-town master mariner struggling in his arms, a woman who came to the village of her own free will; the scene is watched over by two justices who themselves have been torturing the woman by making her stand with her arms outstretched, and who take no action against the Indian but remand the woman to jail for invisible crimes allegedly committed by her against Mary Walcott, Abigail Williams, and Mercy Lewis at this very session of the court in which she herself is being assaulted. These crimes had not even been committed when the woman arrived in the village, or indeed when she was summoned to appear before the magistrates.

The drama in which Elizabeth Cary lucklessly starred suggests a deliberate and explicit repudiation of class structure and hierarchy; of prevailing concepts of decorum and decency; of religious principles, social taboos, and conventions; of the very fabric of the communal values of the time. Her husband expressed his fury to the court: "I being extreamly troubled at their Inhumane dealings, uttered a hasty Speech (That God would take vengeance on them, and desired that God would deliver us out of the hands of unmerciful men)." Nevertheless, she was remanded to prison in Boston. Four days later there were more bizarre scenes in Salem Village.

Sewall's friend John Alden, sixty-five years old but still a man of action, came back from Canada where he had been paying ransom to free his son and a comrade from captivity by the French enemy, only to find himself summoned to Salem to face witchcraft charges. Alden was the son of one of the signers of the Mayflower Compact, and himself had been a founder of Sewall's meetinghouse, the South Church. He spent a lot of his time in the forests, fighting, trading, and negotiating with hostile Indians, and there is a breezy, outdoors quality about the way he described what now happened to him. He refused to be intimidated when he entered the claustrophobic meetinghouse of this stressed-out rural community, keeping his hat firmly on his head while facing his accusers: "Those wenches being present, . . . plaid their jugling tricks, falling down, crying out, and staring in Peoples faces." Like Proctor and Jacobs, he concluded straightaway that the charges were trumped up. One of the girls claiming to be haunted by his specter didn't recognize him, and had to be prompted by a man who was propping her up as she writhed in her torments: "The Magistrates asked her if she had ever seen Aldin, she answered no, he asked her how she knew it was Aldin? She said, the Man told her so."

Instead of dealing firmly with this admission of bad faith, the magistrates sent everyone outside while they consulted. The accusers immediately formed a ring around Alden. One of them cried out: "There stands Aldin, a bold fellow with his hat on before the Judges, he sells Powder and Shot to the Indians and French, and lies with the Indian Squaes [squaws] and has Indian Papooses." The wilderness was the domain of paganism—Satan's kingdom—with the Christian commonwealth of the Puritans uneasily perched within it. As Cotton Mather would put it later that year, "The New-Englanders are a people of God settled in those which were once the *Devils* territories; and it may easily be supposed that the *Devil* was exceedingly disturbed." People like Alden, who fought with and against the inhabitants of the Devil's territories, straddled this divide in a threatening way. In accusing him of lying with squaws and fathering their babies, the person in the ring pointed out another upside-down reflection in the dark tarn, an alternative passional existence in the hidden and hostile world of the Indians.

Alden was taken back into the Salem Village meetinghouse, and made to stand on a chair in full view of everyone. The accusers cried out that he was pinching them, even though he was a good distance away, so one of the magistrates ordered the marshal to hold open Alden's hands to stop his specter doing so. The image of spectral causality prompting this intervention must have been something like the mechanism of a pantograph, a device in which a pointer is connected to a pencil by a flexible lattice in such a way the pencil imitates, on a greater or smaller scale, every move the pointer makes, enabling the clumsiest person to make an accurate copy of an image. Unabashed, "Aldin told Mr Gidney, that he could assure him that there was a lying Spirit in them [the accusers], for I can assure you that there is not a word of truth in all these say of me." Like Mrs. Cary, he was remanded to Boston jail. His predicament caused deep unease to Sewall, newly appointed justice of the witchcraft tribunal.

But in case his resolution faltered, Sewall's minister, Mr. Willard, preached a sermon well calculated to stiffen resolve: ". . . your adversary the Devil as a roaring Lyon gooth about seeking whom he may devour." Three days later, on 2 June, Sewall was in Salem Town for the first case to appear before the Court of Oyer and Terminer, that of Bridget Bishop, a woman in her early fifties who had been accused of witchcraft some years previously and who therefore must have seemed a likely case with which to start the trials. Sewall's brother Stephen was clerk of the court.

The accumulated gossip and rumors of many years were paraded before the justices: a child developing fits in 1680, following a number of apparently purposeless visits by Bishop to his family house; a sow going mad after Bishop was disappointed in a business transaction, and knocking its head against a fence; a claim that poppets with pins in them had been found in a house she once occupied; the black pig that turned into a thing like a monkey; a cartwheel getting stuck in a mysterious hole—the tall stories of a farming community. The court swallowed the "evidence" whole, as did Cotton Mather: "There was little Occasion to prove the Witchcraft, it being evident and notorious to all Beholders."

More relevant to the specified charges was the account of Bishop's alleged spectral manipulation of the "Bewitched" at her examination on 19 April, more of the pantographic effect: ". . . upon some Special Actions of her Body, as the shaking of her Head, or the Turning of her Eyes, they presently and painfully fell into the like postures." This was the nearest that could be got to hard evidence, and the antics were repeated in front of the judges' eyes in the court. The scene at this trial and the ones to follow in the spacious, plain meetinghouse of Salem Town could hardly have provided a more striking tableau of the conflict between order and confusion, those terms for heaven and hell used by the Indian apostle, John Eliot.

On the one hand: the row of grave justices, Sewall among them, in long scarlet gowns with matching hoods, along with attending ministers like Samuel Parris from Salem Village, and Nicholas Noyes from Salem Town, in their black robes, white cravats around their necks conveying the dignity of spiritual office. On the other: the accusers, mainly girls, some of them small ones, shrieking, falling over, going into paroxysms, staring at Bridget Bishop like children do in playgrounds, seeing who will be the first to blink, though here a life depended on it. Then there were the onlookers, fascinated by the spectacle but fearful a finger might suddenly, arbitrarily, be pointed at them. Many were weatherbeaten country people from Salem Village and outlying parts, men in smocks or doublets and knee breeches with worsted stockings, the women with shawls—long handkerchiefs as they called them—their homemade dresses dirty at the bottom where they swirled over miry paths and fields (one of the accused at the next set of trials was charged with supernaturally avoiding getting a "drabled tayle" on a wet day twenty years before). Some better-off townsfolk were sprinkled among them, a glint of brass buckles and buttons on their shoes and surcoats, the women in gowns with virago sleeves, made of patterned, quality material, sarcenet or velvet—imported perhaps by Sewall himself, or Philip English, Salem's wealthiest citizen, now under arrest along with his wife, for witchcraft. Nathaniel Cary was in the crowd, checking out his wife's prospects when her case came to trial, while she remained in prison, clunking about in leg irons that were believed to prevent witches from sending their specters out on haunting missions (they were even being worn by the most diminutive of the accused witches, four-year-old Dorcas Good, daughter of Sarah).

What did Sewall make of it? The task of the court was to decide whether the tormented accusers represented the forces of order in the throes of resisting chaos, or the forces of confusion itself. Back at home, Sewall had his own children, at least two of whom—Sam Jr., coming up to his fourteenth birthday in a week's time, and ten-year-old Betty—had experienced episodes when they were overwhelmed by spiritual anguish, so the sight of the apparently suffering girls would have struck a chord in his parental heart. He would have every reason to transfer his knowledge of his children's sincerity to them. And, despite his constitutional optimism, he was perfectly able to buy into the evolving narrative of the witchcraft, with its vision of a dismal reversal of the Christian colonization of the New World. The collectivization of evil was a prominent feature of this trial. The afflicted had been asked to sign a book that Bishop's "Spectre called, Ours," and Deliverance Hobbs affirmed that "this Bishop was at a General Meeting of the Witches, in a Field at Salem-Village, and there partook of a Diabolical Sacrâment in Bread and Wine then Administred!" Sewall could have moments of despair about the Christian destiny of New England, as demonstrated by the dream he had in the opening months of King Philip's War, when the *sedes beatorum* had dwindled into a furnished chamber at Harvard. True, he believed America was heading for a glorious spiritual destiny, triggered by the conversion of the Indians. But his chiliasm was grounded on the prophecies of Revelation, and their basic dynamic was that of a pendulum, whereby things always got much worse before they got better. Sewall was particularly fascinated by the account of the angels who were ordered to pour out the vials of the wrath of God upon the earth, each in turn bringing down upon the world some terrible disaster or pestilence. At the end of this cycle, there would be a final battle between the Beast and the Lamb, after which the millennium would be inaugurated: Christ would reign for a thousand years (Revelation 16–17). Like many Puritans, Sewall thought the end was near, so it was hardly a surprise to find the Devil on the rampage.

Cotton Mather recorded Bishop's trial, along with those of four other accused witches, in a book called *Wonders of the Invisible World*, which was written within days of the last executions in late September, and had the explicit endorsement of both Stoughton and Sewall. The court had no problem in tracking back the gyrations of the accusers to movements made by Bishop's body. "There could be no collusion in the

Business," Cotton Mather stoutly claimed, as if a hard-nosed empiricism ruled the proceedings. What was really going on was a spectral appearance of empiricism, apparent effects being assigned to apparent causes.

Mather also recorded the search that had been made of Bishop's body for a "preternatural Teat" that, according to ancient belief, enabled a witch to nourish her familiars. On the morning of the trial, nine women examined her, along with Rebecca Nurse, Alice Parker, Elizabeth Proctor, Susannah Martin, and Sarah Good. They reported the discovery of excrescences of flesh between the pudendum and anus of three of the women: Nurse, Proctor, and Bishop herself. The scale of humiliation for the accused witches of Salem covered the gamut of human existence, from religious excommunication down to group inspection of the body's most private parts.

Some skepticism was felt, because the women were examined again at four in the afternoon of the trial date. This time: no teats. And yet for Mather, as for the judges, the evidence of the morning session incriminated Bishop even though it had disappeared by the afternoon. Presumably, the inconsistency just added to the presumption of supernatural involvement, a no-win situation for the accused.

The jury felt uneasy about coming to their verdict, because the chief justice, William Stoughton, made a strange ruling that must have been in response to a query. The court used a formula to express the charges against the accused, one repeated in the subsequent cases: "Ann puttnam . . . was & is hurt tortured Afflicted Pined Consumed wasted & tormented." But, said Stoughton, the jury "were not to mind whether the bodies of the said afflicted were really pined and consumed." According to Sewall's old traveling companion Thomas Brattle, now treasurer of Harvard, the afflicted, when not actually in their torments, were perfectly "hale and hearty, robust and lusty." Stoughton dealt with this awkward circumstance by arguing that the issue was "whether the said afflicted did not suffer from the accused such afflictions as naturally *tended* to their being pined and consumed, wasted, etc." Brattle summed up Stoughton's ruling with terse contempt: "This, (said he,) is a pining and consuming in the sense of the law. I add not."

Stoughton allowed the assumption of criminal intention even though the crime wasn't achieved. It was the completion of a perfectly consistent cycle: spectral crime, established by spectral empiricism, causing spectral affliction. At no point in this system does anything actually happen in the real world, except, unhappily, for the judicial response: hanging by the neck. Six days after the verdict, the General Court ended the legal vacuum in which the colony had pursued its business by confirming that the laws made by the previous governor and legislature of Massachusetts Bay remained in full force. This enabled the death sentence to be confirmed, and Stoughton duly signed the warrant that same day, ordering Bishop's execution two days later, the morning of 10 June.

Shortly after the hanging, Nathaniel Saltonstall resigned from the court. He had refused to sign warrants against women accused of witchcraft in his own town of Andover, and also declared himself unwilling to conduct examinations of the accused Salem witches. Though the conduct of Stoughton, and the acquiescence of the other judges, Sewall included, can be explained away in terms of prevailing beliefs and assumptions and by reference to precedent, one at least of their number was able to see that the emperor had no clothes.

The governor too had his doubts. He put out a request for clerical advice in relation to the trials, a sensible move given that a secular court was handling a spiritual crisis. "The Return of Several Ministers" was drawn up by Cotton Mather with the approval of twelve of his ministerial colleagues. For the most part it was an unmistakable condemnation of the legal process that had hanged Bridget Bishop and remanded so many others in custody. It suggested caution when dealing with accused people of good reputation (like Rebecca Nurse), condemned loud and chaotic scenes in court, challenged the relevance of tests on the accused (reciting the Lord's Prayer without stumbling, and touching the afflicted to see if that would supernaturally end the affliction), and, most important of all, dismissed spectral evidence because a demon can appear in the shape of an innocent, indeed virtuous, person. According to this advice, Bridget Bishop's execution must have been a horrible miscarriage of justice. But then the document backtracked, concluding with the pious hope that more of the accused would be speedily prosecuted.

Cotton Mather was a friend of Sewall's and the other judges—and they already had blood on their hands. And he wasn't above the fray himself, but subject to the same fear they had: that the city on a hill might be overtaken by dark forces from the wilderness. It was a fear shared by other clergymen too. Immediately after Bishop's trial, Sewall took notes of a sermon given by James Bayley, the first of the ministers to have been appointed at Salem Village, to the congregants at the South Church, one that maintained the militant note Willard had struck three days before: "Chr; is y^r: Captain . . . Sat[an]: is a very great & powerful enemie . . . we are bid to storm Heaven take it by violence, we are bid to fight . . . T B a good Christian y^t [that] is ye way to be good soldiers . . . The day grows dark you know not w^t [what] enemies are to come against you." Sewall noted down an equally fiery performance from Willard two days after Bishop's hanging, in which his pastor reverted to the image he'd used two weeks previously: "Your adversarie ye Devil as a roaring Lyon . . . is come down with power & great wrath. The Devil ranges here & takes all opportunities to do mischief unto us to ye very extent of his power."

A couple of weeks after the execution, on 28 June, the court met again for a three-day session to try Sarah Good, Elizabeth Howe, Susannah Martin, Rebecca Nurse, and Sarah Wilds. The suggestions in "The Return" were completely ignored. Martin repeated the point she'd raised in her examination, that the Devil could take the form of innocent people, but in his account of the trial Mather abused her as "one of the most Impudent, Scurrilous, wicked creatures in the world," "impudent" being the key word: she'd made a sound theological case that preempted the clergy and discredited the authorities, and this was not going to be acknowledged by her examiners, or her judges, or by Mather himself.

The depositions in these trials teem with the grudges and puzzles of deep, claustrophobic rurality, of people trapped within tight, unmediated lives. Oxen drown or choke on turnips, hens keel over, cows dry up. There are arguments about borrowing a scythe; the posts and rails of a fence mysteriously break while it's being erected. In Goody Wilds's case, there are problems involving the purchase of bees and the well-being of geese, along with some difficulty with securing a rope on a cart. One deposition in Susannah Martin's trial gives us an insight into the process by which, in this remote countryside, individual confusion could externalize itself into a landscape of threat and terror.

John Pressy of Amesbury, near Sewall's hometown of Newbury, told how, twenty-four years previously, he "was at Amsbury ferry upon a saterday in the eving near about the shutting in of the daylight." After a quarter of a century, he still remembered the moment of being benighted. Pressy's home was a little beyond a field belonging to Susannah Martin and her husband, at a place called Goodall's Hill, several miles off. However, he lost his way and wandered in a circle: ". . . he cam bake againe to the same place which he knew by stooping trees." Again he set out, steering by moonlight, and once more came back to the same spot. Then a third time: the panic of repetitive lostness in the big darkness of early America, where hostile Indians could be lurking, and the index of a man's bewilderment was a clump of stooping trees.

On the fourth attempt, a light appeared on Pressy's left hand. He carried on his way and it reappeared several times, finally manifesting itself directly in front of him. He tried beating it with a stick he was carrying, "and the Light seemed to brust up & wave from side to side as a turky cock when he sprads his tayle." It was light leeching in from another world, with a strange solidity and life of its own, so tangible in fact that eventually it knocked him down. As he continued on his way, he saw Susannah Martin standing to one side (he was, of course, going by the Martins' property, so her presence was perfectly understandable; she may well have shared an equal and opposite fright as his dark shape lumbered up; and she may, of course, have been holding a candle). When he finally got to his own home, Pressy was "seazed with fear coold not speak till his wif spake to him at the dore." The next day, the talk in town was that Goodwife Martin had got herself covered with bruises.

Depositions of this sort illuminate the anxieties that lay beneath the surface of small-town New England life. The farmyard world, with its dry cows and foaming pigs, was one cause of suspicion (Pressy himself, in another deposition, claimed that Martin had once sworn that he and his wife would never own more than two cows, and they never had). The nighttime wilderness, in which light was an anomaly, was another. Samuel Sewall wrote in his diary for 21 December 1691 about how he navigated himself home from an engagement by moonlight—a certain Mrs. Weld had arrived late and delayed his departure. When away from home, people had to glance regularly at the sky to check how long remained before "the shutting in of the daylight."

Years later, Sewall wrote a letter describing the death of Daniel Rogers of Ipswich, justice of the peace, who got lost returning home from a visit just a few miles from Amesbury, where Pressy had experienced such terror:

> He . . . proceeded out of his way to the left hand, and went down to the Sea; and was maroond and bewilder'd upon the Beach and Marishes, and at last benighted. That Saturday night there was a great Gust of wind with Snow and Hail, whereby a vessel in Merrimack River was driven down; her Anchors could not hold her. But near a ledge of Rocks on Salisbury side, call'd the Black Rocks, the Anchors held again . . . 'tis conjectur'd Mr. Rogers saw the Light, and attempted to wade over Black-Rock Cove, to get to it: but he sunk fast, and the rising Tide overwhelm'd and drowned him. Though his Horse and Cane were found, and hundreds sought after him, yet he was not found till January 14[th.] by a gunner, accidentally.

Another man in the dark, deluded by a bright chimera. One could become irrevocably lost in that landscape, and it's easy to see how, in the evolving story of witchcraft examinations and depositions, it could provide a literal, mystical, and metaphorical arena for problems of the spirit.

But witchcraft testimony pointed in two directions: outward toward the farming landscape and the wilderness beyond, inward to the depths of the individual soul. Often the latter course would be triggered by an argument. Samuel and Ruth Perley's daughter began to suffer from fits after a row with Elizabeth Howe and her husband. She would become disorientated and wander into water and fire, getting badly burned at times. Eventually she died, all skin and bones. A family is struck by a mysterious misfortune that causes real fear and suffering, so they track back for a possible explanation: ". . . this goode how [Goody Howe] that is now seised was the cause of her sorows."

What we see in respect of the Perleys' deposition, and also in the authorities' explanation of the torments of the afflicted at the witchcraft examinations and trials, is an assumption that external events can readily be tracked back to the hidden motives of the accused, that a straightforward connection can be made between public and interior realms. Visible suffering on the part of one person is the index of the malignity of invisible motivations on the part of another. Rebecca Nurse had denied this connection in her examination by Hathorne. At one point, accused of not weeping at the torments of the afflicted, she'd replied, "You do not know my heart." Many of her friends and neighbors were sure they did, however, because thirty-nine of them signed a petition on her behalf, at considerable risk of implicating themselves in the allegations. Such pressure, along with Nurse's blameless reputation, must have weighed with the jury at her trial, because they found her not guilty.

It was the only time it happened. The defendant was old and had been taken to her limit. She had tried to respond to the allegations with all the dignity and honesty she could muster. For a moment, she was entitled to huge relief.

Then the afflicted "made an hideous out-cry." What happened next was explained a week after the trial by Thomas Fiske, foreman of the jury. The fact he felt compelled to issue a public statement suggests the confusion and anxiety caused by this case. Stoughton expressed his disapproval of the verdict, and told the jury they hadn't taken on board the words the prisoner spoke against herself when faced with allegations from Goodwife Hobbs and her daughter Abigail (actually, her stepdaughter). Nurse had said, "What, do these persons give in evidence against me now, they used to come among us." The inference is that she was complaining of being betrayed by fellow members of a coven. Two other judges also apparently expressed dissatisfaction with the initial verdict. Several members of the jury, faced with this intimidating backlash, said they were willing to reconsider, and were granted leave to do so by the bench.

Well beyond the boundaries of due process now, this was not an unknown procedure at that time. Nearly twenty years later, when Sewall was chief justice, he presided over the trial at Kittery, Maine, of a man accused of murdering an Indian. The verdict was not guilty. Once again there was huge public interest in what was going on, with an audience of over a thousand people in attendance, and the jury was sent out again to reconsider (they returned with the same verdict).

Fiske, to his credit, continued to feel ill at ease during these further deliberations. When the jury was brought back into court, Nurse had been returned to the bar. Fiske referred to her remark but she made no reply at all, and he took her silence as evidence of guilt. The verdict was reversed.

It's hard to imagine how she must have felt, receiving this blow when she had apparently reached safety. What made it worse, when she understood how it had come about, was that the inexplicable hostility of her accusers had been supplemented by her own unfortunate turn of phrase—and that she had passed up the opportunity to limit the damage her ambiguous statement had caused. In one of the most poignant documents of the whole crisis, she explained what had happened: "I being informed, that the Jury brought me in Guilty, upon my saying that Goodwife Hobbs and her Daughter were of our Company; but I intended no otherways, then as they were prisoners with us, and therefore did then, and yet do judge them not legal Evidence against their fellow Prisoners." It's hard to imagine the judges, Sewall among them, not being moved at her next sentence: "And I being something hard of hearing, and full of grief, none informing me how the Court took up my words, and therefore had not opportunity to declare what I intended, when I said they were of our company."

Nurse had not finished on her vertiginous zigzag course. Four days after her trial ended, she was formally excommunicated from Salem

Town Church. Then, when all hope seemed irretrievably lost, Governor Phips granted her a reprieve. Unbearably, the accusers renewed their clamor, and some "Salem gentlemen" prevailed with the governor to withdraw the reprieve almost as soon as it was granted. The fact that Nurse was found not guilty, then guilty, reprieved, then condemned, testifies to the deep anxiety that her case caused. Precisely because it illustrated the crisis in its ultimate and purest form—an infestation of evil that was arbitrary and inscrutable, located in the heart of the community, even, as Parris had pointed out in a sermon, within the communion of saints itself—accusers and legal authorities alike needed to ensure condemnation. From the accusers' point of view, they had to prove they could win their most ambitious case so far, because there was an even more challenging one, that of Burroughs, in the offing. They had achieved a remarkable hold over their community, and over the representatives of the colony at large, but one failure could shake their credibility forever: after all, they were making the same charges against everyone. If Nurse had not spectrally tortured them at her examination, maybe no one had. And, from the point of view of the authorities, resistance needed to be unrelenting and comprehensive if the malevolent infection they had identified was to be prevented from overwhelming the province; exceptions could not be made. Nurse went to the gallows on 19 July, with the other four women.

Nicholas Noyes, one of Salem Town's ministers, tried to make Sarah Good confess at the point of execution, telling her she was a witch, and knew it. Noyes was a close friend and regular correspondent of Sewall, with whom he exchanged learned analyses of the prophecies in Revelation. He was also an avid poet, but unlike another of Sewall's friends, Edward Taylor, tended to produce reams of doggerel, often on the subject of the dear departed. Good, notorious for mumbling to herself, replied clearly for once: "You are a lyer; I am no more a Witch than you are a Wizard, and if you take away my Life, God will give you Blood to drink."

In Hawthorne's *The House of the Seven Gables*, this curse is attributed to a male character called Matthew Maule when he's on the gallows and eyeball-to-eyeball with the mounted Colonel Pyncheon, who comes across as a portmanteau ogre, an amalgam of various actors in the real drama: Hathorne, the author's despised ancestor; Stoughton, the chief judge; Noyes himself; Cotton Mather, who was to make a horseback appearance at the next round of executions; and even the corrupt sheriff, Corwin, nephew of one of the judges, who had a habit of galloping off and illegally claiming the property of the victims the moment they were hanged. It's a pleasing irony that the last words of this muttering woman would achieve literary permanence.

Five "witches" had been hanged in one day, an event unprecedented in American history. The sheer scale of these executions worked two ways, emphasizing both the enormity of the supposed threat and the extreme nature of the authorities' reaction to it. One can get an idea of how torn and disturbed Sewall felt by his behavior the following day, when he took part in an extraordinary event, a fast at the house of his friend Captain Alden, himself absent from the occasion as he was in prison awaiting his own trial for witchcraft. Fasts were days of abstinence and prayer offered up to God for a particular end. They could be on a community-wide scale, as in the one announced by the General Court before the proceedings began, or be a private observance (Sewall regularly undertook fasts in his own home). This one was in between the two. Prayers were opened by Samuel Willard, the pastor of both Sewall and Alden. Willard had preached a fiercely militant sermon the day after Alden had been remanded, just six weeks before; now, though, he had a more conciliatory approach. Then Sewall read a sermon. After that, more prayers, some of them led by Cotton Mather. When, on 19 May, John Proctor had asked Nicholas Noyes to pray with and for him, "it was wholly denied, because he would not own himself to be a Witch." Yet here were Cotton Mather, Samuel Willard, and one of the justices from the Court of Oyer and Terminer at their devotions on behalf of an accused witch who had no intention whatsoever of confessing.

The members of this community were intricately connected. Here is a web of association established by Sewall in his capacity as merchant and personal banker. On 26 June 1691, he received £30 from Alden, and on 10 October paid him for goods for his own sister Dorothy. Meanwhile, on 30 September, he received a sum of money (amount illegible) from John Hathorne for safekeeping in a sealed bag. Hathorne withdrew amounts from his bag through 1692 and 1693. On 2 March 1692, Sewall gave a redeemed captive called Mrs. Clark a piece of eight at Captain Alden's house; he bought flour from Alden on 1 April 1692, less than two months before his arrest. A week later, he received £13 from William Stoughton for the account of the minister Samuel Torrey.

The fasters at Alden's house sang the first part of Psalm 103—"The LORD doth judgment, justice too, / for all oppressed ones"—and finished at about five o'clock. "Brave Shower of Rain while Capt. Scottow was praying, after much Drought." That was a good omen, like the rainbow that had seemed a harbinger of Sewall's father's recovery.

As it happened, neither the fact that the drought had eased nor that a judge and two clergymen were willing to fast for him put Alden's mind at rest; in September, he escaped from custody and fled. He did not face trial until the Superior Court of Judicature sat on 25 April the following year, when the crisis was over, and his discharge a foregone conclusion. Six weeks after that, Sewall visited Alden and his wife to "tell them I was sorry for their Sorrow and Temptations by reason of his Imprisonment, and that was glad of his Restauration."

It's difficult to say whether the fast shows Sewall's disinterestedness or his favoritism; paradoxically, it seems to prove both at once. Certainly, it illuminates his humanity, and that's important to hold on to in the light of the grim events of the summer of 1692. Unease had begun to percolate into his mind. He wrote to his cousin Hull in London: "Are perplexed p[er] witchcrafts: six persons have already been condemned and executed in Salem." Certain issues must have resonated in his thoughts: Stoughton's ruling that a simple *tendency* to the pining and tormenting of the afflicted was sufficient; Nathaniel Saltonstall's resignation from the court; the way the bench ignored his friend Cotton Mather's advice in "The Return," and refused to listen to Susannah Martin's citation of the precedent of the Witch of Endor; the changed verdict in the case of Rebecca Nurse; above all, the fact that his friend and fellow congregant John Alden had been remanded for trial as a witch. Sewall was respectful of authority—though, as he would prove several times in the course of his life, would defy it courageously on a matter of principle. But he had gone into the trials feeling that he had made a serious judicial error, one caused by being too concerned about how others might think of him. He had pardoned a pirate under pressure from Wait Winthrop, now his fellow judge in the Court of Oyer and Terminer, and later despised himself for his weakness in not holding to what he believed was right. His instinct was now to stiffen his resolve when doubts and merciful feelings sneaked in, to overrule any unease he might be feeling with the implacability he had learned from his colleague and superior, William Stoughton.

One observer felt more than unease. Nathaniel Cary was horrified at what had taken place in the trials so far. "I went thither, to see how things were . . . managed; and finding that the Spectre-Evidence was there received, together with Idle, if not malicious Stories, against Peoples Lives, I did easily perceive which way the rest would go; for the same Evidence that served for one, would serve for all the rest." Ten days after the fast at Alden's house, Sewall noted in his diary that Mrs. Cary had escaped from jail. Cary had successfully plotted to get her out, furious about the bad faith and hypocrisy he had come across, the injustices and cruelty that were being meted out, "which is the more, considering what a People for Religion, I mean the profession of it, we have been."

The essential issue of the Salem witch trials was religion. Cary saw the trials as a betrayal of the religious faith of the colony; the authorities saw them as a defense of it. A secular court had been entrusted with protecting the Puritan community from assault from outside, and erosion from within. The nature of this task was highlighted in the next batch of trials, on 5 August, when one of the defendants was Sewall's former dinner guest, George Burroughs.

CHAPTER SEVEN

The King and Queen of Hell

THE TRIALS OF SIX PEOPLE WERE SCHEDULED FOR 5 AUGUST, four of them men. They were the minister George Burroughs, John Proctor, old George Jacobs, and a local man called John Willard, who had been acting as a deputy constable and had become convinced that the proceedings were misconceived. The women were Elizabeth Proctor and Martha Carrier, who was from Andover, where the witchcraft contagion had spread.

By now, there were a number of embattled communities. Spectral Indians were sighted near Gloucester, a seaport just north of Salem Town, leading Cotton Mather to speculate that the whole crisis might "have some of its original among the Indians, whose chief sagamores are well known unto some of our captives to have been horrid *sorcerers*, and hellish *conjurers*, and such as conversed with *dæmons*." (Two years before the Salem crisis, Sewall had been in correspondence with an expert on Indian matters called Samuel Lee, who gave him examples of their conjurations.)

Mather was interested in the case of Mercy Short, a seventeen-year-old girl who had survived a terrible attack on Salmon Falls two years before. News of this massacre had intensified Sewall's depression in the period following his pardon of Hawkins the pirate, when he'd gone down to New York with Stoughton to help coordinate policy in the war against the French and their Indian allies. Mercy Short's family had been slaughtered, and she was held captive by the Indians till being ransomed, when she came to Boston as a servant. Unluckily, her mistress sent her to Boston jail to deliver some tobacco to a friend who'd been remanded as a witch, and there she had an altercation with the muttering woman, Sarah Good, who tried to cadge some off her. The upshot was that Mercy Short thought Good had cursed her and rapidly became unbalanced, fusing her Indian trauma and her witchcraft encounter so that the Devil—short in stature, of "Indian colour," and in a high-crowned hat (like the small and swarthy minister George Burroughs)—counted French Canadians and Indian sagamores among his devotees, a diagnosis that confirmed Mather's fears, and those of the authorities in general. The external threat represented by the Catholic French and their pagan allies segued naturally into the internal one brought about by apostasy and visions of satanic covenants.

It was in this climate that the case against Burroughs, Martha Carrier, and the others was being prepared. A few days before Carrier faced the court, her sister, Mary Toothaker, contributed to the evolution of this narrative at her own examination: "This May last she was under great Discontentednes & troubled w'h feare about the Indians, & used often to dream of fighting with them . . . the Devil appeared to her in the shape of a Tawny man and promised to keep her from the Indians . . . it was the feare of the Indians that put her upon it." Confessors told the magistrates what they wanted to hear. Toothaker's testimony used the ingredients of personal malaise but tapped into widespread fears and preoccupations. Her account put tawny people on both sides of the equation, establishing a firm correspondence between spiritual malaise and external threat. She described going to a witch meeting at Salem Village where a little man called Burroughs was preaching—a handy observation for the authorities, given the same little man was to come to trial within the week. The assemblage of witches talked of a grandiose plan for "pulling down the Kingdom of Christ and setting up the Kingdom of satan," and their forces were massing: ". . . they did talk of 305 witches in the country." We have come a long way from village children spooking themselves while at play in a parsonage.

On 4 August, Sewall was at Salem getting ready to take the bench for the trials the following day, when he heard of "desolation in Jamaica." A terrible earthquake had taken place at Port Royal two months previously (the news lag again), with "1700 persons kill'd, besides the Loss of Houses and Goods." The scale of the disaster perfectly complemented the apocalyptic atmosphere in New England. Over in Boston, Cotton Mather got the news the same morning and brought it into his midweek sermon on Revelation 12:12, "Woe to the Inhabiters of the earth, and of the sea! for the Devil is come down unto you." In the latter days, the Devil would try to establish his kingdom, but he would be defeated and confined to the bowels of the earth, where his struggles would cause earthquakes. One of these might have caused the Port Royal disaster. Perhaps because of the short notice, Mather hadn't quite integrated this event into his general picture that, based on the recent testimony of Mary Toothaker and other Andover witches, had the Devil still active on the surface of the world, furious at losing his pagan kingdom of the Indians to the Christian settlers, and busily scheming to recolonize New England. A few years later, returning to the subject of Port Royal, Mather was able to provide an account of the disaster that reconciled it to the Salem witchcraft, since it too had been brought about because the inhabitants dabbled in fortune-telling.

The contrast between the trivial and the grand is at the heart of the witchcraft narrative. At his trial the next day, the stories of George Burroughs's feats of strength were rehashed, but by now he'd also been given the dignity of king of hell, with Martha Carrier as his queen. In her testimony to the court, seventeen-year-old Mercy Lewis, once his servant and now one of the most avid accusers, assigned him the role of the Devil and at the same time promoted herself to Messiah, in her retelling of the temptation of Christ in the wilderness: "mr Burroughs caried me up to an exceeding high mountain and shewed me all the kingdoms of the earth and tould me that he would give them all to me if I would writ in his book." Lawson earned his reward for siding with the accusers: testimony was offered that Burroughs had killed his successor's wife and daughter because he resented Lawson's success as a preacher at Salem Village.

Disappointingly, the papers relating to Martha Carrier's case contain little to show why she was given the lofty, or lowly, position of Burroughs's spectral consort. The depositions are full of the usual mishaps to cows and sheep, with the occasional human ailments thrown in. Carrier had a forthright, contemptuous voice, it's true: "They will dissemble if I look upon them," she said, when instructed to make eye contact with her accusers. And in a row with a certain Benjamin Abbott, she threatened to stick as close to him as bark to a tree; according to Abbott's own report, "she would hold my noss so Closs to the grindstone as Ever it was held since my Name was Benjamin Abbut." Nothing, however, makes hers a special case, though Cotton Mather huffed and puffed ("this Rampant Hag") in his attempt to explain Carrier's spectral rank. But in Revelation 17 a woman sits on a seven-headed beast, dressed "in purple and scarlet colour, and decked with gold and precious stones and pearls." She represents "MYSTERY, BABYLON THE GREAT, THE MOTHER OF HARLOTS AND ABOMINATIONS OF THE EARTH." Satan may be masculine, but the embodiment of all the actual evil committed in the world is female. (A month later, Parris would use a sermon on this chapter to put forward his own candidate for queen of evil, Martha Corey.)

As claims grew larger, doubts grew stronger. John Proctor had written to ask five Boston clergymen, including Increase Mather and Samuel Willard, to support an appeal to the governor for a change in the judges. He claimed that he and his son were being mistreated and prejudged: "The Magistrates, Jewries, and all the People in general, being so much inraged and incensed against us by the Delusion of the Devil, which we can term no other, by reason we know in our own consciences, we are all Innocent Persons." This is a natural response to the tortured reasoning that had been offered at his (or rather his wife's) examination, when Sewall was present. Proctor had witnessed what he knew to be a charade when the accusers had cried out that his specter was about to grasp Mrs. Bathshua Pope's feet and, sure enough, Mrs. Pope's feet promptly rose in the air. Hathorne, the examining magistrate, had found himself having to guard against the charge that by calling out the accusers were really relaying instructions to Bathshua Pope to raise her feet at the appropriate moment (which is obviously what did in fact happen). "You see the Devil will deceive you," he'd told Proctor, "the children could see what you was going to do before the woman was hurt. I would advise you to repentance, for the Devil is bringing you out." The Devil was betraying Proctor himself, one of his own, by giving advance warning to the accusers of the intentions of Proctor's Devil-sponsored specter. Why would he? It's an example of the twisted no-win logic Hathorne targeted at his victims, and it adds a further twist to what could possibly be meant by "seeing" in the context of invisible phenomena. Throughout the crisis, juries and judges accepted that the accusers could "see" things nobody else could. But at the Proctor examination, Hathorne suggested that they could "see" the actions of an invisible specter before it had even performed them. Seeing is becoming less and less real, more and more metaphorical. Having been on the receiving end of this process, Proctor takes it a step further. He suggests evil is "Delusion," a form of internal confusion, of illusory and apparent perception, rather than the perception of the invisible. The agency is still the Devil, but by siting the area of operation within the mind, Proctor is relegating him to a metaphorical role and pointing toward his ultimate redundancy.

An even greater challenge to the judges was offered by the granddaughter of one of Proctor's codefendants, George Jacobs, the old man with two staffs. Finding herself indicted for witchcraft, sixteen-year-old Margaret Jacobs had turned confessor, making accusations against her own grandfather, as well as George Burroughs, John Willard, and an accused witch called Alice Parker. Then she retracted her confession. She later explained that the afflicted had fallen down at the sight of her and told her that if she didn't confess she would be put in the dungeon and hanged. She had done as she was told, but "the very first night after I had made confession, I was in such a horror of conscience that I could not sleep for fear the Devil should carry me away for telling such horrid lies."

While the authorities were drumming it into the accused that the Devil was preventing them from confessing, the accused themselves knew that if the Devil was involved at all, he must be on the opposite tack. As Margaret Jacobs makes clear, by the time her case came before the examiners the necessary strategy for survival was quite explicit: confess and accuse others. Nevertheless, she decided she must repudiate her words: "What I said, was altogether false against my grandfather, and Mr. Burroughs, which I did to save my life and to have my liberty; but the Lord, charging it to my conscience, made me in so much horror, that I could not contain myself before I had denied my confession, which I did though I saw nothing but death before me, chusing rather death with a quiet conscience, than to live in such horror, which I could not suffer."

The girl who penned these noble and heroic words could not have guessed at the time that she would not, in fact, hang as a result of her honesty (her trial was delayed because of an "Imposthume [an abscess or cyst] in her head," and by the time it finally took place the following January the danger had passed). Though this letter was probably not written until September, her retraction was known to the judges. She had been forced to confess the truth to the examining magistrates, who did not, of course, believe her. Her grandfather did, however. She was able to ask, and gain, his forgiveness, and the tough old man altered his will to leave her £10.

Despite these pressures, the court wasted no time in finding Proctor, Jacobs, and the other four defendants guilty, though Elizabeth Proctor was reprieved on account of pregnancy. They were sentenced to hang two weeks later, on 19 August.

Sewall didn't attend the executions. Instead, he and Stoughton, along with several other dignitaries, went off to Watertown, just north of the Charles River and to the west of Cambridge, where they took it upon themselves to advise the inhabitants to get on with the task of acquiring a minister. If they couldn't agree on their choice, they could at least decide where to build their meetinghouse: "Many say Whitney's Hill would be a convenient place." In view of the conflict and distress caused by the executions, this was a well-timed public gesture, two judges showing themselves involved in the spiritual development of the community. Problems about obtaining a minister and building a meetinghouse underlaid the tensions and anxiety at Salem Village, and contributed to the climate in which the witchcraft crisis arose. Sewall and Stoughton were making it clear they were prepared to take a cre-

ative part in preventing a future similar occurrence in another neighborhood, the other side of the coin of their punitive role in passing a sentence of death on those found guilty of witchcraft.

When he got home, Sewall promptly contacted Cotton Mather,
who had attended the executions, to get his account and transcribe it in
his diary. A great number of spectators had been present. He noted
down the names of the ministers who'd attended—Mather himself,
Zachariah Simms, John Hale, Nicholas Noyes, Ezekiel Cheever—
hoping perhaps to convince himself that they provided adequate spiritual ballast on his side. However, Thomas Brattle, writing a few months
later, suggested that there had been influential members of the community present who were leaning the other way. The condemned had behaved in an exemplary manner, asking Cotton Mather to pray with
them (Brattle implies that Mather refused). They forgave their accusers, the jury, and the judges, and conducted themselves with such dignity (especially Burroughs and John Willard) that it "was very affecting
and melting to the hearts of some considerable Spectatours, whom I
could mention to you."

It's fair to say that by this point an alternative way of explaining the
crisis, a rival narrative, was beginning to gain ground. The prevailing
story was that the colony was under siege from pagan and devilish
forces intending to reverse the accepted history of European settlement
in New England: the Puritan landfall, the city on a hill, the establishment of a Christian commonwealth in the wilderness. The other possibility, broached by a number of the accused and by Proctor's letter,
given added force by Margaret Jacobs's brave stance and accepted by the
friends and relatives of people like Rebecca Nurse and Mrs. Cary, was
that innocent people were being killed because of a terrible *delusion* that
the colony was under threat in this way. The witchcraft papers contain
details of 156 cases, most of which had been set in motion by this
point. The figure can be used to give alarming credibility to either account.

Sewall goes on to note that "all of them said they were innocent,
Carrier & all." This was one of the most disturbing features of the executions. Admitting guilt had the immense practical advantage of pro-

tecting you from the rope: nobody who did so was hanged during the Salem crisis. More important from Sewall's point of view, it would mean that the condemned could make their peace with God. What motive could they have for holding out to the bitter end, when they were about to confront their maker? "Carrier & all," he marvels, obviously finding her claim the hardest to swallow, which itself suggests that some of the others must have seemed to him more likely. However, "Mr. Mather says they all died by a Righteous Sentence." That reassurance obviously gave him comfort. The fact it did shows us why Cotton Mather, having demolished the assumptions and procedures of the witchcraft trials in "The Return," fudged his conclusion. Denying his support for the judges' actions would have seemed like betrayal.

Sewall concluded his entry with bad news: "Mr. Burroughs by his Speech, Prayer, protestation of his Innocence, did much move unthinking persons, which occasions their speaking hardly concerning his being executed." It's almost like party politics, with the opposition shrewdly garnering support. Standing on the ladder, Burroughs made a speech declaring his innocence, and then prayed. He finished with a masterstroke: reciting the Lord's Prayer without stumbling. It was believed witches could not manage this feat. Beside him on the gallows stood John Willard, who had been condemned in part for his failure to do exactly that. "Can you pray the Lords Prayer?" he'd been asked at his examination.

Yes
Let us hear you.
He stumbled at the thresh hold & said Maker of heaven &
    earth
He began again & mist
It is a strange thing, I can say it at another time. I think I am
    bewitcht as well as they, & laught
Again he mist
Again he mist & cryed well this is a strange thing I cannot say it
Again he tried and mist
Well it is these wicked ones that do so overcome me.

Willard's terrified laugh, as his life slipped away, is one of the bleakest moments of the whole tragedy. Now Burroughs, with the rope around his neck, brings it off word perfectly. In front of them is the discomfited Cotton Mather, mounted on a horse, the man who had explicitly denounced the use of witchcraft tests in his "Return."

For the time being, Sewall's own judgment remained secure. In the margin of his entry he wrote, "Dolefull! Witchcraft." But anxiety about the executions was so acute that someone, probably his brother

Samuel Sewall. Diary entry for 19 August 1692.
Samuel Sewall Diaries, MHS.

Stephen, clerk of the court, appended an odd memorandum to Burroughs's dossier. A confessor called Sarah Wilson told of a meeting of witches the night before the minister's execution. Burroughs was there in spectral form. After the sacrament, "he tooke leave & bid them Stand to their faith [i.e., their satanic faith], & not own any thing." Burroughs had had his own equivalent of the Passion in the Garden. His final words could be used to explain the refusal of the condemned to admit their guilt.

THE COURT of Oyer and Terminer met twice more, on 9 and 17 September. Fifteen more people were tried and found guilty. Eight of them were executed on 22 September. Preliminary examinations continued during this time, and the story of the Devil's deconstruction of New England's Christian settlement reached its maturest form. On 29 August, William Barker described a witch meeting at Salem Village "where he judges there was about a hundred of them, that the meeting was upon a green peece of ground neare the ministers house." The witches had been empowered by the backsliding of the people, and the way he words it almost makes the coven seem to be working as agents of the Lord rather than the Devil: ". . . they mett there to destroy that place by reason of the peoples being divided & theire differing with their ministers." "Satans design," Barker says, "was to set up his own worship, abolish all the churches in the land, to fall next upon Salem and soe goe through the countrey." Here is the gateway, or landfall, story, with Salem's troubles (Barker himself was from Andover) providing merely the first stage of a colony-wide dismemberment of Christianity. A couple of weeks later, in his sermon of 11 September, Parris gave historicity and weight to this vision. "How industrious & vigorous is the Bloody French Monarch, & his Confederates against Christ & his Interest?" he reminded his listeners. Well, we have a similar problem right on our doorstep: "Yea, & in our Land, what Multitudes, of Witches & Wizards has the Devil instigated with utmost violence to attempt the overthrow of Religion?" In short, the Devil was real in much the same way as that old enemy, the king of France; and just like the French armies, the Devil's legions could be supposed to represent a genuine military threat: "No marvail then that the Devil & his Instruments are making this War at this day in our Plantations by Witchcrafts."

In waging war on the plantations, the Devil had a clear and radical agenda. Barker described a sort of fusion of the antinomian heresy (whereby there is no need to live a good life because God has already made his choices) and the Declaration of Independence, still almost a century off: "He [Barker] sayth the Devil promeised that all his people should live bravely that all persones should be equall; that their should be no day of resurection or of judgement, and neither punishment nor shame for sin." He went on to describe the sacrament at the meeting, identifying Burroughs as a ringleader and blower of the summoning trumpet. He provides a rather odd account of the genesis of the crisis: "In the spring of the yeare the witches came from Connecticut to afflict at Salem Village." They had gone home, however, leaving about 307 local witches to continue the work. At this point, he confronts the alternative version of events, according to which innocent people are suffering injustice, remarking that "the witches are much disturbed with the afflicted persones because they are descovered by them, They curse the judges Because their Society is brought under, they would have the afflicted persones counted as witches but he [Barker] thinks the afflicted persones are Innocent & that they doe god good service and that he has not known or heard of one innocent persone taken up & put in prisone." It's obvious the credibility of the accusers is under attack, and there is anxiety and anger about the arrest and confinement of the innocent.

The Court of Oyer and Terminer was becoming embattled. The very fact that the final sessions were so close together suggests urgency, a sense that matters were reaching a climax. What we know of the tactics of some of the accused indicates an awareness of a groundswell of public criticism and opposition. Ann Pudeator, for example, who was tried at the first of these sessions, was a low-caste defendant like Sarah Good, an "ill-carriaged woman." But having been sentenced to death, she put in a petition alleging the unreliability of the witnesses against her, and reminding the bench that "the great God of heaven . . . is the searcher & knower of all hearts." Mary Bradbury, meanwhile, was a different class of accused, the wife of a shipmaker from Salisbury. She too made a written defense of her own virtue; her husband produced another, very movingly written ("she hath bin a loveing & faithfull wife to mee"). Her pastor wrote too, and over a hundred of her fellow towns-people signed a petition in her support: ". . . neither did any of us (some of whom have lived in the town w'th her above fifty yeare) ever heare or knowe that shee ever had any difference or falling oute with any of her neighbors man woman or childe." None of this made any difference; she was condemned. But the judges were affronting substantial communities by this stage in the proceedings. The townspeople of Salisbury must have seen the court itself as the threat to social order. The elderly Mrs. Bradbury managed to escape before her execution, perhaps aided by the strength of her popular support.

The two accused sisters of Rebecca Nurse, Sarah Cloyse and Mary Easty, also wrote a petition to the court at around the time of the trials of 9 September. They too were able to call upon the support of their minister and fellow citizens, "Mr Capen the pastour and the Towne & Church of Topsfield." In addition to this assertion of community solidarity, they made some stringent criticisms of the proceedings of the Court of Oyer and Terminer. They pointed out that they were not allowed to plead their own cause, nor to have the benefit of counsel (counsel were not normally appointed in courts until later in Sewall's career, the provision of a team of judges being assumed to guarantee the appropriate range of questioning and points of view). In these circumstances, they asked the judges themselves to represent their interests—a forlorn hope, but it made the point that defense had become impossible (in Easty's examination, her attempt to plead not guilty had been treated as sheer impertinence).

The sisters' criticism of the fairness and legality of their treatment had no effect, though Cloyse was lucky enough to have her trial adjourned to the safety of the following January. Easty, however, like all the other defendants on 9 September—indeed all the other defendants at all the sessions of the Court of Oyer and Terminer—was condemned to die.

It was inevitable that the procedures of the court were being discredited. Nothing the accused said in their own defense was ever accepted; all that was left for them was to attack the court itself. This response was taken to its ultimate extreme by another of the defendants on 9 September, eighty-year-old Giles Corey. He refused to plead, in effect denying the very authority of the court.

Stoughton was not a man to take insubordination lightly, and the obduracy of this rough-hewn farmer would have caught him on the raw. All the paraphernalia of his court—the dignified judges; the solemn ministers; the fascinated, intimidated spectators; the shrieking, contorting accusers—must suddenly have seemed tawdry and inconsequential, like a children's game when a grown-up walks into the room. According to Cotton Mather's analysis, the whole edifice of the witchcraft crisis had been built on a foundation of children's games.

The court had to find a way to reestablish its potency, its very reality, as an institution, and it scrabbled through old statutes to do so, coming up with a terrifying English sanction to make Corey think again about his stance: *peine forte et dure*, piling heavy stones on a condemned man while he lay prone upon the ground until finally he couldn't breathe.

The threat had no effect; Corey called their bluff. "Much pains was used with him two days," wrote an anguished Sewall, "one after another, by the Court and Capt. Gardner of Nantucket who had been of his acquaintance: but all in vain." As time went on and all the pleading fell on deaf ears, Sewall might have had to hold on to the memory of how disgusted he'd been with himself after succumbing to weakness in the case of pirate Hawkins.

By definition, the mute man's motives can't be known for certain. He knew he had no chance of survival if he pleaded not guilty: his wife, Martha, was sentenced to hang on 22 September. Undoubtedly, he was aware that the corrupt sheriff Corwin stole the possessions of condemned witches as soon as they were executed, so he might have thought he was safeguarding his legacy. But that doesn't seem a strong enough reason. All those who had come before the court so far had refused to save themselves by the topsy-turvy expedient of pleading guilty; he went one better and refused to plead at all. There must have been radical contempt in the gesture. The court obviously thought so, imposing its outrageous sanction for the only time in the history of America. The extreme punishment was patently *pour encourager les autres*, the logic being that of the outlaw (appropriately enough) who commits ever more terrible crimes as he desperately tries to save himself. The court was increasingly being perceived by its victims, their friends and relatives, and people of influence in the community at large as deviating from social norms, let alone legal ones; in Corey's case, it responded by showing itself willing to go to absolutely any lengths in order to try to shore up its position. The court's ferocity was increasing in direct ratio to its loss of standing. Corey was sentenced to face his punishment on 19 September, three days before his wife's execution.

While the prospect of appalling *peine* hung over Corey, and in a different sense over the justices themselves, along came another threat to their morale and prestige. Mary Easty, in prison awaiting her own execution, put pen to paper once more and wrote them a letter. She explained how she had been confined for a month, then released, and then confined again, on account of the "wiles and subtility" of her accusers. Since she knew she was innocent, she knew others of the condemned must be innocent as well. What gave her petition its authority was that Easty chose not to plead on her own behalf—"I Petition to your honours not for my own life"—but for others. This sublime disinterestedness makes the document rank with Margaret Jacobs's retraction as the most heroic of the witchcraft papers. Easty was forthright in her address to the justices—"you are in the wrong way," she told them—and offered two suggestions for putting them back on track. They should keep the accusers apart from each other and then question them rigorously. Also, they should put some of the confessors on trial. The result of these two strategies, she confidently informed them, was that the lies would become apparent and "youle see an alteration of thes things they say."

These suggestions went to the very heart of the problem, but equally significant was the tone in which they were made. Easty had no hesitation at all in passing judgment on the judges, as Proctor did in his petition, as Corey did by his silence. The court had shown itself to be deviant, and a threat to the community, and it was the prisoner's responsibility, through her unique perspective, to set it to rights again. She showed none of the desperation and panic of someone who will hang within days. At the very moment when she faced being expunged by her society, Easty established herself as the protector of its interests and values. She even managed to sound slightly patronizing: "I question not but your honours does to the utmost of your Powers in the discovery and detecting of witchcraft and witches and would not be guilty of Innocent blood for the world."

It's a sign of the desperate position the court was in that this letter had its effect. It didn't save Mary Easty's life, but that was not what she'd asked. At the sitting of 17 September, four confessors were at last brought to trial—Rebecca Eames, Ann Foster, Abigail Hobbs, and Mary Lacy Sr.—along with a fifth woman, Abigail Faulkner, who had made a partial confession. Perhaps Hobbs represented the most significant breakthrough, in that she had spent months cooperating with the authorities and acting as an accuser. But although these women were condemned by the court, none of them was hanged in the last batch of executions that took place on 22 September. The court preferred to keep them in cold storage. Confession was an implicit recognition of its authority and of the reality of witchcraft, and in the end that reassurance was more valuable to it than consistent treatment. The delay in punishment could always be put down to the quest for further evidence from cooperative witnesses.

This message had not got through to one of those tried on the seventeenth, Samuel Wardwell, who had confessed when examined on 1 September but withdrew his confession on the thirteenth, saying that "he: knew he should dye for it: whether: he ownd it or no." He died for it, because in the end he had too much integrity to own to something that hadn't happened. But his short-lived confession is interesting because, in trying to flesh out his lie, Wardwell internalized and psychologized the Devil's arrival in his life. He had once been in a disturbed frame of mind; "the reason of his discontent was because he was in love with a maid named Barker who slighted his love." As a result, he was susceptible to the Devil's offer to put him at ease and get him promoted to the rank of captain. This is a more subtle story than previous tales of demonic tit for tat. Wardwell searched his past to locate a moment when he hadn't felt in control of his own destiny, and therefore could conceivably have been under the sway of malign forces.

One of the confessors who stood trial, Rebecca Eames, also brought love interest into her testimony, explaining that a fellow witch, Sarah Parker, had been crossed in love, "& the Devil had come to her & kisd her" and that she herself had covenanted with the Devil as a result "of her great sin in Committing adultery." Confessors are beginning to see the Devil not as an external force, but as the embodiment of their own emotional confusion.

The other confessors who came before the court on 17 September kept to the main narrative, however: that was what the justices needed to hear. Hundreds of witches abroad; Burroughs in charge of their sacrament; the Devil's plan to recolonize New England. All the confessors survived; those who pleaded not guilty were sentenced to hang along with those convicted on the ninth. They were Mary Parker, who'd told off her husband for being at a tavern, and was rebuked for it by a man called John Westgate, who later found himself pursued by a spectral hog; Wilmot Reed, who had once had words with a Mrs. Syms, and told her she wished she might not *mingere* or *cacere*—urinate or defecate—thus allegedly causing the dry bellyache; Margaret Scott, about whose case, which was hurried through the court at great speed, little is known; and Samuel Wardwell. The evidence against Wilmot Reed might have rung a bell with Sewall. Two years previously, he had received an account from Samuel Lee of an Indian curse whereby a hole was dug and a herb placed in it, with the result that the victim was never able to make water again. Of course, the actual charge in each case was that the accused had spectrally afflicted the regular accusers at their examinations—except, oddly, in the case of Wardwell, who was indicted for spectral haunting before he actually came to court. The judges were being less rigorous in this last act of the drama.

Nine prisoners were scheduled to die on 22 September—those condemned at the later session of the court therefore had only days to prepare themselves. The machinery of justice was dealing with as many witches in as short a time as possible. Nobody knew how long they had left. In the meantime, there was Corey's execution to go through. "About noon, at Salem," Sewall wrote on the nineteenth, "Giles Corey was press'd to death for standing Mute." A detail of the sickening event comes down to us. Corey's tongue was forced out of his mouth by the pressure, as if grotesquely parodying the court's wish to loosen it; Corwin, the sheriff, pushed it back in again with the tip of his cane.

One person at least noticed Sewall's anguish. Thomas Putnam chose to send him a letter the following day, the second time he had directly intervened with the witchcraft courts. He explained that on the eve of the execution, his daughter Ann Jr. was, as usual, being tormented by witches, who threatened to press her to death in advance of the same thing happening to Corey: the clear implication was that the extreme nature of his punishment could be justified by the extreme behavior of his malevolent agents. Ann was then visited by a man in a winding sheet, who explained that Corey had murdered him. Significantly, the man alleged that Corey had pressed him to death with his feet—in other words, killed him in a way that made Corey's execution perfectly appropriate. Corey had got away with the murder at the time because he made a covenant with the Devil under the terms of which he was promised that he would not hang. The Devil's assurances inevitably proved unreliable in the long run: Corey wouldn't hang, but Satan had said nothing about him suffering *peine forte et dure*. God himself clinched the outcome: "God Hardened his Heart, that he should not hearken to the Advice of the Court, and so dy an easy Death."

Putnam pretended to grapple with the mystery of why this past record had not previously come to light. "Now Sir," he told Sewall, "this is not a little strange to us; that no body should Remember these things, all the while that Giles Corey was in Prison, and so often before the Court." Strange indeed, and maddening, to come across a juicy titbit at a point when, except for a daring piece of chicanery, it might have gone to waste. In 1675, Corey had in fact beaten his servant, Jacob Goodale, nearly a hundred times with a large stick. Goodale died a few days later without incriminating Corey, and the violent farmer was only charged with abuse and fined. For some reason, this past episode had been over-looked when he was examined for witchcraft. Having ferreted it out, Putnam knew that if he brought it directly to the judges' attention, his own vindictiveness would be clear. But by dressing up the details of the case with the spectral torments of his daughter, and modifying them to fit more neatly into the events that had just taken place, he could use the information to keep Sewall in line, reassuring him that the punishment was appropriate and that the failure of the court to persuade Corey to change his stance was the result of God's intervention. As is usually the case when an accuser takes credibility to its limits, he drew attention to the unlikely provenance of this intervention: ". . . the thing was done before she [Ann Jr.] was born," Putnam exclaimed in amazement.

Putnam was giving Sewall just what he needed, and Sewall swallowed it whole: "Now I hear from Salem that about 18 years agoe, he [Corey] was suspected to have stampd and press'd a man to death, but was cleared. Twas not remembered till Anne Putnam was told of it by said Corey's Spectre the Sabbath-day night before Execution." One can feel his relief at latching on to that phrase, "press'd to death," It didn't occur to Sewall, any more than it had to him and his fellow judges on similar occasions, to ask why the spectral Corey was so keen to incriminate himself. In fact, so eager was Sewall to alleviate his conscience, he misread Putnam's account, which gave the source of the information to Corey's victim, thereby adding a theological complication to the plot: the specter of a *non*-witch.

Putnam's hard work went to waste; the Court of Oyer and Terminer had passed its last sentences. On 20 September, Cotton Mather wrote to Stephen Sewall to ask him for the papers relating to some of the trials, so that he could write them up—Governor Phips, who'd been away at the wars for the last stages of the crisis, had requested it. The court was being called to account. But there was a sudden gleam of light the next day, as Sewall recorded: "A petition is sent to town in behalf of Dorcas Hoar, who now confesses: Accordingly an order is sent to the Sheriff to forbear her Execution, notwithstanding her being in the Warrant to die to morrow."

She had been tried on 9 September, and pleaded not guilty. But observing that the confessors brought to trial on the seventeenth were spared the rope, she made a last minute bid for survival, and it paid off. For Sewall, it was a breakthrough: "This is the first condemned person who has confess'd." There must have been moments when he had the awful intuition that all those executed were innocent; John Hale, one of the ministers who signed Hoar's petition, later expressed his anxiety that none of those who died chose to seek last-minute mercy for their souls by confession. Twenty people in all allowed themselves to be put to death because they would not perjure themselves by admitting guilt. Hoar's admission made it seem possible her fellow condemned were guilty after all, a token of such importance that even Noyes signed her petition, the day before gloating over the dangling bodies of those who had held firm: "What a sad thing it is to see Eight Firebrands of Hell hanging there."

The condemned were taken through the streets of Salem in a cart, which got stuck on a hill, causing the afflicted to claim that the Devil "hindered it." When Wardwell gave his last address to the crowd from the gallows, reiterating his innocence, he started coughing on smoke from the executioner's pipe, and once again the accusers cried that the Devil was hindering him, though the Devil's motives are not clear here and seem contrary to his wish to stall the cart. More likely the smoke was the last puff of witchcraft miasma.

The day before, Stephen and Margaret Sewall had arrived at Samuel and Hannah's house in Boston, Stephen bringing with him the court papers, which he had agreed to make available to Cotton Mather so he could answer Phips's request. The next morning, while the executions were actually taking place, Mather himself arrived, along with Stoughton, Hathorne, and Captain John Higginson, son of the senior minister at Salem Town, and there was a meeting about Mather's project. Clearly, he had committed himself to a defense of the trials.

At some stage of the discussion, Stoughton left for another engagement. But the sky darkened and it began to rain, so he was forced to return and stay the night at the Sewalls'. As in the case of the Alden fast, so in this very different context, where it was the justices rather than the accused who were needing to defend themselves, the rain came as a benison. "Blessed be God," wrote Sewall. Perhaps he believed it meant that the crisis had passed and the community could begin to heal itself, that the darkness of the rain cloud represented spiritual light (a month before, he'd noted in his journal that there was a fast in the First Church of Boston in respect of both the witchcraft and the summer drought, almost as if the two were opposite sides of the same coin).

He read the first chapter of the first epistle of John before going to bed: "If we say that we have fellowship with him, and walk in darkness, we lie, and do not the truth: But if we walk in the light, as he is in the light, we have fellowship one with another, and the blood of Jesus Christ his Son cleanseth us from all sin" (1:6–7). To repudiate darkness and walk in the light. "Fellowship one with another" is the key phrase here; he suspected the cycle of witchcraft executions was over.

CHAPTER EIGHT

Speaking Smartly About the Salem Witchcrafts

After the hangings of 22 September, Sewall went about business as usual. He sailed over to Hogg Island and sold his current tenant, Joshua Gee, three white oaks for the sum of 30s., agreeing to cart them to the waterside for collection. Then he was off to Newton to check up on Sam, who'd been living with the family of a Mr. Hobart for nearly a year, continuing his education and gaining experience of another household in accordance with colonial custom; with trees still on his mind, Sewall brought home some chestnuts in their burrs for setting.

But the following Friday he rode off to Weymouth with Samuel Willard to visit "loansome Mr Torrey," the minister there, who'd lost his wife the month before. Sewall had started sounding people out about whether the Court of Oyer and Terminer had any future. Samuel Torrcy's sudden return to single life meant they dined in the kitchen. His opinion was it should carry on with its proceedings but rectify any errors committed as soon as they were recognized, though how some sort of self-correcting device could be inserted into its machinery wasn't gone into. Meanwhile, over in Salem Town, brother Stephen had fallen ill—perhaps an omen something was seriously amiss.

Cotton Mather was working on his account of the trials at lightning speed and within weeks had written a whole book. He brought the manuscript round to Sewall to see if he approved. *Wonders of the Invisible World*, in its muddled and rambling way, gave an account of the trials of Bridget Bishop, George Burroughs, Martha Carrier, Elizabeth Howe, and Susannah Martin, along with an overview of the meaning and nature of the crisis. The Christian settlement of New England was a vine planted by God, who had driven away the heathen to make space for it, and ensure it rooted deeply and covered the country, "so that it sent its Boughs unto the Atlantic Sea Eastward, and its Branches unto the Connecticut River Westward, and the Hills were covered with the Shadow thereof." Now Satan had made a bid at "Unsetling" this settlement and rooting up the vine, sending an army of Devils into Salem because it was the original Christian colony (Mather slid over the distinction between Salem Town and Salem Village). This was very much a restatement of Deodat Lawson's analysis right at the beginning of the crisis (all of six months before, though it must have seemed more like years to those involved).

Perhaps Sewall's September enthusiasm for white oaks and chestnuts should be seen in the light of this imagery of colonial planting and uprooting. From the very beginning of settlement, the Christian community had been defined in organic terms—in his sermon on board the *Arbella* in 1630, "A Model of Christian Charity," John Winthrop had become quite anatomical about it: ". . . the ligamentes of this body which knitt together are love"—and the term "plantations" for the colonies referred to spiritual as well as agricultural husbandry. But Mather went on to indicate a shift away from this organicism: ". . . the Devil has made a dreadful Knot of witches in the Country, and by the help of witches has dreadfully increased that Knot: . . . these Witches have driven a Trade of Commissioning their Confederate Spirits, to do all sorts of Mischiefs to their Neighbours . . . Yea, . . . at prodigious Witch-Meetings, the wretches have proceeded so far, as to Concert and Consult the Methods of Rooting out the Christian Religion from this Countrey, and setting up instead of it, perhaps a more gross Diabolism, that ever the World saw before."

The witches had "driven a Trade of Commissioning" others into their ranks. Mather's prose teems with terms emphasizing the collaborative organization of the witches (knot; confederate; concert) in contrast with the vegetable unity of the Christian commonwealth, whose wholeness has begun to disintegrate. This is an understandable response to the testimony provided by the confessors at the witchcraft trials and examinations, as they described, at the prompting of the examiners and accusers, a reversal and debasement of the conversion experience. Over and over again, according to their accounts, God's covenant, sealed with the blood of his Son, was replaced by a commercial deal offered by the agents of the Devil. The concept of grace, of a gift unearned but freely given, had given way to a transaction between two parties each out for their own ends, and clinched by signing on the dotted line. This reflected the secularization of the culture, as the original settlers were replaced by the next generation. Mather was identifying what can only be called the onset of capitalist alienation, an analysis that remains relevant long after literal belief in witches and devils has faded away. At some level or another it would have rung a bell with Sewall (lonesome Mr. Torrey, whom he'd just visited, was the clergyman who came round to the Hull house years before and tried to persuade him to become a minister rather than join the ranks of the merchants). A business paradigm was replacing the "model of Christian charity."

Another part of the book must have also given Sewall pause for thought. Mather explained that the Indians who settled in Mexico were guided by the Devil, and that their journey strangely imitated God's conducting of the Israelites through the wilderness. The Devil took the form of the idol Vitzlipulitzli, and was carried into Mexico on an ark of reeds and housed at night in a tabernacle. This is part of a tradition of seeing the Native American as Simia Dei, the Ape of God. Sewall too was fascinated by such parallels. He did not see them as dark parodies, however, but as evidence of common spiritual ancestry and portents of future convergence. Mather's point, by contrast, was to establish a crossover with the alleged witches, who were also aping Christian observances like baptism and the sacrament of the Lord's Supper (and had been led by the swarthy, small, strong—in short, simian—George Burroughs, their antiminister).

Nevertheless, on 11 October, Samuel Sewall, along with William Stoughton, put his name to a sort of imprimatur, confirming that Mather's book was an accurate reflection of their deliberations: "Upon

Perusal thereof, We find the Matters of Fact and Evidence Truly Reported. And a Prospect given, of the Methods of Conviction, used in the Proceedings of the Court at Salem." None of the other judges lined up with the implacable Stoughton in this way. During the trials, Sewall had kept to the vow he made in 1690 about never again sacrificing judicial integrity in order to please others, and he had used Stoughton as a stern guide. He was prepared to face the consequences of that allegiance.

The witchcraft judges were on trial themselves. Cotton Mather's book was the case for the defense. Other contributions, which now came thick and fast, were far more skeptical. That same day, the manuscript of another book landed on Sewall's desk, this one by Cotton's father, *Cases of Conscience Concerning Evil Spirits.* Increase Mather concentrated on procedural and legal issues, laying great stress on the point so flagrantly ignored by the court: that the Devil can take on the appearance of the innocent (an assertion his son too had made, in his "Return"). To believe otherwise would curtail the power of the Lord, since Satan acts under license from God. His tricks and stratagems must ultimately be instruments of some divine test.

Increase Mather explained how Satan (with God's permission) went about performing these tricks. Participants in the trials kept running up against the paradoxical nature of seeing and blindness when invisible phenomena were at issue. Mather claimed that the Devil "has perfect skill in Optics, and can therefore cause that to be visible to one, which is not so to another, and things to appear far otherwise than they are." He was also a perfect copyist and expert in the use of color.

Once you allow the possibility that the specters could simply be images of innocent people, you begin talking a different, more modern language altogether. In Increase Mather's book, we move on from the notion of the Devil operating as an external force to one of him much closer to home, tinkering with people's mental impressions, an artist whose canvas is the retina. We're on our way to a perception of the Devil himself as an image: toward a psychological view of evil. But if the evil is internalized, it will be found in the psyches of the afflicted. The accused must be innocent.

Increase Mather irritably denied being at odds with his son and indeed, like Cotton at the end of "The Return," ended by advocating "speedy and vigorous Prosecution of such as have rendred themselves obnoxious," not taking on board the fact that the obnoxiousness had always, and solely, been established by the court as a matter of spectral manipulation. He was keen to make it clear that he was still an ally of those elite who were identified with the trials—Sewall, of course, included.

Sewall began by reading Samuel Willard's introduction to Increase Mather's book, then went off and planted the chestnuts he had collected on his visit to Sam: two in Mr. Bromfield's orchard and three in his own.

Willard was writing a book of his own. After some militant sermons in the earlier part of the summer, he had abruptly changed his tune. John Alden, one of the founder-members of his church, had been imprisoned; the accusers had also named Mistress Thacher, widow of his predecessor as minister. At the end of June, someone pointed the finger at Samuel Willard himself, though she was immediately told she had made a mistake (by that stage, the witches' coven had its minister, anyway, and Willard was an intimate of the most powerful members of the community). Not surprisingly, Willard had become a skeptic.

His book was titled *Some Miscellany Observations on Our Present Debates Respecting Witchcrafts, in a Dialogue between S. and B.* The participants were not named, but perhaps the initials stood for Salem and Boston, a distinction maintained by Brattle, who was also contributing to the debate at this time, and who contrasted the skepticism of the Boston intelligentsia with the gullibility—and worse—of what he called the Salem Gentlemen. This distinction would have hurt Sewall, since he was one of the former who would be identified with the latter. A lot had happened since the days when the two of them happily measured public buildings in London, swam in the Thames, shared lodgings, and sailed home together across dangerous waters. Given Willard's own friendship with Sewall, perhaps the judge himself was standing behind that S.—who gets a fair hearing, though doesn't come out on top—with Brattle as his opponent.

Willard's B. talks of the danger of accepting Devil-inspired testimony from the afflicted, and argues that the Devil could represent the likenesses of innocent people. When S. protests that they must be implicated because their likenesses could not be achieved without their consent, B. tells him, "That's a wheedle; none knows anothers heart . . ." There is an echo here of Rebecca Nurse's reply when Hathorne accused

Samuel Willard, by an unidentified artist.
Courtesy of the Harvard University Portrait Collection,
Gift of Robert Treat Paine to Harvard College, 1842.
Photo by Photographic Services.

her of not weeping at the sufferings of the afflicted: "You do not know my heart." Good and evil are hidden within the depths of an individual being; they should not be seen as opposing forces marshaled across a landscape.

Thomas Brattle did indeed make exactly this point about Rebecca

Nurse, when at this same time he wrote: "Some there are who never shed tears; others there are that ordinarily shed tears upon light occasions, and yet for their lives cannot shed a tear when the deepest sorrow is upon their hearts; and who is there that knows not these things? Who knows not that an ecstasye of Joy will sometimes fetch teares, when as the quite contrary passion will shutt them close up? Why then should any be so silly and foolish as to take an argument by this appearance?" The point that was being made by Nurse and Willard and Brattle was that there was no simple correlation between external appearance and internal reality: you cannot, to paraphrase Hamlet's words, pluck out the heart of someone's mysery. In the stress of the witchcraft crisis, these three oddly assorted people—the distressed old woman facing the rope, the troubled minister, and the angry scientist-cum-merchant—together made a stand against the old habit of regarding human beings as allegorical pawns in a larger game, like the laughing or weeping denizens of the afterlife in medieval paintings and frescoes.

Brattle's letter was dated 8 October 1692. Its recipient is unknown. Though addressed to a Reverend Sir, it might not be ridiculous to suppose it was intended to influence Governor Phips, who was gathering informed opinion on the crisis. The letter has the orderly conciseness of a report, and is completely devoid of any personal content. Moreover, Brattle's opening remarks seem to constitute a careful address to the repository of political power. He claims to be nervous of bringing himself into a snare by his freedom with the addressee, talks of his obedience to lawful authority, and reflects on the "great end of authority and government"; then he gets to work.

He begins by pouring scorn on the touching tests that were carried out in the trials, and which some of the justices had defended as exemplifying the doctrine of effluvia, "that by this touch, the venemous and malignant particles, that were ejected by the eye, do, by this means, return to the body whence they came." In other words, the accused created specters of themselves with particles discharged from their eyes; these entered the bodies of the accusers, and were returned to their source through the test of touch. This process was claimed to be Cartesianism, but for Brattle it "rather deserves the name of Salem superstition and sorcery." He finds a touted route to modernity to be just a dead end, outworn magic masquerading as mechanistic empiricism.

He also attacks the use of evidence alien to an indictment, those depositions relating to odd phenomena observed before—sometimes years before—the courtroom hauntings with which the prisoners were actually charged: such tittle-tattle as the cleanness of Susannah Martin's skirts and footwear on a wet day, or George Burroughs's feats of strength, along with the absurdity of the charge that the accused caused the accusers to *tend* to be pined and wasted. In effect, Brattle argues that witchcraft can never be proved in any circumstances—a view that has, after all, carried the day—because all supporting and background evidence is immaterial, and the only approach left, spectral evidence, is self-evidently absurd, allowing the afflicted to talk as though "there was no real difference between G[oody]. Proctour and the shape of G. Proctour."

Like Increase Mather, Brattle reflects on the nature of seeing. The afflicted claimed that they could see specters with their eyes shut as well as open; they were lying, or at best imagining it: "I think this is all that should be allowed to these blind, nonsensical girls." That sarcastic "blind" is particularly telling. The girls (shorthand, he explains, since the group of accusers included men and women, but was dominated by girls) had shown their inability to see reason through their claims that they *could* see invisible phenomena. And if the specters were delusions, then all the other satanic props must be too: ". . . the Devill's book . . . the witches' meeting, the Devill's Baptism, and mock sacraments, . . . are nothing else but the effect of their fancye, depraved and deluded by the Devill, and not a Reality." What the Devil had done was to instill an illusion that he has a realm of his own, a geographical and institutional existence. His only real domain is that of mental confusion. We're a whisker away from seeing him, too, simply as a figment of the imagination, nothing more than a psychological construct.

Brattle put the lion's share of blame on Stoughton for allowing the miscarriages of justice to take place, and significantly Phips repeated this charge in his letters to the home government; also, and this again suggests the letter was intended to influence public policy, Brattle identified by name some of the prominent men who were hostile to the proceedings of the court. They included Simon Bradstreet, the former governor, Thomas Danforth, the former deputy governor, Increase Mather, and Samuel Willard, as well as Nathaniel Saltonstall and various other justices, including some from Boston who followed Saltonstall's footsteps in expressly disassociating themselves from the proceedings (leaving Sewall out on a limb). In short, Brattle gave a very full basis for a strategic decision about the future of the Court of Oyer and Terminer, expressing the hope that when convened in November 1692 it would see the errors it had perpetrated. Otherwise "I think we may conclude that N[ew]. E[ngland]. is undone and undone."

We do not know if Brattle's letter was circulated. If it was, Sewall may have read it. In any case, as an old friend of Brattle's, he was likely to have a pretty clear idea of his stance on the trials. A week after the devastating letter was penned, Sewall visited one of the men identified in it as hostile to the court, Thomas Danforth. It was part of his quest, parallel to Phips's own, for opinions on how to proceed. Danforth had presided over the hearing Sewall also attended, in which Sarah Cloyse and Elizabeth Proctor were examined, and John Proctor was put in the frame despite only attending as an observer. Danforth had had plenty of time to dwell upon that irregularity and all the strange events that followed it. He told Sewall that the court couldn't carry on without "better consent of ministers and people."

The birth pangs of the modern world were taking place on a number of different levels through the crisis—most obviously in the struggles between superstition and empiricism, and between external agency and psychological motivation: between landscape (the wilderness, the pasture by Mr. Parris's house) as the arena of moral conflict, and landscape as a projection of inner turmoil. But, above all, there was the persistent theme of social egalitarianism running through the events of the summer of 1692, one that cropped up on both sides of the judicial divide. The "marriage" of George Burroughs to a low-status woman like Martha Carrier is one example. Satan often presented himself as socially progressive: ". . . the Devil promeised that all his people should live bravely that all persones should be equall; that their should be no day of resurection or of judgement, and neither punishment nor shame for sin." This moral leveling might be sinister, but the emphasis on social equality no doubt rang bells in some quarters. The authorities inevitably protected their dignity against challenges from impudent members of the lower orders, refusing to countenance accusations against their own, people like Mrs. Thacher and Samuel Willard. But witch cases usually involve a belief in the empowerment of marginalized members of the community, women such as Sarah Good and Ann Pudeator; and at Salem this was augmented by the court's reliance on the testimony of a large number of young girls, not a section of society whose experiences and opinions were—are—normally given much weight. Brattle, liberal intellectual though he was, had a lofty view of these "nonsensical girls," but the court took them perfectly seriously and generated a narrative establishing them as the bulwarks of New England's defense against moral and social disaster. Where else in seventeenth-century America, or seventeenth-century Europe for that matter, could a twelve-year-old like Ann Putnam enjoy her day in the sun? Not in any royal court: only in that of Oyer and Terminer. When the examining magistrates allowed the slave John Indian to assault respectable Mrs. Cary in open court, they rightly attracted the furious indignation of her husband; but from another point of view, they could be seen as trying to free themselves from hierarchical assumptions about race and class. Ironically, Sewall's accessibility, his idealism, his principles, and his fascination with other people were qualities that supported rather than contradicted his role as a witchcraft judge.

In case after case, the judges had listened to the tales of petty squabbles and small-town jealousies of the ordinary people of New England. Even a century and a half later, the elite's willingness to share the concerns—and delusions—of uneducated provincial people amazed Nathaniel Hawthorne: ". . . the influential classes, and those who take upon themselves to be leaders of the people, are fully liable to all the passionate error that has ever characterised the maddest mob." But despite this social openness, as the summer wore on the court had lost the confidence of a wide section of the community, from members of the elite like Danforth to the friends and relatives of many of its humblest victims. For a man as involved in the doings of his society as Sewall, this was a bitter pill to swallow.

His gloom increased a few days later, when he paid a visit to his brother's sickbed. Stephen's fever had lasted a month, and he clearly feared death was near because he expressed his wish to live, hoping to serve God better. He was pleased to see his brother. For both of them, the thought must have hung heavy in the room that God was expressing his displeasure at the witchcraft proceedings in which the two of them had played their part.

On 26 October, a bill went before the assembly calling for a fast and a convocation of ministers to determine the right way of proceeding in relation to the witchcraft. It was passed by thirty-three votes to twenty-nine. Sewall could read the runes: they didn't want the Court of Oyer and Terminer to reconvene.

Two days later, the deputy governor, William Stoughton, coming into Boston over the causeway, was caught in the high tide and saturated, so that he had to go to bed while waiting for dry clothes to be sent from Dorchester (several other travelers were drowned). In the afternoon, he asked, as he had done several times previously, to have the advice of the governor and the council as to whether the Court of Oyer and Terminer should sit the following week. He told them this would be his last time of asking. When he had finished speaking, there was "great silence, as if should say do not go."

In that silence, something enormous shifted. The court as a whole had been overwhelmed by the tide. The following day, with Stoughton strategically out of town, the governor confirmed it "must fall."

In November, a bill was passed establishing the powers of ministers and justices to officiate at weddings. Sewall had drawn up an earlier version that confined the privilege to justices in accordance with the traditional practice in Massachusetts (given that for the Puritans marriage was a secular state anyhow, not a sacrament). By now, he was battered by the sustained criticism the Court of Oyer and Terminer had received and reacted petulantly, believing that as a result of the trials, the judiciary was being treated with contempt: "It seems they count the respect of it too much to be left any longer with the Magistrate. And Salaries are not spoken of; as if one sort of Men might live on the Aer. They are treated like a kind of useless worthless folk." He was still in a bad mood two days later, when four-year-old Joseph threw a brass knob at his sister Betty, making her forehead bleed. When called to the scene of the crime by Mother Hull, Sewall found Joseph hiding behind the cradle, a posture that reminded him of "Adam's carriage." Sewall stood in the nursery, his daughter crying, his son skulking, his mother-in-law scolding, and bleakly discerned the fall of man in all the commotion. He had reverted to Salem mode, seeing apocalypse in the trivial, and whipped Joseph smartly, the only time in his diary he ever mentions giving any of his children corporal punishment. The tantrums and naughtiness of Puritan children could always be routed straight back to original sin, a topic on which he was a Harvard expert. As Cotton Mather put it in one of his books, "Are they young? Yet the Devil has been with them already."

It was time to put the judicial system of the province onto a new footing. A Superior Court of Judicature, consisting of five judges, was to be elected by the council, with a Court of Common Pleas and a Court of Sessions put in place below it, and the office of justice of the peace was established (previously, members of the council were magistrates ex officio). Election to the superior court would be another test of confidence. Sewall prayed to God to pardon his sinful wanderings and to bless the choosing of its members; most significantly of all, to "save New England as to Enemies and Witchcrafts, and vindicate the late judges." He couldn't bring himself to ask for a blank check, however; the vindication should be consistent with God's "Justice and Holiness, &c."

The members of the Superior Court of Judicature were chosen on a dark, cold December day, four of them Court of Oyer and Terminer judges: William Stoughton, who became chief justice, John Richards, Wait Still Winthrop, and Sewall himself. Their previous court had been discredited, but they were encouraged to put a brave face on that humiliation by being given the responsibility, as members of a properly constituted permanent body, of clearing the backlog of witch trials. Grit in the oyster was provided by the remaining appointment, Thomas Danforth.

The judges accepted that their former procedures were too "violent and not grounded upon a right foundation." In the first session of the superior court, in January and February 1693, fifty-two defendants were tried and only three convicted, a radically different hit rate from before. Still, it gave Stoughton the chance to wield his lethal quill. He promptly signed their warrants for execution, along with those of the five confessors who'd been found guilty in the Oyer and Terminer proceedings and left on hold. Phips discussed the matter with the attorney general, who saw no watertight distinction between the cases of some of those who had been cleared and some of those sentenced. That was enough for Phips, and he immediately reprieved all the condemned, to the fury of Stoughton, who walked out of the second sitting of the superior court being held at Charlestown. Phips responded by laying much of the blame for the Salem excesses at Stoughton's door when he reported to his English masters. By the April session of the Superior Court of Judicature, the one in which John Alden was finally acquitted, the pendulum had swung so far that a serving woman called Mary Watkins was actually charged with being an accuser, "spreading false and scandalous reports against her Dame Swift . . . that she was a witch and had murdered a child."

Meanwhile, Sewall had involved himself with the affairs of one of the more unlikely casualties of 1692: the disaffected judge, Nathaniel Saltonstall.

Saltonstall lived in Haverhill, a town strategically situated above the Merrimack River, not far from Sewall's home town of Newbury. He was the son of Richard Saltonstall, who had been insulted by Sewall's grandfather and had officiated at the wedding of Sewall's parents. Saltonstall had fought in King Philip's War as a captain of militia and subsequently commanded the northern Massachusetts forces. He was a man of principle, refusing to serve as a member of the council of the Dominion of New England under Andros and getting a short prison sentence for his pains. Haverhill was very much Indian country, and in 1690 the selectmen of the town had designated Saltonstall's house a "place of refuge" in the event of attack. Sewall sent a barrel of salt out of "sympathy with him in his dangers and confinements, dwelling in a fronteer Town as he does." A glimpse across the years: the angry father of a defendant appearing before Saltonstall in 1691 called him "carrott head."

Saltonstall's disapproval of witch trials extended to his own patch. Four women from Haverhill had been accused of witchcraft during July and August 1692, but none of them appeared before him as might have been expected. Instead, their preliminary examinations were carried out by the magistrate from Andover, on the south side of the river. By late summer, the accusers were active in northern Massachusetts, and Saltonstall's stance earned their hostility, because he too was accused of spectral haunting. The charge was serious enough to force him to write some sort of letter in defense.

There were other reasons for him to be depressed. He was deeply upset at being passed over for appointment as a judge, given the fact that Phips and other power brokers of the province were now in effect endorsing his early repudiation of the witchcraft proceedings. He obviously didn't realize that whistle-blowers are rarely rewarded, while profound policy changes are most effectively accomplished under a veneer of continuity. The authorities had lost a huge amount of face and had been challenged by public opinion. It was necessary to demonstrate basic faith in the legitimacy and integrity of the elite, and, however admirable his reasons, Saltonstall appeared to have betrayed his trust by walking away from the Court of Oyer and Terminer. To cap his woes, he had heard rumors that he was to be replaced as major of the North Essex Regiment.

One day in February 1693, Sewall saw him sitting on the bench in the assembly and began polite conversation. Saltonstall seemed merry, and Sewall suddenly realized he was extremely drunk, babbling on about the breakup of the ice on the Merrimack River, and then becoming accusatory. He suggested that Sewall might have influenced Phips to oppose his appointment as a superior court judge, and talked about his fear of being ousted from his commission in the militia. Sewall watched appalled as the man unraveled in front of him.

Two weeks later, Saltonstall failed to appear in the assembly. This stirred Sewall to put pen to paper, assuring him that he believed him innocent of spectral haunting, declaring that he had no part in influenc-

ing Phips to pass him over, and didn't know who had, and doubting that
Saltonstall was going to lose his commission—a firm, caring letter, with
a touch of humor. Having mentioned their conversation about the
breakup of the ice on the Merrimack River, Sewall urged Saltonstall to
break off his drinking; realizing that he used the same verb twice, he
told him that he didn't mean suddenly, like the river, but gradually. He
was worried that Saltonstall's behavior would give ammunition to his
enemies. "Take it in good part from one who desires your everlasting
welfare."

Before he got around to sending it, Sewall discovered that Saltonstall had resumed attendance at the assembly. He therefore went home,
collected the letter, and delivered it personally. Saltonstall insisted on
reading it in his presence, thanked him, and desired his prayers. It
couldn't have been easy standing by and watching Saltonstall read his
letter about how drunk he got, but Sewall believed in showing social
solidarity and concern. Above all, he felt no resentment toward a man
identified with opposition to the Salem trials.

The dramas of family life continued. Joseph, still in his pestiferous
stage, managed to swallow a bullet. Luckily, he later voided it in the orchard. In poignant contrast, two weeks later, Cotton Mather's first son
was born without an anus, and died after three days. In March, the Sewalls' chimney caught fire, and set alight part of the roof. Luckily, they
were able to rescue their roasting pork from the conflagration and made
a merry meal of it. The Sewalls were already wondering whether to
move to a new house or build an extension; the family decided on the
latter, and the old kitchen was pulled down soon afterward. In May, Sewall was reelected to the Governor's Council with more votes than anybody else, seventy-seven. The following month, an English naval force
arrived in Boston from the West Indies, en route to attack the French
and their Indian allies in Canada. Fever had broken out in the ships and
killed thousands of the sailors and infantry being carried on board. It
spread into the town itself, and Sewall recorded deaths and consternation, citizens packing their bags. Late in August, his daughter Jane was
born; she survived a month. Sewall, as always, told himself he should
learn from the experience; he also wrote out a list, with dates, of the

births of all the eleven children who had been born to him and Hannah so far, a totting up of the living, five, and the dead, six.

Indian trouble flared up badly in 1694. There was bloody fishing at Oyster River in New Hampshire, to use Cotton Mather's grim conceit, with more than ninety people killed and thirteen houses burned. Just over a week later, twenty-one were killed in Groton, Connecticut. In August, Sewall and Major Penn Townsend were appointed commissioners for Massachusetts, and joined other representatives from the province, along with those from Connecticut, New York, and New Jersey, in northern New York, where they were to meet twenty-five sachems from the five Indian nations of the American northeast and negotiate a peace treaty. The trip was an encounter with the wilderness. They clopped through dangerous territory, first with a guard of thirty troopers and then, as they entered more threatening terrain, a further sixty dragoons, finally passing through a palisade of sharpened pine logs into the fortress town of Albany. The Indians came into the street designated for the negotiations in pairs, singing songs of peace, and totally took over the proceedings for the first three days. The treaty was agreed to on 22 August, though it had no tangible effect beyond a general assertion of goodwill.

Shortly after his return, Sewall took young Sam to serve as an apprentice to the bookseller Michael Perry, whose shop was by the Town House. The year before, he had installed thirteen-year-old Hannah with a family at Rowley, just south of Newbury, returning with her homesick pleas and weeping ringing in his ears. She was already back with them by this point, and sixteen-year-old Sam's first adventure in the book trade was short-lived too. Within three months he developed swollen feet from standing on the cold shop floor, and his worried father summoned him home.

The year 1694 was one of mixed fortunes for the Court of Oyer and Terminer judges. One of them, John Richards, dropped dead suddenly in April, having lost his temper with a servant. The postmortem revealed his "noble Parts" were all in order, no cause being found for his death. Later in the year, by contrast, the presiding justice, William Stoughton, found himself elevated to acting governor when Sir William

Phips was recalled to England to explain some erratic behavior, including an assault on Mr. Brenton, collector of the Port of Boston, and another in which he caned Captain Short of the frigate *Nonsuch* during an argument about Admiralty jurisdiction. Phips had not been a popular or diplomatic governor, and the Salem trials damaged his credibility, try as he might to put the blame on the very man who profited by his departure. Phips was dead within months. Cotton Mather wrote a hagiographic biography, not surprisingly since his own father had handpicked Phips as Massachusetts's first royal governor. The death of the Mathers' protégé marked the end of direct ministerial input into the government of the province. One of the enduring legacies of the witchcraft trials was to show how disastrous an overlap of spiritual and secular realms could be.

Meanwhile, Sewall had embarked on a pattern of work that was to last him most of the rest of his life, riding through the New England countryside on a circuit that took in Salem, Charlestown, Plymouth, Sandwich, Ipswich, Cambridge, Bristol, Kittery in Maine (which was part of the province of Massachusetts Bay), and, of course, Boston itself. There was a session somewhere most months, sometimes more than one, except for a couple of months in midwinter; most lasted two or three days. Each required a panel of three or four judges, and Sewall hardly missed a single session, whatever the weather, whatever his other concerns and family circumstances, for a period of over thirty years (which is why it is safe to assume he probably attended all the Salem witch trials), ferrying and fording rivers, catching boats, riding horseback along the miry tracks of colonial New England, passing the nights in the houses of local people or in country inns. His suspicion had not been far off: justices were not required to live on air, but the pay was modest indeed for professional men, from £40 to £50 per annum (Ezekiel Cheever received £60 a quarter as a schoolmaster, while Increase and Cotton Mather received £3 per week as ministers). Dispensing justice was an occupation for men of means, clearly perceived more as a social responsibility than a way of earning a living.

On a stormy day in late November, a daughter, Sarah, was born to the Sewalls. The women of the household and those attending the birth celebrated with roast beef, mince pies, good cheese, and tarts, and the next day Sewall put a bill up at the meetinghouse to thank God. The following year, the baby began having fits, and they took her into bed with them at night. Meanwhile, Sewall dedicated a day to fasting for Sam Jr., praying that he would find a master and a calling in which he could abide with God. On 15 March 1695, a fourteen-year-old boy called Tim Clark fell into the hold of a ship in the harbor and died. The event preyed on Sewall's mind, and two days later, the night before young Tim's funeral, he dreamed that all his own children except little Sarah were dead, "which did distress me sorely with Reflexions on my Omission of Duty towards them, as well as Breaking oft [off?] the Hopes I had of them."

Still, hope could be reasserted from time to time. Little Joseph switched his aggression from his sister to a more powerful enemy: on hearing that his father had sentenced two Frenchmen to prison, he vowed to drive the whole lot of them from the country when he was grown up. Sewall himself planted trees around Wheeler's Pond at the south end of the town as spring came on, his favorite gesture of trust for the future; the grateful authorities gave him and his heirs sole rights to lopping them.

One day in April 1695, the Sewalls invited Cotton Mather to dinner in their new kitchen. The day started off warm and sunny, but in the afternoon it began to thunder. Mather remarked that God allowed lightning to strike the houses of ministers more often than those of ordinary people, and wondered why that should be so. Right on cue, a tremendous burst of hailstones crashed through the windows and scattered over the floor. The damage to Sewall's new wing was so severe that people "Gazed upon the house to see its Ruins." "Twas a sorrowfull thing to me," Sewall said, "to see the house so far undon again before twas finished." Despite the Lord's apparently unfavorable view of the ministry, at least in relation to storms, Sewall asked Mather to pray. "He told God He had broken the brittle part of our house, and prayd that we might be ready for the time when our Clay-Tabernacles might be broken." Outside, the ground was white with hail, "as with the blossoms when fallen." Always ready to see weather as a sign, Sewall recalled that hail damage to their windows in the summer of 1685 had coincided with Monmouth's rebellion.

As it happened, this time the ominous repercussions took place on the domestic front. On 21 June, the family read the sixteenth chapter of Revelation, which concludes with a vision of "a great hail out of heaven, every stone about the weight of a talent . . . and men blasphemed God because of the plague of the hail." Even more significant, though, were the words "Behold I come as a Thief!" At one in the morning, the maidservant, Jane, came into the Sewalls' bedchamber. There was something strange about her manner, and for a while she couldn't speak. Then she told them that Judith Hull, Mother Hull, was seriously ill.

Despite his belief in an all-powerful God, Sewall's reaction gives us an insight into the Puritan's spiritual responsibility for physical matters, that knife-edge alertness necessary to keep the world turning, the capacity, both empowering and crushing, that individuals believed had been entrusted to them for keeping the very frame of things intact: Sewall felt that at prayer he had been "wofully drowsy and stupid," his own lack of attention allowing the deadly thief his entry in the night.

Straightaway he was up and off, over to Captain Davies's for treacle water and syrup of saffron. Meanwhile, Dame Ellis baked an herb cake; in the morning, Dr. Oliver Noyes from Cambridge was sent for. During the course of the day, Sewall found a moment when his mother-in-law's bedchamber was quiet and went in to "thank her for all her Labours of Love to me and mine" and ask "pardon of our undutifullness." Her alarming reply, which he recorded in capitals, was "GOD PITY 'EM." She died a little before sunset. Sewall described her in a commemorative poem as "An *Humble* Soul, Trim'd with an High Neglect / Of *Gay* Things, but with *Ancient Glories* Deck't," making her sound like a battered old galleon.

Six weeks later, Sewall held a fast in the new chamber of their extension. After prayers and preaching by Mr. Willard and other ministers, they sang Psalm 27, with Sewall as usual leading with the "Windsor tune": "My father and my mother both / though they do me forsake, / Yet will Jehovah gathering / unto himself me take." The thought of

Mother Hull's death, of Sam's difficulties, of baby Sarah's convulsions, suddenly overwhelmed him, and he burst into tears.

Still, life wasn't all worry and gloom. He and Hannah entertained the formerly lonesome Mr. Torrey, now with a new wife, the Willards, and Sewall's cousin Edmund Quinsey, also recently married, to dinner. Cousin Quinsey was so impressed with the painted shutters in the Sewalls' new quarters that he gracefully claimed he thought he'd got into paradise.

The following January, Sewall held another fast for Sam, hoping for his conversion and his settlement in a trade that would be good for his body and his soul. Then it was Betty's turn again. Sewall arrived home at seven after a day visiting Mr. Danforth in Cambridge, to find Hannah waiting for him in the entry. Just after dinner, Betty, now fifteen, had suddenly given an "amazing cry," so terrible that all the rest of the family had burst into tears in sympathy—hardly a cozy scene, but oddly affecting in testifying to the love the Sewalls felt for each other.

It was the old story—she was afraid she would go to hell because her sins hadn't been pardoned. Apparently, the return of spiritual desolation was triggered by a sermon Sewall had read to the family the week before, on the texts "Ye shall seek me and shall not find me" and "Ye shall seek me and shall die in your sins." A few days later she herself had read a sermon by Cotton Mather on the topic "Why hath Satan filled thy heart," which increased her fear. Mr. Willard was sent for, and he talked and prayed with her. He said she was confused about her spiritual state, an experience he'd had too, in his time.

Over the next months, Betty and Sam alternated in triggering Sewall's fatherly grief. A wealthy merchant, Samuel Checkley, had taken Sam on in his shop, but Sam couldn't settle to it, complaining of being idle too much of the time—he even mentioned being afflicted by a sermon on idleness he had heard, which has the slight ring of a strategic explanation, guaranteed to gain his father's sympathy. He also found it difficult to cope with the shop's goods, because their prices were not marked like the books had been in Michael Perry's shop.

Sewall had done what he could to get his son an education, sending him to school with Ezekiel Cheever, New England's most renowned teacher, but to little avail. Some years later, in 1698, when he was twenty, Sam Jr. began to confront his problems with simple arithmetic in a commonplace book. The struggle went on interminably. When he was twenty-six, he could still bang his head against a calculation like "If I spend £4–11^s-10^d in 1 Year I demand how much is that 1 day with another," resorting to laborious calculations and much crossing out. The aging schoolboy festooned the pages of his book with the decorations and doodles of bored pupils throughout history.

Sewall took along his brother Stephen, long since recovered from his illness, to Captain Checkley's shop to talk to young Sam. During the discussion, Sewall asked his son to fetch in some wood, and Sam fainted because he was so overwrought, which prompted Stephen to say that he should be moved on, perhaps to his own care in Salem. Shortly afterward, Sam was weeping and too upset to go to work, so Sewall went back to Captain Checkley's to end the arrangement and thank him for trying.

A week or two later, Betty came into his bedroom as soon as he was up, to tell him about her terror that she was not elected and would go to hell. The two of them prayed together, both weeping. There is a strange counterpoint between the tenderness of family life and the uncompromising nature of the religion at its center. Four days later, Sewall prayed with Sam for God to direct him to a calling.

For a while things quieted down; then, in May, Betty could hardly read her designated chapter of the Bible because she was weeping so much, and explained that she had gone back to how she was before, unable to taste the sweetness of the word. Again, she and her father prayed together alone. Later that month, Hannah had a stillborn baby, and Sewall shed more tears over a "sweet desirable Son . . . who had none of my help to succour him and save his Life." However much tragedy they faced, he never lost his capacity to feel pain.

Of course, public matters regularly took his attention away from family troubles. On 11 June, he tried to persuade the council to pass a bill removing the pagan names of the days of the week and calling them by number instead, since "the Week only, of all parcells of time, was of Divine Institution." Nobody would second his motion. It was a matter of the English language, according to some; they'll think we're Quakers, said others. Since his trip to Albany to meet the representatives of the Five Nations in 1694, Sewall himself had used the number system for the days of the week in his journal.

In July, the Sewalls gave a five-hundred-acre farm in Pettaquamscutt, Rhode Island, acquired through Mother Hull's death, to Harvard College to generate income for poor scholars, whether English or Indian. They had previously sold off another portion of land in the same place to pay for a teacher of reading and writing for the Indians in the town. By the end of the month, he was writing to an acquaintance about "Rumours of War and Slaughter against us both by sea and land," and hoping "the Shepherd of Israel will rescue this his little flock out of the mouths of the Lion and cruel Bear, which gape upon it to devour it," the lion representing the French threat and the bear the Indian one.

As the summer wore on, there was failure with the harvest and bread became scarce; lightning killed cattle, along with an unfortunate person; insects blighted the pea crop, and Sewall heard an ominous anecdote about a pregnant woman who could not resist eating peas even though she knew they had been affected by the bug. As a result, when her baby was born, he had a pea in his forehead. One morning, the growth was "empty as the Pea used to be when the Bugg is fled." It was a time of bad news and disturbing portents. The injustices of 1692 were coming home to roost.

An incident happened in August 1696 that caused Sewall heartache. Jacob Melyen, leather dealer and Boston constable, spoke to him in the street "very smartly about the Salem Witchcraft." Melyen made the strange point that "if a man should take Beacon hill on 's back, carry it away; and then bring it and set it in its place again, he should not make anything of that." He was talking about the Burroughs case, where much was read into allegations that the minister had remarkable physical strength. People should not evoke the supernatural to account for unusual attributes or behavior—there was real anger in Melyen's hyperbole. A month later Sewall used the same adverb, "smartly," to describe comments on the topic in a sermon delivered by Willard to the governor, the council, and the assembly: "Spake smartly . . . about the Salem

Witchcrafts, and that no order had come forth by Authority to ask God's pardon." Since the acting governor was the unrepentant William Stoughton, one can imagine the tense atmosphere in the Town House, where the service was held.

An insight into the way the procedures of the judiciary had been discredited comes with the trial of Thomas Maule that November. The proceedings were actually begun the year before, when Maule, a Salem tailor and a Quaker, came up in front of Sewall for writing a defense of his faith and an attack on the way the authorities had treated the sect, entitled *The Truth Held Forth and Maintained*. Maule was a brave, contentious man who had been whipped nearly thirty years previously for calling John Higginson, senior minister at Salem, a liar and promoter of the Devil's doctrines. Sheriff Corwin was ordered to seize all the copies of the book he could (a task to which he brought a wealth of experience), and Maule finally faced trial before Sewall again, sitting with Thomas Danforth and Elisha Cooke, who'd replaced the late John Richards.

In answer to the charge that he had made "divers slanders against the churches and government of this Province," Maule chose a breathtakingly cheeky line of defense, parodying the whole issue of the identification of the Salem accused with their spectral likenesses. His argument was that a book was itself a sort of specter, "and my name to my book made by the Printer does not in Law evidence to prove the same to be Thomas Maule, no more than the Spectre evidence in the Law, is of force or validity to prove the person accused by said Evidence to be the Witch; therefore Jury look well to your work, for you have sworn True Tryal to make and just Verdict give, which if you miss of doing me justice, the fault will lie on your part, for these my Accusers on the bench, are but as Clerks, to conclude your work with Amen."

Poor Sewall could only look on in embarrassment as the fallacy of spectral evidence was held up to mockery, along with an implication that judges wanted to influence juries unduly, which they certainly had in the case of Rebecca Nurse. Even worse, this preposterous argument won the day. The jury found Maule not guilty, with the foreman, John Turner, saying that "they were not a jury of divines, which this case ought to be." The idea that theological expertise is needed to establish a relationship between an author and his text seems like an odd prophecy of some of the more arcane issues in modern literary theory; it shows how the witch trial abuses had made the whole concept of evidence problematical.

In response to Mr. Willard's criticism of the authorities' failure to ask God's pardon for the errors of 1692, the council asked Cotton Mather to draw up a proclamation for a fast. It was a dismal moment in the province's history. After the bad harvest, a severe winter had set in, the coldest in memory. Three days before Mather presented his draft of the bill, two Harvard undergraduates, William Maxwell and John Eyre, went skating on Fresh Pond and fell through the ice. News of their deaths arrived in Boston at the time of the lighting of the candles. Over the darkening streets, Sewall heard the sound of Eyre's father crying out bitterly at his loss. That sudden grief, in an icy season, provided the context in which the legacy of the witchcraft trials had to be confronted.

In his proposal for a fast day, Mather gave a long list of reasons why "God hath vexed us with all Adversity, until at Last the symptoms of an Extreme desolation Threaten us." He was obviously trying to bury witchcraft in a whole tally of evils. He began with backsliding from religious faith and fervor, which, of course, could be seen as the underlying cause of the crisis that took place, and went on to itemize excessive drinking, selling drink to Indians, swearing, vanity in apparel, profanation of the Lord's Day, and decay of family discipline. Only then did he slip in the dangerous admission: ". . . those Errors, whereby Great Hardships were brought upon Innocent persons, and (wee fear) Guilt incurr'd, which wee have all cause to Bewayl, with much confusion of our Face before the Lord." After this the list continued, tacitly demoting the Salem crisis so that it becomes just one of a crowd of evils, including piracies, uncleanness, failure to thank God for harvests, fraud, the discouraging of magistrates and ministers in performance of their duties, falsehood, and slander.

The tactic was ingenious and suggests Mather's anxiety to minimize his own responsibility. But it backfired. The catalog was too much for the council to swallow. Its members could not accept the extreme and general pessimism about the current state of New England it expressed and also objected to an amendment or "streamer" that had been added in the lower house, castigating the standards of justice in the courts. Sewall was asked to prepare another one. This he did, confronting the issue in a much more focused way. God had shown his anger by cutting short the harvest, and in "more ways than one, Unsettling of us." A fast day would be appointed for 14 January 1697, so that iniquity could be put away, "and, Especially, that whatever Mistakes, have been fallen into . . . referring to the late Tragedie raised amongst us by Satan and his Instruments, through the awfull Judgement of God; He would humble us therefore, and pardon all the Errors of his Servants and People that desire to Love his Name; and be attoned to His Land." But then he added his own Indian twist: asking that God "would bring the American Heathen [into the Christian fold], and cause them to hear his voice, and so revive that joyful Proverb in the world, One flock, one Shepherd."

Sewall's bill articulated the official view that Satan caused the crisis of 1692—not, however, because he was making an attempt to colonize the colonies through an entrance in Salem Village, but simply because he whipped up widespread fear that that was his intention. But Sewall also addressed another component of the witchcraft narrative, the crossover between the Devil as Black Man preying on the fears and weaknesses of the Christian community, and those dark-skinned heathens who were the original inhabitants of New England, and threatened its physical and spiritual integrity. He reversed the direction of flow, substituting for the terror of an external paganism that could join forces with the secret Devil-worship of the witches a notion that the religious faith of the Christian community could convert the Native Americans and unify the nation.

This vision was too utopian for the council. The deputies told him to insert the words "and obey" after "hear" in the last sentence, and delete the final clause so that the bill ended with the word "voice"— "That he would bring the American Heathen, and cause them to hear and obey his voice"—giving it a more coercive and less celebratory effect. They didn't see how the conversion of the heathen would, of itself, make things good again, by creating "One flock, one Shepherd."

A few days later, there was another family tragedy. On a terrible winter's day, with deep snow on the ground, baby Sarah became ill again, and Sewall had her brought into his bedchamber. He then left her with the nurse while he went off to care for his wife, who herself was lying sick in their new extension. About break of day, the servant girl, Jane, called him with the news that Sarah had died in the nurse's arms. Nurse Cowell was frantically sorry and upset; she'd promised to let them know if there was a change, and hadn't expected the sudden death. Sewall, though, took the blame upon himself as usual, sadly reflecting "that I had not been so thorowly tender of my daughter; nor so effectually carefull of her Defence as I should have been."

The next day, young Sam read to him from the twelfth chapter of Matthew. "The 7th verse," Sewall wrote, "did awfully bring to mind the Salem Tragedie." It goes: "But if ye had known what this meaneth, I will have mercy, and not sacrifice, ye would not have condemned the guiltless."

This was the most important moment of Sewall's life. Over the next year, he would confront the Salem tragedy in a quite unique way, dealing with his sorrow and guilt and then finding a way to reassert the millennial destiny of America, following through the two plans of action outlined in the Fast Bill he had drafted for the council. No one else would provide such a complete and creative response to the witchcraft crisis.

CHAPTER NINE

Judge Sewall's Apology

THE SEWALLS WOKE BEFORE DAYBREAK ON THE MORNING OF the New Year, 1697. As dawn came up, a trumpeter played a reveille outside their window, and called out season's greetings, but the two of them just lay there, unable to face the day, the year, too depressed to climb out of bed and return the compliment. Baby Sarah had been buried only a few days before—on Christmas Day, in fact—so their gloom was hardly surprising, but part of the problem seems to have been to do with their other bereavement of 1696, the stillbirth of a son in May.

When Sarah's coffin was put in the grave, Sewall had taken the chance to inspect the arrangement of the family tomb. He described the disposition of the coffins as if the dead were reclining in some dim drawing room, and he could socialize with them once more: "I was entertain'd with a view of, and converse with, the Coffins." Sarah's was placed at her grandmother's feet, while "the little posthumous was now took up and set in upon that [coffin] that stands on John's [the baby's brother John, who died in 1678, nearly twenty years before]." The "little posthumous" was the baby who had been born dead seven months previously. In his entry for 1 January, Sewall wrote, rather obscurely, that "on the 22th of May I buried my abortive son; so neither of us were then admitted of God to be there, and now the Owners of the family admit us not."

The "Owners of the family" were his pastor and fellow congregants at the South Church, who had a service at the Willards' house that New Year's Day from which the Sewalls were excluded, old friends and loyal parishioners though they were. Only a week previously, Mr. Willard had prayed over Sarah's body and accepted a funeral ring worth 20s. from Sewall. The issue that had come between them seems to have been the reinterment of the stillborn infant.

Willard must have regarded the baby as outside the congregation. The whole question of the spiritual status of the newly born was a thorny issue for the Puritans. They strongly disagreed with the Baptists that admission to the church should be delayed till maturity, when it would have the full force of a willed decision. They believed babies could be baptized into outward membership of the congregation; then, when they grew up, a conversion experience should establish their elect status so that they could become full, inward members. Implicit in this belief was the notion that a broad Christian identity could be inherited; as one of the leading divines, Thomas Shepard, explained, God covenanted that he would recognize both church members and their seed. The covenant applying to children is limited but "not *meerly conditional*"; there "is something *absolute* in it." But the little posthumous had not lived long enough to be baptized—indeed, had not lived outside the womb at all—and the original solitary burial suggests he wasn't seen as part of a saintly communion. Puritan funerals at this period were normally plain affairs, without singing or preaching at the graveside, and there was no concept of hallowed ground. However, in deciding to place the coffin with those of his family members, Sewall was now asserting that, like them, the child was awaiting resurrection. If this claim was denied by Willard, Sewall might have concluded that both he and his child were excluded from the saved family of Hulls and Sewalls, and the spiritual community of which it was part, by the "owners"—the child because he did not qualify, and the father because he had defied his pastor. "It may be," Sewall glumly reflected, "I must never more hear a sermon there." He was a man who detested exclusion, which was precisely why it was so necessary for him to place his child's body in the family vault.

There was another reason for Sewall's sense of exclusion. Five years

had now passed since those girls in the Parris parsonage began to be-
have strangely, five years in which the woes of New England and of his
own family seemed to have multiplied inexorably. He was deeply implicated in the tragedy and had come to feel singled out by God and man
as a cause of the troubles that had descended on his community. Now
the fast for the witchcraft abuses was looming. That was an occasion for
self-examination, an opportunity for confronting the sins of the past.
Thirty years previously, he had botched a similar chance when making
his case for admittance to the South Church of Boston. Then too he
had had a sense of floundering in spiritual darkness, and had told himself that when the time came, and he was speaking to the congregation
gathered in the meetinghouse, he would make a confession of his sins,
washing himself clean of them so as to make a new start. But under the
pressure of the moment, that plan had gone clean out of his head, and
as a result he had been dogged by fears that the congregation, and the
Lord, might have rejected his membership.

He could not risk letting anything like that happen again. The official witchcraft fast of the province of Massachusetts was a turning
point, the moment when he had to perform the single most important
act of his life. On the afternoon of 14 January, Sewall took his place in
his pew. When the minister went past on his way to the front of the
meetinghouse, Sewall gave him a paper to read out on his behalf. During the course of the service, Mr. Willard duly read it to the assembled
worshippers, while Sewall stood up in full view of everybody.

> Samuel Sewall, sensible of the reiterated strokes of God upon
> himself and family; and being sensible, that as to the Guilt con-
> tracted, upon the opening of the late Commission of Oyer &
> Terminer at Salem (to which the order for this Day relates) he is,
> upon many accounts, more concernd than any that he knows of,
> Desires to take the Blame & Shame of it, Asking pardon of Men,
> And especially desiring prayers that God who has an Unlimited
> Authority, would pardon that Sin, and all other his Sins; per-
> sonal, & Relative: And according to his infinite Benignity, &
> Soveraignty, Not Visit the Sin of him, or of any other, upon

himself or any of his, nor upon the Land: But that He would powerfully defend him against all Temptations to Sin, for the future; and vouchsafe him the Efficacious, Saving Conduct of his Word & Spirit.

Samuel Sewall. Diary entry for 14 January 1696/7.
Samuel Sewall Diaries, MHS.

When Willard had finished, Sewall bowed his head to the congregation. He was one of the wealthiest and most important men in Boston, a judge of the Superior Court of Judicature. Some of his fellow congregants were people of his own social sphere, like Wait Still Winthrop, Elisha Cooke, and, of course, Willard himself; others were members of the lower classes—tradesmen, servants. It's difficult to say which group was the hardest to bow to; in any case, a tendency toward egalitarianism had been one of the features of the witchcraft crisis.

Sewall's recantation was not, on the face of it, unique. Other people involved in the witch trials apologized in their own fashions for the parts they had played. Samuel Parris, faced with demands for his dismissal from his post, had addressed his parishioners two years previously, conceding that "God has been righteously spitting in my face," and apparently taking blame on himself in no uncertain terms: "I do most heartily, fervently and humbly beseech pardon of the merciful God through the blood of Christ, of all my mistakes and trespasses in so weighty a matter: and also all your forgiveness of every offense in this or other affairs, wherein you see or conceive I have erred and offended." Parris wriggled energetically on this hook, however. He was prepared to concede errors that were attributed to him, but was hardly aware himself of having done anything wrong. After all, this was a matter "so dark and perplexed as that there is no present appearance that all God's servants should be altogether of one mind." What he did, he said, "as I apprehended was duty"—however, "through weakness, ignorance, &c., I may have been mistaken." Parris somehow managed to give himself credit for contrition without quite conceding he had anything to be contrite about in the first place. In the end, any blame could be attributed to Satan, "the Devil, the roaring lion, the old dragon, the enemy of all righteousness."

Given the shattering events that had taken place in his parish, and the continuing presence of those members of his congregation who suffered directly or lost relatives in the calamity, it's hardly likely that even a heartfelt confession would have kept Parris in his post. As it happened, the end came in the summer of 1697, when the Court of Common Pleas appointed Wait Winthrop, Elisha Cooke, and Samuel Sewall himself as arbitrators between him and the disaffected members of his congregation. Parris was accused of a lack of charity in believing the Devil's accusations against blameless and godly persons, of consulting people who had a familiar spirit (by this was meant the afflicted, not the accused; a full reversal had taken place) in denial of the providence of God, and of being the "beginner and procurer of the sorest afflictions, not to this village only but to this whole country, that did ever befall them." The arbitrators gave him his salary arrears and the sum of £76 9s. 6d, in return for resigning his post and vacating his claim on the parsonage and its land, that pasture which had acted as the pagan inversion of the Christian meetinghouse, dark center of the witchcraft narrative.

Also in 1697, Thomas Fiske, the jury foreman who had expressed his unease about the proceedings against Rebecca Nurse, was joined by other jurors in producing a paper admitting their role in the miscarriage of justice that had taken place: "We do therefore hereby signifie to all in general . . . our deep sense of, and sorrow for our Errors, in acting on such [insufficient] Evidence to the condemning of any person." The point was, though, that they had acted "Ignorantly and unwittingly," since they had been "under the power of a strong and general Delusion, utterly unacquainted with, and not experienced in matters of that Nature." By their own estimate, they were victims too.

Nine years later, in 1706, came the last major confession, Ann Putnam Jr's. She was a twenty-seven-year-old woman by then, and her statement was read out to the congregation of Salem Village by the minister who had replaced Parris, Joseph Green. Unlike his predecessors in that ill-fated post, Green had the happy knack of uniting his parishioners, and he devoted his pastorate to healing the wounds of the damaged community. In persuading Ann Putnam to make a public confession, he achieved the last and most significant stage in that process. Again, Putnam used the language of intense contrition: "I desire to lie in the dust, and be humbled for it, in that I was a cause, with others, of so sad a calamity." Again, however, she was careful to marshal adverbs of limitation to qualify her guilt: "I justly fear I have been instrumental, with others though ignorantly and unwittingly, to bring upon myself and this land the guilt of innocent blood." Given her age at the time of the trials, along with her family background, she was perhaps entitled to her plea of mitigation: "I then being in my childhood, should, by such a providence of God, be made an instrument for the accusing of several persons of a grievous crime, whereby their lives were taken away from them, whom now I have just grounds and good reason to believe they were innocent persons."

What unites these confessions is that they all see guilt as a matter of external manipulation. Parris, the jurors, and Ann Putnam insist that they were well meaning but had been deceived and made use of by a malignant power. Putnam used the word "instrument" three times in her statement, and it provides the key to the perspective evident in all these confessions. The individuals concerned were simply conduits for a force greater than them. But, as we have seen, the whole basis for the assignation of guilt at the witch trials themselves rested on a parallel assumption. The specters were the agents of the accused; the accused were the agents of the Devil. Puppets were being operated by other puppets, who in turn were being controlled by the master puppeteer, invisible in his surrounding darkness. And even Satan was a puppet in the end, only able to exercise his power by permission of the ultimate puller of strings, equally invisible in his city of light. (Willard emphasized this point in a sermon given on 29 May 1692, and noted down by Sewall: there is an innumerable company of devils striving to turn the world upside down, but "God overules & enlarges or Stratons their Power as he pleases.") The confessors have invoked this system of causality to explain away their own behavior. They are pawns in a larger game.

The witch narrative emphasized growth and scale, from the passage of the yellow bird from person to person to the teeming sacrament on Samuel Parris's pasture. The "Infernal enemy," as Stoughton put it in his preface to Cotton Mather's *Wonders of the Invisible World*, "hath been coming in like a flood upon us." But as a countercurrent to this large-scale view of human behavior, there was a developing notion of psychological complexity, of interiority: the jettisoning of a public allegorical stage on which the war between good and evil is fought out, and the relocation of such upheavals in the depths of an individual being. It was this lesson that Sewall's apology took on board. Like his rival confessors, he could easily have established a collegiate context for his mistakes—after all, he was only one of a team of judges. But he did the opposite, insisting that he was "more concerned than any that he knows of," and desiring "to take the Blame & Shame of it" on himself. It was only when Sewall was considering the effects of sin, rather than its causes, that he evoked a larger context, praying that God will "Not Visit the Sin of him, or of any other, upon himself or any of his, nor upon the Land."

In short, his confession confronted the witchcraft crisis on two levels. It admitted his own guilt, which was hard enough. The pain of an apology (apart from the damage to pride) is that it feels like a destructive process, repudiating the past: a past act, the past self. But the other side of that coin is creative: acknowledging change and growth, both in oneself and in the community at large. By its very structure, Sewall's statement implied that the assumptions about the nature of guilt that underlay the trials rested on an inadequate view of human nature, and therefore made possible a more complex perspective. His act of penance is significant not just because of what it reveals about him—his conscience, his integrity, his sense of responsibility—but because of the way it crystallizes and defines the cultural shift that was taking place in New England during the 1690s. Ironically, given that he was taking the blame upon himself, his gesture represents a moment when an individual's experience merges with that of the community as a whole, when a single person manages to speak for his generation.

None of the other witchcraft judges ever made a public recantation, which makes Sewall's insistence on taking the blame on his own shoulders even more remarkable. If we jump forward nearly two years, we can get some idea of how far out on a limb he had gone.

ON 29 DECEMBER 1698, after attending the Thursday service at the South Church meetinghouse, Sewall invited two of his friends in the congregation, Major William Vaughan (recipient of a cheese Sewall brought all the way from England in 1689) and Mr. Partridge, to dine with him at Mr. Dering's establishment. The meal turned out to be disappointing—"Had only a piece of rost Beef, Minct pye and Tarts"—

but even worse was the information he gleaned from his guests that the acting governor, Stoughton, had invited the council to dinner at his house the following day. Sewall, though a member of the council himself, had heard nothing of it.

He must have sat there, plump and owlish, gazing across his unsatisfying plate in dismay after his companions had dropped the bombshell that he had been left out. Other members of the council turned up and joined them. One, Elisha Cooke, rubbed salt into the wound by asking him point-blank if he had been invited. Another, Wait Winthrop, gave the discomfited Sewall a good stare just as he was leaving, and then told him—almost angrily—that he should go anyway.

The following day, Sewall waited in hopes that even at that late stage the invitation would finally appear, forlornly monitoring his disappointment right up to mealtime (midafternoon on winter days when darkness sets in early): ". . . 'tis now Decr. 30$^{th.}$ past 3 *tempore pomeridiano*," he wrote, registering the moment when all hope had gone.

Sewall hated bad feeling and always tried to take the sting out of any snubs he received. But this rebuff, he believed, would be gossiped about, with the result that the new governor would hear tell of it when he arrived and identify him "as a person deserted and fit to be hunted down, if occasion be . . . in the mean time shall goe feebly up and down my Business, as one who is quite out of the Lt Govr's favour." This mournful self-image of a weakly Samuel Sewall compelled to go through the motions in the half-life of official disapproval says a lot about his ambition and desire for public approbation. But it says even more about his courage in the meetinghouse when he stood to listen to Mr. Willard reading his apology. He was a man who needed a rich social medium as a fish needs water, yet he had taken blame exclusively on himself, to the lasting fury of at least one—the most powerful one at that—of his fellow judges.

DESPITE HIS SENSITIVITY, Sewall never hesitated about expressing his opinion. Within a fortnight of the witchcraft fast, he was arguing with

Samuel Willard about candidates for appointment as junior minister at the South Church. Willard was strongly opposed to the candidate Sewall favored, Simon Bradstreet, while Sewall didn't approve of Willard's favorite, Ebenezer Pemberton, who in due course secured the post and eventually took over from Willard, becoming the cause of much strife and difficulty to Sewall. "I told him my heart; as I said I always did," but the two men managed to keep more or less on terms: "I think parted good friends." Just a month after his despair at losing the regard of his minister, Sewall was prepared to put their friendship on the line by backing his own judgment.

One day in February, Sewall was sawing wood, fuel for the icy weather, when his children came running toward him through the old hall "with a very amazing Cry," his wife along with them. They'd all been scared out of their wits by something that had suddenly come into the house. The something turned out to be a certain Goodwife Duen, who had enveloped herself in a rug, presumably as a way of saying boo to the children—even colonial Boston could experience an occasional attack of zany behavior. But her accidental parody of the Salem hauntings was a painful reminder of Sewall's guilt: "The Lord save me and his people from astonishing, suddain, desolating, Judgmts."

When asked to draw up the bill for the fast day, Sewall had addressed two themes. The first was that of confronting the wrongs of the past, atoning for the errors of Salem. The second was anticipating the millennial future, to be brought about by the conversion of the Indians. He had himself fulfilled the first part of this agenda, and was now busily at work on the second, writing a book about the nature of history and of American destiny, and the part played by Native Americans in those great matters. Sewall had a keen interest in Indian culture and ritual. In March, a certain Thomas Mumford told him about how, eighteen years previously, the daughter of the chief Nimerad acquired her name at a ceremony that followed his death. She terminated her mourning in a purifying dance at which she announced that Wenoquaspouish was now her name. She called up members of her tribe in turn, giving each a string of peag (or wampum). Her tribesmen each made a speech wishing her prosperity with her new name, then shouted three times. When the men had all been received, it was the turn of the tribeswomen, who responded without a speech, but simply with the three shouts.

Sewall was fascinated by this ritual that asserted the possibility of a fresh start after grief, finding four examples of mourning dances in the Bible (Psalms 30:11, Jeremiah 31:13, Lamentations 5:15, and Luke 15:25—this last perhaps not a true analogue because it celebrated the return, *apparently* from the dead, of the prodigal son). He noted that Wenoquaspouish means "Bright Lady," significantly enough the symmetrical opposite of the Black Man who had haunted the witchcraft trials.

On the very day Sewall reflected appreciatively on these cultural and anthropological matters, a terrible event was taking place in northern Massachusetts. Indians attacked the town of Haverhill, and murdered or captured about forty of the inhabitants. This was the community of Nathaniel Saltonstall, disaffected witchcraft judge and sometime heavy drinker. His house had been designated a place of refuge at times of Indian attack—two years previously, the town had managed to hold off a marauding band of eighty Indians and Saltonstall, despite his earlier fear of losing his command, had been promoted to colonel of the North Essex Regiment. This time their resistance was less successful, and he was later rebuked for failing to get all of the community to the shelter of his fortified premises in time, though he remained in charge of the town's defenses.

The Indians brained the newly born baby of a woman called Hannah Dustin in front of her eyes, then carried her off into captivity, along with the child's nurse, Mary Neff. The two women ended up as slaves to an Indian family of twelve on an island at the point where the Contoocook and Merrimack Rivers meet, and were joined by a boy called Samuel Lennardson, who'd been captured the year before. Shortly they would be forced to march northward to Canada, where they would have the horrific prospect of running the gauntlet. This meant they would be stripped and made to run through lines of Indians, being scourged as they went. According to Cotton Mather, the Indians claimed that "This was the *Fashion*, when the Captives first came to a Town; and they derided some of the Faint-hearted English, which, they said, fainted and swooned away under the *Torments* of this Discipline."

One night, when the Indian family was asleep, Hannah and Samuel stole hatchets and killed ten of them, allowing only an old squaw and a small boy to escape. Then the three self-liberated captives set off for home. After they had gone a short distance, Hannah stopped, realizing they could claim bounty if she had proof of what they had done. Back she crept to the site of the massacre, entered the silent, bloody wigwam, raised her ax again, and methodically scalped each of the bodies, remembering perhaps the way her own child's head had been swung at the wall of her house just weeks before (six of the Indians she and Samuel had killed were children).

On 29 April, the trio, with their ten scalps, arrived in Boston to petition for their reward. They were greeted as heroes, showered with gifts, feted by the town. They put in a petition to the General Court, and in due course Hannah Dustin was awarded £25, with £12 10s. each going to the other two. On 12 May, the Sewalls invited Mrs. Dustin to dinner, a strangely domestic occasion for this refugee from an elemental world (made even odder by the fact that Sewall had been one of the judges when her sister, Elizabeth Emerson, was tried for child murder and executed, only six years before). Sewall had spent the day printing off and correcting the first half-sheet of his book. He listened fascinated to his guest's story.

The Indian to whom she had been assigned had once been servant to Joseph Rowlandson, the pastor at Lancaster whose wife, Mary, had herself been captured by Indians during King Philip's War, a coincidence that shows how precarious life could be in the smaller settlements. In the Rowlandson parsonage, he had learned to pray English style, though had subsequently come to prefer the French (i.e., Catholic) method. One evening in the camp, he unwisely explained to young Samuel Lennardson his method for knocking Englishmen on the head and scalping them, a lesson that before the night was over had been put to practical use by the boy and by Hannah Dustin. This was a different, more savage, study in comparative anthropology from the one

Sewall had recorded so gleefully just weeks before, the name ceremony of the daughter of Chief Nimerad: we seem a long way from the woman who called herself Bright Lady.

Nevertheless, *Phaenomena*, the book at which Sewall worked during the course of this year, would build on his respect for Indian traditions and his delight at discovering analogues for Christian, or at least Jewish, practices in their rituals. He jettisoned fear of their savagery and alienness and celebrated them as the key to America's future. The full title is *Phaenomena quaedam Apocalyptica ad aspectum novi orbis configurata*, which means "Some Apocalyptical Phenomena Configured in Relation to the New World," loosely translated in Sewall's own subtitle as *Some Few Lines Towards a Description of the New Heaven as it Makes to Those Who Stand upon the New Earth.*

It is an obscure, convoluted work, which feels to a modern reader much longer than its sixty pages, full of arcane facts and odd shifts of logic, endeavoring to ground a theory of providential history upon theological exegesis, with much learned reference to other scholars of Apocalypse in a way that now inevitably seems strained and cranky, though it represented the fullest statement of a belief in American destiny that Sewall held dear, and which preoccupied him for much of his life. Nowadays, what still strikes a chord is a single sentence of transcendent beauty almost at the end of the work, one of the earliest and most rapt evocations of what has become known as the American Dream. That phenomenon is normally unremittingly retrospective, even in its seventeenth-century manifestations, tinged with sadness at what might have been. Sewall's version, by contrast, is prospective, optimistic, utopian. Amid the gloom that surrounded the Salem crisis, he discovered the strength to make an assertion of hope. If his apology came out of an exploration of an individual soul's dark interior, in this passage he found a language to represent a collective sense of promise and possibility in a hymn to the beauty of America:

As long as *Plum-Island* shall faithfully keep the commanded Post; Nothwithstanding all the hectoring Words, and hard Blows of the proud and boisterous Ocean; As long as any

Salmon, or Sturgeon shall swim in the streams of *Merrimack*; or any Perch, or Pickeril, in *Crane Pond*; As long as the Sea-Fowl shall know the Time of their coming, and not neglect season-ably to visit the Places of their Acquaintance; As long as any Cattel shall be fed with the Grass growing in the Medows, which do humbly bow down themselves before Turkie-Hill; As long as any Sheep shall walk upon *Old Town Hills*, and shall from thence pleasantly look down upon the River *Parker*, and the fruit-full Marishes lying beneath; As long as any free and harmless Doves shall find a White Oak, or other Tree within the Town-ship, to perch, or feed, or build a careless Nest upon; and shall voluntarily present themselves to perform the office of Gleaners after Barley-Harvest; As long as Nature shall not grow Old and dote; but shall constantly remember to give the rows of Indian Corn their education, by Pairs: So long shall Christians be born there; and being first made meet, shall from thence be Translated, to be made partakers of the Inheritance of the Saints in Light.

In reading these biblical cadences, we seem as far from the injustice and bad faith of the witch trials as Nimerad's daughter's assumption of the name Bright Lady is from the savagery perpetrated upon Haverhill and reimbursed with those hatchets stolen by Hannah Dustin and Samuel Lennardson. And yet Sewall's celebration of the pastoral de-lights of his childhood home of Newbury was a deliberate attempt to dispel the despair that both produced and followed the Salem tragedy, as was shortly recognized by the most outspoken of the hostile com-mentators on the witchcraft trials, Robert Calef.

Robert Calef was an obscure Boston merchant and a friend of Thomas Maule, the Quaker from Salem. In a book called *More Wonders of the Invisible World*, which he published in 1700, Calef devoted con-siderable energy to criticizing, and indeed baiting, Cotton Mather, au-thor of the first book of *Wonders*. The gleeful nature of Calef's attack comes across very differently from the closely reasoned critique penned by Thomas Brattle in the immediate aftermath of the trials: Calef's satirical edge anticipates the eighteenth-century world of Pope and Swift. The main difference was obviously one of timing: where Brattle had to be meticulous about making his case, Calef, publishing his work eight years later, was able to assume a skeptical consensus about witchcraft allegations and trials. His tone can be illustrated by a brief passage near the beginning, where he lambasted Cotton Mather's own account of the events at Salem: ". . . we are told in *Wonders of the Invisible World*, that the Devils were walking about our Streets with lengthned Chains making a dreadful noise in our Ears, and Brimstone, even without a Metaphor, was making a horrid and a hellish scent in our Nostrils." There is a world of significance in that apparently casual aside, "even without a Metaphor": Calef is taking it for granted that satanic paraphernalia is no more than a representation of psychological upheaval.

Though Calef's prime target was Cotton Mather (and to a lesser extent Increase), he showed no sympathy for Sewall, either. He professed not to have the wording of Sewall's apology to hand, and his terse summary implied that Sewall was guilty of exactly the sort of evasion and defensiveness that characterized the other confessors: "It was to desire the Prayers of God's People for him and his, and that God having visited his Family, etc., he was apprehensive that he might have fallen into some Errors in the Matters at Salem, and pray that the Guilt of such Miscarriages may not be imputed either to the Country in general, or to him and his family in particular." There was nothing there about accepting the blame and shame of it all.

But it is at the end of the book that Calef's hostility toward Sewall becomes fully apparent. He galloped briskly through the witchcraft trials, letting the absurdities and injustices of the story speak for themselves, before turning the full armory of his contempt upon the assumptions that underlay the proceedings, giving a list of the fallacies, stupidities, and evils apparent in the whole affair. But what is truly extraordinary is the mode in which he chose to express his outrage. He parodied Sewall's serene evocation of the loveliness of his home, and of his faith in the potential of America.

As long as Christians do Esteem the Law of God to be Imperfect, as not describing that crime that it requires to be Punish'd by Death;

As long as men suffer themselves to be Poison'd in their Education, and be grounded in a False Belief by the Books of the Heathen;

As long as the Devil shall be believed to have a Natural Power, to Act above and against a course of Nature;

As long as the Witches shall be believed to have a power to Commission him;

As long as the Devil's Testimony, by the pretended afflicted, shall be received as more valid to Condemn, than their Plea of Not Guilty to acquit;

As long as the Accused shall have their Lives and Liberties confirmed and restored to them, upon their Confessing themselves Guilty;

As long as the Accused shall be forc't to undergo Hardships and Torments for their not Confessing;

As long as Tets for the Devil to Suck are searched for upon the Bodies of the accused, as a token of guilt;

As long as the Lords Prayer shall be profaned, by being made a Test, who are culpable;

As long as Witchcraft, Sorcery, Familiar Spirits, and Necromancy, shall be improved to discover who are Witches, etc.;

So long it may be expected that Innocents will suffer as Witches.

So long God will be Daily dishonoured, And so long his Judgement must be expected to be continued.

By appropriating the rhythms and rhetoric of Sewall's great passage, he showed that he understood something that would not necessarily be obvious to a reader nowadays: in writing about Newbury, Sewall was also addressing the issue of Salem.

Significantly, Sewall opened with a prefatory letter to Stoughton, explaining that he wanted to demonstrate that America will be the

"Seat of the Divine Metropolis" and that here "*in these latter Ages*" God "*hath begun in a Terrible, and Wonderful Way, to form a people for Himself*." For Sewall, the most terrible aspect of this development is represented by the slaughter that took place during the Spanish Catholic colonization of Central and South America, but perhaps, writing to a fellow judge, he's thinking of the pain of the witch trials too.

The little book begins grandly: "Not to begin to be; and so not to be limited by the concernments of *Time*, and *Place*; is the prerogative of GOD alone." For us, in a time-bound world, there are beginnings and endings, though some things have been in continuance so long that they have been "time out of mind." Boston and Massachusetts, however, have come upon the scene quite recently. For most of his book from this point on, Sewall set forth a theory of providential history that he believed pointed to the fact that America (including Spanish Central and South America; Sewall thought of the two continents as one) will provide the location for the New Jerusalem. His argument is a complex one, dependent on a close but imaginative reading of biblical prophecies, particularly of the sixteenth chapter of Revelation, which depicts seven angels, each pouring out a vial upon the earth and bringing down a plague as a necessary prelude to the dawn of a new heaven and a new earth. Sewall was participating in a long tradition of chiliastic scholarship in seeing these calamities as a necessary spiritual cleansing before the arrival of the millennium.

His particular spin was to assert that the first five vials had already been poured. These were, respectively, one discharged upon the earth to bring a sore upon the bodies of those who worship Satan; the next upon the sea, turning it to blood; the third upon the rivers and fountains with the same effect; the fourth upon the sun, giving it the power to burn people up; and the fifth upon the kingdom of the beast. He gave evidence from history to support his claim that these therapeutic catastrophes had already taken place, though they were part of an ongoing process and, having been poured once, continued to flow: "Not but that they hold on with their course still; and will do so until the Confluence of them all do with irresistible Force ingulf AntiChristianisme in utter Ruine."

But the moment was nigh—and this was a belief he held to throughout his life—for the sixth angel to pour out his vial. This would be discharged on to the great river Euphrates, with the result that it would dry up, so that the "way of the kings of the east might be prepared" (Revelation 16:12; the point is that the Euphrates is a river that never, in the natural order of things, actually dries up). Sewall claimed that this prophecy could be distinguished from that concerning the third vial, with its general scope affecting all the rivers of the world; by contrast, the Euphrates "is one individual River," though in the tradition of Revelation typology this by no means compelled it to correspond with its geographical namesake. We are dealing after all with a prophetic book, and there is necessarily a symbolic displacement to take into account, a sort of refraction index of interpretation. As far as Sewall was concerned, the location of that specific river, the Euphrates, could be fixed in the American continent, "thereby to keep it as it were within its banks." Being American is precisely what was specific about it. It was an assertion he made over and over again: a central belief of his life. He wrote to a correspondent in 1702 that "Euphrates is but One River; and I have been ready to imagin it to be Rome's American New-River Water." Three years later: "A River is an Individuum, bounded with its Banks." Therefore, "I propose the Spanish Interests in America for Euphrates." The Catholic imperialism of Spain in the American continent will give way to a Puritan paradise.

Sewall's most clear and consistent point, articulated from the beginning, had to do with his belief that the Indians held the key to American destiny. In some notes preceding his drafting of *Phaenomena*, he related the drying up of the Euphrates to certain developments in the grand project of the conversion of the Indians: Eliot's translation of the New Testament into "Indian" in 1658; Daniel Gookin's appointment as the first "Indian magistrate" in 1656; Sewall's own conviction that several Indians did in fact "fear God, and are true believers"; and John Eliot's preaching to Indians in September 1674 from Psalm 24:7—"Yee gates lift up your heads, / and dores that last for ay." Those gates and everlasting doors will open for the King of Glory to come in.

Sewall argued that the dispute over the whereabouts of the New

Jerusalem would soon be at an end if "Mr *Eliot's* Opinion prove true; *viz.* that the Aboriginal Natives of *America* are of *Jacob's* Posterity, part of the long since captivated Ten Tribes; and that their Brethren the *Jews* shall come unto them." We have seen how the Black Man of witchcraft lore and legend merged with the tawny pagans inhabiting the New England wilderness. Sewall's *Phaenomena* was a conscious and elaborate attempt to reverse that interaction, to restructure cause and effect, so that the Indians provided the means whereby Christian America would achieve its spiritual destiny.

Given the historical treatment of Jews by Christendom, the identification of American Indians with the lost tribes might not seem much of a promotion. But Sewall himself showed no sign of anti-Semitism, as we saw when he visited the Jewish cemetery in London and drank a sociable tankard of beer with its keeper. The Bible claimed the Jews were God's chosen people; the Puritans believed they themselves were; the two groups must therefore, in due course, coincide. For Sewall, the true meaning of the word "Jew" was not sectarian, national, or cultural, but had to do with an inner state of spiritual devotion and enlightenment.

The *Revelation* doth not so much regard what Nation a man is of: but whether he be a follower of the LAMB, or no. *For he is not a* Jew [in this Spiritual sence] *which is one outwardly* [only] *But he is a* Jew *which is one inwardly*. Rom. 2. 9. In this glorious State of the Church which *John* introduceth, the *Jews* must needs be very much concerned; because Christs Receiving them again, is a notable means reserved of God, to revive, and bring on the Spring of the Gentiles, and to cause them to flourish, as is herein described. *Rom.* 11. 15. And yet *there is no difference between the* Jew *and the* Greek: *for the same LORD over all, is Rich unto all that call upon him.*

Sewall is following directly in the footsteps of his teacher in Newbury, Thomas Parker, whose closely argued book, *The Visions and Prophecies of Daniel Expounded*, tried to estimate when the New

Jerusalem would be established. According to his unriddling of Daniel, two dates were possible: 1649, just three years away at Parker's time of writing, and 1859. Either way, it would be marked by the conversion of the Jews. The point, according to Parker, was that "all that is called *Israel* in the Old testament, unto whom the Promises are made, are not *Israel* according to the flesh, but mystical *Israel*, the whole church." As part of this process of reconciliation, the lost tribes of Israel shall be reunited with their brethren: ". . . the Jews that first began to run, shall come in last, and bring distinct and perfect tidings of the fall of Antichrist, and all enemies universally." This will lead to New Jerusalem, which will be a true form of Catholic Church, "advanced to the state of glory, wherein there is no distinction of Jew or Gentile, Grecian or Barbarian." The inclusion of the barbarians and the reinstatement of the lost tribes coalesced into a powerful equation in the young Sewall's mind, bringing about the conclusion that the American savages were in fact the missing Jews, and held the key to the New Jerusalem.

The *Phaenomena* developed two supporting arguments. The first was that Jews have been making their way to the New World in (no doubt unconscious) anticipation of their eventual reunion with their Native American relatives. The numbers may not have looked substantial, but Sewall had a theory that many of the settlers in South America might actually be Jewish, "tho covered with a *Spanish* Vail." As far as he was concerned, it was too much of a coincidence that they were driven out of Spain in 1492, the very same year that Columbus discovered America. He quoted a theory that the Indians of the West Indies actually spoke Hebrew. In his copy of Thorowgood's *Iewes in America*, he made a marginal note about a discussion he had had on the topic: "Ponampam an ingenious Indian Scholar at Harvard Colledge, told me ye Indians used affixes after ye manner of eastern Languages; Hebrew &c." Sadly, the ingenious Indian scholar had concluded that there would have been more vestiges if the mother language had indeed been Hebrew: ". . . yet thought y^t [that] could not be Hebrew; bec. Footsteps of y^t Language not remaining." From the beginning of settlement, there had been interest in the relationship between Indian and Old World languages.

Thomas Morton, for example, in his *New English Canaan* (1637), claimed that Indian words have elements of Greek and Latin in them, and concluded the original Native Americans were refugees from the fall of Troy. Samuel Lee, with whom Sewall corresponded on Indian matters, claimed their language came partly from "ye African Phœnicians" and partly from "ye Eastern Tartars from Japanward."

Sewall's second main point was that although Satan appeared to have been in possession of the culture of the Native Americans (of the house of America, as he put it), there were nevertheless signs of ultimate reconciliation between the Indians and the settlers (the story of the Bright Lady appealed to him precisely because its biblical analogues suggested such a connection). Sewall referred to another example of the essential compatibility of Indians and immigrants, one that powerfully suggested a happy outcome to the great American experiment: the story of Squanto, which took place at the very beginning of colonization and which immediately and permanently took on the power and meaningfulness of myth.

All through the long winter after the first settlers landed at what became Plymouth Plantation near Cape Cod in December 1620, there was a desperate struggle for survival in what seemed to them to be a "hidious & desolate wildernes, full of wild beasts & wild men." Most of the colonists fell sick, especially—inevitably—from scurvy, as their arrival at the onset of winter had prevented them from planting fruit or vegetables, and many more died from exposure since they had not had the opportunity to build themselves proper shelters. During this desperate time, when they were staring disaster in the face, "Indians came skulking about them," sometimes showing themselves at an aloof distance, and once venturing near enough to steal some of their tools. In their first forays ashore from the *Mayflower*, the colonists had run into hails of arrows, so they had no reason to think that either this land, or its inhabitants, had any good to offer them.

And then an extraordinary thing happened. An Indian came striding up to the embattled little group and spoke to them in their own language. For a people looking for signs and tokens of God's favor, this was a sweet moment, indeed. His name was Samoset. It turned out he'd picked up his broken English from British fishing vessels, but he told them of another Indian by the name of Squanto who could speak the language much better than he did. The nearest we can now get to re-creating this shock of the familiar would be to imagine arriving at a sinister, faraway planet to find that its inhabitants, strange and hostile though they appear, are able to say hello. A short time later, Samoset went away and returned with the sachem Massasoit, accompanied by Squanto as he had promised.

Squanto, it turned out, had been carried off to Europe, along with fellow tribesmen, by an adventurer who hoped to sell them off into slavery. Instead, Squanto finally ended up at the home of a merchant in London, and here he now was, ready to act as intermediary and guide to the New World. How bizarrely reassuring it must have been to find an inhabitant of this remote and threatening landscape who knew his way about the streets of London.

In *Phaenomena*, Sewall related the later and sadder part of Squanto's story. Squanto soon fell out with Massasoit, who then sought his life, leaving him with little choice but to throw in his lot with the English. Then he fell sick and asked Governor Bradford to pray for his soul, saying he wanted to go to the "English-mans *God in Heaven.*" He died in 1622, only two years after the *Mayflower* landed, and the year a great drought broke on the very day the colonists had set aside for fasting and prayer. This demonstration of the efficacy of Christian belief had an impact on the local Indians, who, Sewall reported, were forced to conclude, "*Surely, your God is a Good God!*" Meteorological signs and portents were dear to Sewall's heart.

Sewall believed "Unparalleld Providences" might be awaiting the Indians. This was hardly the usual argument: indeed, the providences lying in wait were more often of a dire kind, whether one consulted Edward Johnson's *Wonder-Working Providence* (1655), where a plague that decimated the Indians was seen as a sign of God's favorable attitude toward the Puritans, or jumped forward to Benjamin Franklin's acid remark in the *Autobiography* that "if it be the design of Providence to extirpate these savages in order to make room for cultivators of the earth, it seems not improbable that rum may be the appointed means." Nevertheless, Sewall had a tradition on his side too, as he made clear, one that stretches from Squanto through the Indian College at Harvard and the missionary work of John Eliot, to that of the New England Company, an organization devoted to spreading the gospel to the Indians. The *Phaenomena* is dedicated to the governor of the company, "who in shewing Kindness to the Aboriginal Natives of *America*, may possibly, show kindness to *Israelites* unawares." The other dedicatee is Stoughton: the dystopian past and the millennial future neatly encapsulated. Toward the end of *Phaenomena*, Sewall referred to the founding of Salem in very much the same terms as Cotton Mather had done before him: ". . . in the Year 1628, the first Town in the *Massachusetts* Bay, was begun by Mr. *John Endecott*, and was called SALEM." While Mather emphasized how the promise of this beginning was betrayed by the Satanic events of 1692, Sewall still awaited its fulfillment, continuing, "which may give occasion to hope, that GOD intendeth to write upon these Churches the name of *New Jerusalem*," the name Salem being contained in that of the millennial city.

Sewall was sharply sensitive of the significance of the time in which he wrote *Phaenomena*. Society was just moving beyond the biblical life expectancy of the very first generation of Americans, those born in the 1620s and 1630s. He listed examples: Mary Brown, the firstborn of Newbury, the mother and grandmother of many; Captain Peregrine White, who was born in November 1620, about the earliest date on which it was possible for a European to be an American too, and who "is yet alive, and like to live"; Major William Bradford, son of Governor Bradford (who came over on the *Mayflower*), who was seventy-three. Among others: Elizabeth Alden and her brother John, both over seventy. The witch crisis was never referred to directly, but it is significant that one of the accused got his mention, as a survivor, on the very last page of Sewall's book.

With the passing of this first generation of Americans, the country would become an historical entity in its own right, an organism that was bigger and longer-lived than the people who at any given moment inhabited it. And its achievements were promising enough: "Faith . . . is no where more Unanimously, Skillfully, and Resolutely defended than here." Just a year previously, Sewall had found himself making the New England case. Mrs. Martha Oakes, wife of Dr. Thomas Oakes, had been visiting the Sewalls with her stepdaughter, and at some point had given her a slap. As in the case of Nathaniel Saltonstall, Sewall responded in a straightforward letter, going right to the point: ". . . your striking your daughter-in-law [i.e., stepdaughter] before me, in my house, is not justifiable: though twas but a small blow, twas not a small fault." Some other unpleasantness had taken place too. Mrs. Oakes had only recently arrived in New England and apparently was not impressed. Sewall put her right in no uncertain terms: "As for New England, It is a cleaner Country than ever you were in before, and, therefore, and with disdain to term it *filthy*, is a sort of Blasphemie, which, by proceeding out of your mouth, hath defiled you."

This clean and fruitful country, "where *Ash, Chesnut, Hazel, Oak* & *Walnut* do naturally and plentifully grow," had more riches to offer yet. Ensign James Noyes had discovered a body of marble at—where else?—Newbury, which would provide lime much more conveniently than using oyster shells or limestone from the West Indies (that was Sewall the merchant writing; the ketch *Endeavour*, in which he had a half share, had returned from Jamaica in March 1686 with a cargo that included four tons of limestone, a bulky consignment that used up valuable space for a return of only 18s.). The starving were being assisted by initiatives in Rhode Island, Narragansett, and Connecticut; most of the ministers in the colony were American educated—that is to say, the spiritual life of the community was becoming self-propelling. There had been some bad omens—"the Blast, the Worm, the Frost, the Drought, the War"—the same ominous symptoms that led Sewall himself and many of his contemporaries to the conclusion that the community was being punished for the witchcraft injustices. Despite this, faith was holding up, and new meetinghouses were being built.

The book ends on a more muted note that nevertheless establishes once and for all that it was intended to provide comfort and reassurance, a rebirth of a belief in destiny, during a dark time: Sewall hopes that the outcome of events in New England "will be such as was with *Job*; Because the Language of this Thing seemeth to be, *Tho He Slay us, yet will we Trust in Him.*"

What Sewall did, through *Phaenomena* and his act of contrition in January, was confront his own demons and those of his country, with more literalness than that expression usually carries with it. Sewall's response to the crisis of his time was to claim that demons were indeed a personal matter. He looked at the Indians and concluded that despite the horrors of the ongoing conflicts between them and the settlers, they were not agents of the Devil, but embodiments of millennial hope; he looked at himself and concluded that he was directly responsible for judgments made at Salem.

The previous year had ended with Sewall insisting on the reality of Christian inheritance. His stillborn son had been transferred to the family tomb, an action that offended Willard but was consonant with Shepard's assertion that God's covenant extended to the seed of believers in a limited but absolute form. A couple of weeks later, Sewall had confronted his role in the Salem tragedy, taking the blame and shame of it on himself. This enabled him, by the following autumn, to publish his assertion of the organic continuity of the Christian tradition in America, implicitly repudiating the Salem narrative, which had claimed that the legacy, through backsliding, had lost its legitimacy and surrendered to the pagan forces implicit in the landscape, those "*Devils* territories," as Cotton Mather called them. On the contrary, *Phaenomena* insisted, Christ's kingdom was passing from the original settlers to the generations that followed; moreover, the primeval landscape of America wasn't the Devil's plantation but had belonged to God all along, though its inhabitants were not aware of the fact. The Puritan presence in the landscape was legitimate and purposive because it would restore the Indians to their true though forgotten inheritance and, as a result, guarantee the salvation of the settlers too.

Just as Sewall's little unbaptized son had not died in a state of nature but was part of God's commonwealth, so the Indians, living in their wilderness, would be citizens of the Christian utopia that was unfolding. Sewall had rediscovered the hope he expressed before the trials ever began: "Mr. Eliot believ'd the Americans to be of the Ten Tribes; if so, He that shall come will come and will not tarry—here will be a very beauteous Bride, and they will be extream happy who have been any way imployd in wooing Her for Christ."

Sewall was determined to get his message across to everyone he knew. In a commonplace book, he listed two hundred names of people he'd given copies to. And on 9 November, Sewall recorded the sale of the first copy of his book in Mr. Wilkins's bookshop, where his own son Sam was now the assistant.

Part Two

AMERICAN COMEDY

. . .

*Y*ET THIS DARKNESS is irradiated with the
brightness and solace of the concomitant Rain-bow.
And tho' the Storm increase and grow never so
Violent; yet this Angel persists with Courage
and Constancy to Proclaim the certain
approach of a Fair day.

—SAMUEL SEWALL,
Proposals Touching the Accomplishment
of Prophecies

CHAPTER TEN

American Pastoral

❦❦❦

$\mathcal{B}$EFORE SEWALL HAD PUT THE FINISHING TOUCHES TO *PHAENOM-ena*, there was an Indian attack on Lancaster. This town, some forty miles west of Boston, had been the scene of a famous Indian massacre years before, when Mary Rowlandson had been captured. It was also the place where the Indian captor of Hannah Dustin had served as a servant to Mrs. Rowlandson's husband, the minister. Now the current pastor, John Whiting, was shot and scalped. Four days later, returning from his judicial rounds, Sewall heard news of military engagements and maneuvers, and reflected on the precariousness of small-town Massachusetts: "Blessed be God who hath carried us out and brought us home safely and that preservs so many of our Towns like Flocks of sheep in a howling Wilderness, naked and defenceless."

A fortnight later, off he went on a picnic to Hogg Island. Hannah was poorly and couldn't go, but the children were there: Sam (nineteen), Hannah Jr. (seventeen), Elizabeth (sixteen), Joseph (nine), and Mary (six), along with the three sons of a friend, Jeremiah Belcher, the Willards with their four children, and a couple of others. The Willards had lost another of their children only three months before: thirteen-year-old Richard had gone for a swim in the Charles River and drowned. He had just applied for Harvard and his acceptance letter was found in one of his pockets. Perhaps this excursion was to help the family recover. They had a first meal of butter, honey, curds and cream, and later a dinner of "very good Rost Lamb, Turkey, Fowls, Applepye."

After dinner they sang Psalm 121 ("I To the Hills lift up mine eyes, / from whence shall come mine ayd"). Hannah had sent along a bottle of spirits, so as to be with them in spirit, presumably, and Simon Willard knocked a glass of it off a joint stool. Sewall couldn't resist commenting that the accident was a lively emblem of our fragility and mortality, but on the whole the mood was jolly, youthful, sunlit. They were hopeful Americans enjoying curds and cream in plain air, inhabitants of another land from the one in which Mr. Whiting had met his terrible fate just three weeks earlier. Sewall's peculiar talent was to live in both versions of the American pastoral simultaneously, the towns like flocks of sheep in a howling wilderness, and Hogg Island on an early autumn picnic— engaging with the first while insisting that the spirit of the second would prevail.

A harsh winter set in. On 23 January 1698, it was "Very cold. . . . Very thin Assemblies this Sabbath, and last; and great Coughing: very few women there. Mr. Willard pray'd for mitigation of the wether; and the south wind begins to blow with some vigor. My clock stood still this morning, and yesterday morn, which has not done many years." The frozen clock, the coughing in church, God's concession of a warm wind in response to Mr. Willard's prayer: Sewall's alertness to detail allows us to enter, for a moment, the lived experience of three centuries ago. There's no more poignant evocation of the past than transient, never-to-be-repeated weather. Where are the snows of yesteryear? Answer— in Sewall's journal. On 3 February, that south wind still blowing, Sewall wrote, "Day warm though blustering; the sun much qualifying the Aer," and the lovely final phrase makes us feel a layering of warmth and cold. Later in the year, Sewall had an odd experience while in bed: "Last night, lying awake, but with my eyes fast shut, Lightening flash'd in my face, I could not certainly tell what Light it should be; but presently heard a loud clap of Thunder." The next day, "between the ringing of the morning Bells, it Thundered several times, but with a more confused and rumbling noise. Much Rain, Mist." Lightning through shut eyes (perhaps in the interval before the answering clap, Samuel Sewall, head on pillow, eyes still closed, waited in hope or fear for a divine revelation), different categories of thunder: he had an extensive portfolio of weather.

In the spring, he received some queries about the argument of *Phaenomena* from the Reverend John Wise of Ipswich, Massachusetts. He modestly pooh-poohed Wise's flattery—"you had overvalued the crazie fining Pot, when as you ventured to pour into it so many and great Hyperboles of Praise" (a fining pot was a crucible for refining metal: his is of poor quality, with a fractured glaze)—and went on to counter Wise's doubts about the lost tribe theory, restating his faith that the conversion of the Indians will be the key to the future. As so often, the prospect of this millennial outcome gives rhetorical power to his writing: "And possibly this place that was lately none at all; and is still last of all, may in time, be made the first." The following month, however, the Indian College at Harvard was pulled down, an experiment that had failed. The replacement building was funded by and named after William Stoughton, that implacable enemy of alleged followers of the Black Man.

On 28 June 1698, Sewall officiated at the Salem court, with a wealthy local merchant, Major William Browne, acting as president. As darkness fell, they adjourned to the Ship Tavern. Just as candles were being lit, there was a cry of fire. A serving girl had gone into a nearby warehouse to draw rum or check on a leaking barrel and her candle set light to the spirits. The barrel exploded; bales of cotton caught fire; these in turn set light to a nearby house belonging to Francis Willoughby. Unfortunately, there was a barrel of gunpowder in Willoughby's attic; it blew, taking the roof with it, and widely scattering "the flaming particles"; the wind took many of them across to Major Browne's house on the other side of the road.

He and Sewall, hotfoot from the tavern, stood aghast as the night lit up with flames and sparks. Browne's home was burned to the ground, along with his adjoining warehouse. Five houses were destroyed in the first serious fire ever to afflict Salem. Browne was devastated—Sewall estimated he'd lost three or four thousand pounds in the conflagration.

Two weeks later, Sewall's old friend and former bedfellow, Edward

Taylor, came to visit. Taylor had been ministering to the frontier town of Westfield, Massachusetts, for a quarter of a century by this point, acting as the little community's physician and general administrator as well as its religious leader, and growing vegetables for his family in his large garden. Westfield was a tiny place: when the church covenanted in 1679, Taylor himself was one of only seven people to make their profession of faith and comprise the elected congregation. The town lived in fear of an Indian attack, and was occasionally raided by "skulking rascalds," as Taylor called them. His own house, like that of Nathaniel Saltonstall in Haverhill, was designated the town's fortress in the event of danger. Westfield was one of those little sheeplike towns in the howling wilderness, a rough-hewn place where Taylor painfully transcribed books Sewall lent him, to provide reading matter for his isolated intellect to play upon. He and Sewall corresponded regularly, often sending poems to each other.

One morning during his stay, the two friends walked along Cotton Hill, Beacon Hill, the pasture, and the stone wall; then, on their way back, they sat on "the great Rock" and Taylor told Sewall the story of his courtship of his first wife. He also recounted an anecdote about someone praying for a wife, and asking God "to bring his Affection to close with a person pious, but hard-favoured," a Puritan request of the grimmer sort. This earnest entreaty not to be distracted from higher things triggered a strange reflection on Sewall's part: "Has God answered me in finding out one Godly and fit for me," he asks his diary, "and shall I part for fancy?"

The diaries testify to Sewall's love of his wife and the happiness of their marriage, and though with no portrait we can't tell whether Hannah was "hard-favoured" or not, it somehow seems unlikely. But not even a Puritan judge is immune from moments of sexual restlessness, of wanting to succumb to "fancy" and feeling a twinge of dissatisfaction at what, or who, the good Lord had provided for him. When he arrived home, Hannah gave him a letter from his brother-in-law Jacob Toppan about the latter's eighteen-year-old daughter Elizabeth. We don't know what it said—perhaps something to do with matters of love and sex (she was eighteen and wouldn't get married till the comparatively late age of twenty-three). Whatever the content, it caused Sewall to reflect further on his talk with Taylor, who had apparently prayed "for pardon of error in our ways." This, Sewall claims, "made me think whether it were not best to overlook all, and go on." Some slight wobble seems to have occurred in the otherwise smooth progression of his marriage.

The talk with Taylor must have covered other topics too, probably the fire that had just taken place in Salem, because at some time or another Taylor wrote a poem that seems to have been richly informed not simply by the imagery of the event but by its very setting. It's called "Let by Rain," "let" in this case meaning hindered (or kept indoors), and the poem depicts a moment of spiritual confusion or indecisiveness. Taylor is thinking particularly of the challenges facing the Puritan pastor:

> *Wager thyself against thy surplice see,*
> *And win thy coat: or let thy coat win thee.*

While "surplice" can mean an overcoat, its primary meaning then as now was a priest's vestment. From a minister's viewpoint, the dilemma is whether to be defined by one's office or to take the responsibility, as a Puritan minister should, of defining it oneself. The Puritans were deeply suspicious of ornamentation, including the wearing of clerical vestments. In 1634, Richard Mather, father of Increase and grandfather of Cotton, was summoned before the ecclesiastical authorities in Wigan to answer charges of nonconformity. He confirmed that he had never worn a surplice in the course of his ministry, which led one member of the court to remark, "It had been better for him that he had gotten Seven Bastards." Increase Mather followed in his father's footsteps by refusing to wear a cap or hood during his master of arts ceremony at Trinity College, Dublin, a stance that caused cries of "Precisian" and some loud humming (though luckily Mather interpreted the latter as a signal of support).

If you fail to disclose your values and express your nature, the poem suggests, the soul will build up pressure within the prison of the flesh. This seems to bring to mind the conflagration of the spirits in the

Salem warehouse. It will ferment like liquor in a barrel and then explode:

> *As bottle ale, whose spirits prisoned nursed*
> *When jogged, the bung with violence doth burst.*

Taylor switches metaphors to a blacksmith's shop, where the sparks rise high then, like the flaming particles from Mr. Willoughby's house, drop on a nearby building, in this case God's temple. The verses themselves seem to float across the page:

> *One sorry fret,*
> > *An anvil spark, rose higher,*
> *And in Thy temple falling almost set*
> *The house on fire.*
> > *Such fireballs droping in the temple flame*
> > *Burns up the building: Lord forbid the same.*

If the source of this imagery was the unlucky chain reaction at Salem, then the content of the poem might be tracked back to Salem too, to its courthouse (after all, the current president of that court was the chief victim of the conflagration), to the trials there of six years previously, and the events in the neighborhood that triggered them, the spiritual hopes and fears that exploded with such tragic consequences during that long summer. The poem is about the dangers of enthusiasm, religious excess generated by too much baffled and pent-up spiritual emotion, a syndrome brought on readily enough in the claustrophobic atmosphere of colonial Puritan society, and taking a peculiar form, rampaging to terrible effect, in Salem in 1692.

If this interpretation is correct, this was yet another attempt by Sewall to grapple with the trauma of the witchcraft crisis, providing Taylor with an outward sign, the recent fire, and an inward meaning, the witchcraft crisis of six years before, his own presence as a circuit judge the connecting link, these elements being fused together by Taylor's poetic gift. The events of 1692 still provided a reference point for emotional anarchy. In March, Sewall had intervened in a furious argument between Theophilus Frary and his brother-in-law, Seth Perry, who had called him "Rogue, pittifull Rascal, &c." Sewall added fuel to the flames by sending a letter to Frary that put him into such a state "almost as the poor creatures were at Salem"—the afflicted girls having become a byword for uncontrollable emotions. Frary burned the letter, unable to read it through to the end, though later he joined Perry in asking Sewall to resolve their quarrel—an example of the respect a person could have for Sewall's integrity, even when he disliked what he had to say.

On at least one previous occasion, Sewall had made surrogate use of his friend's talent. When little Hull died in 1686, Taylor sent him an exquisitely wrought poem, and three years later, while in London, Sewall had it printed (along with a sermon by Cotton Mather that also dealt with the child's death), thereby becoming Taylor's first publisher by a margin of two and a half centuries:

> *I pausing on't, this Sweet refresh'd my Thought*
> *Christ would in Glory have a Flower sweet, prime;*
> *And having choice, chose this my Branch forth brought*
> *Lord, take't; I thank thee thou tak'st ought of mine.*

Babyhood was dangerous in late-seventeenth-century America. Infant mortality was high in households where children were loved and desired; but infanticide was common among girls who became pregnant outside wedlock and couldn't cope with the shame and ostracism they faced (after all, the greatest novelistic treatment of colonial America, Hawthorne's *The Scarlet Letter*, deals with the disgrace and isolation that adulterous motherhood brought about). That autumn, Sewall was on the bench for the trial of nineteen-year-old Sarah Threeneedles, who was found guilty of killing her illegitimate baby. She was brought into the South meetinghouse for a service immediately before being taken to the gallows, as was the custom. Cotton Mather was guest minister. The South Church had been chosen because of its capacity, but it was so full that he had to use heads as stepping-stones to clamber to the pulpit. Those who couldn't get in were standing pruriently outside on the street. Mather had been quite put out that the execution had originally been scheduled for the previous week when someone else was in the pulpit, as that would have deprived him of the opportunity to shine. His sermon lasted two hours, and as usual Sewall set the tune for the singing of the psalm: "O God, God of my health set me: / free from blood-guiltiness."

There was an odd mixture of voyeurism and caring during occasions like this, the ultimate objective being that the community learn from the plight of the condemned, and that she should have the opportunity to repent and find salvation. Two years later, Sewall was one of the judges in the trial of Esther Rogers, also accused of murdering her illegitimate child. She lived in Newbury and had drowned her baby in the village pond behind the meetinghouse. After sentence had been pronounced, Sewall pointed out to the condemned woman that her mother hadn't treated her as she had her own child, and that the biblical Esther had been a savior while she was a destroyer. Then, characteristically, he relented, telling the doomed woman that he was not trying to "insult over her, but to make her sensible"—fleeting patriarchal sympathy from judge to condemned prisoner. On another occasion, he wrote a heartfelt letter to Cotton Mather about a young black woman he had had to condemn: "There is one case wherein I would bespeak your compassions; Elizabeth Negro born in Col. Shrimptons house, late Servt. to Col. Winslow was condemned at Plimouth on account of the death of her Bastard Child. She beg'd some Time with Tears; and probably, this may be the last entire day of her riefed [reprieved] time; the next light will show her dead and buried. I hope she will hear a Lecture to morrow; Pray that she may hear the Voice of the Son of God, and Live." He showed similar concern for an Indian by the name of Sam Chapen, who had to use crutches: "It was sad to see or hear how swift his wooden feet were to shed innocent blood—with a short knife wherewith he stabd his Neighbor." Luckily, Cotton Mather secured Chapen's conversion after "Unwearied Endeavours" (Sewall's contribution was to lay out 11s. on the murderer's shroud and coffin). The witchcraft executions had been so traumatic because the condemned did not repent, which meant that they were eternally damned—or, as had now become clear to most people, innocent.

We get a glimpse of Boston as the seventeenth century wound down through the eyes of a visitor from England, the Grub Street hack Edward Ward. The houses were neat and handsome, terraced in places in the London style, with pebbled streets; but the religious atmosphere of the town was hardly to his taste: "In Boston there are more *Religious Zealots* than *Honest-men*; more *Parsons* than *Churches*; and more *Churches* than *Parishes*." Worse still, there was a law against kissing in public, which was regarded as equivalent to fornication. "A Captain of a Ship, who had been on a long Voyage, happen'd to meet his Wife, and kist her in the Street; for which he was fin'd Ten Shillings . . . What a Happiness, thought I, do we enjoy in *Old-England*, that can not only Kiss our own Wives, but other Mens too, without the danger of such a penalty." Boston women were as attractive to randy Ned Ward as the London variety, and indeed had better complexions, but the men were "generally *Meagre*; and have got the *Hypocritical* knack, . . . of screwing their Faces, into such *Puritanical* postures that you would think they were always Praying to themselves, or running melancholy Mad about some Mistery in the *Revelations*."

Sewall, of course, spent his life pondering a mystery in Revelation, but showed no sign of running melancholy mad, or even being melancholy. Nevertheless, it was as a result of the providential theory of history he derived from Revelation 16 that he lent support to one of the great disasters of late-seventeenth-century colonization—the Darien adventure.

In late December 1698, the buzz in Boston was about the arrival in Jamaica of some of the fleet of the Scotland Company. "'Tis rumor'd," Sewall wrote, "they intend to settle on the American isthmus, or on Golden Island just by it." This was a commercial endeavor backed by massive public subscription in Scotland, and the idea was to colonize a stretch of the isthmus connecting North and South America. The territory in question was known as Darien and appeared to have been overlooked by Spain. It was situated on the north, or Caribbean, side of the isthmus, not far above the South American mainland, and consisted of a peninsula curving from east to west like a protective arm round a small bay, with Golden Island some distance beyond to the west. The colonists had little idea what they were sailing into—but the same could have been said of the Pilgrim Fathers, and it was undoubtedly that analogy that excited the attention of Samuel Sewall and his fellow Bostonians. Obviously, the colony could develop enormous strategic and trading importance when it had been established—the "door of the seas and the key to the universe," as its promoter, William Paterson, proclaimed, a heady prospect and one eagerly taken by upwards of two thousand Scottish men, women, and children in search of a better future. Expectations were fed by seafarers' tales, particularly legends spread by buccaneers, of a land teeming with fruit and fauna, a romantic place that could still stir the imagination more than a century later, when Keats used poetic license to picture the Spanish conquistador, "stout Cortez," gaining his first sight of the Pacific, "Silent, upon a peak in Darien." A visitor in 1681 described a country teeming with pineapples, rabbits, quam (a fat bird like a partridge), even, symbolically enough, honey, and inhabited by the friendly Cuna and Choco Indians. But it was a very wet country with swarms of mosquitoes, "uneasy vermin." In the excitement of colonizing a new Eden, these contraindications were passed over. People didn't seem to ask themselves why its Spanish conquerors took so little interest in the place.

The factors that sold the scheme to the Scots would have sold it to the author of *Phaenomena* also. The plan chimed in with his view of America's status as the final installment of God's historical plan, and the prospect of muscling out the Catholic Spanish and creating a rapport between good Scots Covenanters and amenable Indians was perfectly attuned to the prophecies in Sewall's book. His immediate reaction was to send a dozen copies to Francis Borland, one of the four appointed ministers of the colony, who would be going out in the second phase of the expedition the following year. William Paterson, the leader of the enterprise, read it and wrote of the parallel between his ideas and those expressed in print: ". . . am glad to see the Spirit and Hand of Almighty God at this time in so eminent a manner, as it were moving in the minds of so many men, and inclining and preparing them (although in so many and various circumstances, and different and distant places) to this great Work."

Some months later, Sewall wrote to the ministers in Caledonia in warm support of their enterprise, and reflected on the marvelous coincidence between their plans and his theories: "I cant but revolve in my mind . . . the Synchronisme there was between my Meditation and the Scots Action." He points them to his account of the sixth angel. This angel is about to pour out his vial, which will bring about the drying up of anti-Christian values in the New World. "It was above a year after the printing of this," he excitedly tells the colonists, "before I heard the least inkling of the Scots company. So soon as I was informd of it, and of their Expedition to Darien, I said within my self Surely the Company of Scotland is the Sixth Angel." He concludes by expressing his faith that Christ "will lead you on to glorious Conquests."

The first settlers were welcomed by the Indians (as Squanto had welcomed the Plymouth settlers), who saw them as allies against Spanish oppression. The settlers built huts and began to construct a fort. They had brought along four thousand periwigs, ascending in order of elaboration from plain bobs to "magnificent structures which . . . towered high above the foreheads," as if anticipating the cool streets and comfortable drawing rooms of Edinburgh rather than the blazing heat of this frontier land. The rain and the tropical sun beat mercilessly down; exhaustion and fever took their toll. The Spanish plotted to reclaim what they regarded as their territory. The English government issued proclamations declaring the settlement illegal. Unlike their stubborn North American counterparts, this first cohort of settlers had had enough within a few months. Ill and sick, they clambered aboard their ships and set sail for home, leaving behind just six men who were too weak to make their escape.

In ignorance of the collapse of the settlement, the second swathe of colonists set out from Scotland. Borland described their dismal landfall: "Expecting to meet with our friends and countrymen, we found nothing but a vast howling wilderness"—that phrase again, a sort of anti-description, evoking landscapes with nothing in them to succor or accommodate; asserting emptiness, and threat, and the threat of emptiness—"the Colony deserted and gone, their huts all burnt, their fort most part ruined, the ground which they had cleared adjoining to the fort all overgrown with weeds: and we looked for Peace but no good came, and for a time of health and comfort, but beheld Trouble." Four days later, five hundred of the men and all the women were sent off to Jamaica. The remainder immediately managed to provoke enmity from the previously welcoming Indians. The British king made known his displeasure in the whole enterprise, and within a few weeks the Spaniards had started to attack. By the end of March 1700, the adventure had ended in ignominy. The articles of surrender were written in Latin because none of the Scots spoke Spanish (typical of the expedition's total lack of preparedness, since it was after all an attempt to conquer Spanish territories). They were given two weeks to get their ships ready, and then had to leave. Sewall copied the articles, in their original Latin, into his letterbook, a gesture of long-distance empathy.

Meanwhile, Sewall had received his second commission as judge of the superior court from the new governor, Lord Bellomont, on 25 July 1699. He hurried home expecting congratulations from his nearest and dearest only to discover the house empty and unimpressed. The reconfirmed superior court judge, a little stout, fond of food, used to being served, had to poke about for odds and ends in the pantry: "I came in . . . and made shift to find a solitary dinner of bak'd pigeons and a piece of cake." It wasn't his nature to be disappointed for long. As he ate his cold pigeons and cake, he pondered his judicial responsibilities: "How happy I were, if I could once become wise as a Serpent and harmless as a Dove!"

These were qualities that needed to be brought into play on the domestic front too. Betty was seventeen, and had begun to attract the attention of suitors. Early in January 1699, Captain Zachariah Tuthill declared his interest. Sewall made inquiries and discovered he was an eligible match. Betty disagreed, however: one night, when Tuthill came to pay court, she disappeared. The family knocked at the doors of several houses, trying to track her down. After several hours she popped out of the coach that was standing outside, where she'd hidden herself, looking "very wild."

In the next few days, Tuthill paid more visits, and spoke with the flustered Betty in her father's presence. On one occasion, Sewall sent him away because he wanted to find out what Betty was thinking. Then, on 20 January, Captains Brown and Turner came for breakfast, to plead Tuthill's cause. After the meal, Sewall asked Betty to serve wine. As soon as she had done so she disappeared again, much to his consternation. He had the bright idea of suggesting they should have some almonds and raisins, his favorite snack, which gave him an excuse to leave the room. He found Betty and brought her back in to serve the refreshments, persuading her to make a toast to Captain Turner. However, despite this nimble improvisation, the courtship petered out.

No ill feelings, apparently: a few days later, the Sewalls went off on a family excursion in a coach—presumably the very one Betty had hidden in. The excursion took them to the Turk's Head at Dorchester, where they had sage cheese, beer, and cider. And in March, Tuthill rented a house from Sewall for himself and his mother, so he didn't bear a grudge.

Having escaped from Captain Tuthill, Betty soon found herself on the receiving end of more overtures, this time from a Salem merchant called Grove Hirst, whom she had got to know while staying with her uncle Stephen and his wife, Margaret. On 28 September 1699, a blisteringly hot day, Sewall arrived home after an incident-filled trip. Land on Point Judith, some of it owned by him and Hannah, had been formally transferred to Indian ownership as represented by the person of a certain Block Island Harry. As Sewall left the signing ceremony, someone fired a pistol so close to the calash in which he was riding that the horses panicked and broke one of the poles. When he finally got to his house, relieved as usual to have arrived safely, Sewall discovered his wife had a cold and Betty had turned Grove Hirst down. Another anticlimax, like the cold pigeon and cake: "The Lord sanctifye Mercyes and Afflictions."

A month later, the issue came to a crunch, with an awkward meeting between the two fathers. William Hirst came to thank Hannah and Samuel in valedictory fashion for having let his son have the freedom of their house. Sewall suggested that all might not be lost and that Grove should go and see Betty, who was staying at Braintree. Hirst replied that his son would be only too willing to do so if there was any hope of a satisfactory outcome, but as things stood it would make people think he was in so deep he wouldn't be free to follow other possibilities.

This sticky encounter prompted Sewall to write to Betty two days later, saying that Grove was willing to wait on her if she would agree to see him. He began in stern mode, reminding her that rejecting her suitor after what had passed between them could damage her reputation and put off "persons of worth" who might otherwise pay court to her (both the fathers concerned were sharply conscious of the marketability of their offspring). He gave advice about balancing out the good with the bad, then characteristically offered a way out: ". . . if you find in yourself an immovable, incurable Aversion from him, and cannot love, and honour, and obey him, I shall say no more."

This intervention did the trick, and the meeting in Braintree took place. By the following summer Grove Hirst had become courtly indeed, writing to Elizabeth in the character of Strephon, and sounding like some lovesick swain in the pastoral landscape of a Shakespeare comedy—"Subscribe not my Name, you are not unacquainted with the hand." But even now, the course of true love refused to run entirely smoothly. Ten days before the wedding, Grove managed to do something (undisclosed) that caused huge offense on the part of the normally tolerant Sewall, who said he would only forgive him as long as Grove never forgave himself. Nevertheless, the nuptials took place in the new parlor on 17 October 1698, and the assembled party sang Psalm 128, "Thy wife like fruitfull Vine / Shall be by thine house side"—prophetic words (she would have eight children), even though Sewall accidentally set them to the wrong tune.

While Betty's mating dance was going on its way, Sewall had another, very different, one to deal with. It would rapidly lead to one of the great moral challenges of his life, and to one of his most extraordinary achievements.

CHAPTER ELEVEN

The Selling of Joseph

⚘⚘⚘

IN APRIL 1699, JUST MONTHS AFTER A WILD-EYED BETTY HAD hidden from the advances of Captain Tuthill, a friend of Sewall's called John Wait approached him on behalf of his slave Bastian. Bastian wished to marry Jane, a slave belonging to Nathaniel Thayer. A few days later, Mrs. Wait called on the same business.

Bastian did Sewall errands from time to time, fetching Sam Jr.'s trunk home after a job fizzled out, setting Sewall's vines, bringing him fuel, rushing up to tell him about the sickness of friends, going to Hogg Island and gathering pumpkins with him. These were vicarious favors, courtesy of his master, but there's something easy and familiar about the diary references that suggests warmth between Sewall and Bastian. A year after the initial approaches from the Waits, Sewall was moved to undertake one of the most surprising and courageous acts of his life: he wrote *The Selling of Joseph*, one of the first antislavery tracts ever written in English.

He'd been worried about the slave trade for a long time and had got to the point of putting pen to paper, but then the mood wore off (Sewall's frankness never lets us see the past as cut and dried: we watch certainties and commitments ebb and flow, see clusters of possibilities underlying hard facts and accomplishments, look back beyond a finished life toward the unfinished, untidy experience of living). Now, though, he was galvanized into action. A number of issues had converged, in addition to the negotiations about the slaves' marriage. A committee in Boston was agitating for a punitive tax of 40s. per head on all imported slaves, in order to discourage the trade. Cotton Mather was writing a paper exhorting owners to convert their slaves to Christianity. The case of a slave called Adam who had been promised his freedom and was being unjustly kept in bondage had been drawn to the attention of the General Court. The issue was in the air. Sewall's own reinterpretation of the witch trials made him alert to cultural shift and development, to the bigger historical picture, above all to injustice. Now the moment was come he acted rapidly: he decided to tackle the subject on 19 June 1700, and five days later his pamphlet had been printed.

There were only about a thousand slaves in New England at this time, against a white population of ninety thousand, but the number in Massachusetts Bay was expanding rapidly and would reach two thousand by 1715. This trend, and the "Uneasiness" of slaves under their yoke, made it timely to question the institution as a whole. The current cause célèbre involving the slave Adam triggered some learned reflections by Sewall on the Adamic inheritance in the Bible. We are all descendants of the original Adam, slaves included. True, covenanted Christians are also heirs to the second Adam, Christ, who provides an upgraded legacy, ultimate salvation, but unconverted blacks still have entitlement to liberty as their inheritance from the original one. We have a vested interest in respecting this universal privilege. Genesis 37 tells how the Ishmaelites bought Joseph for twenty pieces of silver. Such a transaction, by turning a person into a commodity, involved denying the original inheritance on which the Ishmaelites' own status as human beings depended: "For he that shall in this case plead *Alteration of Property*, [i.e., the passing of a commodity from one person to another for payment] seems to have forfeited a great part of his own claim to Humanity."

The witchcraft trials produced some fleeting intuitions of egalitarianism and civil rights, and above all taught the lesson that people should not be seen as pawns in a game but as possessors of their own interior universe, owners of their souls. Sewall had taken the lesson to heart: "There is no proportion between Twenty pieces of Silver, and LIBERTY," he declared " 'Tis pity there should be more Caution used in buying a Horse, or a little lifeless dust; than there is in purchasing Men and Women." Men and women are different in kind from material that can be traded; liberty cannot be quantified or qualified; it is an all-or-nothing concept.

Sewall did not envisage reconciliation and harmony with the blacks. For him, they were racially distinct and could not be integrated: ". . . they can never embody with us, and grow up into orderly Families, to the Peopling of the Land." Unlike the Indians, they would not be participants in a glorious destiny for America. They belonged elsewhere. But belonging itself mattered hugely to Sewall, rippling out from him in concentric circles—family man, Bostonian, Massachusetts citizen, New Englander, Englishman . . . and he empathized eloquently with the horror of dislocation: "It is . . . most lamentable to think, how in taking Negros out of *Africa*, and Selling of them here, That which GOD ha's joyned together men do boldly rend asunder; Men from their Country, Husbands from their Wives, Parents from their Children. How horrible is the Uncleanness, Mortality, if not Murder, that the Ships are guilty of that bring great Crouds of these miserable Men, and Women."

The colonists were no better than the Africans who kept white people in captivity on their own continent; and in terms of gritty economics, the expense of redeeming white captives (not to mention the cost in lives), added to that of buying black ones, might not be balanced by the overall profits of the trade. That unconvincing argument was skewed slightly by personal experience, since Sewall had spent two years (1686–88) negotiating a ransom for Joshua Gee, a Bostonian held captive in Algiers. Gee came in person to thank him for his efforts and presented him with a pair of garters he had bought in North Africa.

Some people justified slavery on the grounds that according to Genesis, the posterity of Ham—that is, the blacks—were cursed (Genesis 9, 25, 26, 27). Against this, Sewall argued that the last role one would ever want to take on would be "Executioner of the Vindictive Wrath of God." For the Puritans, God could be furious as well as benevolent. As Edward Taylor put it, in a meditation written in June 1703, "such as will not with thy rule Comply / Thou with thy iron Scepter down wilt smite." The most popular American poem of the seventeenth century, Michael Wigglesworth's *The Day of Doom* (1662), graphically depicted the terrors of God's vengeance on sinners. Wigglesworth's dislocated sentences accidentally mimic their panic and torture, verbs coming at the end of lines like the final struggles of squashed insects:

> Some to the Rocks, (O Senseless blocks)
>   And woody Mountains run,
> That there they might this fearful sight
> And dreaded Presence shun.

In 1741, a lifetime after *The Day of Doom* and eleven years after Sewall's death, Jonathan Edwards, the great preacher and theologian, would stand up in a church in Enfield, Connecticut and deliver his sermon "Sinners in the Hands of an Angry God," causing panic in the congregation, with people crying out and moaning with terror. "The Wrath of God burns against them," he announced, "their Damnation don't slumber, the Pit is prepared, the fire is made ready, the Furnace is now hot, ready to receive them; the Flames do now rage and glow."

The Almighty's capacity for ineluctable fury had provided a precedent for the Salem authorities when they themselves dispensed harsh justice. They were dealing with spiritual rather than earthly issues, quite literally acting as divine agents. Half a century later, Edwards looked back toward Puritan certitudes and in his sermon constructed a God who embodied them in the inexorability of his rage: ". . . he will have no compassion upon you, he will not forbear the Executions of his Wrath, or in the least lighten his Hand; there shall be no Moderation or Mercy, nor will God then at all stay His rough Wind. . . . Nothing shall be withheld, because 'tis so hard for you to bear." This is about inflicting ultimate suffering; it is also—and more importantly—about having the absolute confidence to inflict it; and above all it is about having absolute confidence, as church members, in God's absolute confidence. Edwards's emphasis on God's implacability acts as a kind of transferred metaphor for the unwavering faith he insists his congregation should espouse. His project, in this sermon and in his ministry in general during the 1730s and 1740s, was to reinstate a lost fervor of belief, as part of a revival known as the Great Awakening. The Salem trials marked the very point where the certainty of condemnation reasserted by Edwards had originally been discredited, at least as enacted by ministers, jurors, and justices in their capacity as agents of divine displeasure.

The problem with this role, according to Sewall, is that we cannot know the wrath's duration or scope, so that we might be providing an ugly footnote long after the sinners in question have been forgiven; worst still—and this touched a painful spot—we might end up persecuting those against whom he had no animosity in the first place. It is possible that the curse in Genesis may have been confined to the Canaanites, and not apply to the descendants of Ham at all. Unsurprisingly, the man who in 1697 apologized for his part in the condemnation of the alleged witches, warns others, four years later, of the dangers implicit in acting as executioner of God's fury.

Sewall has no time for the argument that the blacks (he uses the word "Nigers") were being taken out of a pagan country into a Christian one: evil can't be condoned on the grounds it leads to good—the end, in other words, does not justify the means. As for the claim that the slaves were lawful captives in African wars, "Every War is upon one side Unjust." Imagine a party of Boston gentlemen sailing off to the nearby Brewster Islands in order "to take the Air, and Fish," and finding themselves attacked by a stronger party of men from the nearby town of Hull (there was a long-standing dispute between the Boston and Hull authorities about the ownership of the islands). The Hull men might then sell their captives as slaves, to form the cargo of some outward-bound ship. The victims, Sewall sardonically suggests, would "think themselves unjustly dealt with; both by Sellers and Buyers." Choosing an example so close to home shows his faith in the connectedness of humankind and the universality of human experience.

Finally, there is the argument that Abraham bought servants. Sewall's verdict is that it cannot set a precedent because we do not know enough about the circumstances to draw any conclusions. The Old Testament model of slavery was something of a hot potato. There were two sorts of servitude in ancient Israel: Jewish servants who went free after six years, and Gentiles who were slaves for life, though protected by Mosaic Law from severe ill-treatment. The Puritan commonwealth oscillated uneasily between these two precedents, and indeed tried to effect a compromise between them. That's why slaves were usually called servants, and why in many cases they were freed after six years of service (especially in the seventeenth century).

The point is that God expects Christians to be ingenuous and benign. Holding one's neighbor in bondage would be an ironic way of demonstrating one's own "Spiritual Freedom." In celebrating the way New Testament values enriched those of the Old, Sewall shows his awareness and appreciation of cultural transition, that great issue of his life and his time: "Our Blessed Saviour ha's altered the Measures of the ancient Love-Song, and set it to a most Excellent New Tune, which all ought to be ambitious of Learning."

Unlike *Phaenomena*, *The Selling of Joseph* made no attempt to discover a grand pattern connecting the past and the future, because as far as Sewall was concerned the races under discussion had separate destinies. Yet, in its own way, the pamphlet did confront the temporal process, reaching back to ancient spiritual verities, taking on contemporary issues and perspectives, and picking up, like some delicate seismograph, the emergence of new values in the future. Judge Sewall, lover of home and family, celebrator of the original New England impulse, easily put out at having to make do with a cold pigeon supper and quickly demoralized when snubbed by those in authority, nonetheless backed his way toward the future, his willingness to exorcise past ghosts ensuring that he was open to new perspectives, the possibility of social change, and the amelioration of his community. Within a year, the selectmen of Boston had voted that "the Representitives ar . . . desired To Promote the Encourrageing the bringing of white serv^{ts} and to put a Period to negros being Slaves."

Negotiations about the fate of Bastian and Jane resumed a few months after the publication of *The Selling of Joseph*, when a delegation arrived at Sewall's house. It consisted of Bastian's owners, John and Eunice Wait, and Mrs. Debora Thayer, mistress of Jane, along with the slaves themselves. John Wait wanted to go ahead with the publication of the banns. Mrs. Thayer was worried about the financial implications if Jane should produce a family, and wanted the Waits to give Bastian one day a week off to support her and any children. Mr. Wait would not agree, but offered to pay Bastian an allowance of £5 a year toward the maintenance of his offspring, in addition to supplying his food and clothing. Sewall took up this offer and persuaded Mrs. Thayer and Jane herself to agree to it. Mrs. Thayer then gave the Note of Publication (the banns) to Mr. Wait so he in turn could give it to the town clerk and have it officially published.

That wasn't the end of the saga, however. Three months later, on a January morning, Mrs. Thayer was working her water pump (Jane obviously didn't have to do everything) when she suffered a stroke, and she died later that day. Obviously, this threatened the carefully negotiated arrangement, and on 10 January, John Wait called on Sewall to ask him to hurry the wedding along before the opportunity was lost. On 13 February 1701, Samuel Sewall finally married Bastian and Jane. (Over the course of the following summer, Cotton Mather married two black couples, but they were free people, not slaves.)

The extent to which Sewall had gone out on a limb, in defiance of the attitudes of his contemporaries, can be registered by an odd and rather unsavory episode that took place in Mr. Wilkins's bookshop that October.

Increase Mather was president of Harvard College, but for years there had been problems about his tenure of the post. He was unwilling to take up residence because it would mean neglecting his Boston congregation. He had in fact made two attempts at living in Cambridge (nowadays just a few minutes by subway from the center of Boston) but had given them both up. Quite simply, he loathed being there. It was "the place, which of all under Heaven, was most abominable to him," according to his son Cotton, and caused his spirit to be "prodigiously unfram'd, unhing'd, and broken." The matter caused disquiet and was debated in council. Mather agreed to live in Cambridge again but would not commit himself to lead prayers and expound scripture to the students, on the grounds that such a commitment could conflict with his duties at the North Church of Boston. Sewall complained that this half-cocked arrangement would actually make matters worse, because Mather's lack of involvement in Harvard worship would be more obvious if he was in the vicinity while it was going on.

Cotton Mather, always a passionate supporter of his father, was infuriated by Sewall's stance. He strode into the bookshop, knowing young Sam worked there, and "talked very sharply against me as if I had used his father worse than a Neger; spake so loud that people in the street might hear him." In his pamphlet, Sewall too had used the word "Niger," which of course meant black, as does the form it had modulated into by 1786, "nigger." The pejorative associations of the latter are sourced by the *Oxford English Dictionary* at that date, but implications are a matter of tone and context, and the word seems to carry its full modern freight of contempt and disparagement as it comes from Mather's mouth. He buttonholed young Sam, and told him that a certain person had been very busy taking up the cause of the Negroes, and yet at the same time had treated his father worse than one—and that person was his, Sam's, father. It was one son venting his feelings on another.

Cotton Mather's own attitude to slavery is displayed in a proposal for an all-black congregation he drafted in 1693, though didn't publish until 1714, when he left a copy at Sewall's house for his perusal. The rules of this society included the stipulation that no shelter should be provided for blacks who ran away from their masters; instead, they should be handed over for punishment. And if any slaves should pretend to their masters that they were at meeting when they were really doing something else, their fellow congregants "will faithfully *Inform* their Owners." He seems at least as interested in their status as property as in their spiritual welfare.

Sewall detested ill-feeling and hostility, and when Sam Jr. reported back, as Cotton Mather had known he would, Sewall experienced the same woe and panic as when he was snubbed by Stoughton two years before. In the margin of his diary he wrote: "Opprobrium. Mr Cotton Mather speak hard words of me." But that wasn't the whole story. Sewall had worried about his attitude to disapproval for years, certainly since the reprieve of the pirate. His conduct during the witchcraft trials might well have been influenced by a need to stand firm, an "ambidexter" position, reflecting both a need to defy opprobrium and a desire to be respected by his peers. His public recantation had been the bravest possible exorcism of this inner demon. But his long and painful struggle had made him sensitive to the complexity of his own response to the issue; and in any case, one of the great lessons of the whole crisis had been to heighten awareness of psychological processes, and the tangled motives informing human behavior.

First, he remembered some improving words he had read only that morning: "Sanctified Afflictions are good Promotions." In other words, hardships bestowed by God are for our own benefit. Next, he thought back to his reaction to the recent loss of both his parents, and the comfort provided by Psalm 27:10: "My father and my mother both / though they do me forsake, yet will Jehovah gathering / unto him self me take." The disturbing news from his son had made him yearn for the security of his own parents, and then remember that God would protect him in their absence, and understand that this was consonant with the notion that sufferings are good for the development of the soul. The spiritual logic up to this point was linear and classically Puritan: trust in the Lord.

But for Sewall, examination of the issue didn't end there. One of the legacies of Salem was a critical attitude to religious enthusiasm, a need—to paraphrase Taylor's verse—to wear one's surplice rather than be worn by it. Suddenly, the notion crossed Sewall's mind that his process of thought, and his emotional investment in that process, might in fact be a sort of egotism: "It may be it would be arrogance for me to think that I, as one of Christ's Witnesses, am slain, or ly dead in the street."

He realized he had turned a personal slight into a spiritual drama, which is what one would expect a Puritan to do, since all matters, big or small, good or bad, were seen as part of one's spiritual journey. When Cotton Mather got a toothache, for example, his pain had to have a meaning; in fact, it yielded two. He must have indulged in excessive eating, and he must have spoken evil—teeth being used in the formation of speech. But Sewall's analysis was of a different sort: it was self-reflexive. During the witch crisis, the insistence that large effects were generated by small causes had led to disaster, with evidence about dry skirts in wet weather or the shooing away of a cow seen as relevant to capital charges. Sewall continued to believe, like other Puritans, that the details of life are of crucial importance (we'll see that in the next chapter), but a healthy sense of proportionality is apparent in his thinking here. He was aware of the dangers of exponential acceleration from little to big in the context of religious belief. It might be, he realized, that he had been guilty of pride in attributing his petty distress to his allegiance to Christ, and succumbing to a martyr complex.

Of course, there is nothing more authentically Puritan than a capacity for self-doubt, but Sewall once again seems modern in his need to scrutinize his faith from the outside, so to speak, and question his own motives in this way. This was exactly what his current antagonist, Cotton Mather, had not learned to do, despite the example of the trials. He was only too willing to humble himself and grovel in the dust (in the dust on his study floor, in fact, where he would often lie in self-abasement), but he had not acquired the ironic self-awareness that would enable him to inspect that groveling, and feel doubts about it. When attacked by the "*Sadducee*," Robert Calef, he undertook no serious self-examination, but simply convinced himself that the cavalry would come over the hill any moment: "And I now beleeve, That the *Holy Angels* of my Lord Jesus Christ, whose Operations this impious Man denies, (which is one great Cause of his enmity against mee!) will do a *wonderful Thing* on this occasion!" As it happened, Mather made no mention of the incident in the shop, recording merely that he went in to leave a couple of treatises to be published as *Christianity to the Life*, a title somewhat out of kilter with the ensuing shenanigans.

As soon as Sewall eliminated religious purpose and dignity from his reaction, resentment swooped in to take its place, and he remembered that only eleven days previously, "I sent Mr. Increase Mather a Hanch of very good Venison." He could not resist adding sarcastically, "I hope in that I did not treat him as a Negro." Even while angry thoughts were seething in him, however, he was penning a placatory letter to Cotton, thanking him and his wife for visiting the previous Thursday, mentioning the incident in the shop, and asking for a meeting there the next day at half past nine in the morning, where they could resolve their quarrel in the presence of friends. Sewall could be petty, alarmed, serene, self-questioning, angry, embittered, placatory, in bewildering succession. Because he confronted his crises with his whole personality, he both embodied and transcended the assumptions of his age.

It was rather like a duel. Sewall's detailed record gives us each thrust and parry, three centuries later. At the appointed time, nine thirty, Sewall appeared in Mr. Wilkins's premises with the seconds, Major Walley and Captain Checkley, to meet Cotton Mather. Sewall, Mather's senior by nearly eleven years, made the opening move. "Rebuke not an elder," he told him sternly, quoting the first book of Timothy.

"I considered that," Mather told him.

"You have published a book on kindness." A cunning point, worked out in advance. Sewall knew how much Mather's publications meant to him. "Does your behaviour correspond with it? Or with Christ's laws?"

Mather dodged the issue. "I have spoken with you about my grievance before," he complained.

Sewall had a shrewd interpretation of that reply. Mather was saying that because he had given a warning shot across his bow, he was subsequently entitled to revile him as much as he wanted to behind his back.

Now Mather surrendered to fury: "The Council are liars, hypocrites, tricksters."

Sewall took the opportunity to try a bit of sarcasm. "Does that claim show sufficient meekness?" he asked.

"Yes," Mather unexpectedly replied. Sarcasm is a conspiracy: it needs the other person to acknowledge it. Perhaps Sewall winced at the low blow. Now Mather got to the heart of his complaint: Sewall's criticism of his father for offering to live in Cambridge on condition he didn't have to expound the scriptures. (In other words, Sewall in particular was a liar, hypocrite, trickster.)

Sewall admitted he had said it.

Mather became snide. It was not just a matter of his own grievance. Jonathan Corwin of Reading had taken him to task for even being friends with a man like Sewall (perhaps he was reminding Sewall here that his fellow judges at Salem, Corwin included, had cause to resent his apology). Mr. Corwin had exclaimed, in obvious bafflement and disapproval, "This is the man you dedicate your books to!" Sharp revenge for Sewall's temerity in reminding him about his book on kindness: Cotton Mather is an important author who has lowered himself by associating his works with Sewall.

Sewall tried asking Mather how he would feel if the boot was on the other foot. If Mather had done something he, Sewall, disapproved of in the exercise of his church responsibilities, would it be right to shout about it in the public street?

At this point Cotton Mather became so enraged that Mr. Wilkins tried to usher him to the back of the shop, but he refused to go.

Sewall admonished the apoplectic clergyman: "You have done much unbecoming a Minister of the Gospel." That was his clincher. He had to go off to council, no doubt to Mr. Wilkins's huge relief. There, ironically enough, he found himself authorizing a payment of £25 due to Increase Mather. Also (and the choice of verb gives his feelings away) he "Hammer'd out an Order for a Day of Thanksgiving."

Spitefully, Increase Mather went into Wilkins's bookshop the next day and said (knowing that young Sam would again report back), "If I am a Servant of Jesus Christ, some great Judgment will fall on Capt. Sewall, or his family." However, the feud blew over in the end, as these things will. When Cotton Mather and his father actually read the report of the council meeting they calmed down a little, though their basic grievance continued and was in due course exacerbated when they discovered that Increase's successor at Harvard, none other than Sewall's minister, Samuel Willard, was himself not going to be required to take up residence in the college.

The Mathers had actually been jealous of Sewall's support of Negroes. One of the immediate stimuli that caused Sewall to take this public stance, the case of the slave Adam, had brought him into conflict on another front altogether, since Adam was owned by a fellow member of the bench. In 1694, Judge John Saffin had leased Adam, along with a farm, to a certain Thomas Shepard for a period of seven years. The deal was that if Adam worked "chearfully quietly and industriously" during that term, he would be given his freedom. This was the same arrangement that governed indentured servants, and, as we have seen, often applied to slaves in attempted conformity with Puritan understanding of Old Testament practice.

As the term of the instrument approached, it became clear that Saffin didn't intend to honor it—or rather that he was claiming Adam himself had not honored it. Saffin must have gnashed his teeth at Sewall's repeated references to the first and second Adam, and the self-righteous seventy-five-year-old published a response to Sewall's pamphlet, *A Brief and Candid Answer to a Late Printed Sheet*, attempting to counter Sewall's main arguments and listing the grievances he had against his slave.

Saffin argued against Sewall's claim that Adam's descendants have an equal share in liberty. There were social distinctions, after all; and these he claimed had divine sanction. He referred to a passage in 1 Corinthians in which Paul said that even the lowliest parts of the body have their own indispensable function and therefore should be entitled to "abundant honour" (12:23). Saffin managed to reverse the obvious gist of Paul's argument, claiming it proved that God supported social distinctions, and that it would be a "breach of good manners to treat a Prince like a Peasant." Sewall himself would not be happy, he slyly, and no doubt accurately, suggested, "if we should show him no more Defference than to an ordinary Porter."

Having established to his own satisfaction the biblical basis for social hierarchy, Saffin assigned Negro slaves a place at the bottom of the heap (he had in fact been a slave dealer himself while living in Virginia in his youth). The true ancestry of the Negro race is unimportant, he claimed, since any heathen people can be enslaved; and it was actually a moral process to bring them into a Christian country, where they can be "Eternally Saved." Naturally, Abraham's household arrangements, about which Sewall showed such caution, were a precedent for Saffin. But there was no parallel between the case of Joseph and that of Negro slaves, because the latter were simply unworthy of the comparison. Saffin fancied himself as a poet and general man of letters, and he conducted this argument in a series of despicably racist couplets:

Cowardly and cruel are those Blacks *Innate*
Prone to Revenge, Imp of inveterate hate.
He that exasperates them, soon espies
Mischief and Murder in their very eyes.
Libidinous, Deceitful, False and Rude,
The Spume Issue of Ingratitude.
The Premises consider'd, all may tell,
How near good Joseph *they are Parallel.*

Not surprisingly, Adam had got wind of his owner's intention to renege on the agreement, and while Saffin was out of town in March 1701, he fled. Saffin himself was summoned to Sewall's house on his return and found himself faced not just by Sewall but also by Isaac Addington, secretary to the council. The two men took Saffin to task, telling him that he should give Adam his freedom. As in the case of Sewall's pamphlet, their arguments were pitched on two levels, one reflecting prevailing attitudes—"there was much to be allowed [i.e., excused] in the behaviour of Negroes, who are so ignorant, rude and bruitish"— and one asserting a permanent truth—"liberty was a thing of great importance, even next to life."

The next day, Saffin returned to Sewall's house with heavy-duty company in tow, council member Penn Townsend. Townsend was willing to bind Adam over to appear at the May term of the superior court in Boston. Dick, a free Negro, was offered as surety for Adam's appearance. At this hearing, the case was adjourned to the next superior court at Bristol, since Bristol County was the residence of the parties. In the meantime, on 1 August 1701, Saffin managed to get himself appointed to the Superior Court of Judicature, though a number of deputies disapproved, and Sewall was suspicious of his motives.

Sure enough, Saffin ended up sitting on the bench at Bristol for his own case, and also, apparently, contrived to get one of his tenants onto the jury by bribing the foreman. Thomas Shepard testified to Adam's

"Vile Refrictory" behavior, though other witnesses spoke of his good conduct. Not surprisingly, the jury found Adam guilty. Nevertheless, Sewall was able to persuade his fellow judges to hear the case again, and Adam was remanded to his master pending the Bristol superior court sitting the following year.

For the time being, Adam was leased out to work for a certain Captain Clarke, but this arrangement soon ended in disaster. The two men had a row, and Clarke knocked Adam's pipe out of his mouth and hit him with a stick. The logic of slavery dictated that Adam was responsible for having been assaulted in this way, and Saffin's response was to order him to be transported out of New England, but Secretary Addington ruled that this would be illegal. When the case came up again in September 1702, Adam was sick with smallpox. In November, it was ruled that the case could not be tried because it was founded on Saffin's complaint rather than the king's—in other words, because the administration of justice wasn't impartial but compromised by personal interest (the court was a little behind the times since hearings were in the queen's name now: Anne had succeeded William III in March of that year). The court appointed Thomas Newton and Joseph Hearne to consider Adam's claim for liberty pending a hearing at the Court of Common Pleas, where Adam brought suit against Saffin. Here Saffin again tried to have him transported, but the court ruled he should be left in peace until in due process of law found to be a slave.

Saffin's promotion to the superior court had been a stopgap measure: he was filling the vacancy caused by Stoughton's death. In May 1703, Saffin was elected to the council, which confirmed him in his role as a superior court judge; that same day, not being one to neglect his own interests, he petitioned the council for ownership of Adam. Perhaps this blatant self-serving was just too much for the new governor, Joseph Dudley, because he annulled Saffin's appointment to the council the following day, along with that of several others, on the grounds that different appointees "might have served the Queen better than they did." The council then refused to hear Saffin's case and referred it to the next Court of Sessions for Suffolk. On 1 June, Adam was again arrested, prompting Sewall to try his hand at some retaliatory couplets:

Superanuated Squier, wigg'd and powder'd with pretence,
Much beguiles the just Assembly by his lying Impudence.
None being by, his bold Attorneys push it on with might and main
By which means poor simple Adam sinks to slavery again.

Somehow the clunky metrics catch his spluttering fury at Saffin's attempts to manipulate the judicial process more effectively than the polished heroic couplets of an Alexander Pope ever could. As in the case of Wigglesworth, the very lack of artistry makes the poem more accurate as a record of colonial emotions.

On 2 November 1703, at the Superior Court of Judicature, the case was heard by Sewall, Hathorne, and two other judges. They found in favor of Adam and ruled that "the sd Adam & his heirs be at peace & quiet & free with all their Chattles from the sd John Saffin Esqr & his heirs for Ever." Saffin later appealed to Dudley again, but to no avail (he claimed in his bitterness that Adam had once threatened to wring his neck, and that his legal expenses had been more than £60). It had been a long, tortuous process, but woven like a bright thread through all the legalities was Sewall's vigorous and eloquent support of the slave in his fight for freedom.

Meanwhile, Bastian and Jane had had a daughter, also called Jane. She was baptized the following day. Joseph, Sewall's thirteen-year-old son, was at the meeting, and reported how Bastian held her up in the church. A year later, Sewall reported on the progress of his own fourteenth—and last—child: "Judith is very well weaned, and by a late addition can now shew eight Teeth. Little Jane, Bastian's daughter, died last night 2 hours after midnight." He continued, with the poignant contrast of those two outcomes in his mind, and also perhaps with an awareness of the larger issues raised in his pamphlet and in the ongoing Saffin case, "God is pleased to dispense himself variously."

But if, as a good Puritan, Sewall was prepared to accept inequalities of destiny when they could be traced back to the inscrutable will of God, it continued to be a different story whenever the human dispensation went awry. In 1705, an act was put before the council "for the Better Preventing of a Spurious and Mixt Issue." It would outlaw marriage and fornication between races, with "extraordinary penalties," as Sewall described them, for offenders. "If it be pass'd," he said, "I fear twill be an Oppression provoking to God, and that which will promote Murders and other Abominations." He immediately set to work trying to dilute it, persuading the council to remove any reference to Indians, and to reduce the penalties for Negroes. He also managed to insert a clause that would help blacks who found themselves in the position Bastian and Jane had been in: "And no master shall unreasonably deny marriage to his negro with one of the same nation, any law, usage, or custom to the contrary notwithstanding."

The year before, Sewall had been browsing in a bookshop when he came upon a book called *The Athenian Oracle*, recently published in London, which contained a discussion of the question "Whether Trading for Negros . . . be in it self Unlawful, and especially contrary to the great Law of Christianity." It was another antislavery polemic, one that supported his own pioneering pamphlet; indeed, there is some evidence that Sewall himself had posted the leading question to its authors. Now he decided to extract and republish the piece in the light of the unfair bill on miscegenation. His edition came out on 5 December, the day the bill passed into law. He received "Frowns and hard Words" for his pains, but undeterred wrote to the aged minister John Higginson, thanking him for his support: "By the interposition of this Brest-work, I hope to carry on and manage this enterprise with Safety and Success."

That optimism was ill-founded. A setback occurred a decade later, on 22 June 1716, when Sewall fought unsuccessfully to block the passage of a new bill that rated Indian and Negro slaves, for taxation purposes, in the same category as horses and hogs. Three years after that, Samuel Smith of Sandwich faced trial for killing his Negro. As in the case of Saffin, Sewall was alert to the danger that the judicial process could serve the interests of the privileged and sent a memo and a covering letter to Judge Davenport, one of the justices hearing the case, reminding him that "the poorest Boys and Girls within this Province, such as are of the lowest condition; whether they be English, or Indians, or Ethiopians, They have the same Right to religion and Life, that the Richest Heirs have. And they who go about attempting to deprive them of this Right, they attempt the bombarding of HEAVEN: and the Shells they throw, will fall down upon their own heads." Along with this robust admonition, Sewall enclosed copies of *The Selling of Joseph* and of his extract from *The Athenian Oracle*. At the trial, Smith admitted beating his slave, but claimed that he had died from swallowing his tongue, either while asleep or in a fit of rage. Despite Sewall's intervention, Smith was found not guilty and discharged after paying costs of £5 1s 6d.

While this long battle was going on, Sewall was fighting on another front altogether. He seems farsighted and liberal in his campaign against slavery; in this simultaneous struggle against periwigs he comes across as obsessive, even ridiculous. But it was a cause that consumed as much time and emotional energy as the other, though we have to make an intellectual and imaginative leap in order to begin to understand it. His attack on slavery has a route through to our own time; his assault on periwigs seems ring-fenced by the assumptions of his own.

CHAPTER TWELVE

"Wigg'd and Powder'd with Pretence"

LATE ONE NIGHT IN NOVEMBER 1687, AN INHABITANT OF Boston by the name of William Clendon climbed up into the watch house. The last thing on his mind was keeping guard over his fellow townsfolk during the hours of darkness. Staggering drunkenly through the streets, he had needed a refuge from the chilly air. Sometime during the course of the night, he died.

A miserable end, according to Sewall, the man being "almost eat up with Lice and stupified with Drink and cold." Somewhat gleefully, he reported that the body remained seated in its vantage point for most of the next day, gazed on by passersby. The familiar Samuel Sewall, generous in spirit, quick to mourn even the children of slaves, is strangely absent from this journal entry. The reason lies in Clendon's job description: "Barber and Perriwig-maker."

Wigs, all the rage in the late seventeenth and early eighteenth centuries, were an abomination to Sewall. He noted their appearance among his fellow Bostonians as if they were the early symptoms of some terrible plague. Perhaps, for him, in a religious and moral sense at least, they were (in his poetic attack on John Saffin he described him as "wigg'd and powder'd with pretence"). The year before Clendon's death, Sewall had had to visit Mr. Hayward, the public notary, on business, and took the opportunity of speaking "to him about his cutting off his Hair, and wearing a Perriwig of contrary Colour." The vanity of changing one's image in this way was a direct defiance of Christ's words (slightly misquoted): "Can ye not make one Hair white or black." Sewall also read out a relevant passage from a sermon on the subject by Vincent Alsop, an English minister who had attacked those willing to take a "way of unrighteousness" in pursuit of lost youth, "a false, an imaginary, hour." All poor Hayward could offer against this heavy artillery was a limp excuse: "He alleges, The Doctors advised him to do it."

Sewall was by no means alone in his horror at the sight of pates adorned with artificial hair. The Puritan pamphleteer William Prynne inveighed against wigs in 1628, long before the Restoration made them fashionable: condemning those "who dislike the quantitie, or qualitie of that Haire, which God's wisdome hath assigned to them, and therefore purchase the haire excrements of some other person, to Adorne and Beautifie their heads with all." The College Laws of Harvard in 1655 didn't deal with hair excrements as such but took a strong line against fussy hairstyles: students were forbidden "to weare Long Haire, Locks or foretops, nor to use Curling, Crisping, parting or powdering their hair." In 1677, John Mulliner, of Northampton in England, wrote an impassioned tract entitled *A Testimony against Periwigs and Periwig-Making* in which he explains why he left off his "*Imployment of* Borders [hairpieces] *and* Periwig-making" and was moved to burn a wig in front of the two men he employed, by way of setting an example. In this mood of renunciation, he also set fire to his musical instruments, including a treble viol. He saw a recent fire in his town as the result of a general failure of the populace to repudiate such frivolities. Increase Mather went so far as to suggest that the wearing of "monstrous and horrid Perriwigs" by men, and borders and false locks by women, had angered God so much that it had helped to bring about King Philip's War. While wigs can't be directly blamed for the Darien disaster, the mountain of them the Scottish colonists brought along were an index of their utter cluelessness.

Some of Sewall's early sightings, first symptoms of the epidemic to come. On 8 July 1677, there was a sensation at the South meetinghouse. A Quaker woman interrupted the service in the middle of the sermon. In the seventeenth century, the Quakers were a much more confrontational and enthusiastic sect than they subsequently became, and repeatedly ran foul of the New England authorities. The Massachusetts General Court made Quakerism a capital crime in 1658, and two years later a Quaker missionary called Mary Dyer, who persisted in defying the authorities and who returned to the province after being exiled from it, was hanged on Boston Common. The intruder on this later occasion had made her face as black as ink and was wearing a canvas frock; worse still, the imp of the perverse had "her hair disheveled and loose like a periwig," nature aping the careful abandonment of art.

In 1685, two new members of the South Church congregation, Benjamin Davis and Samuel Checkley, were received into it with periwigs on their heads. Shortly after this dubious induction came the confrontation with Mr. Hayward, and the appropriately lice-ridden death of the poor wigmaker. However, in the next act of the drama of Bostonian head arrangements, the tables were suddenly turned on Samuel Sewall himself—as sometimes seemed to happen when he occupied what appeared, to him at least, to be the moral high ground.

There was a time lag between English fashion and American adoption of it, and wigs weren't widespread in New England until around 1690. In March 1691, Sewall attended a sermon by Cotton Mather on the subject of the servant who threw in his portion with the hypocrites. A hypocrite, Mather claimed, was someone who strained at a gnat and swallowed a camel (Matthew 24:48–51). You could recognize him by the bulge in his throat. Then he gave an example: a person might be zealous in his hostility toward an innocent fashion, yet not worry at all about committing a grave immorality. Sewall knew exactly what he was getting at: "I expected not to hear a vindication of Perriwigs in Boston Pulpit by Mr Mather." The text concerned an evil servant who had smote his fellows and got drunk, and then been consigned to join the hypocrites; the last thing Sewall had expected was to find that story being fired off in his direction. He regularly did his share of watch duty, patrolling the poorer parts of town to "prevent and redress disorders" and taking a keen interest in the goings-on in ordinaries and inns. His response was to ask the Lord to help him know and do His will, "that my Heart and [charming touch, this] Head may be his."

What made the sermon particularly disagreeable to Sewall was the

fact that hypocrisy—that is, pretending to be something you are not—
was precisely his own grievance against wig wearers. Perhaps Cotton
Mather was the hypocrite, or at least he was speaking out of self-interest.
In the one portrait we have of him, painted near the end of his life, his
own wig cascades like a great waterfall down each side of his head.

Cotton Mather (1663–1728). Mezzotint by Peter Pelham, Boston.
MHS #2454.

It became a battle, waged for the sake of Puritan decorum. On 13
October 1696, Sewall wrote, "Mr. Simms dined with me to day, spake

of the assaults he had made upon periwigs; and of his Repulses. Seem'd to be in good sober sadness." Good sober sadness was just the frame of mind in which to undertake assaults, and receive repulses, in this difficult area of human conflict.

In May of the following year, Sewall entertained Hannah Dustin, Indian captive, Indian killer, and—most significantly of all—Indian scalper. Ironically, the cutting of Indian hair was seen as an important part of the conversion process. Sewall, though unusually tolerant of Native American customs and always anxious to discover homologues to Jewish anthropology, nevertheless drew the line at the women's hairstyles: "The Hair upon the foreheads of the young females is cut in such a fashion from time to time, that one may defie what form Nature has plac'd them in."

Shortly after entertaining Mrs. Dustin, Sewall went off on his judicial rounds to Salem where the patriarchal pastor, John Higginson, presented him with a treatise he had written on the subject of periwigs. When Higginson died twelve years later at the grand age of ninety-three, his fellow Salem minister Nicholas Noyes celebrated his defiant baldness in a suitably terse couplet:

For Rich Aray car'd not a Figg
And wore ELISHA'S Perriwigg.

Elisha's "periwig" was baldness. He was the Old Testament prophet ridiculed on account of being follically challenged: ". . . and as he was going up by the way, there came forth little children out of the city, and mocked him, and said unto him, Go up, thou bald head; go up, thou bald head." Elisha failed to adopt the same stoical attitude to the situation as Noyes celebrated in his New England successor, Elisha's reaction being to curse the cheeky infants in the name of the Lord, so that two she-bears promptly came out of the woods "and tare forty and two children of them," a pretty drastic punishment for naughty behavior, even by Old Testament standards (2 Kings 2:24–25).

As the seventeenth century drew to its end, Sewall began to lose his own hair. He was in his late forties, after all. The problem came to a head, so to speak, in mid-December 1699 when he was confined to bed with an ague in his face. There had been some cold weather, including a severe ice storm on the last day of November that had broken down many trees—"my little Cedar [is] almost quite mortified" (he had an almost parental love for trees he'd planted). His illness must have been quite serious because he was visited by a whole posse of New England dignitaries: his pastor, Samuel Willard, who led prayers for him, Cotton Mather, Moses Fisk, and Ezekiel Cheever. Perhaps as a result of all this heavy duty moral support, he shortly had ease and "was let out of the stocks."

His solution to his newfound vulnerability was a black cap, almost a sort of bonnet, to fit over the top, sides, and back of his head. No doubt, having taken a stand on the matter of wigs, he felt somewhat self-conscious appearing in public in this headgear for the first time, which he did on 21 December. "Went to Lecture, wearing my black cap," he solemnly recorded, without saying anything about the reception he met with.

Another eighteen months were to pass before Sewall found himself facing the greatest periwig crisis of his life. It involved Sam Jr.'s close friend, Josiah Willard, son of his pastor. Josiah was considerably more intellectual than Sam and a graduate of Harvard, but that didn't prevent the two young men from getting into a number of scrapes together. In the spring of 1700, for example, they nearly met with disaster on a fishing trip in Boston harbor with some other friends. They saw a ship coming in and immediately rowed toward it to find out who was on board—arrivals were likely to be people you knew, or knew of, or would get to know in due time.

The Boston ship was traveling at a good pace with a fair wind behind it, and the captain rapped out orders at the hapless young men in their boat (Sam was twenty-one, Josiah nineteen), who did the clear opposite of his instructions, and collided with the ship. Their mast was broken off, the boat filled with water, and two of them, Samuel Gaskill and Josiah himself, fell overboard. Gaskill couldn't swim and soon disappeared beneath the surface. Luckily, a local man named Richard Fifield jumped into his boat and rowed out to the scene of the accident.

Gaskill's hat bobbing on the water marked the point where he'd gone under, and Fifield was able to haul him and Josiah out. Meanwhile, Sam and the others scrambled to safety up the big ship's rigging. It was the second time he had nearly drowned in the company of Josiah Willard, and just the month before Sewall had recorded the drowning of three young men who "went in a Canoo a Gunning before day-light."

Josiah spelled danger, and one day in 1701 news came that he'd compounded his acts of folly by shaving off a full head of hair and adorning himself with a wig. Promptly the following morning, Sewall trotted around to the Willard household and informed Josiah's mother of his concern. She called her son down to explain himself. Sewall asked, "What Extremity had forced him to put off his own hair, and put on a Wigg?" Slightly sarcastically, he was inviting the medical defense, but Josiah didn't bite. It was an aesthetic matter: "None at all. But his Hair was streight, and . . . it parted behinde." He was willing to take his much older and more formidable adversary on, arguing "that men might as well shave their hair off their head, as off their face." This didn't cut any ice for Sewall. Shaving wasn't a valid precedent. Women and young males don't have facial hair at all, so it isn't an integral part of human identity: "Men were men before they had hair on their faces, (half of mankind have never any)."

Then came the crunch argument. "God seems to have ordain'd our Hair as a Test," Sewall explained, "to see whether we can bring our minds to be content at his finding: or whether we would be our own Carvers, Lords, and come no more at him."

The word "carvers" seems to be a particularly significant one. Sewall is surely thinking of the biblical injunction against worshipping graven images. Cutting off one's own hair and replacing it with a wig involves the attempt to re-create, and therefore ultimately to create, oneself as a physical entity, blasphemously assuming God's prerogative, and appointing oneself one's Lord. The temptation exists because hair doesn't register pain: "If disliked our Skin, or Nails; 'tis no Thanks to us, that for all that, we cut them not off: Pain and danger restrain us." But meddling with hair apparently poses no physical risks, despite the terrible spiritual ones involved.

There was a lot at stake in this debate because Josiah was planning to follow his father into the church. Sewall reminded him that his calling would be to teach men self-denial, and listed distinguished members of the community who had resisted the blandishments of periwigs: Josiah's own father, his brother Simon (the same who had once knocked a glass of spirits off a joint stool while picnicking with the Sewalls on Hogg Island), Ebenezer Pemberton, Michael Wigglesworth, Thomas Oakes, Oliver Noyes, Thomas Brattle. "Allow me," Sewall asked, after spelling out this impressive register of allies, "to be so far a *Censor Morum* [arbiter of manners] for this end of town."

Josiah said that he would stop wearing his wig when his hair had grown back. Or at least "seem'd to say." Sewall could sniff intransigence in the wind. A day or two later, Pastor Willard soothed his ruffled feathers. He'd had a word with Josiah, who'd confirmed he was willing to discard his wig as soon as his hair was long enough to cover his ears. If he, Willard Sr., had known what was going on, he'd have put a stop to it. He recounted a nice bit of parental moral strategy: Mrs. Willard, it turned out, *had* known all along of Josiah's intention, in the way that mothers somehow do, but was frightened to order him not to carry it out in case he did so anyway, which would have compounded the fault by adding disobedience to it.

But Sewall failed as *Censor Morum* with respect to Josiah Willard. On Sunday, 30 November, Josiah took the pulpit at the South Church as deputy for his father's assistant minister, Mr. Pemberton. He was still wearing his wig.

Sewall had been warned in advance and absented himself in protest, going instead to the Manifesto Church. This had been set up the year previously with a list (or manifesto) of more liberal policies than the other Congregational churches in Boston, in particular allowing right of membership to be based on visible virtue (the covenant of works) rather than testimony of a conversion experience (the covenant of grace). Progressive and logical Thomas Brattle, dismantler of the misconceptions behind the Salem witch trials, paralleled Sewall's role as precentor here, setting the tunes for the Psalms.

Sewall was a devoted member of his own, orthodox, congregation but had been driven to make this gesture by the gravity of young Willard's misbehavior: "He that contemns the Law of Nature is not fit to be a publisher of the Law of Grace" (in those pre-evolutionary days, the laws of nature and grace were interlocking and compatible rather than in conflict with each other). As usual, however, he sought to accentuate the positive. Quite apart from making public his feelings on the matter of Josiah's delinquency, he was pleased to set an example by holding communion with a church that despite its radicalness was in line with the New England tradition of renouncing the cross at baptism and refusing to celebrate holy days. The pioneering congregation greatly appreciated his presence: he was *Censor Morum* after all. As it turned out, Josiah didn't follow the ministerial path. Instead, undeterred by his escapades with Sam Jr., he became a sea captain and was twice captured by privateers. In due course he was appointed secretary of the Province of Massachusetts, with an office in Faneuil Hall.

Wigs continued to spring up all over New England, like a species of noxious, hardy weed. Sewall glumly noted his sightings in his diary. In January 1704, it was Major John Walley. Three days later the delinquent major was one of a small group of men who met at Sewall's house before going off to visit the "disorderly poor" of Boston, the others being Constable Franklin, Robert Calef (as usual, Sewall was able to forget bad feeling), and Captain Timothy Clark. Before they left on their rounds, Captain Clark put his wig on (the weather had been snowy). Sewall sternly referred him to a verse in Isaiah about the way certain proud people tried to tart up their surroundings: "The bricks are fallen down, but we will build with hewn stones: the sycamores are cut down, but we will change them into cedars" (9:10). Captain Clark "seem'd startled," as well he might.

Two years later, another acquaintance, Jonathan Belcher, succumbed. Belcher's excuse was that he needed more than his own hair as protection on his journey to Portsmouth, New Hampshire, where he was getting married, and that "other provision" (a barb directed at Sewall's black cap) would hardly be suitable for a wedding. Sewall noted that Belcher had possessed a fine head of hair, though he conceded it had grown a little thin.

Soon enough the *Censor* had trouble of his own. On his legal rounds a couple of months later, he was in Plymouth with Major Walley (no doubt still bewigged). Sewall walked to the local meetinghouse, then returned to his lodgings so exhausted that he didn't pray with his serving man, but instead retired to bed. He couldn't find a chamber pot, so called out for one. When he used it in bed during the course of the night, the bottom came off, causing pee to run all over him. "I was amaz'd, not knowing the bottom was out till I felt it in the Bed. The Trouble and Disgrace of it did afflict me." As soon as daylight came, he called his man, who made a fire and warmed him a clean nightshirt— "and I put it on and was comfortable." No matter how trivial or embarrassing an episode, it could only tend in one direction: "How unexpectedly a man may be expos'd! There's no security but in God, who is to be sought by Prayer."

That October, Benjamin Wadsworth wore a periwig to the midweek service, the Thursday lecture, to the distress of ninety-two-year-old Ezekiel Cheever, colonial New England's most celebrated schoolmaster, whom Sewall visited, as a gesture of moral support, the following day. Two years later, Sewall was attending his deathbed, and gave an account that is warm and touching even by his standards, illuminating both the humanity and the spirituality of the two men. In August 1708, the old man had gone to hear Cotton Mather preach. Sewall understood the significance of the occasion: "This is the last of his going abroad." The next day, Sewall visited him. He spoke, and Cheever asked him to speak again. This time it struck a chord. "Now I know you," he said, and "speaking cheerily mention'd my Name." Sewall asked a blessing for himself and his family. Cheever, graceful in two senses of the word, told him he was blessed already, and it couldn't be reversed. Nevertheless, as Sewall left, Cheever asked blessing for him.

A week later, Sewall visited him on his way to the lecture, thanking him for all his kindness. Cheever was affectionate, taking his hand several times. He gave his friend the distilled essence of his long New England odyssey (he had come over from England in 1637, when he was twenty-three): "The Afflictions of God's people, God by them did as a Goldsmith, Knock, knock, knock; knock, knock, knock, to finish the plate: It was to perfect them not to punish them." Years of teaching experience behind the exposition, seventy years of it; years of encountering and trying to cope with human suffering, ninety odd years of that, culminating in the lovely, optimistic simile. Suffering put the final patina on the human soul: there was a kind of alchemy in pain. It was news from the very gate of heaven, and Sewall hurried off to relay it to Mr. Pemberton, who was to preach that day.

The following afternoon, Cheever was much weaker. He called his daughter in and asked her if the family was composed. They guessed he was worried because there had not been any prayers that day, and asked Sewall if he would lead them. He did not want to, believing that Mr. Cheever's teaching assistant should be sent for to do the honors; that would be "most natural, homogeneous." But they insisted, so he prayed. Afterward, he told Cheever that the last enemy was death, and God had made that a friend too. Cheever put his hand out of bed and held it up to show he understood and agreed, like a child in one of the classes he had taught right up to the end. He sucked a piece of orange, then put it neatly in his mouth and chewed it, afterward taking the fibrous part out again.

Perhaps, for us, that's where the true alchemy can be found: in the human homely detail, observed with kind eyes that make it precious, the dying man's careful transfer of the orange segment to his mouth ("orderly" is the adverb Sewall used); the removal of the intractable part (the "core," as Sewall called it) after the goodness of this last of earth's fruits had been chewed out. Seeing his pleasure in the orange, Sewall brought along the best figs he could find after dinner, along with a dish of stewed fruit, but by this time Cheever was beyond speech. He died that night.

Sewall wrote a little obituary in his diary, detailing the main facts of Cheever's life, and concluding: "A rare instance of Piety, Health, Strength, Serviceableness. The Wellfare of this Province was much upon his Spirit. He abominated Perriwigs."

On 19 October 1713, Mr. Winslow arrived in town and attended council in his own hair. The next day, "he appears with a Flaxen Wigg. I was griev'd to see it, he had so comly a head of black Hair." Just days before, Sewall had inspected the bodies of a pair of conjoined twin girls; a lesson perhaps that we should respect the formal integrity of nature. A couple of weeks later, Colonel Thomas Noyes made an appearance in a "swash Flaxen Wigg." Two years after that it was Mr. Pemberton's turn, Sewall's own minister also choosing to appear in flaxen. In 1717, Thomas Prince arrived back in Boston after years of traveling and preaching abroad. His first act was to attend a service at South Church. Sewall himself was in the congregation, but because Prince wasn't in his thoughts, and because he was wearing not only a wig but a russet coat, Sewall didn't recognize him.

That was the problem in a nutshell. Wigs alienated the familiar; they distorted one's perception. (The fact that in 1688 Increase Mather had avoided arrest when he left his house because he had disguised himself in a wig and a long white cloak and thereby discombobulated "one of Randolph's creatures" who was lying in wait for him only served to prove the point.) Just six months before, Sewall had mourned Prince's apparent loss on the ship *Amity*, only to discover that he had missed both the boat and an untimely death. Now, in quite another sense, Prince had gone missing. In one of his notebooks, Sewall had transcribed a long diatribe against periwigs by his friend Nicholas Noyes: "A man with his Hair cut off, and anothers put on, looketh not as he did before . . . So that he that wears a Perriwig doth in effect put on a Vizzard, and disguiseth himself." At the same time, the disguise will be futile. You can't escape who you are. The discontinuity between a man's natural coloring and his prosthetic adornment will be such that "he that hath skill in Physiognomy, shall be able to know that this hair could not grow upon that head, no more than Salt-Marsh hay can grow upon a hill."

Even as old age approached, the preoccupation with wigs continued. In 1722, Sewall wrote to Solomon Stoddard, the great liberal Congregationalist of western Massachusetts and grandfather of Jonathan Edwards (who would one day repudiate that liberalism in his heroic attempt to reassert old Puritan verities), asking permission to reprint a letter about periwigs. On the same day, he sent a letter to the Reverend

Hugh Adams, minister at Oyster River, New Hampshire. Adams had once appeared before Sewall in court, when bringing an action of defamation against an innkeeper named Ebenezer Hawes. Hawes, described by his affectionate fellow citizens as "the most forwardest, forthputtingest and noblest man that wee have in our town," had won the day at an earlier hearing, declaring that the court rated Adams no more highly "than a little black dogg." This time Adams prevailed, but that didn't prevent Sewall from meting out some stern advice: "Seeing you have Justice done you, hope it will incline you to Govern your Tongue, and govern your Pen." Government of Adam's pen was on the agenda on this occasion too, the subject being his verses against periwigs, which adumbrated the theory that those wearing them were likely to be scalped by Indians. Sewall's editorial advice evokes a strangely exotic and wide-ranging poem: ". . . earnestly advised him wholly to obliterat Zimri and Cozbi; Names and Text. Leave out Madam Maintenon; I have heard no such character of her."

Three months later, he was writing to his nephew Samuel Sewall *de Stephano* as he called him, since he was the son of his brother Stephen. It is a charming and affectionate letter on what might be conceived to be a related subject, that of wearing spectacles: "Well! But Cousin, By Counsel learned in the Law, I am advised that a man can't be entituled to the use of Spectacles, under Fifty years of Age; and you have not quite run out Thirty three." But in fact he has no problem with this. After all, in a sense spectacles do the opposite of wigs. Instead of replacing part of the body, they restore it to its previous utility. Perhaps remembering his own self-consciousness when he first appeared in public wearing his black cap, the doting uncle assures his namesake that he has nothing to fear from public scrutiny: "So that I am surpris'd to hear how dexterously you put them on, and how handsomely you wear them! Nay, I am informed the Beauty of it has been charming to the whole Town."

SEWALL'S CRUSADE against slavery seems noble and even modern. By contrast, there's something absurd about his obsession with the evils of the periwig, even though the fashion itself now seems foolish too. His attitude comes over as petty and neurotic, like Cotton Mather's assumption that a toothache must be a punishment for evil speech (though somehow Sewall manages to give charm and warmth even to his idées fixes, like some puritanical oyster covering its irritant in pearl).

Though, as we saw in the previous chapter, the post-Salem Sewall tried to get some sense of proportion in his thinking and avoid the trap of religious excess and enthusiasm, he remained enough of a Puritan to have a sense that any of life's details could be significant. As Increase Mather put it: "*Hence see the reason why little inconsiderable things do occasion great matters to be brought to pass amongst men in the world.* It is because he that sits upon the throne doth wonderfully over rule all. He maketh little matters like the small wheel of a clock which sets all the rest a going or like the hinges of a great gate upon which all turns."

In an early journal, Michael Wigglesworth told how he was troubled by the fact that a neighbor let a door of his house swing back and forth in the wind. He had mentioned it to him, and the man made light of it. This sent Wigglesworth into paroxysms of uncertainty and even despair. Perhaps the fact that he had got involved meant that he wanted to meddle in other people's affairs. There might be a good reason why the door should be left to swing. Yet perhaps he should do something after all. The quandary made him feel that God was eclipsing the "sweet beam's of his love, he hideth his face and I am troubled." That is a perfect example of the sort of egotistic self-flagellation that Sewall had rejected when he was smarting from Cotton Mather's wrath, religious enthusiasm that leads to a martyr complex. But there was another side to the story. Wigglesworth believed the hinges of an annoying door might also be hinges of that invisible great gate on which the largest moral questions turned; and behind that belief is a sense that all the details of the world are knitted together in a coherent way that makes each one unique and irreplaceable.

A good way to evaluate the relevance of this perspective is to apply the test of time. A century and a half later, the poet Emily Dickinson offered herself as in some respects the heir to this aspect of the Puritan sensibility, with her sharp eye for the significant smallnesses of life:

"Faith" is a fine invention
When Gentlemen can see—
But Microscopes *are prudent*
In an Emergency. (Poem 185)

But what about Walt Whitman, the celebrated "disgraceful" poet as she called him (no doubt ironically, because there was nothing puritanical about her moral judgment), the man who loafs and invites his soul? "I lean and loafe at my ease observing a spear of summer grass." On the face of it, his self-proclaimed lazy and casual attitude to life is as far as can be from the stern notice to visitors that hung over the door of Cotton Mather's study: BE SHORT. But when Whitman declared, "I believe a leaf of grass is no less than the journey-work of the stars," or "there is no object so soft but it makes a hub for the wheel'd universe," he was declaring his own Puritan descent. He too celebrated the way inconsiderable things can occasion great matters to be brought to pass in the world. Sewall's complaint was that wearers of periwigs are implying dissatisfaction with the body God gave them; Whitman made very much the same argument but simply used more provocative examples:

I do not press my fingers across my mouth,
I keep as delicate around the bowels as around the head and heart,
Copulation is no more rank to me than death is.

The closed and restrictive Puritans helped to make it possible for Whitman to articulate his barbaric yawp, his yes to life, his openness to all experience.

This leveling tendency in the Puritans' perspective did not inform their social organization. There was a clear class system in colonial New England, and John Saffin had been accurate enough in his suggestion that a man like Sewall, however tolerant and generous, would be taken aback if treated with no more deference than a porter (though as we have seen, Sewall's siblings and children could serve relatively humble apprenticeships as part of their preparation for life). There were even sumptuary laws in place to prevent the lower orders from buying expensive clothes, in case they were mistaken for their betters. But the colonists' rejection of religious hierarchy, their belief that God's grace cut across class distinctions, and their respect for the significance of life's smallest details, ultimately helped to bring about the democratic principles of a later generation. One respect in which Sewall (along with other Puritans) certainly anticipated Whitman's earthy egalitarianism was in his refusal to use the title "saint," as in Saint Luke, on the grounds that it wasn't scriptural, and was "absurd and partial." He rejected such hierarchy, arguing it would lead to the celebration of holy days. All through his life he rejoiced when he saw shops open and deliveries being made on Christmas Day. He extended his objection to secular celebrations too, particularly April Fool's day, writing to his old friend Ezekiel Cheever on the subject on 1 April 1708, just months before Cheever's death. Here is Sewall the Puritan at his most grumpy and intolerant. "If stated anniversary days for solemn Religious exercises, are unwarrantable," he sternly argued, "Without controversy, anniversary days for sinfull vanities, are damnable." The nub: "I have heard a child of Six years old say within these 2 or 3 days; That one must tell a man his Shoes were unbuckled (when they were indeed buckled) and then he would stoop down to buckle them; and then he was an April Fool." It's hard to avoid the suspicion that precisely this had happened to Sewall himself, the well-upholstered judge folding himself futilely in the middle while some gleeful urchin looked on (otherwise, surely, it would have made more sense to write to the schoolmaster in advance of the actual day in question, to give him time to warn his pupils). There is distinct cantankerousness in Sewall's final remark: "If you think it convenient, as I hope you will, Insinuat into your Scholars, the defiling and provoking nature of such a Foolish practice: and take them off from it."

Sewall did not want to set apart particular individuals or particular days: everybody, every moment, was equally important for him, as for other Puritans. It was this sense of existential focus and urgency that drove Edwards's sermon "Sinners in the Hands of an Angry God": "And it would be no wonder if some person, that now sits here, in some seat of this meetinghouse, in health, quiet and secure, should be there [in hell] before tomorrow morning." Sewall took notes of a similar sermon while on his judicial circuit in 1716. It was preached by Peter Thacher, minister at Weymouth, who told his congregation that it would be great folly to defer their repentance until their deathbed. If they take that lazy and cowardly course they "run a dreadfull Hazard. The delaying this Sabbath, may be your Ruine. God only can help you to Repent; will you not take his Now!"

The Puritans had to keep faith with God's Now, the privileged but fleeting moment. Whitman would simply continue this assault on hierarchy, flattening out human categories—"I do not call one greater and one smaller, / That which fills its period and place is equal to any"—and advocating the primacy of the immediate moment:

> *There was never any more inception than there is now,*
> *Nor any more youth or age that there is now,*
> *And will never be any more perfection than there is now,*
> *Nor any more heaven and hell than there is now.*

The Puritans bequeathed the modern world many of the democratic principles behind its social and political institutions; they also encouraged us to see the individual phenomena of life freshly and without categorical assumptions, however doctrinaire and blinkered they sometimes seem to have been themselves. The other side of Sewall's extended war on periwigs was his desire to keep his attention and his grip on his world as it was, without vanity or evasiveness, to accept God's Now.

CHAPTER THIRTEEN

"Impartial Light"

❧❧❧

*T*HEIR FATHERS AND MOTHERS HAD COME OVER THE OCEAN to seek a city on a hill. But that city was receding into the past, because the present could never live up to it. "What's the meaning . . . of your Pancakes, of your Friters?" demanded Increase Mather. "To my knowledge, the first Generation of Christians came into this Wilderness with hopes that their Posterity here would never be corrupted with such vain Customs. Ask such of the old Standers as are yet living, if it were not so."

The Puritans' nonhierarchical way of perceiving the objects around them meant that pancakes and fritters, like wigs and banging doors, could be taken perfectly seriously as threats to the moral and religious basis of their community. They looked back wistfully and unironically to a time when no one would dream of eating pancakes to mark the beginning of Lent (though, of course, when in Rome . . . ; Sewall had thoroughly enjoyed Lent cakes, stuffed full of currants, during his trip to Oxford many years previously). But the daily experience of individual lives told another story, a much more pragmatic and uncertain one, involving the grind of establishing and maintaining a community between the stormy Atlantic, with all the political uncertainties that lay beyond it, and the continental wilderness, with its savage inhabitants.

For Samuel Sewall, as New England's first century gave way to its second, the task was to keep faith with the original vision while coping with the challenges life threw at him. Here he is, operating on three fronts: dealing with the Indians on one side, those embodiments of the wilderness; with pirates on the other, products of international tension and antagonism; and with family and social concerns in between.

IN THE SUMMER of 1699, Boston jail was crammed with pirates, including the most famous of them all, Captain Kidd. His story hinges on a conflict between private and public interests (after all, Massachusetts Bay itself was originally founded as a commercial enterprise). In 1695, he went to England to negotiate a royal commission as a privateer. An article of agreement was drawn up with the Earl of Bellomont, soon to be governor of Massachusetts, under which Kidd received the royal warrant, Bellomont provided the lion's share of the cost of buying and fitting a ship, and profits were to be distributed amongst the interested parties. Crew members would get six hundred pieces of eight for the loss of an arm, one hundred for an eye: the piratical props of patch and hook had a precise price tag.

But despite this businesslike arrangement, Kidd and his crew descended into piracy in the Far East, arousing the wrath of the East India Company. Kidd actually murdered one of his own men. The ship's gunner, William Moore, was sitting on deck grinding a chisel and talking to his fellows about capturing a nearby Dutch ship. Kidd called him a lousy dog; Moore replied that if he was, it was Kidd who'd made him one. Kidd picked up a wooden bucket with iron hoops and hit Moore such a savage blow that he died. Kidd wasn't fazed: "I have good Friends in England, that will bring me off for that." In due course, most of his men deserted and Kidd decided to take advantage of the situation by returning to America with the few sailors he had left, blaming his absent crew for any crimes that had come to the notice of the authorities.

Kidd arrived off the American coast at a time of great excitement caused by the escapades of another pirate, Joseph Bradish. Bradish had participated in a mutiny on the ship *Adventure* while it was moored in the Spice Islands. While the captain, Thomas Gullock, was ashore, Bradish took over and made off with a substantial cargo. He anchored off Block Island and scuppered the ship; men and booty were smuggled ashore on sloops, where they split the loot, and scattered over New England on horseback.

By the time Kidd in turn arrived off Block Island in June 1699, Bradish and a fellow pirate, the one-eyed Tee Witherley, were locked up in Boston jail, which was in the charge of one of Bradish's kinsmen, Caleb Ray. After a short spell inside, the pirates were sprung from the prison by a young woman called Kate Price. The following November, Sewall was one of four judges who heard the case against Caleb Ray and Kate Price (along with that of an Indian called James Speen who was alleged to have acted as the pirates' guide). Ray was found not guilty, and the other two were discharged.

Meanwhile, the new governor, Lord Bellomont, had his work cut out trying to decide how to handle the awkward presence just off the coast of his business colleague, Captain Kidd. He wrote to him reassuringly, offering a sympathetic reception in Boston, and taking an optimistic view of the outcome: "I make no manner of doubt but to obtaine the King's pardon for you . . . tho this I declare before hand that whatever treasure or goods you bring hither I will not meddle with . . . they shall be left with Such trusty as the council advise until I receive order from England."

Bellomont admitted that he had hoodwinked Kidd into returning to American shores: "Menacing him would not bring him but rather wheedling and that way I took." He stood to gain a larger share of Kidd's booty if he was proved to be a pirate than if he was vindicated and the treasure divided as per their original contract, because by making the arrest he was entitled to a third of any valuables he seized. Bellomont emphasized his zeal to punish pirates by offering a reward of one hundred pieces of eight for the recapture of Bradish and Witherley. This propelled an Indian sachem called Essacambuit, who'd been visiting Boston on behalf of the Kennebec tribe, into hot pursuit of the two renegades as they headed for wild country to the north.

Kidd, having salted much of his booty away in various hiding places along the New England coast like some nautical squirrel, made his case at a number of appearances before the council in early July, but Bellomont committed him to prison anyway. Sewall, with four others, was ordered to take responsibility for Kidd's treasure, to act as the trustees Bellomont had promised. The world of lurid seafaring adventure had intersected with the orderly procedures of Sewall's civic responsibilities in New England.

There were "Gold, Pearls &c." in an iron chest along with "40 Bails of east-India Goods, 13 hogsheads, chests and case," as Sewall described the spoils, as well as "one Negro Man, and Venturo Resail, an East-Indian born at Ceilon." On 25 July, Sewall took it upon himself to show Lady Bellomont around Boston. They rode up to Cotton Hill, and as they "came down again through the Gate I ask'd my Lady's Leave that now I might call it Bellomont Gate. My Lady laugh'd, and said, What a Complement he puts on me! With plesauncy." Sewall, custodian of treasure stolen in exotic waters, now the courtier, taking his ungainly bow. Perhaps he pinked up at my lady's "plesauncy."

In October, Bradish and Witherley were captured in Maine and brought back to jail in Boston. William III had been "very pleased" to hear of Kidd's capture, and the ship *Advice* was sent from England to bring him and the other pirates back for trial. Bellomont convened the council to approve their dispatch to England.

Courtier though he liked to be on occasion, Sewall was willing to cross the authorities on matters of legal principle (and indeed on matters of moral and religious principle as well), and did so now. He told the council that he knew of no powers he had to send men out of the province. The Boston courts were English; why should their prisoners be sent over the Atlantic to be dealt with in the mother country? (Behind that argument lay the contrary notion that American courts had separate loyalties and responsibilities and should handle business in their own way.) Since Bellomont wanted Kidd as far away as possible, Sewall's intervention was the last thing he needed.

In any case, Sewall had the support of only two members of the council, so Kidd, Bradish, Witherley, and another pirate called Kelley were put aboard the *Advice*. Twelve days later the treasure was shipped off too, ironically enough on Kidd's own sloop the *San Antonio*, to Sewall's enormous relief: "I look upon it as a great Mercy of God, that the

Store-house has not been broken up, no fire has happened." The weight of gold agreed precisely with the original record, and Sewall scurried about finalizing the paperwork. The *San Antonio* rode at anchor beyond the outward wharf of Boston Harbor, and Captain Winn of the *Advice*, who was in charge of the transportation, wouldn't supply a receipt until he'd seen the goods arrive on board, so Sewall watched anxiously while the treasure was taken out. Captain Gullock, victim of Bradish's depredations, disapproved so vehemently of the dispatch of his own consignment of treasure he spent the night in jail for his insolence. It was the Crown who profited from all this booty in the end: Kidd's treasure yielded £6,471, which went toward the building of Greenwich Hospital.

Bradish, Witherley, and Kelley were promptly tried and executed after their arrival in England; Kidd's due process, because of those important connections of which he had boasted, was a more leisurely affair, and it took a year before he finally faced trial, when he was found guilty of murder and piracy. When he was executed the rope broke, so he was hanged twice. Sewall, regretting his earlier reprieve of another pirate, had longed for this day, "when the Earth and Sea shall be cleared of such professed Enemies of God and man."

IN 1699, two years after dedicating *Phaenomena* to the governor of the New England Company, Sewall reaped his reward and became one of its commissioners. The company took it for granted that the best that could be done for Native Americans was to provide them with Christian beliefs and European values and customs, though at least that agenda assumed some sort of equalization of condition and status at the end of the road; for Sewall, by contrast, the final outcome would be a mystical reunion of the lost tribes of Israel, the inauguration of a religious millennium.

The company's most extraordinary achievement, Eliot's Indian Bible, sums up both its ambition and its limitations. The word of the Lord could be accommodated to the Algonquian tongue, but only in the expectation that the Indians in turn would ultimately be accommodated to the word of the Lord. Sewall enthusiastically welcomed the second edition of the Bible in 1685, and as we shall see, did what he could to bring about a third one in the new century.

The biggest community of praying Indians was on Martha's Vineyard, the island lying to the south of Cape Cod. One and a half thousand of them were living there in 1694. They were ministered to by successive generations of the Mayhew family, most importantly by Experience Mayhew, who began to preach there in March 1694, and spent his life serving the community. He never became their official pastor, believing that role should be filled by Indians themselves, even though he could speak their language. Despite his devotion, he didn't share Sewall's millennial expectations. Toward the end of his career, with Sewall's encouragement, he published *Indian Converts: . . . the Lives and Dying Speeches of . . . the Christianised Indians of Martha's Vineyard.*

Mayhew's dismal subtitle is a reminder of Puritan priorities. Life does not reach its apogee with youth and middle age, only to decline toward a gentle exit stage left, but rises relentlessly toward the moment when the individual goes to meet his or her maker—which is why Sewall was addicted to deathbeds and funerals. As Samuel Willard had put it in his sermon on the death of John Hull, "He [God] takes order that his People shall always die in the best time for them: it may be a bad time for the World to lose them in, but it is a good time for them to leave it in." Mayhew took a restrained view of the success of his own mission. "The Grace of GOD . . . hath effectually appeared to some of these," he wrote in his introduction, but on the other hand, "the Indians are generally a very sinful People." In 1698, Grindal Rawson and Samuel Danforth were commissioned by the New England Company to tour the province inspecting arrangements for teaching and ministering to the Indian communities. They found about thirty religious settlements in all, some of them with just a handful of people, others with dozens or even hundreds, almost all of them with their own Indian preacher.

By the summer of 1700, Sewall had reflected sufficiently on his appointment as a commissioner of the New England Company to write to Sir William Ashurst, its governor, with some important recommendations. He supported the policy of training and paying Indians to teach school and act as ministers. "When God intends Good to a Nation, He is pleased to make use of some of themselves, to be instrumental in conveying of that Good unto them." He also made the important point that peace would never be achieved until a satisfactory territorial settlement had been made: ". . . convenient tracts of land" should be allocated to the Indians, with "plain and natural Boundaries, as much as may be; as Lakes, Rivers, Mountains, Rocks, Upon which for any Englishmen to approach, should be accounted a Crime. And it will be a vain Attempt for us to offer heaven to them, if they take up prejudices against us, as if we did grudge them a Living upon their own Earth." The history of Native Americans would have been radically different if Sewall's suggestions had been carried out, in his own time and the centuries to follow.

Boston marked its entrance into the eighteenth century on 1 January 1701, logically enough in mathematical terms (though for Sewall and the rest of his contemporaries, using the old calendar, the date was in any case 1700, still three months away from the turn of the year). Nevertheless, Sewall was determined to celebrate in style. Four years previously, he and Hannah had woken to a wretched dawn. They had just buried their baby daughter, and were worried too about the repercussions of reinterring their stillborn son, who had died six months previously. The shadow of Salem still hung over Sewall, and two weeks later he would make his public act of contrition. Neither he nor Hannah could respond when trumpeters played a levett (or reveille) at their window.

Now, four years on, he decided to exorcise the sad beginnings of 1697 and draw a line under the troubled last decade of Massachusetts's seventeenth century. This time he arranged for a group of trumpeters to give a blast as day broke. Just before they did, the bellman read—or possibly sang—some verses Sewall had composed for the occasion:

> *Once more! Our God vouchsafe to shine:*
> *Correct the Coldnesse of our Clime.*
> *Make haste with thy Impartial Light,*
> *And terminate this long dark night.*

Give the poor Indians Eyes to see
The Light of Life: and set them free.
So Men shall God in Christ adore,
And worship Idols vain, no more.

So Asia, and Africa,
Eurôpa, with America;
All Four, in Consort join'd, shall Sing
New Songs of Praise to Christ our King.

It's a heartfelt poem, one of Sewall's best, looking forward to the end of conflict through shared faith, to the reconciliation of whites and Indians, then of the continents, in the equalizing love of God. It's patently a product of its own time, of the traumas that Sewall and his community had gone through, but it taps deeply enough into American utopianism to have been sung, again to the accompaniment of trumpets, two centuries later at Boston State House, ushering in the twentieth century while simultaneously recalling a colonial moment, and so knitting together the hopes of past and future in a way that might have given its author comfort.

Sewall's reference to the poor Indians is patronizing by modern standards but humane too, a far cry from the suggestion of the Puritan minister Solomon Stoddard that Indians should be hunted with dogs: "They act like wolves and are to be dealt withall as wolves." The poem's high point, that phrase "Impartial Light," evokes the chilly hopefulness of midwinter dawn. The clarion opening of the first verse, with an appeal for a return of God's favor to New England, is a reminder that Sewall led the singing of the psalms at the meetinghouse and at home, and knew all about the ways in which musical effects could heighten the drama of language. For him, the task for the new century is a specifically American one: the conversion of the Indians, and their consequent liberation and transformation into equals, into "Men." This union of pagan and colonist will trigger a larger harmony between the continents, and bring about a global concert in two senses of the word.

———

ON 5 MARCH 1701, Lord Bellomont died, his estate much encumbered despite those seafaring investments. That year, Sewall noted the deaths of twenty-eight people and attended the funerals of seventeen of them, including his mother's (his father having died the year before). When he motioned with his hand for her grave to be filled, he could "hardly speak for passion and Tears."

A couple of months later, William Stoughton, lieutenant governor and chief justice, was dying too. During his last illness, he expressed the wish to attend Harvard commencement one last time, but Sewall and others dissuaded him. He then asked Sewall to present the silver bowl he had had made for the occasion. Sewall drank a toast from it to the Harvard president, Increase Mather, saying that he presented this cup in the place of "him who was the Firmament and Ornament of the Province." Nothing could show more clearly that when Sewall said he took the blame and shame of the witchcraft trials on himself, he meant exactly that: he simply wasn't interested in implicating others. Two and a half years previously, he had been in despair because Stoughton had snubbed him; now he was acting as his representative. When he visited the chief justice for the last time, Stoughton lifted himself up on his couch and held out his hand, which Sewall kissed, giving him his own. "Pray for me!" Stoughton asked. Three days later, the senior justice of the witch trials was dead. Who knows whether he spared a deathbed thought for Rebecca Nurse, and that terrible moment when the jury was asked to reconsider its verdict of not guilty.

In that tighter world, Sewall might not know everyone who died, but he would know *of* almost all of them, from Lord Bellomont ("The Town is sad") to Will, formerly Captain Prentice's Negro, who was thrown from a horse on to hard frozen ground on 9 February 1700. "I saw him panting," Sewall recorded, "as came from visiting Captain Foxcroft," and he reflected: "He was much delighted in Horses, and now dies by a horse." Will had once saved his master from a bear. One doesn't need to ask for whom the bell tolls when the community is too small to allow for complete strangers; the same day as he saw Will dying, Sewall went to meeting and encountered Captain Belcher, whose nineteen-year-old daughter had just died in childbed. Sewall told him, "I was sorry for the cropping of his desirable flower." The sincerity of his grief did not become eroded by the frequency of his mourning.

After the truncated and unsuccessful governorships of both Phips and Bellomont, it was time for a period of consolidation, and to provide it Joseph Dudley managed to maneuver himself back into power and hold on to it for the next fourteen years, despite being regarded with suspicion by much of the populace because of the part he'd played during the charter crisis. His portrait almost looks like a satirical image of aristocratic disdain. He peers out from a huge, violently curling dark wig with a condescending smile, smirk almost, and heavy-lidded eyes, as though what he is looking at—the world in general, the present and posterity—is not quite worth the effort of opening them fully. But Dudley's roots went right back through the history of the colony. Strangely, he was the half brother of the poet Anne Bradstreet, née Dudley, a first-generation New Englander who came over on the *Arbella* with Winthrop and had been dead thirty years by this point (she was born around 1612; he in 1647). Bradstreet's learned, courtly verse suggests a conflict between the patrician perspective of a family like the Dudleys (never was a man more conscious of his status than Joseph) and the nitty-gritty of American life, which receives more authentic expression in the glum prophecies of *The Day of Doom* or the knotty and idiomatic metaphysics of Edward Taylor's verse. She wrote about an idealized pastoral landscape that had little to do with either the beauty or the threat of the New England she encountered. There she was, the first European poet on American shores. What did she see?

> *Some time now past in the Autumnal Tide,*
> *When Phoebus wanted but one hour to bed,*
> *The trees all richly clad, yet void of pride,*
> *Were gilded o'er by his rich golden head.*
> *Their leaves and fruits seemed painted, but was true,*
> *Of green, of red, of yellow, mixed hue.*

The blazing, astonishing red of New England maples in the fall makes little impact here. What still survive for us are her domestic writings, love poems to her husband, passionate ones ("His warmth such frigid colds did cause to melt. / My chilled limbs now numbed lie forlorn"), verses about her love for her children, a poem about the loss of

Joseph Dudley (1647–1720). Oil on canvas, ca. 1701.
MHS #132.

her house and possessions in a fire (broadcast on the BBC during the London blitz): "Under thy roof no guest shall sit, / Nor at thy Table eat a bit." What mattered most to her was the maintenance of family life, and beyond that the life of township and community. That's what was important to Sewall too, and what would link him to Bradstreet's brother, Joseph Dudley, in the years to come.

During 1700, Sam Jr. had managed to do something constructive:

fall in love with Rebeckah Dudley, Joseph Dudley's daughter. While Sewall was trying to hurry up the wedding of the slaves Bastian and Jane, he found himself taking on an even more intimate role as romantic facilitator, writing a letter to Rebeckah on behalf of his son, and enclosing a silver coin, the Spanish piece of eight, as a symbolic gift. When romantic matters cropped up, the perfumed air of Illyria would drift into the bracing atmosphere of colonial New England:

MADAM,—

The inclosed piece of Silver, by its bowing, humble form, bespeaks your Favor for a certain young Man in Town. The Name [Real]* the Motto [Plus ultra] seem to plead its suitableness for a Present of this Nature. Neither need you to except against the quantity: for you have the Mends in your own hand; And by your generous Acceptance, you may make both it and the Giver Great. Madam, I am

Your Affect¹ Friend S.S.

His playful reference to the quantity of silver suggests that he was prepared to supply rather more than a single piece of eight if the relationship blossomed: perhaps necessary reassurance for a highborn woman who was being courted by a bookseller's assistant.

The Sewalls' family was completed in January 1702 with the birth of their daughter Judith, second of that name. Five years had passed since the death of the stillborn son whose burial had caused the rift with Mr. Willard. There were six survivors in all, the others being the two boys, Samuel Jr. (now twenty-three) and Joseph (thirteen), and three girls, Hannah Jr. (twenty-one), Elizabeth (twenty), and Mary (ten). Their mother, Hannah, was coming up to her forty-fourth birthday. It had been a troubled pregnancy, and she and her husband had decided it would be the last. To celebrate, Hannah gave a dinner for all the

---

* The square brackets in this note are Sewall's. "*Plus ultra*" means "more in prospect."

women who had attended her over the years: Madam Usher (who carved), "Mrs. Hannah Greenlcf, Ellis, Cowell, Wheeler, Johnson and her daughter Cole, Mrs Hill our Nurses Mother, Nurse Johnson, Hill, Hawkins, Mrs. Goose, Denning, Green, Smith, Hatch, Blin," the honorifics and lack of them reminding us of social distinctions, and the length of the list demonstrating the inclusiveness of the Sewalls' gratitude. The proud father was as keen to list the goodies consumed as the names of the consumers: "Boil'd Pork, Beef, Fowls; very good Rost-Beef, Turkey-Pye, Tarts." He must have slid into the feminine celebrations to steal a plateful. There was a good fire in the stove that warmed the room. A few months later, he would compare little Judith's progress with the sudden death of the slave Bastian's baby daughter, Jane.

That spring, he went to Cape Cod and Martha's Vineyard on a fact-finding mission for the New England company, of which he was now treasurer. He visited a wigwam and admired the "goodness" of it. One of the Indian schoolmasters, Jonas Hassawit, held Baptist beliefs and Sewall discussed with Experience Mayhew the possibility of publishing a treatise in Algonquian to stop Christian Indians from succumbing to such notions.

A month later, in May, Sewall addressed his troops at a shooting competition. He had returned to military—or at least militia—service two years earlier, becoming captain of the Ancient and Honorable Artillery Company, a tricky role for an individual without military ambition or ability. Sixteen years before that, he had resigned his commission in the South Company of Boston on a question of principle: the image of the cross in the colors. When Sewall took up his new command, Colonel Pynchon presented ceremonial staves; on receiving his, Sewall made an unfortunate joke: "I said I was surpris'd to see that they had mistaken a sorry pruning Hook for a Military Spear." Nevertheless, he tried to be gracious about his commission; he would rather make a fool of himself, he told his men, than slight the faith the company had placed in him. To the most experienced of his sergeants, Thomas Finch, he expressed the deference of novice officer toward battle-hardened noncom: "Doubted not but if I could give any thing tolerable words of command, he would mend them in a vigorous and speedy performance." Finally, he had performed the military duty he was best able to do: he took the whole company home and entertained them with bread, beer, and wine syllabub.

Now, more at ease with his men, he reminded them that the last time they had all shot at a mark he himself had completely failed to hit it. As punishment, he would impose on himself a small fine, the amount a judge was allowed to charge when sitting on a case alone, and donate it to the winner, Ensign Noyes, who'd managed to hit the bowels of the man-shaped target (though a little to the left-hand side). He also presented Noyes with a cup that he'd had inscribed with a text about the drying up of the River Euphrates.

In June 1702, Joseph Dudley sailed into Boston harbor to take up his duties as governor, and Sewall made a speech of welcome. The very next day, Dudley called at the Sewall house to thank them all for the kindness they had shown to his family. The following month, Sewall visited Madam Dudley, perhaps to prepare some ground, because three days later young Sam called on the Dudleys' daughter Rebeckah, whom he had been courting (with his father's assistance) for more than a year.

Sewall's sister Mehetabel Moody died not long afterward. He does not describe her in the diary but records frequent visits, as with all his siblings. He heard the news shortly after parting with Dudley, and wrote to him straightaway, expressing shock and sadness: she was "but a little crazy Cistern, and the breaking of it so soon (37. years 3 mots) is a Rebuke directing me to the FOUNTAIN of Living Waters." His sister was only a small cracked vessel of holy water (the original meaning of crazy was flawed, liable to fall apart): despite her passing he still has access to the living fountain. This imagery of cistern and fountain comes from Jeremiah 2:13, and perhaps helps to explain the outgoing nature of a man like Sewall. The Puritans might come over as mean-spirited, totting up individual allocations of grace like spiritual misers, but in reality they were thoroughly social in outlook, community builders, architects of that city on a hill or—the dark obverse—defenders of a faltering Christian commonwealth from imaginary invaders entering through a portal in Salem Village. This contrast between the individual reservoir and the total flow is a watery equivalent of John Donne's great metaphor "no man is an island."

Crazy also had its other meaning at that time, and there's something heartfelt, loving, and forlorn about Sewall's description of this "ingenuous, tender-hearted, pious creature," his crazy little cistern of a sister. He's aware of how much he has let his emotions show to his grand correspondent: "I ask your Excel.s pardon that I have wept these Tears in your presence: Griefs disclôsd divide." As we would say: a trouble shared is a trouble halved. Of course, such confidences reflect—and can create—intimacy. He is inviting Dudley into family concerns. On his way to the funeral, he reproved a certain David Simons for tending his flax without any clothes on.

A week later, Sewall gave the town clerk notice of the intended marriage of Sam and Rebeckah Dudley. No doubt both families felt themselves the gainers, though on the face of it the unsettled Sam—bookshop assistant, sufferer from aching feet, cause of fatherly anxiety—wasn't a great catch (as it turned out, Rebeckah proved to be even more wayward than him). But Dudley had been imprisoned by his fellow citizens; now he would be connected to one who was known for his loyalty to the New England cause, and who was an influential and popular member of the community, his reputation only enhanced by his public apology, and who always scored high on elections to the council. And it was only three years since Sewall had been in despondency at being snubbed by Stoughton; now he would have family ties with the governor.

But this arrangement wasn't as cozy as it might seem. Dudley was a proud, arrogant man, hugely sensitive about his dignity and with a bad temper on a hair trigger, as Sewall and others would frequently discover. Moreover, Sewall wouldn't hesitate to give him cause to fly off the handle if a controversial issue cropped up. On 15 August, having been taken to the Town House in Dudley's calash to receive the renewal of his commission as a justice, he listened skeptically while Dudley promised he "would never insert himself to influence any proceeding." Which "he has many times done with great Vehemency," Sewall commented sardonically, immediately joining with his fellow justices in appointing Elisha Cooke their clerk, and swearing him in. Cooke had been a member of the council that imprisoned Dudley, and Dudley took a long revenge by consistently overruling Cooke's election to the council during the years of his governorship.

That September, while on his judicial circuit, Sewall was lying awake in his lodgings at daybreak when he heard someone ride up to the house. His heart plummeted. "Thought I, I fear there may be some bad News from Boston." The man knocked, and when a person of the household answered, the messenger asked if Captain Somebody-or-other was there. Sewall couldn't make out the name, but Captain as he was himself, though poor at target practice, "I took it he said me." The man said that the captain must come with him at once, because his daughter was very bad. Sewall immediately thought something had happened to Betty, who was in the late stages of pregnancy. He prepared himself to make a sorrowful journey back to Boston, as he had once done on being told about the stillbirth of his son. But suddenly he was let off the hook: a Captain Brown was the one destined to get the bad news. Sewall saw the funeral the next day, as he went on the ferry. It was only a temporary reprieve, however: two months later, Betty gave birth to a dead child.

On 15 September, Sam Jr. and Rebeckah were married. The ceremony took place in the dining room of Governor Dudley's house, with singing from Sewall's turkey leather psalmbook.

A totting up at the end of the year: Sewall weighed himself on Colonel Nathaniel Byfield's scales. He recorded 193 pounds (thirteen stone eleven pounds). And that was wearing just his "close coat." But never mind, Colonel Byfield was an impressive 63 pounds heavier. "The Lord add, or take away from this our corporeal weight," Sewall prayed (as long, of course, as it was to the advantage of spiritual growth). Add, was the Lord's eventual decision: nineteen years later, Sewall tipped the scales at 228 pounds.

Sewall, man of affairs, conducted a hard-nosed correspondence with Dudley about a settlement for their married children, the upshot being that he and Hannah provided land at Muddy River, a few miles to the west of Boston, while Dudley paid for the erection of a house on it. The Sewalls' gift was a generous one. The land in question, three hundred acres in all, had passed to them from her father, John Hull. They had to apply to the council for permission to use part of the family inheritance in this way, and accordingly an act was passed approving the transaction on condition that the Sewalls compensated their other children for the loss of their shares of the inheritance to the tune of £1,000 in total. In February 1703, Sewall sent Rebeckah a piece of gold with an engraved motto: *Florent Concordia Regna*, "agreement makes kingdoms flourish," as he explained in an affectionate note ("Dear child"). Spend the gold but keep the motto, he told her, since it was the only one he had, and "even a family is a little Kingdom" (and like a kingdom, prone to civil war, as they would all discover).

Sewall the unworldly: in January 1704, he asked his wife to take responsibility for his cash, an odd request from a man who was private banker to his friends and acquaintances, as well as treasurer of the New England Company. When he needed some he would borrow it from her, because she was better than he was at managing such business. Wisely, he awarded himself 24s. pocket money before handing over the rest of his cash in hand, £4 3s. 8d., as the first installment under the new regime.

Meanwhile, Queen Anne's War had broken out, bringing a decade of conflict between France on the one hand, and England, Austria, and Prussia on the other. As far as the northeastern region of America was concerned, this renewed the old conflict with the French and allied Indians. There was sporadic violence in Maine, and then, on 29 February 1704, the Deerfield massacre took place in Massachusetts, when a force of 350 Indians and French attacked a small frontier town of 300 inhabitants.

A few nights before the assault the villagers heard, or thought they heard, a trampling sound round the fort, "as if it were beset by Indians." As in the case of the spectral sightings of Indians in the Gloucester marshes in 1692, bad dreams and genuine threats could overlap and merge in undifferentiated terror. This time the noises in the darkness could have been a premonition of what was to come, or the actual sounds of a scouting party. On the night of the attack, deep snow had drifted up against the palisades, allowing the Indians to use it as a ramp to scale the community's defenses. Fifty inhabitants were killed, and over a hundred carried off as prisoners, including the minister, John Williams. His wife, Eunice, was one of the dead; she was the niece of Increase Mather and sister of Eliakim Mather, who had lived with the Sewalls for some years in the late 1680s, and probably acted as a clerk. The Williams's daughter, also called Eunice, was captured too. Williams was released two years later and came to Boston, where Sewall treated him to dinner. His daughter married an Indian, however, and resisted all attempts to get her back.

The resumption of hostilities with the French and their Indian allies couldn't dent Sewall's confidence in the millennial future of America. While earthly battles went on all around, his mind was focused on a grand scheme that gave purpose and harmony to history. He entered into lively debate with Nicholas Noyes of Salem about his interpretation of Revelation 10, the prophecy that the angel of the Lord will set his right foot on the sea and his left foot on the land. For Sewall, the vision was of a great figure straddling, and conjoining, east and west. The ancients had had no reason to suspect that the west contained the continent of America, and that was why they had described the right foot as being in the ocean. Thus the reconciliation of Old and New Worlds, and the reconciliation of races implicit within it—including, of course, union with the Indians—could be given a biblical foundation. In Thomas Thorowgood's *Iewes in America*—a book Sewall carefully annotated—the author conjectured that the Jews had been able to get to America because the continents were originally joined together (a theory now endorsed by modern geology, though on a rather different timescale) or only slightly separated: ". . . time and the sea two insatiable devourers have made the gap wider." Sewall approvingly marked Thorowgood's concluding sentence, which could almost be seen as a gloss on the image of the straddling angel: "It is an indubitable thing, that the one world is continued, and joined with the other." (The claim gave unity to Sewall's own story, as a man born in England and living in America.)

The following month, he referred to this linkage in a letter to Richard Henchman, with whom he was in the habit of exchanging verses, explaining that he believed the key events in Revelation—"the Appearance of the Angel, the Slaughter of the Witnesses, the Drying of the Euphrates, and the Calling of the Jews" (this last to include the Indians)—were to take place inside a short time span, and it was necessary to get ready to welcome the Lord Jesus.

Sewall's teleological concerns never diminished his appetite for mundane matters. In April 1704, the *Boston News-Letter* was launched, the first regularly issued newspaper in America (it continued until the Revolution). It was a significant event, a step away from the parochial: news in itself. Behind it lay a recognition that the community was getting big and complex enough to need more than word-of-mouth communications. Even Sewall, with tendrils out to every section of his society, each one ready to twitch sensitively at sightings of periwigs, disasters by fire, rumors of Indian attacks, and particularly at news of illnesses or deaths, recognized this need, and became an enthusiastic subscriber, making marginal notes and constructing his own index. His fervor was enhanced by the fact that the newspaper offices were next door to his house. He visited Harvard on 24 April to check up on some books about Revelation in support of his theories, and while there listened to Mr. Willard give a sermon to the students (among whom was Sewall's son Joseph). He took the opportunity of giving Willard a copy of the *News-Letter*, "the first . . . that ever was carried over the River."

Within weeks, the paper had a juicy story to tell: pirates again, this time the notorious Captain Quelch and his crew, and once more Sewall had his own part to play, though the star of the drama was his brother Stephen.

A briganteen called the *Charles* was fitted up as a privateer by a group of Boston merchants and commissioned by Dudley to attack French shipping off the northern American coast. Its captain, Daniel Plowman, sensed a piratical tendency in his crew before they ever set sail but fell ill, and command was taken over by his deputy, John Quelch. The ship headed south rather than north, and Captain Plowman ended up overboard. The *Charles* preyed on Portuguese ships off the coast of Brazil, in defiance of a treaty of friendship between England and Portugal. In May 1704, it returned to New England. Presumably Quelch, like Kidd, thought he could brave out the authorities and justify what he had been doing. Such doomed confidence reflected ambivalent attitudes toward piracy in the New England community but also testifies to a transition between old and new times. It was difficult for pirates to picture how crimes committed in faraway seas could come home to roost in law courts in London or Boston; how the planet was getting smaller as a result of the colonial interests represented by the East India Company or America itself; how narratives and accountability could travel, albeit slowly, to the very ports the pirates put into; above all, to get their heads around the developments in communication that Boston's first newspaper itself represented, as it scooped the closing scenes of Quelch's story.

Sewall had been on his judicial rounds, and discussing apocalyptical matters with Nicholas Noyes in Salem. On his way home, he stopped for a meal at Lewis's tavern in Lynn, where he bumped into Paul Dudley, attorney general and son of the governor. Dudley had just taken one of the Quelch crew into custody and sent him off to Boston. Now that he had a fully fledged judge to hand, he called his prisoner back, and Sewall was able to formally remand him for delivery into the custody of Secretary Addington.

This was just the beginning of Sewall's involvement. A few days later, the governor commissioned Colonel Nathaniel Byfield, Paul Dudley, and Sewall himself "to search for and seize Pirats and their Treasure, and to hold a court of Enquiry for this end at Marblehead" (Marblehead was a port just to the south of Salem). Two days later, while the pirate commissioners were still abed in Marblehead, an urgent message arrived saying that "9. or 11. Pirats, double arm'd" had been spotted at Cape Ann. The commissioners got up immediately and sent out orders for militia to go there. Dudley sailed off in a boat while Colonel Byfield (all 256 pounds of him) and Sewall set off on horseback, calling at Salem on the way.

Here Sewall's brother Stephen commandeered a shallop, appropriately enough called the *Trial*, along with its crew of four fishermen. He gathered a dozen men and set sail for Cape Ann too, towing a small pinnace that could be used as a landing craft, while Sewall and Byfield continued by land with a party of troops. Just before they arrived on the cape, a messenger galloped out with news that the pirates had set sail in a ship called the *Larrimore Galley*.

Captain Abbott was asked to take charge of the chase, but was reluctant; Captain Herrick requested that his troops should be excused, and "matters went on heavily." Then Stephen Sewall arrived and came up trumps. He would take command himself. That freed the logjam: man after man offered to join him till they had a party of forty-three in all, crammed into a small fishing boat. The men "gave us three very handsom cheers." No dramatic exit was possible because the wind had died, so the *Trial* was rowed out of harbor after sunset.

The next day, Sewall and Byfield set off for Salem, where they dined with Stephen's wife. She was "very thoughtful what would become of her husband. The Wickedness and despair of the company they pursued, their Great Guns and other war-like Preparations, were a terror to her and the rest of the Town." After comforting her as best he could, Sewall made his way to Boston. Meanwhile, first thing that morning the *Trial* had reached the Isles of Shoals. The *Larrimore Galley* was moored near one of them, Star Island.

Stephen Sewall got his men to lie down so that only the four bona fide fishermen were in view. Six men from the pirate vessel clambered into a boat and set out for the shore of Star Island. When the *Trial* was spotted, the pirates still aboard the galley began to run about, pulling the covers off the guns and drawing out their tampions, long plugs inserted down muzzles to keep them clean and dry. At this strategic moment, Stephen Sewall got his men to reveal themselves, intimidating the depleted pirate crew. He took a boarding party over in the pinnace and took the pirates into custody, along with forty-five ounces of gold.

Sewall concludes his account of these events with a significant reminder to himself: "See the News-Letter." This marks a crossover from personal investment in community events to the imprimatur of external record, from diary anecdote to news report: a stage in the long process of separation of public from private. "GOD save the QUEEN," the *Boston News-Letter* announced excitedly at the head of its account.

Stephen Sewall brought the pirates into Boston under strong guard, and they were remanded to jail, the gold being transferred to the care of Sewall's committee. Dudley convened a Court of Admiralty to try the case, with Sewall sitting as one of the team of twelve justices. The trial took place promptly, and twenty pirates were sentenced to death, with John Quelch and six others scheduled to hang on 30 June.

The executions took place on the flatlands by the Charles River estuary. There were crowds of onlookers and perhaps 150 boats and canoes on the river. Sewall was amazed at the numbers. The pirates were brought by boat to the gallows. They climbed up the ladder and stood on the scaffold while Cotton Mather said prayers from the boat, a well-crafted spiritual contribution to the last act of a seafaring drama.

To no avail: according to the newspaper, the pirates "dyed very obdurately and impenitently, hardened in their sin." Ropes were hung from the frame—only six, as one of the men, Francis King, received a last-minute reprieve from Governor Dudley, and climbed shakily back down the steps. When the trap fell, "there was such a Screech of the Women," Sewall remarked, "that my wife heard it sitting at our Entry next the Orchard, and was much surprised at it; yet the wind was sou-west. Our house is a full mile from the place." The following year, the surviving pirates received the queen's pardon on condition they went into her service, another example of how it was possible to toggle between buccaneering and privateering.

Road rage in a horse-drawn era: one day in early December 1705, the governor was in his coach heading north from his home in Roxbury on province business, when he had a face-to-face encounter with two carts. It had been a bad year for him in transport terms: two overturned sleighs and a near shipwreck. (Sewall had parallel problems: in August he and Mrs. Willard tumbled out of the calash in which they were riding, and the following week little Judith was thrown into some dirt and then, later the same day, run over by a horse, though not badly hurt.)

Neither party would budge for the other. The carters challenged Dudley's status, one of them saying, "I am as good flesh and blood as you."

"Sirrah, you rogue or rascall, I will have that way," the governor insisted. "Run the dogs through," he cried, and stabbed one of them in the back (presumably superficially) while he was calming the horses. The carter grabbed Dudley's sword and broke it in two. The other carter shouted to the onlookers that he was acting in self-defense.

"You lie, you dog; you lie, you divell," Dudley cried.

"Such words dont become a christian."

"A christian, you dog, a christian you divell," roared the governor, "I was a christian before you were born."

The carters said they would get on their way. "No, you shall goe to Gaole, you Dogs," Dudley replied.

They asked what would become of their horses, in that case.

"Let them sink into the bottom of the earth," was Dudley's clincher.

It so happened that Sewall met the governor two days later and was regaled with his version of events. On his way home, Sewall encountered a mysterious third carter, whose vehicle was apparently between the other two, and who must therefore have had an uncanny knack for keeping a low profile. He showed him where the carts had been, and Sewall formed the opinion that the carters were essentially in the right, because they couldn't turn and the governor's coach could easily have passed them on a parallel, slightly higher track.

The next day, the fathers of the two carters came to Sewall and asked him to release their sons from prison. There followed more than a week of difficult negotiations, as Paul Dudley, shamelessly acting in his father's interest, did all that he could to block bail. The attorney general had the same imperious outlook as his father. One day he was driving in his carriage toward Boston when he realized he'd left a law book at home. He pulled up beside a laborer and asked him to go and fetch it. "*Can* one fetch it?" the man asked. "Oh yes," Paul Dudley replied. "Then go yourself," the man replied. Sewall had no doubt that continued detention was inappropriate, and when he thought (slightly prematurely as it turned out) that he'd succeeded in freeing the carters he wrote, "I am glad that I have been instrumental to Open the Prison to those two young men, that they might repair to their wives and children and Occasions." He wrote to John Hathorne "to desire him, an experienced Traveller, to help us to steer between Scylla and Charibdis." He quoted Coke's statutes, which specified that only felony or treason could prevent bail.

Sewall felt vulnerable trying to administer justice in the teeth of Dudley's anger—and with reason. In January 1706, he visited the failing James Bayley, his old school fellow from Newbury days, the first ever minister of Salem Village and the only one not to be sucked into the witchcraft crisis, and gave him two pounds of currants, gratefully received. Bayley was in terrible pain from the stone, and over the next year Sewall came regularly to comfort him, dutifully recording his agonies: "New Pains: Cryes out, My Head! My Head! What shall I doe?" Over in Salem another friend of Bayley's, Nicholas Noyes, monitored the progress of his suffering too, but because of the distance couldn't be sure when it would end, so wrote an elegy on the off chance: *"To my Worthy Friend, Mr. James Bayley, Living (if Living) in Roxbury."* The poem was written eight months before Bayley's actual death. In the course of this odd obituary, he pictured Bayley's destiny in the afterlife: "Thy Soul from thence forth shall be blest; / Thy Dust be safe; for Christ shall find it, / And leave this cruel Stone behind it." The doctrine of the resurrection of the body had been fine-tuned to include the possibility of a sort of posthumous surgery.

After leaving Mr. Bayley, Sewall met John Leverett, a fellow judge involved in the case, and discovered from him that Dudley had made a declaration relating to the accused and had himself sent for Hathorne. Sewall clearly felt that a potential ally was being appropriated, and that events were being manipulated in advance of the trial. He hurried off to the governor's house, but only Madam Dudley was there. From her he received shocking news: "Scandal." The charge was that he, Sewall, was going around saying he had seen quarts of blood running from the carters' horses. Sewall had "never seen, nor thought, nor reported, any such thing."

At the council next day, the governor read out his declaration. He was obviously furious about judicial delay: ". . . he did not know whether he should live to the time of the court." He brought up the quarts of blood allegation against Sewall, who gave as good as he got, mentioning a claim that the local magistrate, who had taken the carters into custody, had landed a blow himself, "which was inconvenient for a justice of the peace." He did well, the governor riposted.

This episode illuminates a number of issues: the conflict between private and public roles, Dudley's choler and Sewall's willingness to stand up to it, the attempt by some members of the elite to maintain their privileges against the leveling tendency of America. One of the carters would eventually be appointed chief justice of Massachusetts, while the other became the first representative of the town of Brookline. Occupations did not necessarily define position in the social hierarchy, as the case of Sam Jr. demonstrates. The discipline of colony building was creating a more open society, one capable of triggering the patrician wrath of a member of the Dudley clan.

The problem rumbled on for most of the year. In April, Sewall tried a bit of detective work. He came upon the governor's coach one day after he'd been visiting poor Mr. Bayley, and followed it. When it got to the point where the standoff occurred, the coach took the higher track, the very one it had refused to use when meeting the carters. In other words, Dudley had just been bloody-minded—and, of course, still was. Two months later, he exploded at Sewall in council: ". . . the Govr brake forth into a passionate Harangue respecting the Roxbury Carters. He might be run through, trampled on, & no care taken of him."

There is something comic about this fretful petulance, the way Dudley expected people to believe he spent his days in trepidation at the thought of those ferocious carters. Their case finally came to the superior court in November 1706, before Justices Sewall, Hathorne, Walley, and Leverett, who discharged them. The entries detailing these two "Solemn Proclamations" are the tersest in the record of the court's sitting and unlike other cases are not given a marginal gloss, perhaps to emphasize the lack of credible evidence. Despite his tetchy prophecy, Dudley managed to remain alive to see his case collapse.

Before long though, his probity would be tested again, and he and Sewall would be involved in acrimony indeed.

CHAPTER FOURTEEN

"The Concomitant Rain-bow"

🙢🙣🙢

THE BIG BATTLE BETWEEN SEWALL AND DUDLEY BEGAN IN 1706. Its background was the much larger battleground between the New England colonists and the French and their Indian allies, Queen Anne's War. Many prisoners had been taken by both sides, including those captured during the Deerfield massacre in 1704. A mission led by an officer called Samuel Vetch, and including Dudley's son William, was sent to Canada to effect an exchange. On their return, Vetch and another officer, John Borland, were charged with using the opportunity provided by these negotiations to conduct their own business with enemy Indians. Vetch was "confined in ye stone cage, for fear he should get away." Given the awkward possibility of guilt by association, Dudley supported his son's colleague.

Instead of being sent to the superior court, the case went before the General Court (comprising the Governor's Council and the House of Representatives), which as a legislative assembly was only empowered to hear misdemeanors. The charges against Vetch and his colleague John Borland amounted to treason, which meant that the General Court lacked the authority to deliberate on them. Sewall believed Dudley was pulling a fast one. If the hearing was unconstitutional, a guilty verdict and the ensuing sentence would be wide open to appeal.

The men were duly found guilty, and large fines imposed (£200 in the case of Vetch; £1,100 for Borland). Sure enough, they promptly appealed to the Privy Council in London, which set aside the verdict and demanded that the superior court should try the case. By this time, Vetch was commanding another expedition against Canada, and the charges were dropped altogether.

This piece of finessing caused outrage. Twenty leading New Englanders, headed by Nathaniel Higginson, son of the pastor of Salem and friend of Sewall, signed a petition to the queen and Privy Council calling for Dudley's dismissal. They used certain "luxuriant words," as Sewall called them, to claim Dudley had manipulated the legal process for his own treasonable ends. The charge wasn't simply that Dudley had got Vetch and Borland off the hook, but that he himself had had an interest in their treacherous dealings with the enemy. He had deliberately dragged the legal proceedings out so that hostile Indians could benefit from their ill-gotten gains: "The Govr. delayd their prosecution till the Ammunition, with which he had furnished the Enemy, was used by them; to the destruction of your Majs good Subjects; and that Colony thereby put to Thirty three Thousand pounds charge." It's hard to imagine a more serious allegation, a cocktail of corruption and treason. Its extremeness makes one aware of the deep distrust in which Dudley was held by many of the citizens of Massachusetts. He had identified himself with the oppression visited on the colonists (as they saw it) by the representatives of the British Crown during the period when the charter was withdrawn. It wasn't such a leap to imagine him playing a perfidious part in alliance with the current enemy, the French and Indian alliance in Canada. Naturally—and from a survival point of view, inevitably—Dudley urged the council to pass an "abhorrence" of this petition.

Sewall wanted more time to investigate the matter, but Dudley pushed the issue to a vote posthaste, and the council gave him its unanimous support. There was little choice. The charges were so grave they could hardly be endorsed without a proper period of investigation and reflection. Over the next couple of weeks, Sewall grew increasingly uneasy about what had happened, particularly when Dudley used the fact that the council had voted for the motion of abhorrence to bully the representatives into doing the same. Late in November 1707, Sewall interviewed Borland and decided that Dudley had indeed been guilty of conniving at trade with the French, "which has open'd a Tragical scene that I know not when we shall see the close of it."

The more Dudley emphasized the two houses' support, the more Sewall felt that he himself was in an anomalous position and, being Sewall, said so to Dudley's face: "At the Conference, his Excellency was pleas'd to say, that every one of the Council remain'd steady to their vote, and every word of it: This Skrewing the Strings of your Lute to that height has broken one of them; and I find myself under a Necessity of withdrawing my Vote." Dudley was not fitted by temperament to take such rebellion lying down, as Sewall ruefully noted: "The Govr often says that if any body would deal plainly with him, he would kiss them; but I rec'd many a Bite, many a hard Word from him."

It was a tense time. Pugnacious Cotton Mather published a long pamphlet exploring Dudley's alleged perfidy, *The Present Deplorable State of New-England, with the Many Disadvantages It Lyes Under, by the Male-Administration of Their Present Governour, Joseph Dudley*. Sewall, however, did what he could to keep things civilized. The council invited the governor to dinner, and Sewall drank a toast to him and presented his duty. But two days later, matters came to a head. Dudley suggested printing a record of the vote taken by the council in the Vetch case to prevent false reports. As the vote had been unanimous, this amounted to listing the members of the council as supporters of Dudley. Sewall had to remind him that he had since withdrawn his vote. As usual, Dudley took this opposition badly: "I pray God judge between me and you," he said. Colonel Penn Townsend mightily upset Sewall by accusing him of temporizing, on the grounds that he wanted to replace Dudley with Nathaniel Higginson. Sewall immediately felt compelled to fire off an earnest prayer: "Lord, . . . fly to me in a way of Favourable protection!"

Townsend's charge hurt because he had nailed exactly what Sewall did want to happen. "There is none in England I have eat so much Py in partnership with, as your self," Sewall told Nathaniel Higginson, "therefore I Trust you." Anticipating the Privy Council's acceptance of the petition and the consequent fall of Dudley, Sewall wrote to Sir Henry Ashurst explicitly asking for him to support Nathaniel Higginson for governor. Then he wrote again to Higginson himself, explaining, "I should much rejoice to see you succeed him [Dudley]."

But the very fact that his preference was so clear hardly suggests temporizing. Sewall was prepared to mix it with the governor at every turn. In response to Dudley's decision to publish the votes in order to ram home to the public that he had the support of their representatives, Sewall decided to publish his own reasons for withdrawing his vote, accusing the governor of having personal involvement in the trading, and defending Nathaniel Higginson's petition. It was a difficult, public act, one that fully vindicates Sewall's integrity. Some days before his document went to press, Sewall dozed off in the council chamber. When he awoke, Colonel Townsend was by him. Townsend, acting on behalf of Dudley, wanted Sewall to back off. He asked him "pleasantly"—one can almost see ominously glittering teeth—to withdraw his paper, and put it in his pocket. Sewall answered—"pleasantly"—that he could as easily put Colonel Townsend himself in his pocket. He published his reasons for withdrawing his vote on 10 December 1707.

Despite his "Mount Etna Eruption," as his brother Stephen termed it, Sewall continued to do his best to stay on terms with Dudley when they weren't at each others' throats about public matters. This wasn't hypocrisy: it was a reflection of his nature and of his Christian belief. About this time he had a serious row with a tenant, Nathaniel Henchman, who was interested in buying the tenement he was renting but wanted it at a knockdown price Sewall wasn't prepared to accept. The two men had known each other for years (Henchman had rented Sewall's warehouse during the latter's stay in England), and this disagreement didn't stop Sewall from trying to make sympathetic conversation with the man when his wife died: "I cross'd the way near our house, and ask'd him how he did: He only shew'd his Teeth." Dudley survived: the Privy Council dismissed the charges against him as frivolous.

In addition to his responsibilities as a member of council and of the Superior Court of Judicature, Sewall was deeply involved in local matters, regularly attending meetings of justices and selectmen to make decisions such as highway modifications, planning consents, the removal of indigent or undesirable people from Boston, and the granting of liquor licenses. Taverns and ordinaries blossomed in early eighteenth-century Boston, and the names of some of the license holders have a warm glow reminiscent of Ben Jonson or Charles Dickens: "Exercise Conant, all sorts of drink, out of doors; David Gwin, both within and without doors; Capt. Grigory Shugers, out of doors; . . . Mehitabell Pumery may keep a victualling house and sell liquor." Sewall himself enjoyed eating and drinking in them, but he also monitored public behavior there when on watch duty.

One day in 1708, Edward Bromfield, a fellow councillor and justice of the peace, showed Sewall a letter concerning certain debaucheries that had taken place at the Exchange Tavern. Sewall had had a spot of bother there a few years previously, when he broke up a card game one Saturday night, and the gamblers took their revenge the following Wednesday, scattering playing cards all over his yard. The letter came from the landlord's wife and maid, and Sewall was "surpris'd to find my self unaccountably abused in it." Immediately, he said that he shouldn't meddle with the business: "I must not be a Judge in my own Cause." Presumably, he was being blamed for heavy-handed interference and creating bad feeling.

Antagonism between those in search of a good time and those committed to religious observance and social regulation dated right back to the earliest years of colonial settlement. Almost from the moment Europeans set foot on American soil there were attempts to establish a Bacchic alternative to the austerity of official culture. In the spring of 1627, Thomas Morton and a group of followers had set up a maypole at Merry Mount to celebrate the death of winter. They brewed a barrel of excellent beer and danced hand in hand around the maypole singing an appropriate song:

> *Drinke and be merry, merry, merry boyes,*
> *Let all your delight be in the Hymen's ioyes; . . .*
> *Make green garlons, bring bottles out*
> *And fill sweet Nectar freely about.*
> *Uncover thy head, and feare no harme,*
> *For hers* [here's] *good liquor to keepe it warme.*

It didn't take long for a group of militia led by Myles Standish (Morton disrespectfully called him Captain Shrimp, on account of his short stature and pink complexion), to overpower the hapless revelers, one of whom was so drunk he stabbed himself in the nostril with his sword, and Morton was sent back to England posthaste.

When the incident at the Exchange Tavern came to court, a certain Thomas Banister, Harvard graduate and general thorn in the flesh, proved the star culprit. He had lied (fined 20s.), cursed (another five), and thrown the pots and scale box at the maid (10s. for breach of the peace). Undeterred, this lord of misrule would play a significant role in another pub fracas a few years later.

Boston was getting bigger, and in 1708 it was decided that there should be a wholesale naming of streets. The time when Sewall could simply address a letter "To his dear Wife Mis. Hannah Sewall at Boston in New-England" had passed away. As the owner of the most substantial house on his road, he was able to choose the name himself, and did so in homage to his boyhood home: Newbury Street. The population of the town was eight thousand, and the Long Wharf, stretching about eight hundred feet into the harbor (soon chockablock with shops and warehouses), was built that year to cope with the massive increase in shipping. America was evolving from a wilderness to a built environment, from the domain of rural tragedy, as Sewall had expressed it in his long-ago letter to a Harvard classmate, to that of urban comedy.

He had been keen to produce a third edition of Eliot's Indian Bible for some time, and now he decided to make his case. It soon became apparent he was a lone voice in promoting this cause, a measure of the change that had taken place in the colonial perspective on Native Americans. There were still attacks and massacres generated by the war with the French. Indians raided Haverhill, and murdered the minister Benjamin Rolfe, his wife, and one of their children (a servant concealed their two little daughters in tubs in the cellar, however, and they survived). But despite savage incidents like these, there was a general awareness of the decline of Native American society and culture. The Mathers, along with Nehemiah Walter (Increase's son-in-law), had written a letter on the subject in 1705: "The Hand of God, has very strangely wasted them; and the *War* . . . [of] 1675 [King Philip's War] hastened a strange Desolation upon whole Nations of them." This awareness of decline (perhaps that repetition of "strange" suggests some sense of guilt) made ensuring that the gospel was available in Algonquian less relevant. Cotton Mather's own view was that the money would be better spent on teaching the Indians English. He was contemptuous of "*Indian* Long-winded words" and devised a mock one of his own to characterize ferocious warriors: "*Bombardo-gladio-funhast-flami-loquentes.*" He believed that the retention of their own language would keep other undesirable cultural baggage in place too: "They can scarce retain their Language, without a Tincture of other Savage Inclinations, which do but ill suit, either with the Honor, or with the design of Christianity."

The petering out of Eliot's great enterprise is epitomized by an incident that took place in July 1709. As Sewall got contentedly into bed, he reminded his wife of the goodness God had shown in providing them with—here he must have looked about his bedroom—a chamber, and—getting between the covers—a bed, and—perhaps clasping his wife—company. One of those moments in life when you count your blessings, forgetting how this tempts fate. Sometime between two and three in the morning he was woken by Hannah, who could smell smoke. Sure enough, the bedchamber was full of it.

Sewall swung himself out of bed, pulled on all his clothes (except his stockings) and ran from room to room, finding them all fine except for his bedchamber. Then he went up to the garret and woke his servant David, who fetched him a candle. Hannah was frightened the brick wall had caught fire and the children were in danger, so she rushed off to wake them while Sewall patted his bedroom closet and was unnerved to find it was warm.

The question was whether to open it. Perhaps that would "cause the Fire to burst forth in an Unquenchable Flame." He plucked up courage and did so anyway. Inside he found his deal box of wafers—the strips of wax used for seals—"all afire, burning livelily; yet not blazing" (note the subtle distinction: it was a society used to conflagrations). He called for a bucket of water, and salvaged some papers that were in danger of catching fire. By the time the water was brought, the closet was almost too hot to approach, but he managed to throw several bucketsful over it and quenched it. "Thus with great Indulgence GOD saved our House and Substance, and the Company's Paper." He'd been storing paper for the new edition of Eliot's Bible, more than a thousand reams of it, in the closet immediately below the one that had caught fire, just in case the company relented. Sewall in forensic mode: he worked out that a mouse might have taken a lit candle from the candlestick on the hearth, dragged it under the closet door, and deposited it behind the box of wafers.

Despite his disappointment with Eliot's Bible, Sewall did bring off one smaller achievement in this line. He gave a night's lodging to an Indian preacher, John Neesnummin, and the following morning sent him on his way to Natick with a letter of introduction. A few days later, on one of his frequent days of private fasting, he prayed for the New England Company in general and Neesnummin in particular, as part of a huge range of prayers devoted to his family, church, and province—and not forgetting the household servants ("Make David a man after thy own heart, Let Susan live and be baptised with the H[oly] G[host], and with fire"). In due course, the New England Company decided to publish the Psalms and the Gospel of Saint John in an edition derived from Eliot's translation. Cotton Mather, Nehemiah Walter, and Sewall were appointed to the committee, and they employed John Neesnummin and Experience Mayhew to take charge of the translation, producing English and Algonquian versions in adjacent columns. James Printer, like Neesnummin an Indian but unlike him given a convenient English name after his trade, was employed to do the printing, though Sewall was so involved in the project he did some himself. The edition came out late in 1710.

Sewall took his job as commissioner and treasurer of the New England Company very seriously. His meticulously kept account book shows him making payments to nearly four hundred individuals engaged in preaching to or teaching the Indians, including Neesnummin—in effect, he was responsible for the financial administration of New England's biggest employer.

As always, though, he gave equal attention to domestic matters. In February 1709, Samuel Gerrish, Boston bookseller, asked permission to court Sewall's daughter Mary, now eighteen. Gerrish passed his first test, getting protocol right by toasting her in third place (after her parents) at dinner. But Sewall remained alert for his child's interest, worrying about the fact that young Gerrish had previously courted another girl, and spluttering in sympathetic outrage one day when Mary got herself ready for him and he failed to appear: "In the evening S. Gerrish comes not; we expected him, Mary dress'd herself; it was a painfull disgracefull disappointment." Nevertheless, the two were married in August, and next day Sewall invited the governor and the council around to his house, gave them "a variety of good Drink," and presented each with a large piece of wedding cake wrapped in paper to take home.

The following year, Mary gave birth to a daughter. A few days later, she began to seem unwell. Hannah sent some of their dinner over to her house and she apparently managed to eat it. Both parents went to see Mary that evening, and Sewall prayed with her at her request. When they got home again, the chimney in the new part of their house caught fire, a regular occurrence "which made a great Uproar, as usual." In the early hours of the morning, Samuel Gerrish arrived to tell them that Mary had become dangerously ill.

All the family assembled together in the Sewalls' bedroom. Sewall himself hurried off with Gerrish to his house and was appalled to find Mary already beyond speech. At four in the morning, "my dear child expired, being but Nineteen years and twenty days old," the small change of her life totaled up with care, the more valuable for being so meager. Sewall returned to the family, who were still waiting and praying in his bedroom. When he told them the news, "a doleful Cry was lifted up."

Just when his guard was down, a crisis erupted with his pastor, Ebenezer Pemberton, sole minister at the South Church since Willard's death three years before. There had been tension between him and Sewall since the spring. That had been a time of grain shortage in Boston, and when a ship laden with wheat attempted to leave harbor, it was intercepted by rioters who cut its rudder cable. In conversation with Pemberton, Sewall had expressed disapproval of the speculators and sympathy with the saboteurs. Mr. Pemberton was known for tolerance in religion, but not in social issues: "They were not God's people but the Devil's people that wanted Corn," he ranted. "There was Corn to be had; if they had not impoverish'd themselves by Rum, they might buy Corn." Sewall was "stricken with this furious expression."

Now matters got even worse. Two men, John Banister, brother of the man who'd wreaked havoc in the Exchange Tavern, and Aaron Stuckey, were hauled before Sewall for publishing libels about the Mathers. One of them was about Cotton Mather's magnum opus, *Magnalia Christi Americana* [The Great Things—or Doings—of Christ in America], a huge rambling history of New England, for which he'd recently been awarded an honorary doctorate at Glasgow University:

> *My belly's full of your Magnalia Christi.*
> *Your crude Divinity, and History . . .*

Pemberton, as a liberal cleric, disapproved of the Mathers' religious conservatism, and asked Sewall what had happened in court. When Sewall told him he'd fined the two men, Pemberton exploded with fury, "capering with his feet" and claiming that if the Mathers told Sewall to shoot him—Pemberton—Sewall would agree to do it. (Sewall managed to be abused by Cotton Mather for alleged hostility toward his father and by Mr. Pemberton for alleged partiality toward the Mathers: testimony to his integrity, perhaps.) Sewall told Pemberton he was in a passion. He said he wasn't in a passion. A little later while they were walking down the street, Pemberton resumed the attack and had to be hushed by another member of the party. The following Sunday, Pemberton took mean revenge, ordering the first five verses of Psalm 58 to be sung in the meetinghouse. They represent a scorching attack on the integrity of judges:

> *Your wicked Hearts and Judgements are*
> *Alike by Malice sway'd;*
> *Your griping Hands, by weighty Bribes,*
> *To Violence betrayed.*

"I think," Sewall said, "if I had been in his place and had been kindly and tenderly affectioned, I should not have done it at this time." Sewall was, after all, in mourning. "Tis certain, one may make Libels of David's Psalms; and if a person be abused, there is no Remedy." But the one thing Sewall could not bear was to leave bad feelings to fester—dealing with unfinished business was the great repeated motif of his life. He went round to Mr. Pemberton's house a week later to sort things out, and they called a truce. Six years later, while Pemberton lay dying, it was Sewall whom he wanted at his bedside.

Later that winter, an Indian boy called Benjamin Larnell turned up on Sewall's doorstep, as John Neesnummin had done three years before, bearing a letter from Grindal Rawson, one of the New England Company missionaries, who had himself taken Larnell in as a boarder and sent him to school. This was in accord with the New England Company policy, strongly supported by Sewall, of educating promising Indian boys for the ministry by placing them with white families. Sewall too offered the boy his hospitality, and Larnell lived on and off in the Sewall household for the next three years. Sewall persuaded Nathaniel Williams, master of the Boston Latin School, to accept him as a pupil, and in 1712 Larnell was admitted to Harvard.

Here he attracted attention for his intellectual abilities, and President Leverett called him "an acute Grammarian, an Extraordinary Latin Poet, and a good Greek one," high praise indeed, particularly for one who had taken a journey hardly any human had ever made before, from the Algonquian tongue to Latin verse. Larnell was noticed for other reasons too, unfortunately, and made an appearance in Cotton Mather's journal in 1713 as one of a number of reprobates who had "fallen into dreadful Snares of Sin, and of Death."

These snares were sufficient to cause him to be thrown out of the college and returned to Rawson, who wrote a "very pathetical letter" to Sewall, asking for him to be reinstated in his household. Sewall agreed. Larnell then made a public confession and was readmitted to Harvard. But there was no happy ending to this particular experiment in cultural accommodation. One day in 1714, Larnell went for a swim in cold water and caught a chill. He died at Sewall's house, despite family prayers being offered up for him. The funeral was a formal one, the bearers, all of them Larnell's fellow students at the college, being provided with white gloves and scarves. Sewall accompanied the Harvard president at the head of the mourners, following the body to its grave.

Meanwhile, the New England Company had finally decided to take the action Sewall had been advocating for some years and purchase land on Martha's Vineyard for the use of Native Americans. The cost was £600, money well spent if it could prevent the Indians from returning to the mainland and reverting to pagan ways. The decision then had to be made as to what to do with the land—whether to let the Indians organize their community or to let it out and use the income for evangelizing them. Sewall was consistently in favor of giving Indians freedom to run their own affairs, so he advocated the first policy. Cotton Mather had much less faith in their capacity, and advocated the second.

Sewall decided to place these difficult matters in a larger prophetic context and in the summer of 1713 published *Proposals Touching the Accomplishment of Prophecies*, a short, intense book restating his vision of America's great destiny. Sixteen years had passed since *Phaenomena*, but his faith that reconciliation with, and conversion of, the Indians, would open the door to an American-led millennium was as passionate as ever. He gave his own version of the parable of the sower. Some seed fell by the wayside; some on stony places; some among thorns; and some on good ground: this predicts (and gives a pecking order to) the four dispensations of gospel teaching in Asia, Africa, Europe, and America. It was a progressive historical process, with America providing the glorious finale.

For Sewall, the cause of the Indians was inextricably bound up with that of America itself. If all parts of the earth belong to God, all peoples of the earth must too. Sewall repeated his view, expressed years before in his discussions with Nicholas Noyes, that when the angel puts his right foot on the sea and his left on the earth, as predicted in Revelation, the right foot will in fact be on America, the land that lay hidden in the western ocean. His own divided identity, as a New Englander and an Englishman, indeed as a Hampshireman, becomes apparent as he consoles Europe for its apparent loss of status: "Let not the Old World, let not Europe, let not England, let not Hampshire, let not any Shire be grieved that the Angel takes possession of the New World with his Right Foot; but rather rejoice that he keeps possession of the Old, with his Left." (Nicholas Noyes had gone one step further, calling Old England a "*tottering Empire*" both in terms of history and apocalyptic history.)

But despite this consolation the angel is in fact striding forward into the New World. In his copy of Thorowgood's *Iewes in America*, Sewall approvingly marked up a heady assertion of the two American continents' possibilities for native people and settlers alike: ". . . there is New *Spain*, New *France*, New *Netherland*, New *Scotland*, New *England*, why should there not be solicitous endeavours that all the Natives of that New world, should be made a world of New creatures." Sewall assures his reader of the approach of this transcendental moment, despite the troubles and difficulties of the present: "Yet this Darkness is irradiated with the brightness and solace of the concomitant Rain-bow. And tho' the Storm increase and grow never so Violent; yet this Angel persists with Courage and Constancy to Proclaim the certain approach of a Fair day." The angel had a rainbow on his head, its arc obviously reflecting the stance of his legs (Revelation 10:1). Sewall's journal is full of the sightings of rainbows—in the two years before publishing his book he recorded six of them. The ones in June 1711 were particularly impressive: "A very glorious Rainbow appears, being compleat, and of long continuance"; "Just as I had written this I went to look of the Rain at my East-Chamber window, and saw a perfect Rainbow." As a result of these metereological events, Cotton Mather published two sermons on the subject, and Sewall enthusiastically—and rather surrealistically—distributed *Rainbows* to friends and acquaintances, as well as *Fountains* (a sermon by Samuel Willard on the conversion of the Jews).

True to these reassuring symbols, Sewall's pamphlet presented a tolerant and inclusive God, whose will is not circumscribed by caste or class or race; Indians, therefore, can be saints as readily as anyone else: "There is the fair Possibility of their being made the happy Subjects of this Royal Privilege and authority: for all Saints are *born not of blood, nor of the Will of the flesh, nor of the Will of man; but of GOD*." This generous view of the scope of the doctrine of election cuts across the possibility of spiritual complacency and cliquishness. At the same time, it also counters the doubt and despair that comes with the thought that the company of elected saints might be strictly limited in scope. Sewall's household was familiar enough with the terror it might not be numbered among the chosen people, as was apparent in an incident that occurred just months after Sewall published his essay. He spilled a can of water just as he was going to bed. In the true Puritan economy nothing was wasted, not even spilled water. It provided an opportunity to reflect on the fact that "our Lives would shortly be spilled." That night, in the early hours, Sewall and Hannah were woken by a knock on their bedroom door. It was Susan Thayer, their maid. She told them she couldn't sleep and was frightened of dying, "Which amaz'd my wife and me." The kindly pair fetched Susan in, blew up the fire, wrapped her up warm and sat her by it, then got back into bed. Susan stayed by their fire until nearly morning, and then felt better and went to her own room. Sewall was startled to think that his own reflections on death had been paralleled by Susan's, though this casual glimpsing of apparent deep structural patterns itself provided security against the cold and darkness. But more effective still was the warm fire, the mutual reassurance of that little group in the bedroom. Those qualities of warmth and solidarity were what he celebrated in his pamphlet.

He concluded with a reprise of his poem written to summon in the new century, with amplification to include references to transplanted Englishmen and the conversion of the Jews. The header is significantly devoted to spelling out its original occasion: "WEDNESDAY, *January* 1. 1701. A little before Break-a-Day, at Boston of the *Massachusetts*." For Sewall, in 1713 as in 1701, the spiritual day was about to break.

By the autumn, the New England Company had worked out a compromise in relation to the Indian settlement in Martha's Vineyard. Some land would be assigned to the Indians, and the rest would be leased out, the rents being used to defray the cost of schooling. Sewall and Penn Townsend were ordered to go to the island to make the appropriate arrangements, but on the appointed day Sewall discovered someone had stolen his horse from the stable. This setback, combined with unpromising weather, led to the postponement of the trip; winter came on, and Sewall didn't set off until the following April, when Townsend wasn't able to go with him (perhaps some awkwardness still lingered from the time Townsend had accused Sewall of temporizing). But a couple of months before he finally set out, Sewall faced an unpleasant crisis in another of his many roles: custodian of civic order.

At about nine o'clock one Saturday evening in February, his neighbor Colson, the assistant constable, knocked on his door to tell him that there was disorder in John Wallis's tavern nearby. By this time, of course, Sabbath day abstemiousness ought to have set in. They collected Edward Bromfield and hurried over. The tavern was crowded and the drinkers refused point-blank to disperse, telling Sewall they'd come to drink the queen's health (it was Queen Anne's birthday) and, Sabbath or not, still had plenty more healths to drink, including his. A certain John Netmaker then insisted on drinking to Sewall (Netmaker was well named, given that he would shortly spin a web to catch the unwitting judge). Sewall told him he wasn't drinking himself, upon which Netmaker desisted. Then a young man called Francis Brindley put his hat on his head just to cause offense. Sewall made him take it off. At this point he decided to threaten the rowdy crowd with imprisonment, but they were unimpressed, pointing out that the statutes only set a fine of 5s. for failing to observe the Lord's Day, and this they were willing to pay.

New Englanders behaving badly. It's so easy to gauge the atmosphere: laughter, high spirits, and teasing just this side of menace and violence, like a saturated solution that could crystallize any moment. Sewall upped the stakes by informing them they might be guilty of riot, and Mr. Bromfield threatened to raise some men to quell them. He got himself quite worked up, which Sewall felt was unwise. He himself tried a more businesslike approach, taking down the names of the troublemakers. Unfortunately, he didn't have pen and ink with him and was forced to resort to a less impressive pencil. To compound matters, he didn't know how to spell people's names, so they gleefully took his paper away and wrote them down themselves. To compound the cheek, Netmaker observed to the council member and superior court justice that the Province of Massachusetts had not passed one good law.

Thomas Banister was there, the man who'd caused such trouble in the Exchange Tavern a few years before. Despite that, Sewall decided to appeal to him, as leader of the pack. He told Banister that as he'd been a resident and freeholder longer than any of the others, he should set a good example. He avoided reminding him that he had been a trouble-maker longer than any of the others too—since he was a Harvard un-dergraduate, in fact, when he was notable for paying record fines for breaking window glass. Banister had also been prosecuted in Connecti-cut for traveling on the Sabbath. On the other hand, he would later write a respected pamphlet on colonial commerce and appear as an ex-pert witness before the Board of Trade and Plantations in London. Se-wall was obviously hoping to tap into this more mature side of his character. To his relief, Banister agreed to invite everyone back to his own house, and the whole lot trooped off. "The Clock in the room struck a pretty while before they departed," Sewall wrote, revealing the tension the long-drawn-out scene had induced.

On the Monday, Sewall and Bromfield gave the penciled list of of-fenders to the constable, Henry Howell, telling him to fine those will-ing to pay, and order the rest to appear before them at 3:00 p.m. Four of those who then appeared (all of them from the professional and middle classes)—Andrew Simpson, ensign; Alexander Gordon, surgeon; Fran-cis Brindley and John Netmaker, gentlemen—were duly fined 5s. for breaking observance of the Lord's Day, but all appealed, and Thomas Banister stood bail for each of them. A ship's captain who was about to sail, and a visitor from New York, "who had carried it very civilliy," were let off. Netmaker was fined an additional 5s. for saying "God damn ye" to Colson, when the latter refused to join him in drinking the queen's health.

But at this point the plot thickened. Sewall and Bromfield de-manded that Netmaker arrange two bonds of £10 apiece to stand as surety for his appearance before the next Suffolk general sessions, on a charge of contempt for, and vilification of, the government of the province. Banister wouldn't stand surety for this; nor would anyone else. Sewall inferred, rightly, that this refusal was intended to embarrass the justices. Netmaker was then given till ten the following morning to provide the sureties. He turned up late, without them, and refused to offer any of his own. Bromfield and Sewall tried to reason with him but to no avail, so sent him to prison. He didn't go quietly but threatened the constable with physical violence.

After this difficult scene, Sewall went into town. Near the Town House he met William Payne, commissioner of excise, who was alarmed to hear that Netmaker had been put in jail, and offered to pay his fine for him. Sewall explained that the situation had got beyond a fine. He did not seem to have intuited from Payne's concern that he had fallen into a trap.

That afternoon, he was summoned to a meeting of the council. Afterward, he and Bromfield found themselves sitting in front of a small fire next to General Francis Nicholson, who was acting as a representative of the queen. Nicholson began questioning them in an alarming manner:

Did they know that he was bearer of the Great Seal of
England?
Yes, they knew that.
Did they not know that Mr. Netmaker was his secretary?
Sewall (cautiously): 'Tis generally so received.
Then with a roaring noise: I demand JUSTICE against
Mr. Sewall and Bromfield for sending my Secretary to
prison without acquainting me with it.

You can see Sewall jump with shock at that "roaring noise."
The keeper of Boston jail was sent for, and he produced the warrant that Sewall and Bromfield had both signed. The secretary of the council immediately declared that it was not binding (in terms of expediency, if not law), and the governor ordered Netmaker's release forthwith, to Sewall's fury and embarrassment. The merrymakers had taken their long revenge on Captain Shrimp. (Two years later, Thomas

Banister was drowned when the ship *Amity*, returning from England to Boston, foundered off Dungeness in Kent. Never one to bear a grudge, Sewall went around to his widow's house to console her.)

After these difficult civic responsibilities, it was a relief to be off to Martha's Vineyard to attempt to sort out Indian land rights in accordance with the policy established by the East India Company. The voyage to the island had a whiff of colonial adventure about it: they were becalmed, and the sloop was rowed shoreward to a part where they had not intended to land. It anchored some distance out, and their horses had to leap into the sea. By the time they got ashore and calmed the animals, night was falling. They made out some sort of presence farther along the beach. In the gloom, they thought it was a group of men and horses, but it turned out to be a solitary Indian mounted on his horse with a net resting on his shoulders. He was Thomas Paul, who was planning to do some fishing by night. Sewall, though, was the fish he caught, and Paul guided him to his host, Ebenezer Allen.

Sewall was pleased to hear that the Indians had fenced their land in Gay Head, a peninsula in the far west corner of the island. He sat in a wigwam and ate roast alewife, a fish like a herring, and some "very good Hasty pudding." He attended a service for more than a hundred Indians and was impressed: "The Women especially were attired with a very surprising Gravity and Decency." When he asked if any present could read English, two young men came forward. He gave one of them his psalmbook with red covers and promised a Testament to the other. He also settled a number of legal disputes.

One night, just before he left, an Indian called Samuel Toon went in his canoe to fetch two fish from the sloop in the harbor, missed his footing climbing on to the larger vessel, and was drowned. The next morning, when Sewall arrived on the wharf to catch the same sloop back to Boston, he saw the coroner and his jury inspecting the body. The man was about twenty-six years old. The fact that this person of a different generation, culture, and race had shared his name gave Sewall pause. "Thus I, in many respects, a greater Sinner, am suffer'd to go well away, when my poor namesake, by an unlucky Accident, has a full stop put to his proceedings, and not half so old as I." Of course, moral drawing to one's own disadvantage was a compulsion with Puritans, but it still seems surprising that Sewall was prepared to compare himself unfavorably to a dead Indian.

While he was staying at Martha's Vineyard, his host, Ebenezer Allen, mentioned he would like to have first refusal on some pasturage in Gay Head, if any was likely to be let out and if the arrangement (rather a pious note struck here) were to be compatible with the main plan of helping the cause of the Indians. Sewall was opposed: "I . . . could not find it convenient as yet, to let out any part to an Englishman." Unfortunately, as it turned out, the other commissioners disagreed. They ordered six hundred acres leased to Ebenezer Allen for ten years at £50 per year. It was only after they had committed themselves to the transaction that they discovered Indians were actually living on the land in question, and were forced to add a codicil: ". . . if any Indians be aggrieved, the Commissioners will Consider them."

The issue dragged on for years. Allen applied for a lease on another thousand acres, claiming he would pay compensation to the Indians for taking any land to which they had a claim. The Indians took direct action against his encroachment, impounding his cattle and pulling down his fences. Since the Indians were unable to produce any title to the disputed property, the commissioners brought action of trespass against them, but lost the case on a technicality. Matters weren't sorted out until 1727, when there was a formal treaty by which the Indians resigned their claim to eight hundred acres but were given the rest of Gay Head on payment of quitrent of one ear of corn annually to the Company. It was victory of a kind, but hardly the outcome Sewall had sought, and a long way from that rainbowed vision of a new heaven and a new earth.

CHAPTER FIFTEEN

"Wave after Wave, Wave after Wave"

SAM JR. AND REBECKAH, LIVING THE LIFE OF FARMERS ON the estate provided by the Sewalls at Muddy River in Brookline, were having a difficult marriage. Four of their five children died in babyhood, and tension was building, coming to a head when Rebeckah got involved in some way with a certain William Ilsley from Newbury. One February day in 1713, Sam failed to show up on a visit to his parents, and a busybody neighbor reported to Hannah that the marriage was on the rocks and Sam ought to be brought back to Boston. The next day, Sewall set off with his other son, Joseph, to try to get to the bottom of the problem and fetch Sam Jr. to the parental home. When they arrived, at eleven in the morning, Sam was still asleep in bed. Sewall got him up and they dined together.

Later, Sewall waited for a moment when he was alone with his daughter-in-law and asked her, "What might be the cause of my Son's indisposition? Are you so kindly affectioned toward one another as you should be?"

Her answer, ominously simple: "I do my duty." Sewall said no more.

Sewall had a confidential word with the servant, Tom Lamb, telling him he must avoid taking sides in the conflict between his master and mistress, and giving him 2s. as a sweetener. It must have been an awkward visit, particularly for the two brothers: Joseph, good as gold, shortly to be ordained as the junior minister at his parents' church; Sam, difficult, impulsive, weak, a worry to his father all his days. When they left in the coach with Sam, Joseph's pulse was racing so much Sewall worried about getting him home safely.

Joseph was, in fact, more the tortured introverted Puritan than his father ever was. His own diary is mainly a record of his prayers, morning and afternoon, conscientiously divided into prayer spiritual, when he is petitioning for the spirit, and prayer assisted, when he senses it's already at work, though both labels are regularly modified by a cautious "I hope." He blamed himself for sloth and "formality" (going through the forms of worship while neglecting their inner meaning). When, in 1711, he heard he had been elected as Mr. Pemberton's assistant by a margin of forty-seven votes against his rival's twenty, his response was worthy of Cotton Mather himself in its devotional hypochondria: "Who am I a shattered, frail creature?" (He was suffering from a sore throat and stomach upset at the time.) He took many months to accept the appointment and wasn't actually ordained till September 1713.

Dudley called around to ask about Sam. Sewall sent a bushel of his best peas to Rebeckah at Muddy River. Then Rebeckah came into town and called on them. Sewall diplomatically decided he had letters to post and hurried off, leaving her to talk to her mother-in-law alone. The two women went at it hammer and tongs. Rebeckah said she was completely in the right, and if it wasn't for herself, no maid would be able to stay at their house, Sam being so predatory. Finally, she burst into tears and called for her calash. This calmed things down: Hannah said she hadn't intended to upset her.

Relations with the Dudleys were inevitably tense. The next council meeting was held at the governor's home in Roxbury, since he was ill with the gravel, a bladder disorder. Sam had returned to Muddy River, but Sewall glimpsed him at his father-in-law's house. When the meeting was over and pipes had been called for, Sewall hurried down to the kitchen, hoping to catch him. Sam, though, had gone, and his father found himself trapped in the room for a long time with an oppressively silent Madam Dudley. Desperate to break the tension, he pulled out a silk handkerchief he'd bought as a sweetener for Rebeckah the week before, while diplomatically off on his mission to post letters. He had not been able to give it to her because the ructions had brought about her early exit, so offered it to Madam Dudley instead. She took it, but still remained silent. All he managed to squeeze out of her in the end was an inquiry after Hannah.

The following September, Sewall had great pleasure and pride in finally seeing Joseph ordained as colleague minister of the South Church, with a panoply of clergy—twelve New England ministers—sitting at a

Joseph Sewall (1688–1769).
Engraving after a painting, nineteenth century.
MHS #3993.

table by the pulpit. The new minister wound up proceedings with a blessing. There was a large party at Mr. Pemberton's house, but it spilled over, two tables being provided at the Sewalls'. A week later, Sewall had the mortifying experience of being told by Governor Dudley that Sam was the worse for drink in the salt marshes near his farm, exactly the news to bring the proud family down with a bump. He hurried off to discover the truth of the matter and was relieved to find Sam "very Hard at Work mowing up Stalks."

Not long afterward, Sewall was again at Muddy River, suggesting that a clergyman, Nehemiah Walter, should be asked to pray with the unhappy couple. Rebeckah sullenly replied that she didn't see why she should be brought before a minister. Sewall pointed out that he and Dudley could hardly try to act as moderators, because each would be thought prejudiced. Rebeckah said again that she had done her duty, and that she put up with a lot.

In October, Joseph married Elizabeth Walley, daughter of the major who had offended Sewall by wearing a wig. Sam and Rebeckah arrived separately, and Rebeckah insisted on staying at her sister's rather than with the Sewalls. "Mr. Pemberton craved a Blessing and Return'd Thanks at eating the Sack-Possct." The next day there was an ugly development. Rebeckah joined her husband at the Sewalls' for dinner, and they returned home together in the calash. On their way, they were overtaken by William Ilsley on horseback. Sam called out that he was not to lodge at their house. Rebeckah said that she had as much say in the running of the house as he did, and that Ilsley should lodge there. This so upset Sam that he began to feel ill, and the following morning he hurried over to his parents' house to stay. Full of tears, he told his father that his suffering would bring him to the grave. Sewall's consolation: "O Death, where is thy Sting? O Grave, where is thy victory?" Not surprisingly, Joseph made a dismal journal entry: "I hope I see y^t [that] no Creature is able to make me happy." It was only two days since his own wedding.

Clergymen prayed for poor Sam; friends were called in to advise him. The tension continued over the months and years while he shuttled miserably between Muddy River and the parental home. Sewall and Joseph went over to Muddy River one December day a year later and found themselves in an odd tableau, sitting in the bedroom where Sarah Cummins, a friend of Rebeckah's, was confined with a sore leg. They drank cider and ate apples. Sam, not for the first time, left his father and brother in the lurch, busying himself downstairs doing business. Nothing was said about the grievances. There would have been a weight of reticence and mutual disapproval in the chamber where the two pious men had invaded female space: awkward munching, guarded sips. Sewall was oppressed by the alliance of the two women. A few months later, Sarah Cummins was married, and he noted that "This News will damp my daugter of Brooklin [i.e., Rebeckah] her Triumph," a reaction that suggests the degree to which the two women had, at least from his point of view, belittled the institution of marriage. The uncharacteristic gloating shows how far his nerves were being stretched. In January, Sam Jr. went back to Boston, "Intending to live at my Father's until I could find better Treatment in my own."

It was fifty-four years since Sewall first landed in Boston. He had a middle-aged man's sudden sadness for the helpless child he once was, "a poor little School-boy of Nine years and 1/4 old." Now, half the history of the colony later, the town was still growing fast—he had to get a carpenter to install a window on the northeastern wall of his wife's chamber, since new buildings were cutting out the light from the one on the opposite side of the room (the population of the town was approaching ten thousand).

Though times were changing, Sewall managed not merely to maintain an astonishing range of interests and commitments but to knit them together into a whole. A tiny example testifies to his love of poetry, his status as a lawyer and a businessman, his civic responsibilities, his love of family, and his serendipitous knack of connecting himself with figures and incidents in American cultural history. His great-nephew, Joseph Moody, was finding the summer vacation from Harvard rather boring and sent him his Latin verses. Sewall had just written a strange Latin verse of his own. He was one of a committee authorized to sign bills of credit to the tune of £40,000 for the province, and he and the other three signers had to use a specific shifting alternation between black and red to foil counterfeiters, so his poem was a mnemonic designed to ensure he used the inks in the right order while wading through the immense pile of notes. When he returned young Moody's corrected verses, he included four of these bills, to the value of £1 18s., at his own expense, adding another 2s. to round it up. Years later, Moody, by then a minister, was overtaken by mania and began to wear a handkerchief over his face (at eight years old he'd accidentally killed a playmate). He refused to eat with others and prayed with his back to the congregation. He was eventually dismissed from his post, and from then on conducted morning prayers in the houses of his neighbors. Handkerchief Moody became one of the iconic figures of New England Puritanism and the subject of a short story by Hawthorne, "The Minister's Black Veil," in which he is depicted as suffering from an unspoken secret concerning a young lady gone early to her grave, thus providing a perfect embodiment of the dark, guilt-ridden side of the Calvinist sensibility. This stance, at least as mediated through literature, was at the opposite extreme from that of his great-uncle and mentor, who had publicly confronted his demons in the matter of the witch trials and left behind a diary in which we have access to his fears, hopes, and dreams.

Despite the Netmaker debacle, Sewall still went on watch duty, setting out at eleven one August evening in 1715 with a constable and fellow citizens for the ignominiously named Mount Whoredom, one of the three low hills on which Boston was situated, later to find respectability as Mount Vernon. Here they found a party of revelers playing ninepins in the middle of the night and sent them packing, giving the innkeeper a telling off as they did so. The town was in good order on the whole, though when he got home between two and three in the morning Sewall had to consign a notorious burglar called Joseph Griffiths to jail.

A more congenial responsibility took him out of town, to the Indian community at Natick, with a couple of other commissioners of the New England Company to supervise the execution of a deed whereby the Indians took possession of land at Magunkaquog on payment of a nominal sum of £3 apiece to the proprietors. The ratification of legal documents was to become an important part of Sewall's business, because the following December he was licensed by the council as judge for the probate of wills and letters of administration for Suffolk County, making himself available in his own home every Tuesday at ten in the morning except when absent on circuit. Just as he was about to

leave Natick, there was a crisis: one of the Indians engaged in the negotiations had killed himself. As there wasn't a coroner within reach, Sewall agreed to act himself, noting punctiliously that the man had
hanged himself with his belt, which was three feet four inches long,
"buckle and all."

The winter of 1715–16 was terribly severe, and Hannah fell ill with
a fever. She was frightened of dying, as so many of this devout family
were when their spirits were low. Sometimes, no doubt, their faith faltered; more often, perhaps, the prospect of an imminent meeting with
the God they served filled them with spiritual terror. What mattered
was their demeanor and devotion at the instant of dying. While that
belief meant that redemption was possible right up to the last moment,
it also put intolerable pressure on someone who was already physically
weakened. The condition must have been like ultimate stage fright.
Samuel Willard had given the upbeat version with characteristic lucidity in his sermon delivered on the death of Hannah's father, thirty-two
years previously: ". . . the Saint is the Man that hath the least need of
being afraid to die: this glorious promise is a Believers plentiful security
against all the frightful menaces of the King of Terrors; and it may light
a Child of God into and through this dark valley." But a momentary
loss of confidence puts this optimistic assertion into reverse. If, when
you are ill or dying, you succumb to fear and misery, it suggests God has
not elected you. Willard evokes the "King of Terrors" even as he says he
will not prevail.

Perhaps Hannah was weakened from this time on, because on 15
February Sewall visited their daughter Betty, reminded her that her
mother was coming up for her fifty-ninth year (he was in his sixty-
fourth), and gave her 10s. for acting as his treasurer in her mother's
place. Ironically, though, it was Betty who would be taken next. She
had, in fact, been suffering from consumption for several years. When
he visited her on 13 April, he found her "very Weak and low." Three
days later, he spent the evening with her while her husband, Grove
Hirst, was out on business. Earlier that same day, he saw the first swal-
lows of the year, though he thought he had heard them "chippering" be-

fore, the onomatopoeia testifying to their capacity to lift his spirits, even in ominous circumstances like these. His family was limping along, literally in the case of his daughter Hannah, a shadowy figure who never married but lived her life at home. The year before, she had fallen and broken her kneepan, and now she hobbled over to visit her brother Joseph and his wife, the longest walk she'd undertaken since becoming lame. That same day, Sewall had to warn Sam Jr. about going to taverns.

Betty's illness intensified. On 5 June, Joseph led prayers for her, and a few weeks later Sewall attended a prayer meeting for her and two others at Madam Willard's, where several ministers, Joseph included, conducted the service. Over the next days her condition declined rapidly. Joseph prayed with her and reported that she was ready to "fear y^t [that] Shee was actually in ye Agonies of Death." After the panic of that long evening, Joseph tried to recall exactly what was said: "As near as I can Remember, Shee said to me: Y^t Shee wou'd follow God, thô in ye dark."

On 10 July, Sewall sat with her. She was lying on her left side and complained of the cold. A little later, she wanted to be turned over. Sewall asked if her right arm was troubling her; she said not, all was quiet, it was just that she was tired of lying on the same side. She tried to drink but could hardly cope with the spoon. Sewall told her, "When my flesh and my heart faileth me, God is the strength of my heart and my portion for ever." She "Moan'd lower and lower till she dyed, about Midnight." Sewall sent for Joseph, who had kept vigil earlier that evening but had returned home. "This was a dark Night indeed," Joseph wrote.

Sewall spent the rest of the night in Grove's bed, because he couldn't bear to go home and wake up the other members of the family with the terrible news. "Thus have I parted with a very desirable Child not full Thirty five years old. She liv'd desir'd and died Lamented." Those words could be as cold as the gravestones on which they are often carved, but in the pages of the diary, in the context of Sewall's anxious attendance at the deathbed, they carry their full freight of love and grief. As Joseph said, "This Daûter was much His Delight And Shee was indeed very Amiable, The Flower, & Ornament of the Family." Some years before,

Sewall had had a vivid dream about her: "I dream'd that I had my daughter Hirst in a little Closet to pray with her; and of a sudden she was gon, I could not tell how: although the Closet was so small, and not Cumber'd with Chairs or Shelves. I was much affected with it when I waked."

Sam and Rebeckah's marriage continued to weigh him down. Sam was living with his parents again, and in October 1716, Sewall walked over to Roxbury to talk to Joseph Dudley and his wife about their estranged children. Dudley had finally fallen from power the year before, much to Sewall's relief, and was working at his mill when Sewall arrived. Perhaps he was making himself scarce on purpose; Sewall decided to wait until his return. It was a torrid meeting. The Dudleys went through all Sam Jr.'s failings, and then Dudley listed Rebeckah's virtues. He also took Sewall to one side and told him how heinous Hannah was. As far as the indignant Sewall could make out, her crime was telling Rebeckah from the outset that she should only marry Sam if she loved him. Sewall decided it was fruitless to pursue an argument of this sort. He told Dudley he saw no likelihood of the couple getting back together again, and asked him what he proposed.

As usual in such encounters, social niceties were sharpened up for use as weapons. Madam Dudley offered Sewall a drink. He chose beer. Dudley then tried to press a glass of excellent wine on him though he didn't want it. Then Dudley went through the charade of getting his horses harnessed in the carriage to take Sewall home, all the while telling him how many hundreds of times he himself had walked the same route. Sewall assured him he would make a pleasant journey of it on foot. In the diary, he points out that this indeed proved to be the case, because he met Mrs. Sarah Pierpoint on the way, and they had an enjoyable conversation for the rest of the journey. He needed to have even his rhetorical strategies vindicated.

The unrecorded subject of this unpleasant conference with the Dudleys was the fact that Rebeckah had become pregnant outside wedlock. In December, Sewall went to dinner with various dignitaries, including a newly arrived lawyer called Robert Auchmuty, who offended him mightily and hit the sorest of spots by reading out a letter making fun of matrimony, in which it was claimed that the body yearned for freedom and suffered inconvenience by not being uncircumscribed. "Did you read uncircumscrib'd or uncircumcis'd?" Sewall demanded ironically, the pressure of his emotions driving him to risqué wit and a parody of his own increasing deafness. "I think this a little check'd the Career of his Eleuthera [freedom]," he noted with satisfaction. That very night came the news that Rebeckah had given birth to a son.

One cause for satisfaction during a difficult time: on 6 January 1717, Sewall's reclusive and valetudinarian daughter Hannah was finally able to testify to her full conversion experience—at age thirty-eight!—and become a member of the South Church. Given the pressures that must have been on her from this pious family (even her troubled and troublesome brother Sam had become a fully covenanted member of his church in Brookline in 1713), her long delay is a testimony to the spiritual discipline and integrity required.

That spring, while he was on circuit, Sewall agreed to try to sort out John Neesnummin's debts so he could take up the position of minister at the Indian community at Natick. Sadly, though, it was a short-lived appointment, since he died in 1719. Sewall believed Neesnummin was more skilled than anyone else in the colony at crossing the divide between the Algonquian and English languages, so with his death a symbol of the ultimate compatibility of the two cultures was eradicated.

In July 1717, Hannah Sr. became ill, and Sewall had to miss the Harvard commencement celebrations. He'd missed the event the year before because of Betty's last illness. Nevertheless, in August he was able to give his full attention to Indian affairs again, accompanying Governor Samuel Shute and others on a voyage up the coast to treat with the Indians on Arrowsick Island in the middle of the Kennebec River in Maine. On the way, the party stopped in Casco Bay and Sewall took possession of one of the islands there on behalf of the New England Company. He cut down a thorn tree branch, and gathered gooseberries, raspberries, apples, and grass, symbolically appropriating the fruitfulness of the land. As always, he was alive to the millennial and utopian implications of the transaction, never seeing it simply as a matter of legal contract and social policy. The treaty, which was intended to guarantee the safety of frontier settlers in the region against enmity from Indians allied to the French and under the influence of the Jesuit Sebastian Râle, was duly signed. Sewall sent Râle some Christian reflections of his own, no doubt on the subject of an ultimate reconciliation between the races. After festivities in which the Indians fired volleys and joyfully danced, Sewall celebrated the way he liked best: with excellent cider, plum cake and cheese, and canary wine.

The treaty soon lapsed, and within four years the Massachusetts authorities sent a military force against the Indians. Sewall was moved to publish a broadside, arguing that at the Arrowsick conference they'd asked for boundaries to be fixed, but this hadn't been granted. He pointed out that townships renew their own boundaries every three years precisely in order to preserve "Honesty and Peace." The conversion of the Indians is stipulated in the royal charter, and to achieve this "it is Necessary to state and settle plain and lasting bounds between the *English*, and the *Indians*; that so the Natives may have a certain and establish'd Enjoyment of their Own Country: and that the *English* may have DEUS NOBISCUM [God with us] Legibly embroidered in their Banners."

Back home there was a tricky meeting with Dudley on the usual business. The hapless pair were trying to find the basis for reconciliation. On 22 July, Rebeckah had come to see her husband in Boston. Sam Jr. wrote: "Afternoon My Wife came to see me at my Father's & confesseth her faults with Tears. With promises of amendment. The Lord instruct me in my Duty & give me a heart to perform it." He drew a cross in the margin to emphasize the solemnity of the moment. Dudley hoped to get Sam Jr. to recognize Rebeckah's baby as his own, and mentioned Christ's pardoning of Mary Magdalene. Dudley said that God hated putting children out for adoption. Sewall argued that God hated it to happen without due cause and told him bluntly that Sam Jr. did not want the child chargeable to his estate.

One Thursday in October, Hannah was so ill that Sewall asked her if he should stay at home and miss the midweek lecture. She replied she didn't know, so he thought it best not to go, even though Joseph was giving it. On the nineteenth, he called Cotton Mather in to pray for her, along with Mr. Wadsworth. "About a quarter past four, my dear Wife expired in the Afternoon, whereby the Chamber was fill'd with a Flood of Tears."

It had been a long and loving marriage, and for Sewall as a Puritan it was now over, because the marriage bond was an earthly arrangement, not maintained in heaven. Sometime in the early years he had confirmed that very point, though in a way that suggests he regretted it: "Marriage is honourable for yᵉ Solemn Sacredness of it; I mean not hereby Spirituality: for I know it is a civil Ordinance." Certainly, the diaries express nothing but his love for Hannah; nowhere in all those thousands of words is there a single criticism of her. Several times during the course of their marriage he dreamed or feared she may have died; now it had happened. His first response, grief-stricken though he was, was to acknowledge this was another spiritual test: "God is teaching me a new lesson: to live a Widower's Life. Lord help me to Learn; and be a Sun and Shield to me, now so much of my Comfort and Defence are taken away." The next day, Joseph wept in public during the service as he tried to read the note his father had put up on the church door about Hannah's death.

The weather was hot, so Hannah was disemboweled and covered with a cerecloth. She was buried on 23 October. Sewall gave scarves and rings to the governor and bearers, who included the deputy governor, and even to Joseph Dudley—Hannah by birth and marriage was firmly established in the top echelon of Boston society, and her unassuming goodness had only reinforced her rank, despite Dudley's calumnies. Sewall missed the support of his son-in-law, Grove Hirst, who was himself too ill to attend. Four days later, he found himself saying a solemn farewell at Grove's bedside. Grove prayed him to forgive his faults. There had been a problem between the two men before his marriage to Elizabeth, but that was in the past, and Sewall had no difficulty in forgiving his beloved son-in-law. He asked to be forgiven in turn for "Defects, Excesses," those many things in which we all offend. He told Grove that he had been "in a great degree the Stay and Comfort of my Life."

Even by the standards of the time, death rained down. Within two months of Hannah's death Sewall had been a bearer for two of her bearers, fellow council members Wait Winthrop and Elisha Hutchinson. Other deaths included another councillor, two sets of husbands and wives ("Such a sight has not before been seen in Boston"), an old schoolfellow, Jacob Adams, and another friend from youth, Nicholas Noyes, the fat bachelor priest of Salem who had made himself part of the witchcraft legend by his gloating at the last batch of executions, and who may or may not have repudiated his stance later on. Hammer of heretics, Sewall called him, which perhaps suggests not. He and Sewall had delighted in arguing about their interpretations of the book of Revelation. The fact that Noyes, like Stoughton, was that Puritan rarity, an unmarried man, inspired Sewall to some revealing lines, "On his Celebacy":

> Thô Rome blasphêm the Marriage-Bed,
> And Vows of single life has bred;
> Chaste Parker, Stoughton, Brinsmead, Noyes,
> Shew us the Odds 'twixt Force, & Choice:
> These Undefil'd, Contracted here,
> Are gon to Heav'n and Marri'd there.

Sewall's own newly acquired celibacy had been a matter of force, not choice, but of course it is always open to us to accept, and therefore in a sense to choose, what God has ordained for us. This is a perfect example of Sewall's structural optimism: an attempt to accommodate and affirm his new status, and make his widowerhood spiritually fruitful.

Not that his positive stance dulled the intensity of love and loss. On 3 December, he gave Hannah's wedding ring to his daughter-in-law Elizabeth Sewall, Joseph's wife, telling her "I hoped she would wear it with the same Nobility as she did who was the first owner of it." He then helped Joseph prepare a sermon for the press, and while they were busy Elizabeth came in with a jug of sack posset. Sewall pointed out that he had just given her a wedding ring and that this entertainment savored of a wedding, insisting on life's tendency toward celebration in the teeth of bereavement. Then he went home in the rain.

There were humbler items to dispose of. Susanna Nash, mother of the maidservant Susan, stayed at the house during this time of upheaval. She managed to make it known to Sewall, through the offices of his daughter Hannah, that she would be very grateful for Mrs. Sewall's stays, and he duly passed them on to her, along with a stuff coat of his own for her husband, for which she was "very thankfull." He was always alert to the major issues of life, but never one to demean its details.

When Solomon Stoddard wrote him an excellent letter of condolence, he soaked it in tears while reading it. He thanked another correspondent, Gurdon Saltonstall, governor of Connecticut, son of Nathaniel (who had been rebuked by Sewall for drunkenness) and grandson of Richard (who had been treated with contempt by Sewall's grandfather Henry), for his letters of condolence in terms that give a sense of the cataclysm he had experienced: "When the BREAKERS were passing over me, Wave after Wave, Wave after Wave, in a most formidable succession, your Honour and your good Lady came early to my Succour, and by your Excellent Letters of Condolence did very much towards keeping my Weary head above Water."

He had used the same metaphor in an address to the grand jury at Charlestown a couple of weeks previously, turning toward the vacant chair of the late chief justice, Wait Winthrop, as he did so. It was the opening of a serious reflection on the duties of the court, quite clearly intended to set out his stall for the vacant position, but also trying to make sense of his own experience in the administration of justice, stretching back to 1692:

> The Jurors must be sure so to hear and Consider their Evidence, as to avoid all Favour and Affection; . . . The Attorneys must always Remember the solemn Obligations they are under to the Court, as well as to their Clients; the Witnesses that they speak the Truth with all Integrity. The Parties that they behave themselves with that temper and Moderation as becometh Men, and Christians; and beware of disturbing the Court with Unseasonable, or Tumultuary Noise and Clamor. . . . Gentlemen of the Grand-Jury, Your Return sometimes is *Omnia bene*; which is the

Best Return, and most Acceptable to the Court, if it be True. For the Court do not come with a desire to find Faults; but to prevent and correct them.

Avoid prejudice; bear witness truthfully; beware of tumult and clamor; understand that the most desirable verdict is not guilty: lessons originally learned in the witch trials of Salem.

The following month, Sewall wrote directly to the governor, pointing out that he was the only remaining one of the judges designated in the new dispensation of 1692, and asking for the post of chief justice. In April, he was promoted to that office. By then, he was already thinking of getting married again. He was sixty-five years old, but life was still a challenge and an adventure for him.

CHAPTER SIXTEEN

Putting to Sea in Wintertime

It WASN'T EASY FOR SEWALL, THE PROSPECT OF COURTING IN his mid-sixties after a long and happy marriage. There was a practical plane, the question of baggage, human and inanimate—interests of children, disposition of property. On top of that, the awkward matter of sexuality, compatibility, love. And—perhaps more embarrassing and worrying than either—was the vexed business of demeanor, etiquette, manners, of trying to be a supplicant without seeming awkward or gawky, attempting to assess the mood and feelings and stance of the other party, undertaking that myriad of maneuvers and adjustments necessary to move toward an understanding and, ultimately, an arrangement.

He had written his poem in praise of celibacy. Those exemplary bachelors, now dead, were "married" in heaven, indeed could be seen as married simply because they *were* in heaven ("gon to Heav'n and Marri'd there"). Perhaps there was a way of achieving a spiritual equivalent of—or substitute for—the married state while still alive. Perhaps Christ himself should be regarded as the potential spouse (despite the awkward gender implications, it was Christ the exemplary bachelors had married in heaven). "This morning wandering [*sic*] in my mind whether to live a Single or a Married Life; I had a sweet and very affectionat Meditation Concerning the Lord Jesus; nothing was to be objected against his Person, Parentage, Relations, Estate, House, Home! Why did I not resolutely, presently close with Him!"

He wrote this just three months after Hannah's death. Already his marital prospects were becoming a matter of public concern. A Mrs. Willoughby "seem'd to hint persons had need be ware how they married again." Sewall, just coming up to his sixty-fifth birthday, gave solid endorsement to this arch comment: "I said, (to humour it), They that had been at Sea should be carefull how they put to Sea again, especially in winter time. Meaning of Old Age." He must have looked out of the window after writing this explanatory gloss and added, "Rains, I think, all day long."

Age, like the weather, was closing in. Four days later, he set the York tune for the psalm singing at church and during the repeat the congregation wandered off into the Saint David tune. It was the second time in three weeks he had failed to lead them through the music. Time to quit; God had been long-suffering during his twenty-four years as precentor, but was now calling him off, his voice too enfeebled to continue. He told Thomas Prince (who had been elected minister of the South Church as Joseph Sewall's colleague) how long he'd set the tune. "Do it Six years longer" came the affectionate reply, but Sewall was too honest with himself to accept that as a final answer.

But however much he sighed about the ills of age, Sewall was intrigued by marital possibilities. He visited Nehemiah Walter, pastor of Roxbury, in late February, primarily to talk about Sam Jr.'s problems. Walter's advice was that Sam should make it up with Rebeckah. Sewall had hoped to visit an eligible widow called Martha Ruggles on the same excursion but hadn't had time. Mr. Walter agreed she was a very good woman, but said he had another one up his sleeve, Madam Winthrop, widow of the late chief justice himself.

It seems extraordinary that Sewall could find himself homing in on Wait Still Winthrop's bed as well as his judicial post, but Mr. Walter took a strictly practical view. Winthrop had been the second husband of the lady in question. She had originally been married to John Eyre, and after his death in 1700 she had generously provided Mr. Walter with her late husband's suit of black cloth, which had proved an excellent fit. All these years later, Mr. Walter was still wearing Mr. Eyre's silver shoe buckles.

Just as Mr. Walter had been able to inherit the first husband's clothing, Sewall might inherit the second husband's widow. Walter added
that Joseph Dudley had also "laid out" Madam Winthrop for him. That
was slang for matchmaking (the clothing metaphor being rather appropriate in the context of this conversation), an absorbing hobby in colonial New England. When he got home, Sewall sent some of Increase
Mather's sermons to a friend, as was his lifelong habit. In this case,
though, he might have been trying to convince himself to remain celi-
bate. One of the sermons was "about believers being married to Christ."

A couple of days later, he consulted Nathaniel Williams, music master and doctor, about his voice, and Williams authoritatively agreed that
it was much weakened. Sewall told him to communicate this information to John White, who he wanted to replace him as precentor. The
same day there was a family meeting. Sam Jr. and Rebeckah signed an
agreement that Sam should go home to his wife, and it was witnessed
by Sewall and Dudley, after which Sewall drank Rebeckah's health with
a glass of canary. The illegitimate baby had been adopted, but Sewall
used a shorthand code to describe the arrangement so that readers of
his diary would not be able to track down those concerned. Dudley then
took Sewall to one side and gave him £100 in bills of credit to pass on
to Sam, a sweetener for letting bygones be bygones. Joseph Sewall
prayed with his father and brother (Rebeckah comes across as being
somewhat anticlerical), and Sewall reminded himself that it was his
own wedding anniversary, a good omen. He had married Hannah forty-
two years previously.

It's interesting to compare how these two privileged families han-
dled their wayward offspring with the treatment meted out to people
from the bottom of the social pile. In 1721, Sewall presided over the
trial in Boston of a woman called Jemima Colefix. Even then, all these
years after the Salem trials, criminal charges included the formula "by
the instigation of the Devill." In this case, the Devil had instigated
Colefix to commit adultery, but, unlike Rebeckah, she was a laborer's
wife, and her corespondent was a free Negro. She was found guilty and
sentenced to sit upon the gallows for the space of an hour with a rope
around her neck, the other end of which was to be cast over the gallows;

then to be severely whipped thirty-six stripes on her way back to the common jail, and finally "forever hereafter wear a capital A of two inches long and proportional bigness cut out in cloth of contrary Colour to her cloaths and Sewed upon her upper Garment on her back in open view," under penalty of a further fifteen stripes. Hawthorne's *The Scarlet Letter* would feature an adulterous woman sentenced to wear a similar A, but his novel was set nearly a century before the Colefix trial.

Early in March 1718, Sewall asked Mr. White to lead the psalm singing. Embarrassed, White refused, pretending he was suffering from a cold. Sewall was adamant. It was the first Sabbath of the spring, and he was a man of winter. When the psalm was appointed, he stood up and turned to White, who then led the singing. "I thank'd him for restoring York Tune to its Station with so much Authority and Honor." The following day, Sam Jr. went back home.

The cause of Madam Winthrop was taken up in earnest. On 10 March, while Sewall was delivering a letter, Madam Henchman highly recommended her to him. Four days later, he was told Madam Winthrop's relatives wanted him to pay court to her. On 17 March, Cotton Mather sent him a letter asking him to do his duty by the local widows; two days later, the president of Harvard told him that his wife had laid out Madam Brown for him, though he himself rather favored Madam Winthrop, having been most impressed by the way in which she had shown generosity to the late Wait Still's family in waiving the requirement of a marriage settlement.

This was an economically aware society, one that valued its suits and buttons, was much concerned about dowries, and above all disliked the untidiness of having spare people washing about when they could be neatly paired off. Some news came in that would soon prove to be significant: a William Denison of Roxbury had died.

Mrs. Dorothy Denison came to town so that Sewall could prove her late husband's will, which he had drawn up for him only three days before his death. It was one of five wills Sewall proved that day. He was teased by a colleague, who "smiling said Mr. Denison's Will look'd as if it was written by me [Sewall]." Sewall responded indignantly, "Yes, but there was not a tittle of it mine but the form." A week later, Sewall was nominated for the post of chief justice. The following day, Mrs. Denison arrived at his house, and he gave her a book with her name in it.

Early in June, the new chief justice was in Roxbury, consulting Mr. Walter on matters of courting protocol. Sewall was all for paying Mrs. Denison a surprise visit. By this time, she'd been widowed for two and a half months. Walter counseled against it, just in case he should surprise her undressed. In a society where washing clothes was more inconvenient than it is now, there was a chasm between outfits worn to receive visitors and everyday wear. Reluctantly, Sewall agreed.

Mr. Walter told him that the lady would be in Boston on Thursday. She did not turn up, and the anxious Sewall wrote to Mr. Walter to find out what was going on. At nine o'clock in the morning of 9 June, Mrs. Denison arrived at Sewall's house, and he took her up to his chamber to talk. He told her he intended to visit her the following Thursday. She said people would gossip. Sewall was not to be put off: "In such Cases, persons must run the Gantlet."

When he kept his promise, he brought with him the volume of Increase Mather's sermons, telling her, somewhat suggestively, that "we were in it invited to a wedding." Earlier in the year, he had been hoping for a spiritual marriage that would transcend earthly considerations; now he was seeing that more as a hint of, or precedent for, one in the here and now. Mrs. Denison responded by giving him some good curds.

Over the next weeks, the courtship went on smoothly enough. Sewall made frequent visits to Mrs. Denison, sometimes accompanied by members of his family, and often bearing gifts: an English crown, knives and forks in cases, shoe buckles, a "Pound of Raisins with proportionable Almonds"—that snack first given to him by an uncle when he was a nine-year-old boy setting out for America. By 1 November he was ready to publish the banns, and borrowed Sam Jr.'s horse to go out to Roxbury in order to make the final settlement.

It was at this point he got a shock. He asked her what allowance he should make. She did not reply. He suggested that he should leave her £250 a year for the rest of her life if he died before she did. She said she had better keep as she was, rather than trade certainty for uncertainty.

What was worrying her was the expense of living in Boston. She would "pay dear for dwelling" there. Sewall asked for her suggestions, but she offered none. Sewall was shocked at hitting this unexpected impasse. "May God, who has the pity of a Father, Direct and help me!"

He kept away for four weeks. Then he had a consultation with the inevitable Mr. Walter, obviously an authority on matters of the heart, who advised him to go and speak with her. Off he went. He records the ensuing fraught conversation in wonderful detail.

He began by asking her how she had been since they last met, then told her he had interpreted the conversation they had had then as meaning they should not proceed any further.

She said he should please himself, and went on to blame him for not telling her at that previous meeting that their courtship was over. Someone had since come around expressing an interest in renting her property but she had not known what to reply.

Taken aback by this unexpected reversal of responsibility for the breakdown, Sewall repeated her words of 1 November.

When she heard the bit about paying dear she started, as if she had never said such a thing. But she quickly picked up the adversarial thread once more. "She thought twas hard to part with *all*, and have nothing to bestow on her kindred."

Sewall immediately reassured her that her movables, indeed all her personal estate, would remain in her possession.

She shifted ground: he had been in a hurry when they last spoke, which was why she had made no suggestions of her own.

He pointed out he had asked her long before that to give him her thoughts on the matter in writing.

She took offense. He, who had never written her a letter, had had the impudence to expect her to write *him* one.

It was an awkward moment. She tried to defuse it: there's a switch in tone, from stridency to low-key politeness. She asked him if he would like something to drink. He said he would. She provided cider, apples, a glass of wine. But this was a valediction rather than a reconciliation. She produced the little presents he had given her and offered them back to him. He refused them, and said he wished her well. He would be glad to hear how she was getting along. She implied that she would not get herself involved in this way again with anyone, and asked his prayers. Then her brother and his wife called, and brought the meeting to an end. Sewall went home by moonlight.

At the back of that sparring, those tactical offensives and withdrawals, there was feeling. Having got every nuance of their edgy dialogue down on the page, Sewall wrote: "My bowels yern towards Mrs Denison." But his background as a businessman and judge of probate encouraged respect for contracts and agreements: he reminded himself that in the beginning she had said that if they could not agree, they must break it off. QED: "God directs me in his Providence to desist."

A freezing Sabbath evening, two days later, at about seven o'clock. Sewall had a fire in his hall, and was praying. There was a knock at the door. Sam Hirst, orphaned son of Betty and Grove, who was being brought up by his grandfather, answered it. In came one Thomas Weld. His cousin, Mrs. Denison, was waiting outside. They had walked over from Roxbury. She wanted to have a private word with Sewall. He was startled that she had come so far on foot in such cold weather. He sent young Sam away and let her in himself.

Perhaps he was flattered too. Mrs. Denison's bowels might yearn more for him than he had allowed for. She was anxious people would gossip. That added an extra touch of spice. He assured her that young Sam had no idea who her cousin was, and now the two of them were alone together.

She began by going over their recent encounter. He seemed to be altered in his affections. She was sorry if she had offended him. She did not want the match to break off after they had been keeping company so long (her husband had been dead for just seven months, but courtship has a different rhythm in an age of high mortality). It was all the late Mr. Denison's fault. He had wanted her to hold some of her assets back, just in case some of their friends needed help.

Sewall told her she could keep it all.

She was sorry, but that was not what she understood.

Sewall waited for her to make a suggestion, but none was forthcoming. Instead, she mentioned two glass bottles he had given her.

He said she could keep them, along with his other presents, as long as she understood they would not have the same meaning as they originally possessed. He was worried about how cold she had got on her journey and suggested they have supper. That might allow a more convivial mood to develop. She refused. The best he could do was fetch a tankard of cider and drink to her. Then she was off into the cold night for her long walk back, no moon shining. It was a moment of great pain. He kissed her hand when she left.

There cannot be many records that contain such detailed ebb and flow of thought and emotion, such intricate interplay between two people. It is worth recalling this was a community without theater. When Sewall heard rumors that a play might be performed at the Council Chamber, he was incensed: "Let not Christian Boston go beyond Heathen Rome in the practice of shamefull Vanities." Yet his meticulous records of his romantic encounters show full awareness of the irreducible dynamic of conversation, the fact that the meaning lies in the dialogue itself, rather than in any extractable content. To understand that is to accept that discourse is dependent on context, and to operate in a different world from that of the fatal allegorists of the witch trials, who took allegations at their face value, never allowing for the human circumstances in which they had originated. Here was a very human conflict, between money, prudence, and the status quo on the one hand, and the desire for new experience, love, and companionship on the other, caught in all its complexity by Sewall's pen.

Boston, twenty years into the eighteenth century, was a different world from that of Salem—and indeed of Boston itself—in the 1690s. Sewall had moved from the arena of rural tragedy, as defined in his long-ago letter from Newbury to his Harvard classmate, to a complex urban scene where the comedy of social intercourse can be played out, where the intricacies and velleities of courtship seem perfectly in place. There was now a forest of masts in the harbor—"a kind of Wood of Trees like that which we see upon the River of Thames"—into which, like a nautical highway, the Long Wharf jutted nearly a third of a mile from shore, its warehouses and the shops that continued along King Street into the heart of the town offering a cascade of goods to the

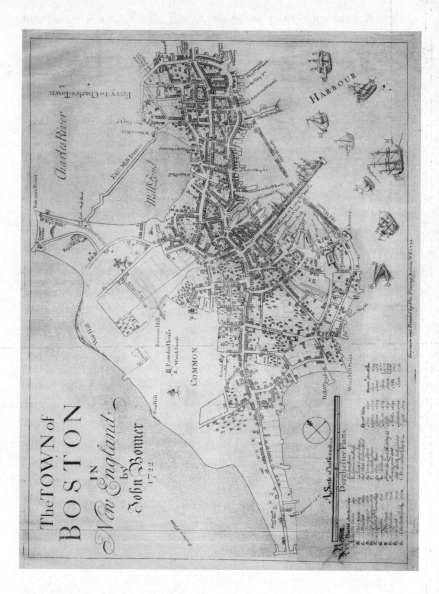

Francis Dewing, after John Bonner, *The Town of Boston in New England*
(engraving), 1722, 53914: I.N.

*Phelps Stokes Collection, Miriam and Ira D. Wallach Division of Art, Prints and Photographs,
The New York Public Library, Astor, Lenox and Tilden Foundations.*

passing public: muffs and necklaces, jewels and paintings, cider and wine, silks and fine cloth, books galore and fashionable spectacles to read them with. You could go to horse races, watch bear baiting, see apparently moving pictures in peep shows or magic lanterns, relax in coffeehouses or taverns. Boston was the biggest town in America, with a population of about twelve thousand spread over three thousand houses, a third of which were built out of stone or brick, giving them a substantial air (along with some protection from Boston's periodic conflagrations). Markets were held every Tuesday and fairs twice a year. On their own small scale, Boston's fashions, furniture, and buildings, its bustling commercial life, bore comparison with London.

Sewall's next courtship was a different matter entirely. On 1 April 1719, he was sent a present, one of a number he had recently received: four oranges, two pieces of salmon, and some of Madam Foxcroft's wedding cake. He loved such give and take, but this gift was in a class of its own: very good white kid gloves, and a gold ring with a motto, *Lex et Libertas* [Law and Liberty], along with the initials A.T. They stood for a woman called Abigail Tilly.

It was quite acceptable for a woman to make the opening move in courtship. Sixteen-year-old Hannah Hull had settled on Sewall before he'd even noticed her, and Mrs. Tilly was a mature widow of fifty-three. By August, they were courting. That month, Sewall's newly born grandson Joseph, named after his father, died and was buried in the family tomb, and Sewall was able to get a glimpse of Hannah's coffin: "May I be prepared to accompany her in that dark house." His second visit to Mrs. Tilly occurred ten days later, and four days after that, on 2 September, he asked her to marry him. There was none of Mrs. Denison's resistance: "She expresses her unworthiness of such a thing with much Respect."

He ate almonds and raisins with her, as he had done with her predecessor, and by mid-October the banns were being published. The whole affair became a bit of a rush. He asked Increase Mather to marry them, but the old man was not keen (he did not like going out in the evenings), and Sewall realized that Mrs. Tilly's plans were so far advanced they couldn't brook delay, so they were married by Joseph instead, on 29 October, at the bride's house. After the celebrations and the distribution of cake, Abigail went upstairs. A little later, her friend Mrs. Armitage, who had been living with her and sharing her bed, formally escorted Sewall into the bedroom to join his bride. Sixty-seven-year-old Sewall tried to handle this awkward moment with panache, but did not quite manage it: "I thank'd her that she had left her room in that Chamber to make way for me, and pray'd God to provide for her a better Lodging."

Every so often events, big or small, embarrassing or tragic, sprang into Sewall's life and startled him. In a life with its full share of disaster he retained the ability to be horrified. This time it was his wife's illness on her wedding night. After a short time, she felt so poorly she had to sit up in bed. She began to cough consumptively, and spit blood. He hurried out of bed to get some of her petticoats to put around her. He was "exceedingly amaz'd, fearing lest she should have died." She was very upset herself. One begins to suspect that her enthusiasm and haste for this match was triggered by her own fear of the dark house.

A few weeks later, Sewall visited the sick ex-governor Dudley, who was light-headed, rambling on about his days on the Isle of Wight. As Sewall made his way home through the darkness, the weather turned foul. "I met with difficulty in my return by reason of the snow in my face: yet the light of it was comfortable to me." In due course, he formulated the experience into Latin, for the benefit of John Frizzell, a young man studying for Harvard: "*Nocta viatori, comitem nix candida lumen Praebebat; lapidusque malo fuit usus in illo*" (The gleaming snow offered light as a companion to the troubles at night, and was a charming aid in that evil). Perhaps that was a metaphor for the marriage of these two people who had known death and were feeling their own mortality: navigating through the dark by snow light. In December, Abigail had such a violent ague fit she again thought she was about to die, but managed to pull back.

Sewall's fear of losing his bearings comes across a week or two later when he wrote a poem on a subject close to home, the expansion of the border of New Hampshire southward to the Merrimack River.

Though Newbury was on the south bank of the river, Sewall believed his boyhood home could be swallowed up by the rival province. The issue was the important one of maintaining natural rather than artificial boundaries, though in this case Sewall's loyalty to his own past put him on the side of the artificial boundary that represented the status quo. (The border problem between the two states, as they eventually became, persisted well into the nineteenth century.)

Sewall's poem was based on the conceit that the river had mysteriously dried up—"Upon the drying up of that Ancient River, The River Merrymak." The image was one of the great reference points of his life, the prophesied drying up of the River Euphrates, a sign of the approaching millennium, and he begins by calling the Merrimack the Euphrates. But he cannot pursue the optimistic implication of the analogy, because his poem is about the loss of the past, not the rewards of the future. Instead, he links the flow of time to the flow of water and celebrates a pastoral harmony that existed for millennia prior to European settlement:

> *In peace profound our River Run*
> *From his remote, and lofty Head,*
> *Until he with the Ocean Wed.*
> *Thousands of Years ran parallel,*
> *View'd it throughout, and lik'd it well.*

He goes on to evoke the seasonal cycle of animal and vegetable life on the banks of, and within, the river, rather in the fashion of the rapt passage of *Phaenomena*, though without the lyrical power he achieved in the earlier work, and because of this larger temporal perspective without the Christian teleology either. The mood is classical, even pagan:

> *Herbs, Trees, Fowls, Fishes, Beasts, and Men,*
> *Refresh'd were by this goodly Stream.*
> *Dutiful Salmon, once a Year,*
> *Still visited their Parent dear . . .*

He radically revises the Puritan encounter with the dark forces of the wilderness, seeing the landscape as a nurturer of the settlers:

> *The Strangers, late Arrived here,*
> *Were Entertain'd with Welcom chear . . .*

Unfortunately this peaceful coexistence has been unexpectedly shattered: ". . . at one Huge Sup, / Hydropick *Hampshire* Drunk it Up!"

This is an occasional poem aimed at a specifically political objective, but the elegiac tone, and the retrospective nature of the utopia depicted there, perhaps reflects the nostalgic attitude of a man feeling his age and wondering if his and his country's future lay in the past. Unlike his earlier evocations of American destiny, it is a classical piece of American Dream literature, mourning the lost possibility of peaceful accommodation in a virgin land.

His old sparring partner, Joseph Dudley, began to fail rapidly, while family tension continued. Rebeckah gave birth to a son, within wedlock this time, and Sam Jr. rowed with Madam Dudley, who thought he was going to call the baby Dudley. She did not want his given name to be confused with the family name of her other grandchildren, a good indication of how she regarded this marriage. In any case, Sam Jr. "had names of my own relations enough to name it" and called him Henry after his grandfather. By this time, Dudley himself was comatose. Despite all the bad feeling, Sewall went to see him, though he had to sit with the difficult Madam Dudley instead, since the ex-governor was too ill for visitors. That once arrogant, vain man had to be "lifted to and fro like a child." Two weeks later, Sewall was a bearer at his funeral.

By contrast, the following month he had the joy of officiating at the wedding of his daughter, nineteen-year-old Judith, to William Cooper, minister at the Brattle Street church. Like her sister Betty before her, Judith had had a difficult time going through her courtship period. Thomas Prince, Joseph's colleague and a most eligible candidate, had tried and failed to win her hand. He had been dining with Sewall when he excused himself, and went through to the kitchen. Here, he got young Sam Hirst to show him the way to a bedchamber where Judith was apparently hiding out with the family housekeeper, Lydia Kay. He knocked and pleaded at the door for a long time before the women would let him in. "Judith trembled much, and is more and more alienated from him by his rough upbraiding Carriage towards her."

After that, Dudley's son William asked if he could pay court to her, but Sewall—thinking of all the trouble the current marital connection between the families had brought—decided he might cause her "some Umbridge" and told him he would have to ask her first. A couple of weeks later, Dudley himself appeared at Sewall's house in his chariot to reinforce the message, but Sewall stalled him, and the whole thing petered out. Then Judith met William Cooper while out to dinner, and in time-honored fashion he walked her home. They were courting a week later.

Sewall told the groom's mother and stepfather that he had no need to ask who giveth this woman to be married to this man, because their presence at the wedding and his conducting of it answered that question. His address to his daughter captures his gracefulness nicely, perfectly combining the affectionate father and the dignified (chief) justice: "Dear Child, you give me your hand for one moment, and the Bridegroom forever." Joseph prayed, and Sewall, on domestic territory, was willing to lead the singing. Then they all had cake and sack posset.

One night, just two weeks later, Sewall went to bed about ten o'clock. An hour later, Abigail began to feel ill. Her throat was full of phlegm, and she found it difficult to breathe. Sewall got up, lit a candle, and asked his black servant Scipio, who was sleeping by the fire, to get a basin of water. But her condition deteriorated rapidly. He called in his new son-in-law (William and Judith were living with the Sewalls while their house was being made ready), another Negro servant called Philadelphia, and Experience Mayhew, who was also staying. To no avail: Abigail died about midnight, "to our great astonishment, especially mine."

Sewall experienced a great shock of guilt: "May the Sovereign Lord pardon my Sin, and Sanctify to me this very Extraordinary, awful Dispensation." A few weeks previously he had had the disturbing experience of reading about the Salem witch trials in Daniel Neal's newly published *History of New England*. "It grieves me to see New-England's Nakedness laid open . . . The Judges Names are mentioned, p. 502. My Confession, p. 536. Vol. 2. The Good and Gracious God be pleased to save New-England, and me and my family!" The reminder of those events of many years before had caught him on the raw, and the sense that his family was somehow likely to be the recipient of God's displeasure couldn't have come at a more unfortunate time (Neal's summary of the confession mentions Sewall's hope that guilt "might not be imputed to . . . his Family in particular"). The Sunday after Abigail's death, he was still wrestling with guilt, and sounding far more like tortured Calvinists of the Cotton Mather or Michael Wigglesworth variety than he usually did: "God having in his holy Sovereignty put my Wife out of the Fore-Seat, I apprehended I had Cause to be ashamed of my Sin, and to loath my self for it; and retired into my Pue." He put up a note about his bereavement to be read in three churches. That night, at about midnight (the time Abigail had died), he heard a desolate cry in the streets.

JUST OVER three months after that bleak experience, Sewall embarked on another courtship, the most stormy, revealing, and closely documented of them all.

One September day he had a pleasant encounter with Madam Winthrop, the much touted candidate for his affections of two years previously, at Joseph's house; later that month, he asked Joseph's wife, Elizabeth, to tell the lady that if it pleased her to be at home at 3:00 p.m. the next day he would wait on her. No colonial American ever wrote anything more revealing than Sewall's account of what happened next.

He arrived on the dot. Perhaps that in itself made him conscious of being too precipitate. He began by telling Madam Winthrop that his wife having died so recently and so unexpectedly, it was too soon to think of marrying again. However, he wanted this to be seen as a preliminary visit: he had taken a resolution he would not pay court to anyone without discussing it with her first. (He was no doubt thinking of the misunderstandings that had arisen with Mrs. Denison.)

After this rather direct opening shot, the conversation softened and became flirtatious. They discussed the seven ladies who had been in the widows' pew at lecture the previous Thursday: Madam Winthrop suggested first one then another for him (not, presumably, Madam Dudley, who had indeed been one of them: too much water under *that* bridge). None was right, however. She mentioned suggestively that Mrs. Loyd was about her own age (fifty-six; twelve years younger than Sewall). Madam Winthrop had, of course, herself been one of the seven.

Two days later, Sewall was back. She was not there when he arrived. Her heavily pregnant daughter Katherine Noyes, was, however, and he took the opportunity of asking her if she had any objection to his paying court. She was in favor of anything that might give her mother comfort. He kissed her hand and wished her good luck in her confinement.

Then something odd happened. Into the room walked Obadiah Ayers, chaplain of Castle William, the island fort in Boston harbor now named after the late king. Ayers hung his hat upon the hook for all the world as if he lived there, while Sewall watched, "a little startled."

Finally, Madam Winthrop appeared. There followed an awkward interlude as the four assorted people sat in the room. Sewall plucked up courage to say that he would like a word with Madam Winthrop. She suggested they go off into another room, but Mr. Ayers and Mrs. Noyes politely left instead. Then Sewall made his move. He reminded her— Katherine, he called her now—of their previous conversation about the women in the widows' pew, and asked her if she would agree to be the one for him.

Her response was immediate. She had been waiting for an opportunity to say no, but, of course, could not do so until she was asked. That was how she felt, unless she happened to change her mind. But she did not think she would. She could not leave her children.

Sewall was sorry she had made her mind up so speedily. He asked when he could visit her again. She did not give a date, so he suggested the next Monday, a week from that day. He left with a flourish, giving her a copy of Willard's *Fountain*, and telling her that if they both took that book to heart they would meet in heaven, if not in the here and now. She put the sermon in her pocket, and he went.

Just two days later, at three in the afternoon, he called again, unable to wait a week. As luck would have it, Madam Winthrop was out, dining with her daughter Katherine Noyes, and he was shown in by the nurse of little Katee, Madam Winthrop's granddaughter by another daughter, Bethia Walley. There was nothing for it but to give little Katee a kiss and a penny and take his leave. He went off to help his daughter Judith and her husband move into their new house. Later that day, he bumped into Jonathan Belcher, who invited him home to share a pasty with the governor and other notables. At the end of the evening, the governor gave Sewall some of the cake and gingerbread that was part of the feast.

Two more days and Sewall was at Madam Winthrop's again, at six in the evening of 6 October. Once more she was out. He gave 2s. to the housekeeper, Sarah Chickering, and another shilling to the black servant Juno, who brought in some wood. Then the nurse came in and he had to give her 1s. 6d. not having any other change. (It was as if he was paying fines to the household staff for his importunity.) At last Madam Winthrop appeared, with her son-in-law, Dr. Oliver Noyes, the same who had attended Sewall's mother-in-law in her last illness. The two talked together for a long time—till eight o'clock, in fact. One can feel for Sewall, out of place and disregarded. Finally, he could bear it no longer, and said he feared his presence might be an interruption to their business. Taking the hint, Noyes replied graciously that he feared *he* was interrupting Sewall's business, and left the room.

Madam Winthrop immediately began "to harp on the same string. Must take care of her Children; Could not leave the House and Neighbourhood where she'd lived so long."

Sewall: "She might doe her children as much or more good by bestowing what she laid out in Hous-keeping, upon them. Said her Son would be of Age the 7th of August." (The precision of that point has a judicial flavor.) After he reached his majority, he would get married in due course. "I said it might be inconvenient for her to dwell with her

Daughter-in-law, who must be Mistress of the House." He clinched his argument by giving her pieces of Mr. Belcher's cake and gingerbread, which he'd wrapped up in a clean sheet of paper.

It was time to get personal: "My daughter Judith was gon from me and I was more lonesome—might help to forward one another in our journey to Canaan—"

Just as he was in full flow, in came John Eyre, her son, he who would reach the age of twenty-one the following August. He was named after his elder brother, who had drowned while skating on Fresh Pond in 1696. Sewall had heard his father crying out bitterly on being told the news: it had been one of those chilling moments in the lead-up to his great apology.

Time for some polite conversation, and then to take his leave. As he did so, he cheekily claimed that this visit had been in order to remind her that he was due to come over on the Monday night. She said she had not forgotten. He also asked permission to visit her sister, Madam Mico, to entreat her to support his suit. This did not go down well— Madam Winthrop "seem'd surpris'd and displeas'd." Her sister was a widow too, "in the same condition!" She was hardly likely, therefore, to be able to act as an honest broker.

Monday evening finally came around. Madam Winthrop was charming. She gave him wine and marmalade (the word was used for any kind of preserved or stewed fruit). He gave her a copy of the *Boston News-Letter* covering the Thanksgiving celebrations. She told him she had had a visit from Increase Mather earlier and he had informed her that Cotton's chimney had caught fire yesterday.

Buoyed by this amicable encounter, Sewall wrote Madam Winthrop a letter the following day, one that beautifully demonstrates his instinct to place his own fate in the context of a larger American destiny, inaugurated by the European discovery of the continent, and completed by the reconciliation with the Indians.

Madam, These [words] wait on you with Mr. Mayhew's Sermon, and Account of the state of the Indians on Martha's Vinyard. I thank you for your Unmerited Favours of yesterday;

and hope to have the Happiness of Waiting on you tomorrow before Eight a-clock after Noon. I pray GOD to keep you, and give you a joyfull entrance upon the Two Hundred and twenty ninth year of Christopher Columbus his Discovery; and take Leave, who am, Madam, your humble Servt. S.S.

The crisis had come: time for Sewall to make his move. He knocked at Madam Winthrop's door at just before eight o'clock the following evening.

The door was answered by Mrs. Anne Cotton, a friend of Madam Winthrop. She showed him in to a small room where Madam Winthrop was working on some material—"black stuff or silk"—behind a stand. Madam Winthrop pointed to Mrs. Cotton to set a chair for Sewall. Her expression had changed from their last meeting: it was "dark and lowering."

At last the sewing was taken away. Sewall sat himself down and had a bit of strained conversation. Then he took his courage in both hands, got to his feet, and asked her if she would mind him removing her kid glove. She asked why (she'd been doing needlework with gloves on to prevent fingermarks on the silk).

Sewall, sixty-eight years old, the charmer, or would-be charmer: "I told her twas great odds between handling a dead Goat, and a living Lady."

This was gallantry constructed entirely from first principles, the clever symmetry of the rhetoric disastrously aligning the beloved with a butchered animal. Nevertheless, he added with hard-won satisfaction, "Got it off."

Then to business. Would she remove the negative she had laid on him on 3 October? She would not. Indeed, she intensified it. She "could not leave her house, children, neighbours, business." A slightly complaining riposte: "I told her she might do som Good to help and support me." She brought up the fact that he'd once courted the widow Denison. His reply was a robust "Yes!" He went on to say that if she changed her mind and let him continue courting, he would be most grateful. At some point in their conversation, he managed to tap into his passionate vein again. He would rather go to the "Stone-House," the lockup next door, once occupied by Samuel Vetch during the great treason crisis of Dudley's administration, than pay court against her will. He explained why he had only been visiting every other night (she was probably wondering why he came so often): the reason was "lest I should drink too deep draughts of Pleasure." She had mentioned having a glass of canary wine: ". . . her Kisses were to me better than the best Canary."

She avoided being swept away by such torrents of feeling, thanked him for the copy of Mr. Mayhew's sermon, but did not mention the accompanying letter. Nevertheless, he explained to her the significance of the reference he had made to Columbus (at that time, few people gave Columbus credit for discovering America), no doubt hoping to persuade her to look at the bigger picture. "When she insisted on the Negative, I pray'd there might be no more Thunder and Lightening, I should not sleep all night." He gave her a theological work he'd bought for 6s. at a recent sale, one with a suggestive title: *The Church's Marriage and the Church's Carriage*, by John Preston.

At this point the mysterious Obadiah Ayres walked into the room, as he had done on a previous occasion, and once again hung his hat up on a peg and sat down, taking the wind out of Sewall's sails. Then Madam Winthrop left the room and Mr. Ayres followed. John Eyre put his head around the door. Sewall, discomfited, mumbled something—"How do ye, or, your servant Mr Eyre," he couldn't remember which—but got no reply. He was now completely marooned.

Fortunately for his dignity, the housekeeper, Sarah Chickering, took pity on him. She poured him a glass of wine and one for herself, and then drank to him, and he to her, chief justice and servant sharing a moment of solidarity in an embarrassing situation. Then she arranged for Juno to escort him home with a good lantern. Sewall gave her sixpence and told her to thank her mistress on his behalf. The following day, he reported gloomily to his son Joseph and daughter-in-law Elizabeth that "the Weather was not so fair as I apprehended."

He was still prepared to battle on, however. Of course, his pursuit of the elusive widow was very much a public spectacle. A friend, James Hill, wished him joy of the proceedings. Hannah Cooper, the sister of his son-in-law William, applauded his initiative and said she thought she would visit Madam Winthrop to press his case. Sewall was grateful, but then he began to upbraid himself for his preoccupation with earthly affairs and consequent indifference to the love of Christ. Nevertheless, on Monday, 17 October, five days after his last visit, he was at Madam Winthrop's door again.

She was courteous enough, but she had not put on clean clothes to receive him, as she had sometimes done previously. This Boston with its wine and marmalade and gingerbread was still rough around the edges. Clean clothes, clean streets, and clean bodies were not to be taken for granted. In 1692, Susannah Martin had been hanged partly because many years before she had inexplicably failed to get her shoes and skirts muddy on a wet day.

Madam Winthrop complained that she had not known whether to expect him again. Mrs. Denison had made a similar charge in her time: on both occasions, Sewall believed it was the woman in the case who had put a dampener on things. The way he explained his reaction offers a fine example of the rigorous and serious scrutiny he applied to such interchanges.

"I ask'd her how she could so impute inconstancy to me. (I had not visited her since Wednesday night being unable to get over the Indisposition received by the Treatment received that night, and *I must* in it seem'd to sound like a made piece of Formality.)"

He reports using a stock sentence of lovers' discourse, then glosses it in brackets for his own benefit, retailing the pain behind the well-turned language. But he had not been able to present this emotional subtext to Madam Winthrop, as it would have come out like a rebuke. So he had to be content with the bloodless phrasing of his original remark, "a made piece of Formality."

Just as little presents like pieces of salmon and cake wrapped in paper served to enrich social intercourse within the community, so this capacity to inspect and analyze the emotional content—and suppression—of courtship conversation must have contributed to creating an environment in which the subtleties and nuances of social life could thrive. The diary, of course, was not read outside the family for nearly a century and a half, but the man who wrote it brought his complexity to bear on the community in which he lived.

Sewall gave Madam Winthrop a copy of the *Gazette*, Boston's second newspaper, and then listened to the Lord's Prayer as recited by her six-year-old grandson David Jeffries (son of her daughter Katherine Noyes by her first marriage—the latter was still only twenty-six, early deaths creating the same dislocations and complications in family life as divorce would do to a later generation). Madam Winthrop went off to a bedroom to give some medicine to her granddaughter Katee. Young David tried to get Sewall to follow but the judge was aware how indiscreet that would be. Then Katherine Noyes and her husband arrived and sat with him some considerable time. They had just come from visiting Sewall's daughter Judith and son-in-law William Cooper, so Sewall would have felt less of an interloper in the conversation than usual. He was escorted home by Juno.

The next day, Sewall made his call on Madam Mico. Unlike her sister, she appeared in a splendid dress. He was received politely enough, and given a glass of canary. She respectfully remembered his first wife, Hannah. She was not opposed to his courtship, if her sister was not.

The following evening, he was back at Madam Winthrop's. She was out, visiting her son-in-law John Walley (who was the brother of Joseph Sewall's wife, Elizabeth) and daughter Bethia, parents of Katee. Sewall had brought along three oranges provided by his daughter Hannah. He passed them over to Sarah Chickering. He did not know whether to go home or not: he would go and meet Madam Winthrop at Mr. Walley's if Sarah was sure he would find her there. She was sure, so he went and did indeed find her there, with Mr. Walley and his wife. As so often happened, he was surplus to requirements, and hung around awkwardly. At seven, he said he must be going home. At eight, he put on his coat, and this time Madam Winthrop responded, so he was able to walk her home.

When they arrived, she spoke loudly to the servant, as if to establish this was her home. Nevertheless, she let Sewall in. She told him he ought to keep a coach. He explained it would cost a hundred pounds a year to run; she said it would only be about forty. John Eyre came into the room and sat with them for a time. Sewall offered him some sermons of Increase Mather's. John said he already had them. Sewall told him he could have a second copy. John promptly exited.

The next day was a Thursday. At the council meeting, Sewall's old sparring partner Penn Townsend complained about the hood he was wearing, and told him he should get a wig. Sewall stoutly replied that the hood was his chief ornament, which he wore in honor of Lecture Day (his usual headgear being his cap).

Madam Winthrop wasn't at lecture, which gave him an excuse to call on her before going for drinks at the governor's at seven. He found her sitting with her daughter Katherine and a friend. She drank to him, and Sewall drank to Katherine. Sewall asked if he could have a word, and Madam Winthrop picked up a candle and led him into her best room. She closed the shutters and sat down on the couch—there was an expectation of intimacy in these details. But the promise was not fulfilled. She resumed on the topic of a coach. A friend had talked to her on the subject: it was important to give the vehicle full use and not leave it to rust. Then, as if part of a conspiracy, she "spake something of my needing a Wigg."

Next she asked what her sister had said to him. With his usual honesty, Sewall reported that she would not hinder the courtship if Madam Winthrop was for it; but at the same time, she had not said she would be glad to have him as a brother. Aware of his forthcoming appointment with the governor, he tried to rescue himself from this low point by switching to his gallant mode. He would keep her in the cold for the moment, and resume this conversation tomorrow night, if she would be at home, "for we had had but a running feast." She did not rise to the bait: she was not sure whether she would be in or not. Sewall took his leave and hurried over to the governor's. By an odd coincidence, His Excellency took it upon himself to make a jocular point: "In England the Ladies minded little more than that they might have Money, and Coaches to ride in." Sewall glumly replied that in that case *New* England was appropriately named. The governor demurred: "They were not quite so bad here."

The next day, Sewall prayed for his courtship with his son Joseph, and then at six in the evening went off to Madam Winthrop's again.

She was out, and Sarah did not divulge where, even though he gave her 5s. She ordered him a fire, and he settled down to read Dr. Sibbes's *Bowels*, a book of sermons. By nine o'clock, he had read the first two. At last John Eyre came in, and Sewall took the opportunity of asking him if he had any objections to the courtship. He had not. Sewall presented him with the book he had promised, inscribing John's name in it and the date. It had cost him 8s. John said he would go to fetch his mother, who was visiting one of his brothers. A little later Sewall heard Madam Winthrop's voice, asking John something, and then he heard her bang the garden gate shut two or three times. She was a woman who liked to announce her arrivals, at least when Sewall was about.

Finally, she appeared. He teased her about being out at that late hour, and she teased him back about him being out even later. He asked her when their relationship could be made public. She replied that it was not likely to get any more public than it was already. She did not offer him wine. At eleven o'clock, he put on his coat. She did not try to help. He asked if Juno could escort him home. She opened a shutter and said it was a light night. Juno was tired and had gone to bed. "So I came hôm by Star-light as well as I could." The following day, his daughter Judith visited, and at about sunset he walked her part of the way home ("near as far as the Orange Tree"). On the way back, he saw little David Jeffries, who gave him an affectionate look and asked if he was going to visit his grandmother. Not tonight, Sewall told him, and gave him a penny.

The following day, Sewall had to set off for court at Salem. He took the hackney carriage over Boston Common to Madam Winthrop's, as he had arranged to make his departure from there. Sarah answered the door with Katee in her arms, but Sewall was so intent on his imminent meeting that he did not think to take any notice of the baby. Sarah called Madam Winthrop. When she appeared, Sewall made his case. He had been encouraged by little David's loving eyes and sweet words and had "come to enquire whether she could find it in her heart to leave that House and Neighbourhood, and go and dwell with me at the South-end." She said something in a low voice; he thought it was "Not yet." He laid his cards on the table. He was not able to keep a coach. If he tried, he would end up in company with her neighbor Brooker, who had been sent to jail for debt. Nevertheless, he disliked people who were willing to offer themselves but not their estate. He would bestow a portion of his estate with himself. As far as a wig was concerned, God had started to provide him with hair before he was born and had done so ever since, so he could not go to another provider. (He made no mention of going thin on top.)

Madam Winthrop had the wit to turn one of his weapons against him. She professed to admire the book he'd given her, Dr. Preston's *The Church's Marriage*. In it the author had criticized those who took it upon themselves to stand apart from popular fashion.

Once again finding himself on the receiving end in the great wig controversy, Sewall did not have an answer: "I said the Time and Tide did circumscribe my Visit." She gave him a measure of black cherry brandy, along with a lump of the sugar that had crystallized in the bottom of it, they wished each other well, and he set off.

A week later he was back, bringing with him half a pound of sugared almonds (he had actually bought a full pound, at a cost of 3s.). She was out at Madam Mico's. He went there, but she had left. He returned to her house and read the epistles to the Galatians and Ephesians in Latin. Then he started on Psalm 103. Mr. Wendell, a merchant and relative by marriage of Madam Winthrop, came along from his warehouse, and offered to track her down. That would make her angry, Sewall told him, able by now to predict her reactions, not difficult as they were so often negative. Mr. Wendell helped him on with his coat. Sewall left a copy of the *Gazette* tucked into the Bible for Madam Winthrop to read.

Two days later, he was back. Madam Winthrop was pleased with her sugared almonds, and wanted to know what they had cost. They got down to business. He would provide her with £100 per annum if he died first (a lower rate than that offered to Mrs. Denison, presumably because Madam Winthrop had a larger estate of her own); what would she provide him with if she were the first to go? He said that he would give her time to think about it. She said that she had heard he had made over all his estate to his children. He told her that was not the case. Point Judith, for example, belonged to him. It was true that his father had wished him to leave his English estate to his oldest son, but that only amounted to £20 per annum. She had thought it was forty. He wanted not to pursue the topic any further for the present, but she did: ". . . a long winter was coming on." She gave him some canary.

He returned on Friday at about seven in the evening. The Walleys were there, and they all talked about Indian affairs, including the case of an Indian woman slave who had obtained her freedom. Sewall showed them a piece of writing by a Native American called Isaac Moses. Madam Winthrop handed round comfits. Then supper was served. Mr. Walley asked Sewall to say the blessing, giving him perhaps for the first time in his visits to this household a sense of belonging. The Walleys left at nine. Sewall took his chance and asked Madam Winthrop what sort of necklace she would like him to buy for her. "None at all" came the crushing reply. He asked if she had thought any more about the issue of their estates. She said she could not change her condition, and leave her children and the Thursday lectures she attended. Ominously, she quoted the apostle Paul on the merits of the single life. Sewall pointed out that it depended on need. She made it clear that sex would not be part of any marital arrangement, telling him that she could no longer take pleasure in things of that sort. Determined to make the best of any argument she threw at him, Sewall replied, "You are the fitter to make me a Wife," discarding his passionate feelings for the time being. If she did not change her mind, he would have to go home and regret the way he had made more haste and less speed in his pursuit of her. Then it occurred to him that the supper had been a promising sign. He asked if he could call the following Monday, and she agreed.

But there was a sting in the tail. She suddenly accused him of insisting that she would have to dispense with the services of Juno if they got married. He denied saying any such thing. He had never even thought it. She insisted that he had, claiming it had cropped up in the conversation about the freeing of the Indian slave. Presumably, Juno was actually a slave himself, and what had happened was that Sewall had expressed his opposition to slavery and asserted that he would never countenance such a thing under his own roof. (As it happened, Sewall's black servant

Scipio quite literally lived under his roof, because Sewall described going up into his garret on one occasion to observe an eclipse. But in Scipio's case, the term "servant" was not a euphemism for "slave." Sewall recorded an occasion when he paid him £20 in back wages; Scipio returned the money, asking him to keep it safe, and Sewall then gave him a bond for the amount, stipulating the interest he would pay on it.) All he could do now was say lamely that he "would not disturb the good orders of her House." She was not in a good mood when he took his leave.

On the Monday, having prayed once more on the subject with his son Joseph, Sewall went to Madam Winthrop's as agreed. She was rocking little Katee in her cradle. He apologized for coming so late—it was nearly eight o'clock. She arranged an armchair with a cushion for him, opposite her own armchair and with the cradle between them, a promisingly comfortable domestic scene. He gave her the second half-pound of the sugared almonds he had bought. She did not begin to eat them, however, but put them on one side.

He said he had come to see whether she had changed her mind or still felt the same. She told him, "Thereabouts." He said he loved her, and thought she loved him. She replied that "she had a great respect for me," a killer response in any generation. He told her he had asked for her hand without taking advice from others; her problem was she had so many people to consult with that it held her back. Then he made an observation on the hearth that signaled his awareness of the end: "The Fire was come to one short Brand besides the Block, which Brand was set up in end; at last it fell to pieces, and no Recruit was made." This is neither spiritual allegory nor romantic pathetic fallacy; instead, it is an alert reading of the language of gesture, or rather nongesture. A couple of weeks previously she had not let him have Juno to escort him home; now she had put his second batch of sugared almonds to one side, and to top it all was letting the fire, along with their courtship, go out. He made a last try, repeating what he said before about regretting that he made more haste and less speed. He would contain himself, and not try to make her do what she did not want to do. He took his leave.

As he went down the steps, she told him to have a care. He told her—perhaps pronouncing it like a sentence—that she had entered the fourth year of her widowhood. He had no newspaper to give her—he had given her the current *Gazette* already. He did not ask her to take her glove off, as he had done previously, so he could kiss the hand of a living lady. He noticed that her dress was not as clean as it had sometimes been.

"*Jehovah jireh*," he wrote in his diary; the Lord will provide. It was the end of the affair.

On the Wednesday, he went to dine with Simeon and Mehitabel Stoddard. They kindly asked if they should also invite Madam Winthrop. He told them no. That evening he went to a meeting at the widow Belknap's, where he handed out twelve sermons. She had the courtesy to send a servant with a lantern home with him. He noticed Madam Winthrop's shutters were open as he walked past. Another two days went by, but he did not go to Madam Winthrop's: this was "the 2^d Withdraw." The following Monday, he noted that Madam Winthrop had gone to visit his daughter-in-law Elizabeth, wife of Joseph, taking little Katee with her.

Then the envoi. "About the middle of Decr," Madam Winthrop gave a meal for her children, to which she also asked Joseph and Mr. Prince. "I knew nothing of it; but the same day abode in the Council Chamber for fear of the Rain, and din'd alone, upon Kilby's Pyes and good Beer."

THE FOLLOWING YEAR, 1721, brought one of Boston's greatest disasters, and Cotton Mather's finest hour. In April, a ship docked from the West Indies with smallpox on board, and as the summer came on, an epidemic began to rage in the town. The local physicians mostly opposed the new treatment of inoculation, but many of the clergy, including the Mathers, supported it, and Cotton Mather allowed the technique to be applied to his own children. Always sensitive to public criticism, he had to endure vilification for his stance. Dr. Lawrence Dalhonde, one of the leaders of the anti-inoculation group, called him "a credulous vain Preacher." At one point a grenade was thrown through

Mather's window, with a message attached: "COTTON MATHER, . . . *You Dog, And Damn you; I will Enoculate You with this, with a Pox to You.*"

But Mather stayed resolute in his support of Dr. Zabdiel Boylston, the physician who advocated the procedure, and his stance was vindicated. Of the 281 people Boylston and his colleagues inoculated, only 6 died; in the epidemic as a whole, 5,759 uninoculated people contracted the illness and 844 died of it. One of them, sadly, was Susan Thayer, servant to the Sewall household, who, eight years before, had sat up all night in her employers' bedchamber because she was frightened of dying. Funerals became such a financial drain on the population that in September the General Court ordered an end to the custom of giving scarves to the mourners.

Sewall survived unscathed, but he was in his seventieth year and aware of it. One day that spring a tooth had dropped out of his lower jaw just as he was seating himself in his pew, and he slipped it into his pocket: "This old servant and daughter of Musick leaving me, does thereby give me warning that I must shortly resign my Head: the Lord help me to do it cheerfully!" He seems to have regarded his teeth as agents of harmony, rather like harpsichord keys. The year before he had written to Edward Taylor, updating him on the state of his jaws: "My dear Colleague, and Chamberfellow, and Bedfellow! I have lost many of my Organs of Music; my Fore-Teeth, both upper and nether." (Ironically, Sewall's unwilling successor as precentor in the South Meeting House, John White—"he did it very sweetly"—himself died that year.)

The ills of age did not assuage his need for courtship, though perhaps they lowered the key. He wrote a querulous, rather sentimental letter to an old Newbury friend, Timothy Woodbridge, telling him how his daughter Hannah was an invalid (her damaged knee had long ago become chronically infected) and his maidservant had gone to Roxbury to flee the epidemic. He was left with no support but his housekeeper, Mrs. Lydia Kay, and was feeling sorry for himself. His thoughts turned to his long-ago childhood, and to the first stirrings of romantic feeling: "I remember when I was going from school at Newbury, I have sometime met your Sisters Martha, and Mary, coming from their Schoole at

Chandler's Lane, in their Hanging Sleeves; and have had the pleasure of Speaking with them." Fashions change, but one can recognize instantly the remembered magic of those schoolgirls in their hanging sleeves. Martha was now a widow. "I could find it in my heart to speak with Mrs. Martha again, now I am my self reduc'd to my Hanging Sleeves." He was at pains to point out that his quest was for domestic comfort and companionship: "The truth is, I have little Occasion for a Wife, but for the sake of Modesty, and to cherish me in my advanced years (I was born March 28, 1652). Methinks I could venture to lay my Weary head in her Lap, if it might be brought to pass upon Honest Conditions."

Two weeks later, he was around at Martha's house. She was now Madam Ruggles, and Sewall had in fact tried to see her at the start of his courtships. She "express'd her inability to be Servicable," though she did give him some cider to drink. In August, he had one last try. She told him she was determined not to move out of her house in Brookline. "May be of some use there; None at Boston—till she be carried out." He pressed a sermon on her but she resisted, in case it put her under an obligation. The coach was delayed, and he apologized; she said he could stay until midnight, "provided I should solicit her no more; or to that effect." This time he took no for an answer, and erected a post of Connecticut stone in his elm pasture, "in Remembrance of my loving Wife Mrs. Hannah Sewall."

But a few months later, he embarked on another courtship, his last. He paid the woman in question, a widow by the name of Mrs. Mary Gibbs, mainly epistolary visits, as he called his letters, because she spent the severe winter of 1721–22 out of town with her daughter and son-in-law at Newton. The negotiations were quite hardheaded. He required the sum of £100 payable by her children, if she died first; she would get £50 a year for life if he did. She came back with proposals for a jointure. He wrote a tough legal letter about not being liable for any debts she had contracted before the marriage. Nevertheless, all went well. When he got out to Newton, he took her glazed almonds, a dozen cakes, two bottles of canary, an orange. And the niceties were observed: "Mrs. Gibbs help'd me on with my Coat at Coming away; and stood in the Front door till the Coach mov'd, then I pulled off my Hat, and she

Curtesied." Passion may have ebbed away, but he still had enormous zest for the intricate details of social bonding. In a nice piece of tit for tat, they were married on 29 March 1722 by William Cooper, who had been married to Sewall's daughter Judith by Sewall himself.

The marriage was a success. Mary dressed Hannah's leg once a day, Sewall reported, "to do which required a great deal of diligence, skill and Courage," and he noted proudly that at a Lord's Day service "my wife wore her new Gown of Sprig'd Persian." They settled down to exactly the comfortable companionship for which he had hoped. Perhaps it was inevitable that his successful courtships would prove to be less fascinating than his unsuccessful ones.

His records of his pursuit of Mrs. Denison and Madam Winthrop remain extraordinary documents: sad, funny, human, and rich. It is not merely that they record customs and manners in early eighteenth-century New England with unparalleled detail, but that in providing and emphasizing that detail they reveal a consciousness actually contributing to the social infrastructure of an increasingly complex and sophisticated society. In this respect, they continue the work begun by Sewall's reaction to the witchcraft trials, where he helped to create a change of perspective from the allegorical, people as pawns in a spiritual drama, to the psychological, where individuals have to explore the roots of their behavior—and take responsibility for it—within the depths of their individual being. Mrs. Denison and Madam Winthrop were perceived as elusive and mysterious people, to be interpreted as best Sewall could by a close examination of their tersest comments and smallest gestures.

He had had the courage to put to sea in winter. Over a century later, Melville would pen American literature's greatest voyage, *Moby-Dick*. In the context of the great public and spiritual enterprise of the pursuit of the white whale, Melville talks of the "ungraspable phantom of life." But through his pursuit of respectable Boston widows, Sewall too— and, ironically, in a more modern and familiar fashion—conveys that ungraspable quality, indeed in such a way that paradoxically we can actually feel life's slither as it slides through our fingers, and his. Sewall was inventing what it is to be a private citizen.

Others had such experiences, obviously, but it was he who made them significant by recording them. In the next generation, Benjamin Franklin was to deal with some ostensibly personal material in his *Autobiography*, but only to prove the case that the private is after all the public: that both are open to strategic maneuvers in the name of the success ethic. He gave tables for monitoring spiritual imperfections, and described techniques for manipulating fellow citizens—asking to borrow a valuable book, for example, from one of your enemies, so that having done you a favor he will feel warmth toward you thereafter, a curiously cynical, though shrewd, adaptation of Christian notions of forgiveness and reconciliation. What Franklin did was to modify spiritual allegorizing into the exemplary mode, the practical handbook on how to live one's life. And even in the mid-eighteenth century it was still possible to undertake to live one's own life as if it *were* a spiritual allegory, as the great Puritan revivalist, Jonathan Edwards, demonstrated in his *Personal Narrative*. Nobody in America would write about human relationships with Sewall's eye for detail and nuance until the nineteenth century.

Certainly as far as Sewall's generation is concerned, the recognized postures are Michael Wigglesworth's wrestling with doubt and gloom, and Cotton Mather's abasement on his study floor. This is not to say that these men were hypocrites, but they needed that attitudinizing (as we cannot help but see it) for their own benefit. They were setting themselves the example of themselves.

Sewall shared with his contemporaries a belief that the details of his life fell into a grander scheme, though by envisaging that scheme as an American destiny, however buttressed by the book of Revelation, he was, though not himself secularizing, making secularization possible. But he was aware not just that every detail of experience matters, but that it is the interplay of detail that contains the essence of life. He has become a fully social being, finding the meaning of experience in the way people send verbal and physical signals to each other from the shadowy recesses of themselves. Thus we see him not as a frozen hieratic figure but as a man on the move, bobbing through time like a cork on the water, bobbing along in the direction of our own time.

CHAPTER SEVENTEEN

"Rocqued Like a Cradle"

Sewall's unmarried daughter, Hannah, began to fail rapidly in the summer of 1724. She was forty-four and had been an invalid for much of her adult life. He spent long nights at her bedside. During the course of one of them, he picked up a book, just to while away the time and take the edge off his grief. It should have catered exactly to his need: *The British Apollo: Containing about Two Thousand Answers to Curious Questions in Most Arts and Sciences, Serious, Comical and Humorous . . . Performd by a Society of Gentlemen.* But one of these curious questions gave him a horrible shock: *Is there now, or will there be at the Resurrection, any Females in Heaven since there seems no need of them there?*

This misogyny, facetiousness, and contempt were the last things he needed with a beloved daughter dying before his eyes. Hannah was a much less demonstrative person than her sister Betty, who had undergone a whole series of spiritual crises while she was growing up, but she had been troubled about religion too, and only became a full member of the South Church in her late thirties. The suggestion that she could be excluded from her spiritual reward because of her gender was intolerable to Sewall, a protective father to all his children. He penned his own answer to the "malapert Question," an essay called TALITHA CUMI. (The title is taken from Mark 5:41, where Christ raises a little girl from the dead: "And he took the damsel by the hand, and said unto her,

TALITHA CUMI; which is, being interpreted, Damsel, I say unto thee, arise.")

The "society of gentlemen" claimed that in the afterlife our immaterial bodies will not be distinguished into sexes, and referred to Matthew 22:30: "In the Resurrection they neither give, nor are given in Marriage, but are as are the Angels of God." Sewall in response consigned the gentlemen themselves to limbo: there "will be no need for impertinent persons . . . in heaven." The quoted verse means simply that without the institution of wedlock, women will be men's equals in paradise. They will not have the subordinate status implicit in being "given" in marriage. Sewall was furious that "some men, . . . have called into question the possibility of their Salvation; yea some, whether they have Souls, or no." He would rather side with the Roman Catholics in believing that the Virgin Mary is already in heaven and does not have to wait for the day of judgment than accept that she will never arrive there because she is a woman. In a passage that takes us to the very heart of his beliefs, his passion not just for his religion but for his family too, he becomes mystical about Mary's womb, the "Bride-Chamber, wherein the Holy Ghost did knit that indissoluble knot betwixt our human nature, and his Deity. Our glorious Bridegroom will not demolish this Chamber . . . from whence he proceeded; but will Repair it with permanent & Wonderful Magnificence."

He went on to consider the question of whether the sexual organs will be eradicated in heaven. He had embarked on a related argument years before, in an after-dinner conversation with his colleagues while he was on the judicial circuit. On that occasion the province's attorney, Paul Dudley, suggested that the belly would not be resurrected, because there would be no use for it in the afterlife. Christ's body was not corrupted after death, Sewall pointed out, and those of the elect would be the same. God would know how to utilize the body's organs outside their earthly context.

Dudley asked, "What use of Tasting, Smelling?"

"Tis possible the bodies of the Saints may have a fragrancy attending them," Sewall suggested.

"Voice is Laborious."

"As much Labour as you please, the more the better, so it be without Toil, as in heaven it will be."

Perhaps this distinction between labor and toil catches the nature of singing in worship, which Sewall so much loved, energy being invested in the voice, which then lifts and fills space as if effortlessly. As he wrote one winter's day: "Though all things look horribly winterly by reason of a great storm of Snow, hardly yet over, and much on the Ground: yet the Robbins cheerfully utter their Notes this Morn. So should we patiently and cheerfully sing the Praises of God." The singing voice transcends the restrictions of the physical world.

Back to the belly. He must have peered placidly down at his own plump one, patting it maybe: "I dare not part with my Belly, Christ has Redeemed it; and there is danger of your breaking in further upon me, and cutting off my Hand or Foot."

It was a jocular conversation, but serious too, and the next day Sewall meditated on exactly the issue he would broach in "TALITHA CUMI." Mary's womb could not be left to rot. "Her Son, her Father, her God will Redeem it from the prevailing power of the Grave." Sewall's different causes—Indians, slaves, the spiritual status of women, even the evil of wearing wigs, that vexed issue that unexpectedly resurfaced during his courtship of Madam Winthrop—all were related to each other. Many years previously, John Saffin had quoted 1 Corinthians 12:23 in a perverse attempt to prove, in the teeth of the biblical argument, that God had a hierarchical view of the body's organs, and by extension of people: "And those members of the body, which we think to be less honourable, upon these we bestow more abundant honour; and our uncomely parts have more abundant comeliness." By contrast, Sewall was able to do justice to the true sentiments of the epistle, respecting not just people of all races and genders, but also the various organs of the body, the belly, the womb, the hand, the foot, the hair. Every hair on our heads is numbered, so it can be resurrected, and "in vain are they numberd, if some time or other they must be totally left." That was the logic at the heart of the great wig debate. But, he argued in "TALITHA CUMI," if this applies to hair, it must equally apply to genitalia. We are all made in the divine image, men and women both; in being God's "Sons and Daughters" each sex is "as like Himself as can be." The mystical paradox refreshingly cuts through the masculine aura pervading Puritan doctrine and worship: in this respect, as in his attitude to minority races, Sewall was on the side of inclusiveness, a perspective made possible by the contemporary belief that the female genitalia were simply an inversion of the male. God therefore showed a divine economy in basing both genders on the model of himself. Nowadays we attribute the sexes' similarity to the economy of evolutionary anatomy, tracking back to a common source and establishing that "the penis and clitoris, and the scrotal sac and *labia majora*, are homologous pairs of organs."

Hannah died on 15 August 1724. "Her pleasant Countenance was very Refreshing to me. I hope God has delivered her from all her Fears! She had desired not to be embowelled." Her leg was dressed in lime before burial so its infection would not spread.

The following year, he paid a last visit to the ailing Madam Winthrop, who had never remarried: "At coming I said, I kiss your hand Madame (her hand felt very dry). She desired me to pray that God would lift up upon her the Light of his Countenance." Two months later, he was a bearer at her funeral.

He resigned as treasurer of the New England Company in 1724, and handed in all the company's books and records. But he continued to feel passionately about the part to be played by the Indians in bringing about an American millennium. "God will as readily Tabernacle in Our Indian Wigwams," he told President Wadsworth of Harvard in 1726, "as enter into them." "I am of Mr. Eliot's opinion," he explained to Experience Mayhew shortly afterward, "that New-England is a preface to New-Jerusalem." He reissued his *Phaenomena* in 1727. "I abide in the same Opinion still," he told President Wadsworth.

He declined reelection to the Massachusetts council in 1725 and resigned from the superior court in 1727. On 30 October that year, at about 10:40 p.m., came the great Boston earthquake. Houses "rocked and crackled as if they were all dissolving and falling to pieces." People ran into the streets, calling for mercy. Sewall's kitchen "was Rocqued like a Cradle." He was just warm in his bed but not yet asleep. "The young people were quickly frighted out of the Shaking clattering Kitchen, and fled with weeping Cryes into our Chamber, where they made a fire, and abode there till morning." As he lay in bed beside his wife while the young people huddled around the fire, Sewall remembered the story of a bishop and his lady in England, who were buried in their bed in a huge tempest, but he didn't dare tell the refugees in his bedroom about it for fear of adding to the panic. He remembered too an earthquake of 1663, when he was eleven, "and my being shaken by it, as I sat in my Father's house at Newbury in a Jâm of the Chimny."

The South meetinghouse was getting dilapidated, and in 1728 a proposal was put forward that it should be demolished and replaced. Naturally, Sewall was against the destruction of a building in which he had passed so much of his spiritual life, and which had seen so much drama, both inward and outward: the battle against Andros and Randolph during the period of cohabitation, the admission of guilt over the witchcraft trials, the many times when he had prayed for the health of members of his family, and the many times he had mourned their deaths, the speculation about the possibilities for courtship on the widows' row, the introduction of new wives to the family pew, and the endless and to him fascinating and enriching sermons he had heard there and noted down over the years, from his respected pastor Samuel Willard, from the less respected Ebenezer Pemberton, above all from his beloved son Joseph. His objections were overruled and demolition began.

In August, he saw a huge rainbow, which he took as a token of God's covenant to the dispersed Jews and a sign of the New Jerusalem to come. New England was to be the preface; the actual site of the New Jerusalem would be to the south, "where, over and above the huge Empires of Mexico and Peru, there [are] innumerable Royalties of Sachems and Squaw-Sachems throughout this incomparably great, and long-extended Continent." In September, he dreamed of the theft of his watch, perhaps an intimation that time was running out. He was much affected on 19 October by the thought that it was the eleventh anniversary of his wife Hannah's death.

A year later, he was asked by Judge Davenport, on behalf of his son

Addington Davenport, for the hand of his granddaughter, Jane Hirst, Betty's daughter. Sewall recorded his consent on 13 October 1729. It was the last entry in his diary. The two married in December. Three years later, they converted to the Church of England, and Davenport eventually became the first minister of Trinity Church in Boston. But if that repudiation of Congregationalism seems to symbolize the end of one component of Sewall's world, other elements survived. One of his great-great-granddaughters (via Joseph and his wife, Elizabeth) was Abigail May, who married Amos Bronson Alcott, the New England transcendentalist, and embarked with him on perhaps the most picturesque and disastrous of American utopian experiments, Fruitlands, which lasted for six months in 1843–4. And one of *their* daughters (Sewall's great-great-great-granddaughter) was Louisa May Alcott, who wrote the most famous of all celebrations of American family life, *Little Women*. In a very direct way, therefore, both his utopianism and his emphasis on the importance of the private and the personal, the two great values and enterprises (inventions even) of his adult life, lived on, as they also, no doubt, did in more subtle and less visible ways.

Sewall died in the early hours of 1 January 1730. Despite his years administering probate, despite his bookkeeping habits and all those courtship discussions of postmortem arrangements, he didn't leave a will.

Notes

Sources are cited by a key name, plus a key title word if necessary, cross-referenced to the **bold** type in the bibliography.

The abbreviation "np" means "no page."

CHAPTER ONE: *The Shaggy Dog*

4   *He brought "English servants"*: D1, xxix.

4   *"wee must be knit together"*: "A Model of Christian Charity," in *Winthrop*, 2:294–95.

4   *"for as hell is a place"*: Eliot, *Commonwealth*, pref.

4   *As early as 1627*: See Morton, *Canaan*.

4   *the Sewalls were descended*: D1, xxix; D2, 1071–74.

5   *he arranged a legal separation*: D2, 1073.

5   *He got into trouble*: Coffin, 22. See my comments on currency on page xvi for some idea of the swingeing nature of this fine.

5   *Rumor had it*: Ibid., 61.

5   *No such problems*: Ibid., 46.

5   *marriage was a secular state*: Ibid., 46.

6   *many Puritan pastors were appointed*: Winslow, *Sewall*, 12.

6   *"she lavish'd away"*: D1, 444.

6   *the Commonwealth collapsed*: D2, 1074.

7   *his American initiation*: D1, xxx–xxxi.

7   *his boyhood haunts in Newbury*: Sewall, *Phaenomena*, 59.

7–8   *For those Puritans crossing*: See Bercovitch, 115–19, for a discussion of this issue.

8   *that giant stride of the angel*: D2, 1107.

8   *"It was a fearfull sight"*: Bradford, 426.

9   *Indians were the servants of Satan*: See Lovejoy, "Indian," 603–21; Nichols, 72.

9   *There were wolves*: Coffin, 42.

9   *John Indian owned property*: Ibid., 40.

9   *the grown-up Sewall*: D2, 973.

9   *England's Newbury*: Coffin, 9, 17.

9   *He was Sewall's "dear master"*: D1, 42.

9–10   *Parker was famed*: DAB, 17:45.

10   *"Your printing of a Book"*: Avery; letter quoted in Morison, "Parker," 266–67 n.

10   *his own millennial history*: Parker.

10   *the perennial rites of passage*: LB2, 133.

10   *"Chamber fellows and bed-fellows"*: Ibid., 274.

11   *Sewall received his first degree*: Winslow, *Sewall*, 32–33.

11–2   *"Pray enquire," Sewall asks*: LB1, 17–20.

12   *three students remained in residence*: Winslow, *Sewall*, 44.

13   *Sewall's question was*: D1, 7.

13   *he had recited a catechism*: This catechism was devised by James Noyes, inseparable partner of Thomas Parker, Sewall's teacher, and remained so popular it was published in the early eighteenth century. Coffin, 288.

14   *two very similar portraits*: The other portrait is by Nathaniel Emmons (1728), and is owned by the Massachusetts Historical Society.

14   *she immediately "set her Affection"*: D1, xxxii.

16   *Pike himself*: Ibid., 9.

16   *"ignorantly and unwittingly"*: Ibid., 11.

16   *this was excessive*: The norm was between one and a half and one and three-quarter hours. See Silverman, 195.

16   *Sewall marked the following sentence*: In his copy of Thorowgood, 59; now in the Boston Public Library, Rare Books and Manuscripts Collection.

17   *Eliot believed they were descended*: See Sewall's marginal note on this point in Thorowgood's intro., np.

17   *and called him "brother"*: D1, 252.

17   *"Mr. Eliot believ'd the Americans"*: LB1, 122.

17–8   *translating the Bible into Algonquian*: Kellaway, 131–32.

18   *a converted Indian named Piambohou*: Eliot, *Dialogues*, 10.

18   *Harvard's original charter*: Kellaway, 109.

18   *Eliot produced an Algonquian grammar*: Ibid., 137.

18   *It was a substantial structure*: Sewall, "Letter," 600.

18   *only four Indians*: Gookin, 176.

18   "the Indian Oxford": Nichols, 80.

18–9   *Daniel Gookin*: Kellaway, 116.

19-20   *Indians were always going to come off worse*: See Ranlet. See also Mather, I., "A Brief History of the War with the Indians in NewEngland," in Slotkin, 87.

20   *Twelve days later*: Slotkin, 47.

20   *Sewall had a dream*: D1, 12.

20   *the decaying Indian College*: Harvard, lxxxiv.

21   *The Indians are "vile enemies"*: Mather, I., "An Earnest Exhortation," in Slotkin, 171–72.

22   *"Nor were our sins ripe"*: Mather, I., "A Brief History," in Slotkin, 86.

22   *Six months later*: Slotkin, 50.

22   *In September 1675*: D1, 13.

22   *"Mother was exceedingly troubled"*: D1, 12. Hall, "World," 36, claims it was an eclipse, but this took place on 21 December that year.

23   *Six hundred Narragansetts*: Slotkin, 49.

23   *Her father, John Hull*: Hull, np.

23   *Sewall, in his meticulous way*: D1, 15.

24   *she was "as round"*: Hawthorne, *Chair*, 37–38.

24   *introduced to the world of the merchants*: D1, 18.

24   *famous account of the massacre*: Rowlandson, 5.

24   *only four of their communities*: Kellaway, 116–17.

24–5   *Mr. Hezekiah Willett*: D1, 18.

25   *A Narrangansett chief*: Slotkin, 52.

25   *Many captured Indians*: Nichols, 86–87; Slotkin, 3–4.

25   *In September, there were some executions*: D1, 22–23. See also 23 n.

26   *A woman visitor to Boston*: Quoted in Middleton, 156.

26   *"small but pleasant Common"*: Dunton, *Letters*, 69. Dunton in fact plagiarized this passage from a work published a decade earlier, but presumably the description still held. See Josselyn, 162.

26   *he went down to Cape Cod*: D1, 27–28.

27   *He kept this poem*: Boston News-Letter, 21–28 March 1723.

27   *Sewall made room for whimsy*: D1, 23–25.

27   *Sewall's seventeen-year-old sister*: D1, 34, 36.

28   *Seth was the son*: Coffin, 156; for more information on Sewall's practice of taking children into his household, see Graham, 135–43.

28   *Sewall discovered a shaggy dog*: D1, 29.

CHAPTER TWO: *"Our Hithertos of Mercy"*

29   *One day early in 1677*: D1, 35.

29   *The Bay Psalm Book*: *Psalms*, p 66. *The Bay Psalm Book*, as this version
was popularly known, had originally been translated for use in
Massachusetts Bay by John Eliot, Richard Mather, and Thomas
Weld in 1640, but Sewall used the 1651 edition revised by Richard
Lyon and Henry Dunster. See Winship, pp 94–99. I have used the
1651 edition in subsequent references.

29–30   *invited him "(courteously) to their Caballs"*: D1, 32.

30   *Another said*: D1, 36–37.

30   *He was eventually admitted*: D1, 39–42.

32   *Individuals became full (or "inward")*: See Shepard, 1, for example.
This is a book Sewall owned and annotated; his copy is in the
Boston Public Library, Rare Books and Manuscripts Collection.

32   *Many Puritans were uneasy*: Increase Mather, for example; see
Middlekauff, 122.

32   *he visited Urian Oakes*: D1, 42–43.

33   *On the subject of election*: Sewall, Commonplace Book, 1677–98, in
Samuel Sewall Papers, np.

33   *Years later, Sewall explained*: D1, xxxii–xxxiii.

33–4   *In May 1678*: D1, 45–46.

34   *Special cages for Sabbath breakers*: Drake, *History*, 428.

34   *He obtained a press*: It has been suggested that Sewall managed but
didn't own the press; Littlefield, 2:19.

34   *He published* The Pilgrim's Progress: D2, 1107–11.

34   *Cotton has a claim*: Silverman, 37.

35   *In his sermon, Willard*: Willard, *Esteem*, 4–6.

35   *The Hull estate*: Estes, 312–14.

35   *the Board of Overseers*: D1, xxiv.

35–6   *John Dunton*: Dunton, *Life*, 155–56.

36   *in 1685 took charge*: See, for example, Sewall, Diary and
Commonplace Book, 1675–1721 in Samuel Sewall Papers, entry for
31 August 1685.

36   *Sewall felt strongly*: Sewall, Commonplace Book, 1677–98, in
Samuel Sewall Papers, np.

36   *He went to ask Increase Mather's*: D1, 119–20.

36–7   *he wrote an antifrivolous missive*: Sewall, "Letters."

37   *his baby son, Hull*: D1, 96.

37   *Sewall wrote to his uncle*: LB1, 22–23; Thorowgood, 6–10.

38   *he dreamed he was away at Newbury*: D1, 65–67.
38–9   *The visiting bookseller, John Dunton*: Dunton, *Life*, 130–35.
39   *One of life's heroic losers*: D1, 83, 88, 96.
39   *Stepney managed to secure*: Bailyn, 192.
39   *Meanwhile, Increase Mather*: Mather, I., *Arrow*, 4.
40   *Stepney's nerve finally failed*: D1, 118; *Music*, 449.
40   *On 30 March 1687*: Mather, I., "Autobiography," 322–23.
40   *a land on the other side*: Palfrey, 3:338.
40–1   *In 1676, Charles II*: Ibid., 3:333, 339 n, 350 n.
42   *One day on the Boston exchange*: Palfrey 3:364 n; Dunton, *Letters*, 65.
42   *Prophetically, he reported*: Palfrey, 3:340.
42   *In 1683, Sewall*: Seventh Report, 169.
43   *Sewall spent 1 January 1686*: D1, 91.
43   *At eight in the morning*: Ibid., 112.
44   *The gulf*: Ibid., 111.
44   *The change of government*: Ibid., 113–14.
44   *Andros knew exactly*: Ibid., 128.
44   *all titles to land*: Palfrey, 3:513–14.
44   *On 22 March 1687*: D1, 135–36.
45   *A year later*: Ibid., 171–72.
46   *In the early months of 1687*: LB1, 68–73 n.
47   *Sewall and Hannah had gone there*: D1, 121, 136.
47   *Sewall went to the island*: D1, 143.
47   *The bombshell came the following year*: D1, 172–73.
47-8   *a letter to Increase Mather*: Sewall, "Letters."
48   *This frustration didn't stop Sewall*: LB1, 62, 90.
48   *Domestic life*: D1, 143–45.
48   *He wrote a lovely letter*: LB1, 79–81.
49   *On 4 April 1687*: Palfrey, 3:463.
49-50 *a letter purportedly written by Mather*: Murdock, 183–85.
50   *Mather vigorously denied*: Quoted in Palfrey, 3:557 n.
51   *After making his escape*: Murdock, 186–88.

CHAPTER THREE: *The First American Tourist*

53   *On 15 October 1688*: D1, 180–84; Sewall, Indenture; Sewall,
      Account Book, 1688–92, in Samuel Sewall Papers, entry for
      5 November 1688.
53   *some outbreaks of trouble*: Norton, 94.
54   *a handbook for later use*: See the comments by Robert Calef, foot-
      noted in Burr, 124; Silverman, 83–87.

54   *He had also attended Harvard*: D1, 3 n.
55   *Five days out to sea*: D1, 185–92.
55   *in roadside inns too*: See Knight, 48.
55   *Newgate had been the owner*: D1, 170.
55–6 *a piece of eight*: The value of a piece of eight was computed by Isaac Newton, master of the Royal Mint, and published in the *Boston News-Letter*, 4–11 December 1704.
57   *On 13 January*: Sewall's published entries for his visit to England occupy D1, 193–247.
57   *Sewall loved music*: See the *Boston News-Letter*, 16–23 December 1731.
60   *He wrote a short poem*: Sewall, "Holt."
61   *Forty years later*: LB2, 262.
62   Increase Mather had been having a frustrating time: Mather, I., "Autobiography," 330–31.
64   New-England Vindicated: Mather, I., *New-England*, np.
66   *A young man called John Winslow*: Palfrey, 3:574–92.
66   *Cotton Mather stood on its gallery*: Silverman, 70.
69   *a world without Shakespeare*: He did briefly sample Ben Jonson and Dryden; D1, 551; ibid., 136. The latter's work is *The Indian Emperor or, The Conquest of Mexico* (1681); see Sewall, Commonplace Book, 1677–98, in Samuel Sewall Papers. This was perhaps a significant choice given Sewall's interest in the destiny of South and Central America. Confronted by Cortez, Montezuma makes a telling point: "He who Religion truly understands / Knows it's [*sic*] Extent must be in Men, not Lands." Sewall read it as he sailed to Hogg Island on 9 April 1687.
69   *"Corporation-Bill sticks in the Birth"*: D1, 232; see also Sewall's letter to Hannah Sewall of 3 August 1689, in Samuel Mather Papers.
71   *Mather wanted to press*: Mather, I., "Autobiography," 340.
71   *Early in 1691, Mather*: Murdock, 230–31.
71   *The charter related*: Palfrey, 3:76, 4:75–83; Mather entry in *DAB*, 14:688.
73   *On 7 October*: D1, 242–47.
74   *The incident had given Sewall another scare*: LB1, 93.

CHAPTER FOUR: *The Yellow Bird*

77   *Sewall faced a crisis*: D1, 249.
77   *the state of New England*: Some historians have argued that the sense of decline during this period was illusory, though, of course,

that didn't prevent contemporary anxiety about decline from being real enough. See Pope and Moran.

78   *Then, in February, came news*: D1, 249–51.

78   *Thomas Pound and Thomas Hawkins*: Dow, 54–72; *Records*: 305–22.

80   *In April, he went off to New York*: D1, 257–58.

80   *When he got home*: D1, 259.

80   *In May, there was bad news*: Hinckley Papers, 253.

81   *Later that summer*: D1, 264–87.

81–2   *Sewall wrote to an acquaintance*: LB1, 129.

82   *a gloomy sermon*: Sewall, *Sermon* Notebook, 1691–92, in Samuel Sewall Papers, np.

82   *There were strong winds*: D1, 288.

82   *one of the original points of entry*: Drake, 56–57; Mather, C., *Magnalia*, 327; Boyer, *Possessed*, 37–63.

83   *Cotton Mather claimed*: Mather, C., *Magnalia*, 326–27; Hale, 132–33. Norton is skeptical about this explanation (Norton, 23). My view is that Mather's version should be taken seriously, particularly as it suggests that the afflicted caused their own afflictions, an analysis that consorts uneasily with his own allegiances in his accounts of some of the trials.

84   *Mary Sibley*: Rosenthal, 25–27.

84   *initially suggested by Samuel Parris*: Parris, 193.

84–5   *The witch cake diagnosis*: Hale, 23, 123.

85   *Elizabeth Knapp, a maidservant*: Willard, "Providence."

86   *the material went on to provide the basis*: See Cotton Mather's account of Burroughs's trial, which makes it clear that the examination record was used at the trial itself; similarly, his accounts of the trials of Bridget Bishop and Susannah Martin in Burr, 216, 223, 229. Burr's book is an edited anthology of witchcraft accounts and is a more accessible resource than some of the original publications, though I shall refer to the latter for material Burr excludes.

86   *the charge at the subsequent trial*: See Rosenthal, 43.

86   *Two witnesses*: Norton, 205.

86   *Nathaniel Hawthorne*: Hawthorne, *Letter*, 9–10.

88   *Goody Osborne claimed*: SWP2, 610–11.

88   *Tituba Indian*: SWP3, 745–49.

89   *The first pioneers*: Higginson, *Plantation*, 119.

91   *Lawson's old village*: Burr, 152–54.

92   *The next day, Martha Corey*: SWP1, 248–54.

92   *Lawson visited the Parris household*: Upham, 1:279; Burr, 157.

92–3   *At Rebecca Nurse's examination*: SWP2, 587.

93–4   *main thrust of Lawson's sermon*: Lawson, 62.
95   *Ironically, the Salem Village meetinghouse*: Salem 255.
95   *Tituba's second examination*: SWP3, 753–54.
96   *In his sermon on Sunday, 27 March*: Parris, 196.
97   *That same Sunday, Parris*: Salem, 278.

CHAPTER FIVE: *"Vae, Vae, Vae, Witchcraft"*

99   *The hearings had been held*: SWP2, 661.
99–100   *Proctor was a practical*: Boyer, *Possessed*, 200–201.
100   *His solution*: SWP2, 683–84.
100   *According to Sewall*: D1, 289.
100–1   *"The Fall of the House of Usher"*: Poe, 138.
101   *When Elizabeth Proctor was interrogated*: SWP2, 658–61.
101   *the Puritan proscription of the theater*: Point made by Upham. See Upham, 2:112–13.
101   *The following day, Samuel Parris*: SWP2, 677–78.
101–2   *Parris's later confession*: Salem, 298.
102   *Proctor's "jade," Mary Warren*: SWP3, 793–95, 803.
102   *As Hathorne put it to Rebecca Nurse*: SWP2, 587.
103   *As Samuel Parris put it*: Salem, 131.
103   *Mary Warren was left*: Upham 2:121; Rosenthal, 47–48.
103   *The single most important development*: SWP2, 405.
103   *she was fourteen now*: Rosenthal, 139.
103   *The next day, 21 April*: SWP1, 165.
104   *It's hard to imagine a more blatant attempt*: Rosenthal is skeptical of this, but in his discussion of the issue he overlooks the coincidence in timing between Ann Jr.'s vision and her father's letter. Rosenthal, 245 n 3.
104   *Abigail's stepmother, Deliverance*: SWP2, 423.
104–5   *Young man called Nehemiah Abbott*: SWP1, 50.
105   *Susannah Sheldon described*: Ibid., 105.
105   *A defendant called Susannah Martin*: SWP2, 551.
106   *Burroughs would provide the leader figure*: As one commentator put it, "The trial and execution of Burroughs . . . legitimized stories of a coven of witches determined to impose a satanic kingdom in Massachusetts Bay." Rosenthal, 150.
106   *he'd last partaken of the Lord's Supper*: SWP1, 153.
107   *He was consistently sharp*: Salem, 174–77.
107–8   *On Wednesday, 18 November 1685*: D1, 85.

108   *Back in Maine*: SWP1, 153, 160–63.

108   *in the case of Mercy Lewis*: Burr, 261.

108–9 *a certain John Louder*: SWP1, 100.

109   *old man called George Jacobs*: SWP2, 475–76, 483–84; SWP3, 702.

109   *One of the most common witch traits*: SWP1, 104; SWP3, 749.

110   *On 14 May*: D1, 291–92.

110–1 *In 1690, Sewall described*: Kittredge, 155.

111   *the peninsula was 487 acres*: Seasholes, 2.

112   *the formation of the Court of Oyer and Terminer*: Norton, 197.

112   *General Court proclaimed a fast*: De Loss Love, 260.

112   *Mr. Willard's sermon*: Sewall, Sermon Notebook, 1691–92, in Samuel Sewall Papers.

CHAPTER SIX: *Oyer and Terminer*

115   *A woman called Elizabeth Cary*: SWP1, 208–10.

116   *Sewall's friend John Alden*: D1, 282–83, 293 n.

117   *he described what now happened to him*: SWP1, 52–3. *The Salem Witchcraft Papers* attribute this account to Alden, though Rosenthal points out that there is no original attribution, and speculates that the author could be Robert Calef (Salem Witchcraft Trials, Transcription Project [http://jefferson.village.virginia.edu/salem/transcript2.html], note 11, visited 4/5/05). It's true the account uses the third person, but that could simply be to give a disinterested tone, and at one point there is a switch from third to first person. The immediacy and detail of the writing suggest Alden's own authorship, and Calef himself attributes the document to Alden. See Burr, 253.

117   *As Cotton Mather would put it*: Mather, C., *Wonders* 11.

117   *People like Alden*: For Alden's dealings with the Indians, see Norton, 184–91.

118   *Sewall's minister, Mr. Willard, preached*: Sewall, Sermon Notebook, 1691–92, in Samuel Sewall Papers.

118   *Three days later*: Burr, 223–24.

119   *long scarlet gowns with matching hoods*: Earle, 1:258.

120   *The afflicted had been asked*: Burr, 223–24.

121   *On the morning of the trial*: SWP1, 106–8; Rosenthal, 76–78.

121   *The court used a formula*: SWP1, 90.

121   *Thomas Brattle*: Burr, 188–89.

122   *the General Court ended*: Gragg, 95.

122   *He had refused to sign*: Konig, 177.

122   *"The Return of Several Ministers"*: Mather, C., *Diary*, 1:150–51; Middlekauff, 152.

122   *It suggested caution*: Salem, 117–18.

123   *sermon given by James Bayley*: Sewall, Sermon Notebook, 1691–92, in Samuel Sewall Papers.

123   *Mather abused her*: Burr, 236.

124   *Goody Wilds's case*: SWP3, 815–18.

124   *John Pressy of Amesbury*: SWP2, 560–61.

125   *Samuel Sewall wrote in his diary*: D1, 285.

125   *Years later, Sewall wrote a letter*: LB2, 148.

126   *Samuel and Ruth Perley's daughter*: SWP2, 439.

126   *Rebecca Nurse had denied*: SWP2, 585. In a famous discussion of *Hamlet*, T. S. Eliot claimed that the play contained "some stuff that the writer could not drag to light," and coined the phrase "objective correlative" to describe a set of objects or events in the external world that would provide the "formula" of a character's internal processes (Eliot, *Essays*, 145). The Perleys' reasoning, and that of the witchcraft examiners and judges, rested on a belief that perceived events are indeed the formula of hidden internal motives, of active malevolence on the part of the accused; in short there is a consistent assumption of a *subjective* correlative to what has been seen happening, or apparently happening, in the external world.

126   *they found her not guilty*: SWP2, 607–8.

126   *What happened next*: Burr, 358.

127   *Nearly twenty years later*: Sewall, Diary, 1717–1726, in Samuel Sewall Papers. In 1705, the superior court sitting at Charlestown asked the jury to reconsider a verdict, and on that occasion they did change their minds. A person in the courtroom told them to stand by their original verdict and was fined £5 for his pains. See *Boston News-Letter*, 5–12 February 1704/5.

127   *In one of the most poignant documents*: SWP2, 608.

127   *Nurse had not finished*: Burr, 358–59.

128–9 *In Hawthorne's* The House of the Seven Gables: Hawthorne, *House*, 8.

129   *his friend Captain Alden*: D1, 293.

129   *John Proctor had asked Nicholas Noyes*: Burr, 362.

129   *a web of association*: Sewall, Account Book 1688–1692, in Samuel Sewall Papers, np.

130   *in September, he escaped*: Upham, 2:246.

130   *Sewall visited Alden*: D1, 310.

130   *He wrote to his cousin Hull*: LB1, 132.

131   *Nathaniel Cary was horrified*: SWP1, 208–10; D1, 293.

CHAPTER SEVEN: *The King and Queen of Hell*

133   *local man called John Willard*: Upham, 2:173.

133   *Spectral Indians were sighted*: Mather, C., *Works*, 2:620. Two years before the Salem crisis, Sewall had been in correspondence with an expert on Indian matters called Samuel Lee, who gave him examples of their conjurations. See Kittredge, 149–52. Kittredge comments: "We may note that Mr. Lee wrote these words shortly before the witchcraft persecutions at Salem, for which the belief that the Indians had to do with Devils was partly responsible" (182).

133   *the case of Mercy Short*: Burr, 259–60. Extensive accounts of the Indian experiences of those involved in the trials, accused and accusers alike, can be found in Norton.

134   *her sister, Mary Toothaker*: SWP3, 767–69.

134–5   *On 4 August, Sewall was at Salem*: D1, 293.

135   *Cotton Mather got the news*: Silverman, 107.

135   *returning to the subject of Port Royal*: Mather, C., *Magnalia*, 191.

135   *king of hell*: SWP2, 523.

135   *seventeen-year-old Mercy Lewis*: SWP1, 169; see the Bible, Matthew 4:8–9; Burr, 217–18.

136   *Carrier had a forthright*: SWP1, 185, 189.

136   *Cotton Mather huffed and puffed*: Burr, 244.

136   *A month later, Parris would use*: Parris, 199.

136   *John Proctor had written*: SWP2, 660, 689.

137   *An even greater challenge*: Burr, 364–66; SWP2, 491–92.

138   *She was able to ask*: Rosenthal 49, 123.

138   *Instead, he and Stoughton*: D1, 294.

139   *Brattle, writing a few months later*: Burr, 177.

140   *Standing on the ladder*: Ibid., 360; SWP3, 825.

141   *Sarah Wilson told of a meeting*: SWP1, 178.

142   *William Barker described*: SWP1, 66.

142   *Parris gave historicity*: Parris, 201, 204.

143   *Ann Pudeator, for example*: SWP3, 702, 709.

143   *Mary Bradbury, meanwhile*: SWP1, 117–19; SWP3, 981.

144   *The two accused sisters*: SWP1, 288, 303.

144   *eighty-year-old Giles Corey*: Burr, 367.

145   *Corey called their bluff*: D1, 295.

145   *Undoubtedly, he was aware*: Rosenthal, 197–99.

146   *Mary Easty, in prison*: SWP1, 304.

147   *a fifth woman, Abigail Faulkner*: Faulkner may not have been regarded as a confessor but was pregnant in any case, so was reprieved for that reason. See Rosenthal, 156–58.

147   *Samuel Wardwell, who had confessed*: SWP3, 783–84.

147–8 *Rebecca Eames*: SWP1, 281–82.

148   *The other confessors*: SWP2, 343, 624.

148   *They were Mary Parker*: Ibid., 632–33; SWP3, 717.

148   *an account from Samuel Lee*: Kittredge, 152.

148   *the case of Wardwell*: SWP3, 784–85; Rosenthal, 155.

148   *there was Corey's execution*: D1, 295; Burr, 367.

148–9 *Thomas Putnam chose*: SWP1, 246.

150   *Sewall swallowed it whole*: D1, 295.

150   *Cotton Mather wrote*: Ibid., 297 n.

150   *as Sewall recorded*: D1, 296.

150   *John Hale*: Burr, 424.

151   *even Noyes signed*: Ibid., 369.

151   *The condemned were taken*: Ibid., 367.

151   *Stephen and Margaret Sewall*: D1, 296–97.

151   *a fast in the First Church*: Ibid., 294.

CHAPTER EIGHT: *Speaking Smartly about the Salem Witchcrafts*

153   *Sewall went about business*: D1, 297–99.

154   *The Christian settlement of New England*: Mather, C., *Wonders*, 11–13.

154   *Winthrop had become quite anatomical*: Winthrop 2:288–89; Higginson, *Cause*, 12.

155   *lonesome Mr. Torrey*: D1, 36.

155   *Another part of the book*: Burr, 245–46.

155   Simia Dei, *The Ape of God*: Phrase used by the British theologian Joseph Mede. See Lovejoy, "Indian," 608.

155–6 *a sort of imprimatur*: Burr, 250–51.

156   *Increase Mather concentrated*: Mather, I., *Conscience*, 9, 43.

157   *Sewall began by reading*: D1, 298.

157   *he had abruptly changed his tune*: Bromfield Papers; Norton, 215–16; Burr, 253.

157   *distinction maintained by Brattle*: Burr, 185.

158   *Willard's B. talks*: Willard, *Observations*, 16; SWP2, 585.

158–9 *this point about Rebecca Nurse*: Burr, 175–76.

159   *He begins by pouring scorn*: Ibid., 169–99.

160–1   *Phips repeated this charge*: Ibid., 199–201.
161   *Sewall visited one*: D1, 298.
161–2   "*. . . the Devil promeised*": SWP1, 66.
162   *provincial people amazed Nathaniel Hawthorne*: Hawthorne, *House*, 8.
163   *His gloom increased*: D1, 299–300.
164   *the only time in his diary he ever mentions*: Graham, 73.
164   *As Cotton Mather put it*: Mather, C., *Tabernacle*, 59.
164   *were magistrates ex officio*: Palfrey, 4:140.
164   *Sewall prayed to God*: D1, 301–2.
165   *In the first session of the superior court*: SWP3, 864–65.
165   *a serving woman called Mary Watkins*: Records of the Superior Court, 1692–95, 1686–1700.
165   *Saltonstall lived in Haverhill*: Saltonstall, 80:55.
165–6   *Sewall sent a barrel of salt*: LB1, 110.
166   *the angry father*: Saltonstall, 80:55.
166   *Saltonstall's disapproval*: Ibid., 80:52–53.
166   *The charge was serious enough*: D1, 305–6.
167   *The dramas of family life*: Ibid., 306–9.
167   *an English naval force*: Ibid., 310.
167–8   *he also wrote out a list*: Ibid., 313 n.
168   *Indian trouble flared up*: Drake, *History*, 509–10.
168   *Just over a week later*: D1, 314, 319–22.
168   *Sam's first adventure*: D1, 327; for more on the practice of sending children out to work, see Graham, 144–66.
168   *The year 1694*: D1, 318.
168–9   *Sir William Phips was recalled*: Drake, *History*, 506.
169   *a hagiographic biography*: "Pietas in Patriam" in Mather, C., *Magnalia*, 276–359.
169   *the pay was modest*: Records of the Superior Court, 1692–95, 1686–1700, 1700–14, 1715–21, 1721–25; *Eleventh Report*, 32. Sewall's stipend had a spending power of about £4,000 sterling, or US $7,000, in today's values.
169   *On a stormy day*: D1, 324, 337.
170   *On 15 March 1695*: Ibid., 328.
170   *Sewall himself planted*: D1, 329; *Seventh Report*, 221.
170   *One day in April 1695*: Sewall's diary references for the rest of the chapter are from D1, 330–67.
172–3   *sending him to school with Ezekiel Cheever*: Sewall, Account Book, 1688–92, in Samuel Sewall Papers. Entries for 1 October 1688, 10 September 1690.

173   *Sam Jr. began to confront his problems*: Sewall, Samuel, Jr,
       Arithmetick and Commonplace Book, 1698–   , in Samuel Sewall
       Papers.

174   *They had previously sold off*: LB1, 26 n.

174   *Sewall heard an ominous anecdote*: LB1, 165–66.

175   *promoter of the Devil's doctrines*: D1, 341–42 n.

175   *Maule finally faced trial*: Maule, 55–58.

175   *In answer to the charge*: Jones, 24–25; Maule, 62.

176   *a severe winter had set in*: Hutchinson, 2:76.

176   *In his proposal for a fast day*: De Loss Love, 266–67.

CHAPTER NINE: *Judge Sewall's Apology*

179   *The Sewalls woke*: D1, 364, 366–67.

180   *Thomas Shepard*: Shepard, 5.

180   *Puritan funerals at this period*: Stannard, 96–134.

183   *Samuel Parris, faced with demands*: Salem, 297–98.

183   *the end came in the summer*: Upham, 2:497–98.

184   *The arbitrators gave him*: LB1, 16 n.

184   *Thomas Fiske, the jury foreman*: Burr, 387–88.

184   *Nine years later, in 1706*: Upham, 2:510.

185   *Willard emphasized this point*: Sewall, Sermon Notebook, 1691–92,
       in Samuel Sewall Papers, 126–92.

185   *The "Infernal enemy"*: Burr, 213.

186   *On 29 December 1698*: D1, 403.

187–8 *he was arguing with Samuel Willard*: Ibid., 368–69.

188   *a certain Thomas Mumford*: D1, 370; in 1689, Sewall had recorded
       another example (or another version of the same example) of this
       ritual, in which a "great lady" who had suffered calamity summoned
       guests from far and near, danced "a considerable time," and named
       herself anew. See Kittredge, 154.

189   *Indians attacked the town of Haverhill*: Saltonstall, 80:57–58.

189   *The Indians brained*: Mather, C., *Decennium*, 138–43; Drake, *Border*,
       123.

190   *six of the Indians*: Ulrich, 167.

190   *her sister, Elizabeth Emerson*: D1, 282, 310; Ulrich, 196–201; *Records*,
       3:357.

191   *It is an obscure, convoluted work*: The complex scholarship and knotty
       apocalyptic interpretation is shown to be a coherent intellectual
       process, "a story of a particular kind," in Scheiding. See 168.

191–2   *As long as* Plum Island: Sewall, *Phaenomena*, 59.

192   *Robert Calef*: Burr, 297–98, 386–87, 392–93.

194–5   *Sewall opened*: Sewall, *Phaenomena*, np.

195   *The little book begins grandly*: Ibid., 1.

195   *His particular spin*: Ibid., 24.

196   *Being American*: Sewall was specifically confronting the assertion by the English theologian Joseph Mede that the American destiny is dystopian; see Lovejoy, "Hell."

196   *He wrote to a correspondent*: Drafts of letters to Mr. Robert Fleming, 22 August 1702, and Abraham Pierson, 13 December 1705, in Diary, 1675–1721, in Samuel Sewall Papers.

196   *In some notes*: Diary, 1675–1721, in Samuel Sewall Papers.

196   *"Yee gates lift"*: Psalms, 41.

196–7   *Sewall argued*: Sewall, *Phaenomena*, 2.

197   *The* Revelation *doth*: Ibid., 28–29. The square brackets are Sewall's.

197–8   *Thomas Parker, whose closely argued book*: Parker, 138, 141, 155.

198   *Sewall had a theory*: Sewall, *Phaenomena*, 31, 35.

198   *Thorowgood's* Iewes in America: Copy in the Boston Public Library, Rare Books and Manuscripts, 16.

199   *Thomas Morton, for example*: Morton, *Canaan*, 18, 22; Kittredge, 178–79.

199   *the house of America*: Sewall, *Phaenomena*, 41–42.

199   *after the first settlers landed*: Bradford, 95, 103, 114, 116.

200   *Sewall related the later and sadder part*: Sewall, *Phaenomena*, 33–34. Sewall refers to the account in Morton, *Memorial*. At some time he also had possession of the manuscript of William Bradford's *History of Plimouth Plantation*, which gives a long account of the encounter with Squanto. See *D*1: 498 n; Bradford, vi–vii.

200–1   *This was hardly the usual argument*: Johnson, *Providence*, 161, Franklin, 116.

201   *The* Phaenomena *is dedicated*: Sewall, *Phaenomena*, np.

201   *Toward the end of* Phaenomena: Ibid., 59–60.

202   *Just a year previously*: D1, 355.

202   *Sewall the merchant*: Sewall, "General store, 1685–1689, Boston in New England," in Sewall, Ledger.

204   *Sewall had rediscovered the hope*: LB1, 122.

204   *In a commonplace book*: Sewall, Diary 1675–1721, in Samuel Sewall Papers.

CHAPTER TEN: *American Pastoral*

207   *there was an Indian attack on Lancaster*: Mather, C., *Decennium*, 148–49.

207   *Four days later*: D1, 377.

207   *a picnic to Hogg Island*: Ibid., 375, 377–78.

208   *Psalm 121*: Psalms, 275.

208   *flocks of sheep in a howling wilderness*: Bercovitch shows how "howling" and similar fearful terms for the wilderness had to be transcended by the Puritans as they sought to justify themselves by justifying America, creating the concept of national election, a redemptive, indeed millennial, view of the landscape they had colonized. Bercovitch, 102–6.

208   *A harsh winter set in*: D1, 386–87, 400.

209   *He modestly pooh-poohed*: LB1, 196–97.

209   *the Indian College at Harvard*: Sewall, "Letter," 600.

209   *On 28 June 1698*: D1, 395.

210   *Taylor had been ministering*: Taylor, xliv–xlviii.

210   *"skulking rascalds"*: Grabo, 10.

210   *walked along Cotton Hill*: D1, 396.

210–1   *late age of twenty-three*: D2, 1075.

211   *"Let by Rain"*: Taylor, 463. It's not possible to date the poem. The original manuscript volume in which it appears (Taylor, MS Poems) contains most of Taylor's life's work, and "Let by Rain" (the title isn't complete: the page is torn and the first part of it is missing) is one of a set of eight poems clearly written out at some date after their composition. While it's true that the last poem in the series. "Upon the Sweeping Flood," has the date 1683, this has no particular significance because this sequence could be random, or determined by thematic considerations. (Eighteen pages before "Let by Rain" appears, there is a poem dated 1697, "Elegy on Samuel Hooker.")

211   *In 1634, Richard Mather*: Murdock, 16, 61–62.

213   *Sewall had intervened*: D1, 390.

213   *When little Hull died*: Johnson, "Taylor."

213   *Sarah Threeneedles*: Records of the Superior Court, 1692–95, 1686–1700.

213   *Cotton Mather was guest minister*: Mather, C., *Diary*, 1:279; Psalms, 98; D1, 400.

214 *trial of Esther Rogers*: Coffin, 168; *D*1, 451; Sewall, *Joseph*, 50–51; *LB*1, 276.

215 *Grub Street hack Edward Ward*: Ward, 5–7.

215 *"Tis rumor'd," Sewall wrote*: *D*1, 401, 409; Prebble, 20–22, 80–88, 353–54.

217 *Sewall wrote to the ministers*: *LB*1, 227–29.

217 *four thousand periwigs*: Macaulay, 15.

218 *Sewall copied the articles*: *LB*1, 242–44.

218 *Sewall had received his second commission*: *D*1, 413.

218 *Betty was seventeen*: *D*1, 406–8.

219 *Salem merchant called Grove Hirst*: Graham, 133.

219 *Block Island Harry*: For the Sewalls' generosity in this regard, see Blackmon, 170; *D*1, 414–46.

220 *This sticky encounter*: *LB*1, 213.

220 *This intervention did the trick*: *D*1, 416.

220 *Grove Hirst had become courtly indeed*: Ibid., 434–35; *Psalms*, 280.

CHAPTER ELEVEN: *The Selling of Joseph*

221 *In April 1699*: *D*1, 408.

221 *Bastian did Sewall errands*: *D*1, 327; *D*2, 636; *D*2, 655; *D*2, 829; *D*2, 862.

221 *A number of issues had converged*: *D*1, 433.

221–2 *A committee in Boston*: Greene, 79–80, 84; Twomby, 224–42.

222 *some learned reflections by Sewall*: *The Selling of Joseph: A Memorial* is conveniently appended to the Halsey Thomas edition of Sewall's diary; see *D*2, 1117–21. It can also be consulted in Sewall, *Joseph*.

223 *That unconvincing argument*: *LB*1, 28, 34, 38, 45, 49, 76–77, 234–35; *D*1, 157, 158. But Davis, *Slaves*, 23, claims that there were a million white slaves during the period covered by his book.

223–4 *As Edward Taylor put it*: Taylor, 17; Wigglesworth, *Doom*, 4.

224 *Jonathan Edwards, the great preacher*: Edwards, 10, 18–19. See Stephen Williams's account, quoted in Winslow, *Edwards*, 180.

225 *a long-standing dispute*: Drake, *History*, 351.

225 *The Old Testament model of slavery*: See Greene's lucid discussion of this issue, 167–68. Von Frank claims that there was little slavery in Massachusetts until the end of the seventeenth century. His argument is based on his insistence that limited term servitude cannot be regarded as slavery at all. He uses Nathaniel Ward's "Body of Liberties," where reference is made to "such strangers as willingly

sell themselves" for specified periods to prove his point. True, this is obviously a reference to indenture, but Von Frank ignores the next phrase, which clearly refers to slavery: "or are sold to us." If an individual is sold without giving his or her permission, even if only for a fixed term of years, that person is a slave. Von Frank, 259–60. Also see Nathaniel Ward, "The Massachusetts Body of Liberties," in Morgan, 196–97.

226   *Judge Sewall, lover of home and family*: Von Frank makes the point that since full-blown slavery had only recently come to Massachusetts, Sewall should be seen as a repository of traditional Puritan values (266). I agree to some extent (hence my image of him walking backward), but I also feel that his words look toward the future, and the attitude of contemporaries like Cotton Mather toward *The Selling of Joseph* confirms his radical and progressive stance.

226   *the selectmen of Boston*: Eleventh Report, 5.

226   *Negotiations about the fate*: D1, 433.

227   *Three months later*: Ibid., 442–43.

227   *Cotton Mather married two black couples*: Report: Marriages, 2, 5; Greene, 195, 198.

227   *Increase Mather was president*: LB1, 264; Murdock, 339–58.

227   *It was "the place"*: Mather, C., *Diary*, 1:360.

228   *Cotton Mather, always a passionate supporter*: D1, 454–55.

228   *Cotton Mather's own attitude*: Mather, C., *Rules*, np.

228–9   *an "ambidexter" position*: The term "ambidexter" was used by Calef to describe Cotton Mather's own self-contradictory position on the trials. See Calef, 153.

229   *comfort provided by Psalm 27:10*: Psalms, 46.

229   *When Cotton Mather got a toothache*: Mather, C., *Diary*, 1:24.

230   *grovel in the dust*: Ibid., 265, 340, 349, 355, 378, 421.

230   *Mather made no mention*: Ibid., 406.

230–1   *Even while angry thoughts*: Ibid., 455; LB1, 263.

232   *When Cotton Mather and his father actually read*: Murdock, 376; Quincy 1:68–117; Mather, I., "Autobiography," 351.

232   *In 1694, Judge John Saffin*: Towner, 47.

233   A Brief and Candid Answer: Saffin. This rare pamphlet is quoted in part in Moore, 251–56. The remainder of the pamphlet can be found in Goodell, 103–112.

233   *a slave dealer himself*: Sewall, *Joseph*, 35; Von Frank, 255–57.

233–4   *Saffin fancied himself as a poet*: See Saffin, *Book*.

233–4   *despicably racist couplets*: Moore, 256.

234   *Saffin himself was summoned*: Goodell, 88–90.

234   *Sewall was suspicious*: D1: 451–52; Greene, 297.

234–5   *Thomas Shepard testified*: Goodell, 91; Sewall, *Joseph*, 42.

235   *Adam was leased out*: Goodell, 93–97.

235   *some retaliatory couplets*: D1, 487.

236   *On 2 November 1703*: Goodell, 100–2; Greene, 296–97.

236   *Meanwhile, Bastian and Jane*: D1, 483.

236   *In 1705, an act*: D1, 532; *Acts*, 1:578–79.

237   The Athenian Oracle: D2, 1098–99; *LB1*, 326; Sewall, *Joseph*, 58–59.

237   *bill that rated Indian and Negro slaves*: D2, 822.

237   *Samuel Smith of Sandwich*: *LB2*, 101.

238   *At the trial, Smith*: Greene, 234–35.

CHAPTER TWELVE: *"Wigg'd and Powder'd with Pretence"*

239   *Late one night in November 1687*: D1, 126.

239   *Mr. Hayward, the public notary*: Ibid., 82.

240   *Vincent Alsop, an English minister*: Quoted in Godbeer, 15; William Prynne, *The Unloveliness of Love-Lockes* (London: np 1628), quoted in Seaver, 16.

240   *The College Laws of Harvard*: Godbeer, 8.

240   *John Mulliner*: Mulliner, 3–14.

240   *Increase Mather went so far*: Mather, I., "Exhortation," 7. John Eliot shared this belief; see "The Historical Account of John Eliot," in Eliot, *Dictionary*, 5–35.

240   *On 8 July 1677*: D1, 44.

241   *Mary Dyer*: Francis, *Ann*, 31.

241   *two new members of the South Church congregation*: D1, 76.

241   *There was a time lag*: Seaver, 17.

241   *Sewall knew exactly*: D1, 277.

241   *his share of watch duty*: *Eleventh Report*, 170.

241–2   *On 13 October 1696*: D1, 357.

243   *In May of the following year*: Ibid., 372.

243   *the cutting of Indian hair*: Godbeer, 9.

243   *the women's hairstyles*: Kittredge, 154.

243   *the patriarchal pastor, John Higginson*: D1, 373; Perley, 3:384.

243–4   *in mid-December 1699*: D1, 418–19.

244   *the greatest periwig crisis*: D1, 427, 429–30, 448–49.

245   *own Carvers, Lords*: It's possible that being one's own carver could mean helping oneself to communion, without the agency of a minister. The phrase was used in this sense in a criticism of extreme

Puritan practice that was penned in England in the 1580s and quoted in Nicholson, 87. But the meaning would still be that the individual was presumptuous and appropriating a spiritual prerogative that didn't belong to him or her.

246   *On Sunday, 30 November*: *D*1, 421, 458.

247   *Josiah didn't follow the ministerial path*: Sibley, 4:427–30.

247   *In January 1704*: *D*1, 496.

247   *Two years later*: Ibid., 540.

248   *the* Censor *had trouble of his own*: Ibid., 543.

248   *That October, Benjamin Wadsworth*: Ibid., 553, 599–600.

249   *On 19 October 1713*: *D*2, 730–32.

250   *Mr. Pemberton's turn*: Ibid., 796.

250   *Thomas Prince arrived back*: Ibid., 837, 858.

250   *his friend Nicholas Noyes*: Sewall, Diary, 1675–1721, in Samuel Sewall Papers.

250   *Solomon Stoddard, the great liberal*: *D*2, 813; *LB*2, 137; Sibley, 4:326–32.

251   *Samuel Sewall* de Stephano: *LB*2, 138.

252   *As Increase Mather put it*: Mather, I., *Doctrine*, 29–30; Wigglesworth, *Diary*, 71–72.

252–3 *the poet Emily Dickinson*: Dickinson, 87.

253   *But what about Walt Whitman*: Whitman, 49, 51, 67, 72, 89, 94.

253   *Cotton Mather's study*: Mather, C., *Magnalia*, 22.

253   *This leveling tendency*: See Morison, *Builders*, 162–63; Foster, 18–19.

254   *his refusal to use the title "saint"*: *D*1, 601; *LB*1, 370–71.

254   *Edwards's sermon*: Edwards, 22.

254–5 *Sewall took notes*: Sewall, Diary, 1714–1729, in Samuel Sewall Papers, np.

CHAPTER THIRTEEN: *"Impartial Light"*

257   *demanded Increase Mather*: Mather, I., *Testimony*, 46–47, 49.

257   *thoroughly enjoyed Lent cakes*: *D*1, 206.

258   *Earl of Bellomont*: *Articles*, np.

258   *Kidd and his crew descended into piracy*: Brooks, 21, 72; Ritchie, 99–102, 108–117.

258   *another pirate, Joseph Bradish*: Ritchie, 174–75.

259   *locked up in Boston jail*: *D*1, 411; Dow, 42; Records of the Superior Court, 1692–95, 1686–1700.

259   *the new governor, Lord Bellomont*: Ritchie, 174–75, 178; Dow, 43, 76.

259–60   *Sewall, with four others*: Brooks, 32–34.

260   *There were "Gold, Pearls &c.*": D1, 426; Bonner, 196.

260   *On 25 July*: D1, 413.

260   *He told the council*: Ibid., 422–24.

260   *Twelve days later*: Ibid., 426 n.

261   *Kidd's due process*: Brooks, 37, 48; Ritchie, 175, 226–29; LB1, 216.

261   *Sewall reaped his reward*: D1, 415; he had already proved his personal commitment to Indian welfare by generous gifts to Harvard and to the town of Pattaquamscutt (now Kingston, Rhode Island) for the promotion of spiritual and educational welfare. See Blackmon, 170–72.

262   *the second edition of the Bible in 1685*: LB1, 22.

262   *biggest community of praying Indians*: Kellaway, 239–41; Mayhew.

262   *As Samuel Willard had put it*: Willard, *Esteem*, 7.

262   *Mayhew took a restrained view*: Mayhew, xx–xxi.

262   *Grindal Rawson and Samuel Danforth*: See their account in Noyes.

262–3   *By the summer of 1700*: LB2, 231–33.

263   *Sewall was determined*: D1, 440–42.

263–4   *or possibly sang*: Sewall says the verses were "said," but in a musical context that verb could mean "sang"; see Smith, 169–70.

264   *"They act like wolves"*: Dudley, 235.

265   *That year Sewall noted*: D1, 444.

265   *William Stoughton*: Ibid., 449–50.

265   *from Lord Bellomont*: Ibid., 425, 446.

266   *There she was, the first European poet*: Bradstreet, 44, 55, 79.

268   *writing a letter to Rebeckah*: D1, 443.

268   *The Sewalls' family*: Ibid., 460–61.

269   *That spring, he went to Cape Cod*: Ibid., 465.

269   *A month later, in May*: Ibid., 448, 467.

270   *In June 1702*: Ibid., 469–71. Yazawa (164) mistakenly assumes Dudley's family arrived with him from London (whereas they had been in Boston all along), and therefore believes the courtship was a whirlwind one.

270   *Mehetabel Moody died*: LB1, 273–74; D1, 471.

271   *notice of the intended marriage*: D1, 473.

272   *That September*: Ibid., 475, 477.

272   *He recorded 193 pounds*: Ibid., 479.

272   *Sewall, man of affairs*: Details of this negotiation are in Massachusetts Archives, Archive 45, 290–91.

273   *In February 1703*: LB1, 278.

273   *Sewall the unworldly*: D1, 496.

273   *The Deerfield massacre took place*: Penhallow, 24; *D*1, 110, 555; *D*2, 719.

274   *lively debate with Nicholas Noyes*: *LB*1, 289–90; *D*1, 501; Thorowgood, 43–44.

274–5   *a letter to Richard Henchman*: *LB*1, 294.

275   *His fervor was enhanced*: According at least to the reconstruction of Boston in 1722 undertaken by Samuel Clough in 1900. See Clough Papers; *D*1, 501.

275   *A briganteen called the* Charles: Dow, 99–101.

276   *Sewall had been on his judicial rounds*: *D*1, 504–6.

277   *the pirates had set sail*: Dow, 103–4.

277   *"See the News-Letter"*: *Boston News-Letter*, 12–19 June 1704.

278   *convened a Court of Admiralty*: Dow, 107.

278   *The trial took place*: *Boston News-Letter*, 19–26 June 1704; *D*1, 505–6, 508–9, 526; Dow, 110–13.

278   *Road rage in a horse-drawn era*: *D*1, 517, 521, 526, 532, 532–35, 535 n.

279   *The attorney general*: Sibley, 4:47.

279   *Sewall had no doubt*: *D*1, 536–40.

281   *he exploded at Sewall*: Ibid., 547.

281   *superior court in November 1706*: Records of the Superior Court, 1700–14.

CHAPTER FOURTEEN: *"The Concomitant Rain-bow"*

283   *an officer called Samuel Vetch*: Kimball, 116.

283   *the case went before the General Court*: *D*1, 549; Kimball, 117; *LB*1, 334.

283   *The men were duly found guilty*: *Acts*, 6:62–63.

284   *Twenty leading New Englanders*: Palfrey 4:303.

284   *"luxuriant words"*: *LB*1, 361.

284–5   *Late in November 1707*: *D*1, 577–78.

285   *Pugnacious Cotton Mather*: Mather, C., *New England*, np.

285   *The council invited the governor*: *D*1, 581.

285   *"There is none in England"*: *LB*1, 336.

285–6   *Sewall wrote to Sir Henry Ashurst*: Ibid., 359.

286   *he then wrote again to Higginson*: Ibid., 362.

286   *Sewall dozed off*: *D*1, 560.

286   *"Mount Etna Eruption"*: Ibid., 583.

286   *a tenant, Nathaniel Henchman*: Ibid., 592–93.

285   *Dudley survived*: Kimball, 189.

287 *Taverns and ordinaries blossomed*: Drake, *History*, 525.

287 *One day in 1708*: D1, 411, 596. For a brief sketch of Bromfield's career, see Belknap Papers, "The Character of Edward Bromfield," 10 June 1734.

287 *Thomas Morton and a group*: Morton, *Canaan*, 134–35; Winsor, 82.

288 *Sewall could simply address*: letter to Hannah Sewall, Samuel Mather Papers.

288 *Newbury Street*: *Seventh Report*, 50. See Estes for a full account of the position and history of the house.

288 *The population of the town*: Blake, 247; Whitehill, 20; Drake, *History*, 537.

288 *murdered the minister, Benjamin Rolfe*: D1, 601.

288 *decline of Native American society*: Kellaway, 235.

289 *Cotton Mather's own view*: Mather, C., *Decennium*, 154; remark copied by Sewall into his *Letter-Book* (*LB*1, 401).

289 *an incident that took place*: D2, 615–16; *LB*1, 389.

290 *He gave a night's lodging*: Kellaway, 219; D1, 586, 589.

290 *the New England Company decided*: D2, 639; Kellaway, 152–53.

290 *His meticulously kept account book*: Sewall, Account Book of New England Company, 1708–19, in Samuel Sewall Papers.

291 *Samuel Gerrish, Boston bookseller*: D2, 615, 625.

291 *Mary gave birth*: D2, 645.

291 *his pastor, Ebenezer Pemberton*: D2, 637–39; *LB*1, 407; D2, 845–46.

293 *Indian boy called Benjamin Larnell*: D2, 651; Mather, C., *Diary*, 2:231; D2, 725, 763–64; Kellaway, 231.

294 *purchase land on Martha's Vineyard*: *LB*1, 371–72; Kellaway, 219–22.

294 *published* Proposals: Matthew 13, Mark 4, and Luke 8; Sewall, *Proposals*, 4, 6–7, 9; Noyes, 56.

295 *Thorowgood's Iewes*: Thorowgood, 88.

295 *this transcendental moment*: Sewall, *Proposals*, 6; Revelation 10:1.

295 *sightings of rainbows*: On 20 May 1711, 12 June 1711, 30 June 1711, 22 August 1711, 9 May 1712, 5 July 1713 (*D2*, 661, 663, 667, 688, 720).

295 *distributed* Rainbows: Mather, C., *Thoughts*, 37, 62; Willard, *Fountain*; D2, 676–77, 949.

295 *Sewall's pamphlet presented*: Sewall, *Proposals*, 5.

296 *He spilled a can of water*: D2, 731.

296 *a reprise of his poem*: Sewall, *Proposals*, np.

296 *By the autumn*: D2, 728, 749.

297 *Sewall faced an unpleasant crisis*: D2, 742–43; Sibley, 4:496–99.

298 *On the Monday*: D2, 741–45.

299–300   *Thomas Banister was drowned*: D2, 840, 842.

300   *off to Martha's Vineyard*: D2, 750–55; Kellaway, 222–24.

CHAPTER FIFTEEN: *"Wave after Wave, Wave after Wave"*

303   *Sam Jr. and Rebeckah*: D2, 705–7.

304   *His own diary*: Entries for 12 February, 26 April, 12 October, 1711, 16 September 1713 in Journal, 1711–1716, Joseph Sewall Papers.

305   *The following September*: D2, 726–27.

306   *Not long afterward*: D2, 728.

306   *In October, Joseph married*: D2: 732; Entry for 31 October 1713 in Journal, 1711–1716, Joseph Sewall Papers.

306   *one December day*: D2, 779, 791.

307   *Sam Jr. went back to Boston*: Sewall, Samuel, Jr, Arithmetick and Commonplace Book, 1698– , in Samuel Sewall Papers.

307   *It was fifty-four years*: D2, 793; Blake, 247.

307   *His great-nephew, Joseph Moody*: D2, 797; Davis, "Currency," 315–16; Sibley, 4:259–61

308   *one August evening in 1715*: D2, 798.

308   *the Indian community at Natick*: Ibid., 801–2, 806.

309   *The winter of 1715–16*: D2, 810; Willard, *Esteem*, 13. In a funeral poem, Edward Taylor congratulates his late wife, Elizabeth, for her ability to quote the dire warnings of Wigglesworth's *Day of Doom* without succumbing to despair, a perfect example of the deathbed as test of nerve: "The Doomsday Verses much perfum'de her Breath, Much in her Thoughts, and yet she fear'd not Death" (Taylor, 476). For examples of Puritan terror in the face of death, see Stannard, 83–91.

309   *Perhaps Hannah was weakened*: D2, 812; Entry for 10 July 1716, in Journal, 1711–1716, in Joseph Sewall Papers.

309   *When he visited her*: D2, 815.

310   *Betty's illness intensified*: Journal, 1711–1716, Joseph Sewall Papers; D2, 824–25; D1, 592.

311   *Sam and Rebeckah's marriage*: D2, 835–36; D2, 821.

311   *In December, Sewall went to dinner*: D2, 840.

312   *on 6 January 1717*: Sewall, Samuel, Jr, Arithmetick and Commonplace Book, 1698– , in Samuel Sewall Papers.

312   *John Neesnummin's debts*: Kellaway, 237.

312   *In July 1717, Hannah Sr.*: D2, 857, 1123–27.

313   *moved to publish a broadside*: Sewall, *Memorial*, np.

313   *On 22 July*: D2, 859–60.

313   *Hannah was so ill*: D2, 863–66; Sewall, Diary and Commonplace
       Book, 1675–1721, in Samuel Sewall Papers.

314   *his love for Hannah*: As Halsey Thomas points out in D2, 864 n.

314   *the standards of the time*: D2, 864–73.

315   *"On his Celebacy"*: In draft letter to Stephen Sewall: see Sewall,
       Diary and Commonplace Book, 1675–1721, in Samuel Sewall
       Papers.

315   *On 3 December*: D2, 871–73.

316   *another correspondent, Gurdon Saltonstall*: LB2, 81.

316   *used the same metaphor*: Ibid., 87.

317   *The following month*: Ibid., 89–90.

317   *In April, he was promoted*: D2, 893.

CHAPTER SIXTEEN: *Putting to Sea in Wintertime*

319   *Perhaps Christ himself*: D2, 884.

319   *A Mrs. Willoughby*: Ibid., D2, 885.

319   *Age, like the weather*: Ibid., 875, 886.

319   *He visited Nehemiah Walter*: Ibid., 886–87.

321   *he consulted Nathaniel Williams*: Ibid., 887; Graham, 190.

321   *In 1721, Sewall presided*: Records of the Superior Court, 1715–21,
       1721–25.

322   *Early in March 1718*: D2, 887.

322   *The cause of Madam Winthrop*: Ibid., 890.

322   *Mrs. Dorothy Denison came to town*: Sewall's courtship of
       Mrs. Denison is described in D2, 892–912.

322   *one of five wills*: Sewall, Probate Records, in Samuel Sewall Papers.

326   *a community without theater*: For some interesting thoughts on
       Sewall's capacity as a dramatist, see Rosenwald, esp. 338–39.

326   *rumors that a play might be performed*: LB2, 30.

326   *Boston, twenty years into*: Neal, 587; details assembled from adver-
       tisements in the Boston newspapers of the time by Silverman, 280.

328   *Boston was the biggest town*: Drake, *History*, 557.

328   *Boston's fashions, furniture, and buildings*: Neal, 591.

328   *Sewall's next courtship*: Sewall's courtship of Mrs. Tilly is described
       in D2, 921–33.

329   *he retained the ability to be horrified*: See Hall, "World," 33.

329   *the sick ex-governor Dudley*: D2, 934, 943, 943 n. The translation is
       by Halsey Thomas.

329   *In December*: D2, 936.

329   *he wrote a poem:* D2, 973.

330   *The border problem:* LB2, 125, 125 n, 129; Palfrey 4:461; D2,
       1027–28.

331   *His old sparring partner, Joseph Dudley:* D2, 943–45.

331   *the wedding of his daughter:* D2, 919, 929, 931, 935, 948–49.

332   *Abigail began to feel ill:* D2, 950–51.

333   *a pleasant encounter with Madam Winthrop:* Sewall's courtship of
       Madam Winthrop is described in D2, 956–69.

336   *He was named after his elder brother:* D1, 360.

338   *few people gave Columbus credit:* Most of Sewall's contemporaries
       gave Columbus little or no credit for the discovery of America. See
       Handlin, esp. 83–84.

346   *Cotton Mather's finest hour:* Drake, *History*, 562; *Boston News-Letter*,
       13–20 November 1721; Silverman, 361–63; Blake, 61; D2, 982, 985.

347   *a tooth had dropped out:* D2, 976; LB2, 105; D2, 985.

347   *an old Newbury friend, Timothy Woodbridge:* LB2, 133.

348   *she was now Madam Ruggles:* D2, 981–82.

348   *Mrs. Mary Gibbs:* His courtship of Mrs. Gibbs is described in D2,
       989–93.

349   *The marriage was a success:* LB2, 162; D2, 1014.

349   *a change of perspective:* Bercovitch's distinction between the Reform
       and humanistic traditions of the Renaissance is relevant here. The
       Reform tradition emphasized that "selfhood appears as a state to be
       overcome . . . and identity is asserted through . . . submission to a
       transcendent absolute," while the humanistic one emphasized hu-
       man particularity and individuality (Bercovitch, 12).

349   Moby-Dick: Melville, 4.

350   *Benjamin Franklin was to deal:* Franklin, 77–84, 97.

350   *demonstrated in his* Personal Narrative: Included as Section 4 of
       Hopkins.

CHAPTER SEVENTEEN: *"Rocqued Like a Cradle"*

351   *Sewall's unmarried daughter, Hannah:* D2, 1018–21.

351   *gave him a horrible shock:* British Apollo, 200.

351   *an essay called "TALITHA CUMI":* "TALITHA CUMI; or, An Invi-
       tation to WOMEN to Look after Their Inheritance in the HEAV-
       ENLY MANSIONS," in Sewall, Diary and Commonplace Book,
       1675–1721, Samuel Sewall Papers.

352   *the province's attorney, Paul Dudley:* D2, 747.

353   *one winter's day:* D1, 483.

354   *female genitalia*: see Godbeer, 17, though he argues that this perspective involves a downgrading of female status, while I feel it enables Sewall to adopt a (relatively) egalitarian position.

354   *evolutionary anatomy*: Gould, 1261.

354   *the ailing Madam Winthrop*: D2, 1035, 1037.

354   *He resigned as treasurer*: Ibid., 1015.

354   *an American millennium*: LB2, 201, 202, 230.

354   *He declined reelection*: Ibid., 183–84; D2, 1051.

354   *On 30 October*: LB2, 229, 229 n, 230; Drake, *History*, 575.

355   *The South meetinghouse*: LB2, 233–34; D2, 1060.

355   *In August, he saw a huge rainbow*: LB2, 248, 273.

355   *In September, he dreamed*: D2, 1062–63.

355   *A year later, he was asked*: D2, 1066 and fn 1067.

356   *Abigail May*: Francis, *Utopias*, 140–217.

Bibliography

Keyword references to sources, as given in the notes, are in **bold**. The following abbreviations are used for frequent citations:

D1, *D2*: *The Diary of Samuel Sewall*, ed. M. Halsey Thomas, 2 vols. (New York: Farrar, Straus & Giroux, 1973).

LB1, *LB2*: *The Letter-Book of Samuel Sewall, Collections of the Massachusetts Historical Society*, 6th ser., 2 vols. (1886–88).

SWP1, *SWP2*, *SWP3*: *The Salem Witchcraft Papers*, eds. Paul Boyer and Stephen Nissenbaum, 3 vols. (New York: Da Capo Press, 1977).

MANUSCRIPT SOURCES

Belknap Papers, Massachusetts Historical Society
Bromfield Papers, Massachusetts Historical Society
Clough Papers, Massachusetts Historical Society
Joseph Sewall Papers, Massachusetts Historical Society
Records of the Superior Court of Judicature, Massachusetts State Archives
Samuel Mather Papers, Massachusetts Historical Society
Samuel Sewall Papers, Massachusetts Historical Society
Sewall, Samuel, **Indenture** 24 October 1688, Rare Books and Manuscripts Department, the Boston Public Library
Sewall, Samuel, **Ledger**, 1685–89, Baker Library, Harvard Business School

Taylor, Edward, **MS Poems**, Beinecke Rare Book and Manuscript Library, Yale University

Winthrop Papers, Massachusetts Historical Society

PRINTED SOURCES

Acts and Resolves, Public and Private, of the Massachusetts Bay, ed. E. Ames and A. Cheney Goodell, 21 vols. (Boston: Wright & Potter, 1869–1922).

Articles of Agreement Made this 10 day of October 1695 between the Right Honourable Richard Earl of Bellomont of the One Part, and Robert Levington Esq, and Capt. William Kid of the Other Part (London: n.p., 1701).

Avery, Elizabeth. *Scripture-Prophecies Opened* (London: Giles Calvert, 1647).

Bailyn, Bernard. *The New England Merchants in the Seventeenth Century* (New York: Harper & Row, 1955).

Bercovitch, Sacvan. *The Puritan Origins of the American Self* (New Haven: Yale University Press, 1975).

Blackmon, Joab L. "Judge Samuel Sewall's Efforts in Behalf of the First Americans," *Ethnohistory* 16, no. 2 (Spring 1969): 165–76.

Blake, John B. *Public Health in Boston* (Cambridge, Mass.: Harvard University Press, 1959).

Bonner, Willard Hallam. "'Clamors and False Stories': The Reputation of Captain Kidd," *New England Quarterly* 17, no. 2 (June 1944): 179–208.

Boston News-Letter, 1704–76.

Boyer, Paul, and Stephen Nissenbaum. *Salem Possessed: The Social Origins of Witchcraft* (Cambridge, Mass.: Harvard University Press, 1974).

Bradford, William. *Bradford's "History of Plimouth Plantation"* (Boston: Commonwealth of Massachusetts, 1901).

Bradstreet, Anne. *Poems of Anne Bradstreet*, ed. Robert Hutchinson (New York: Dover, 1969).

The British Apollo: Containing about Two Thousand Answers to Curious Questions in Most Arts and Sciences, Serious, Comical and Humorous . . . Performd by a Society of Gentlemen 2nd ed., vol. 1 (London: J. Mayo, 1711).

Brooks, Graham. *Trial of Captain Kidd* (Edinburgh: William Hodge, 1930).

Burr, George Lincoln, ed. *Narratives of the Witchcraft Cases, 1648–1706* (New York: Barnes & Noble, 1952).

Calef, Robert. *More Wonders of the Invisible World* (London: N. Hillar, 1700).

Casaubon, Méric, and ten other divines. *Annotations upon All the Books of the Old and New Testament* (London: John Leggatt & John Raworth, 1645). Sewall's annotated copy is in the Boston Public Library, Rare Books and Manuscripts Collection.

Coffin, Joshua. *A Sketch of the History of Newbury, Newburyport, and West Newbury from 1635 to 1845* (Boston: Samuel L. Drake, 1845).

Davis, Andrew McFarland. "Occult Methods of Protecting the **Currency**," *Proceedings of the Massachusetts Historical Society*, 2nd ser. vol. 13 (1900): 315–27.

Davis, Robert C. *Christian **Slaves**, Muslim Masters: White Slavery in the Mediterranean, the Barbary Coast and Italy* (New York: Palgrave Macmillan, 2003).

De Loss Love, William, Jr. *The Fast and Thanksgiving Days of New England* (Boston: Houghton Mifflin, 1895).

Dickinson, Emily. *The Complete Poems*, ed. Thomas H. Johnson (London: Faber & Faber, 1970).

Dictionary of American Biography [**DAB**] (New York: Oxford University Press, 1999).

Dow, George Francis, and John Henry Edmonds. *The Pirates of the New England Coast, 1630–1730* (New York: Dover, 1996).

Drake, Samuel Adams. *The **Border** Wars of New England* (Williamstown, Mass.: Corner House Publishers, 1973).

Drake, Samuel G. *The **History** and Antiquities of Boston* (Boston: Luther Stevens, 1856).

Dudley Papers, The. Collections of the Massachusetts Historical Society, 4th ser., vol. 2 (1852).

Dunton, John. *Letters from New England* (Boston: Prince Society, 1867).

Dunton, John. *The **Life** and Errors of John Dunton* (London: S. Malthus, 1705).

Earle, Alice Morse. *Two Centuries of Costume in America, 1620–1820*, 2 vols. (Williamstown, Mass.: Corner House Publishers, 1974).

Edwards, Jonathan. *Sinners in the Hands of an Angry God* (Edinburgh: Lumisden & Robertson, 1745).

Eleventh Report of the Record Commissioners of the City of Boston: Records of Boston Selectmen, 1701–1715 (Boston: City of Boston, 1884).

Eliot, John. *A Biographical* **Dictionary**, *Containing a Brief Account of the First Settlers. . . .* (Bowie, Md.: Heritage Books, 1995).

Eliot, John. *Indian* **Dialogues** *for Their Instruction in That Great Service of Christ, in Calling Home Their Country-men to the Knowledge of GOD, and of THEMSELVES, and of Jesus Christ* (Cambridge, Mass.: Marmaduke Johnson, 1671).

Eliot, John. *The Christian* **Commonwealth**; *or, The Civil Policy of the Rising Kingdom of Jesus Christ* (London: n.p., 1659).

Eliot, T. S. *Selected* **Essays** (London: Faber & Faber, 1951).

Estes, Howard. "The Abode of John Hull and Samuel Sewall," *Proceedings of the Massachusetts Historical Society*, 2nd ser., vol. 1. (1884): 312–14.

Foster, Stephen. *Their Solitary Way: The Puritan Social Ethic in the First Century of Settlement in New England* (New Haven, Conn.: Yale University Press, 1971).

Francis, Richard. *Ann the Word: The Story of Ann Lee, Female Messiah, Mother of the Shakers, the Woman Clothed with the Sun* (London: Fourth Estate, 2000).

Francis, Richard. *Transcendental* **Utopias** (Ithaca, N.Y.: Cornell University Press, 1997).

Franklin, Benjamin. *Autobiography* (Oxford: Oxford University Press, 1970).

Godbeer, Richard. "Perversions of Anatomy, Anatomies of Perversion: The Periwig Controversy in Colonial Massachusetts," *Proceedings of the Massachusetts Historical Society*, 3rd ser., vol. 109 (1998): 1–23.

Goodell, Abner C. "John Saffin and His Slave Adam," *Publications of the Colonial Society of Massachusetts* vol. 1 (1895): 82–114.

Gookin, Daniel. "Historical Collections of the Indians in New England," *Collections of the Massachusetts Historical Society*, 1st ser. vol. 1. (1792): 141–227.

Gould, Stephen Jay. *The Structure of Evolutionary Theory* (Cambridge, Mass.: Belknap Press of Harvard University Press, 2002).

Grabo, Norman S. *Edward Taylor* (Boston: Twayne Publishers, 1988).

Gragg, Larry. *The Salem Witch Crisis* (New York: Praeger, 1992).

Graham, Judith S. *Puritan Family Life: The Diary of Samuel Sewall* (Boston: Northeastern University Press, 2000).

Green, Samuel Abbott. *Ten Facsimile Reproductions, Relating to New England* (Boston: n.p., 1901).

Greene, Lorenzo Johnston. *The Negro in Colonial New England, 1620–1776* (New York: Columbia University Press, 1942).

Hale, John. *A Modest Enquiry into the Nature of Witchcraft* (Boston: B. Eliot, 1702).

Hall, David D. "Mental **World** of Samuel Sewall," *Proceedings of the Massachusetts Historical Society*, 3rd ser., vol. 92 (1980): 21–44.

Handlin, Lillian. "Discovering Columbus," *American Scholar* 62, no. 1 (Winter 1993): 81–95.

Harvard College Records, pt. 1. *Collections of the Colonial Society of Massachusetts*, vol. 15 (1925).

Hawthorne, Nathaniel, *The **House** of the Seven Gables* (Columbus: Ohio State University Press, 1965).

Hawthorne, Nathaniel. *The Scarlet **Letter*** (Columbus: Ohio State University Press, 1962).

Hawthorne, Nathaniel. *The Whole History of Grandfather's **Chair**, or, True Stories from History and Biography* (London: Walter Scott, n.d.).

Higginson, Francis. *New-England's **Plantation*** (1629), *Proceedings of the Massachusetts Historical Society*, 1st ser., vol. 1 (1792).

Higginson, John. *The **Cause** of God and his People in New England* (Cambridge, Mass.: Samuel Green, 1663).

Hinckley Papers. *Collections of the Massachusetts Historical Society*, 4th ser., vol. 5 (1860).

Hopkins, Samuel. *Memoirs of the Life, Experience, and Character of . . . Jonathan Edwards* (London: James Black, 1815).

Hull, John. *Diary* (transcription; np), Richards-Child Family Papers, Massachusetts Historical Society.

Hutchinson, Thomas. *History of the Colony and Province of Massachusetts*, ed. L. S. Mayo, 3 vols. (Cambridge, Mass., 1936).

Johnson, Edward. *Johnson's Wonder-Working Providence*, ed. J. Franklin Jameson (New York: Scribner, 1910).

Johnson, T. H. "A Seventeenth Century Printing of Some Verses of Edward Taylor," *New England Quarterly* 14, no. 1 (March 1941): 139–141.

Jones, Matthew Bushnell. *Thomas Maule: The Salem Quaker and Free Speech in Massachusetts Bay* (Salem, Mass.: Essex Institute, 1936).

Josselyn, John. *An Account of Two Voyages to New-England* (London: G. Widdows, 1674).

Kellaway, William. *The New England Company, 1649–1776* (London: Longmans, 1961).

Kimball, Everett. *The Public Life of Joseph Dudley* (London: Longmans, Green, 1911).

Kittredge, George Lyman, ed. *Letters of Samuel Lee and Samuel Sewall Relating to New England and the Indians* (Cambridge, Mass.: John Wilson & Son, 1912).

Knight, Sarah Kemble. *The Journal of Madame Knight* (New York: Peter Smith, 1935).

Konig, David. *Law and Society in Puritan Massachusetts: Essex County, 1629–1692* (Chapel Hill: University of North Carolina Press, 1979).

Lawson, Deodat. *Christ's Fidelity: The Only Shield against Satan's Malignity* (Boston: R. Tokey, 1704).

Littlefield, George Emory. *The Early Massachusetts Press, 1638–1711*, 2 vols. (Boston: Club of Odd Volumes, 1907).

Lovejoy, David S. "Between **Hell** and Plum Island: Samuel Sewall and the Legacy of the Witches, 1692–97," *New England Quarterly* 70 (1997): 355–67.

Lovejoy, David S. "Satanizing the American **Indian**," *New England Quarterly* 67 (1994): 603–21.

Macaulay, Thomas. *History of England from the Succession of James II* (Leipzig: Bernhard Tauchnitz, 1861).

Mather, Cotton. *Decennium Luctuosum* (Boston, 1698).

Mather, Cotton. *Diary*, ed. W. C. Ford, 2 vols. (New York: Frederick Ungar, 1957).

Mather, Cotton. *The Great **Works** of Christ in America: Magnalia Christi Americana*, 2 vols. (Edinburgh: Banner of Truth, 1972).

Mather, Cotton. *Magnalia Christi Americana*, ed. Kenneth B. Murdock (Cambridge, Mass: Belknap Press of Harvard University Press, 1977).

Mather, Cotton. *The Present Deplorable State of **New-England**, with the Many Disadvantages It Lyes Under, by the Male-Administration of Their Present Governour, Joseph Dudley* (Boston: S. Phillips, 1707).

Mather, Cotton. *Rules for the Society of Negroes*, 1693, broadside (Boston: n.p., 1714).

Mather, Cotton. *Small Offers towards the Service of the **Tabernacle** in the Wilderness* (Boston: R. Pierce, 1689).

Mather, Cotton. *Thoughts for the Day of Rain* (Boston: B. Green, 1712).

Mather, Cotton. *Wonders of the Invisible World* (Boston: John Dunton, 1693 [actually 1692]).

Mather, Increase. *An **Arrow** against Profane and Promiscuous Dancing* (Boston: 1684 [actually 1686]).

Mather, Increase. "**Autobiography**" ed. M. G. Hall. *Proceedings of the American Antiquarian Society* vol. 71, no. 2 (1962): 277–360.

Mather, Increase. *Cases of **Conscience** Concerning Evil Spirits Personating Men . . .* (London: John Dunton, 1693 [actually 1692]).

Mather, Increase. *The Doctrine of Divine* Providence Opened *and* Applyed (Boston: Richard Pierce, 1684).

Mather, Increase. *New-England Vindicated* (London: n.p., 1689).

Mather, Increase. *Testimony against Profane Customs* (1687), ed. William H. Peden (Charlottesville: University of Virginia, 1953).

Maule, Thomas. *New-England Persecutors Mauled with Their Own Weapons* (New York: n.p., 1697).

Mayhew, Experience. *Indian Converts: . . . the Lives and Dying Speeches of . . . the Christianised Indians of Martha's Vineyard* (London: S. Gerrish, 1727).

Melville, Herman. *Moby-Dick; or, The Whale* (New York: Modern Library, 2000).

Middlekauff, Robert. *The Mathers: Three Generations of Puritan Intellectuals, 1596–1728* (New York: Oxford University Press, 1971).

Middleton, Richard. *Colonial America: A History, 1585–1776* (Oxford: Blackwell, 1996).

Moore, George H. *Notes on the History of Slavery in Massachusetts* (New York: Appleton, 1866).

Moran, Gerald F., and Maris A. Vinovskis. "The Puritan Family and Religion: A Critical Reappraisal," *William and Mary Quarterly* 39 (1982): 29–63.

Morgan, Edward, ed. *Puritan Political Ideas* (Indianapolis: Bobbs-Merrill, 1965).

Morison, Samuel Eliot. *Builders of the Bay Colony* (Oxford: Oxford University Press, 1930).

Morison, Samuel Eliot. "The Note on the Education of Thomas **Parker** of Newbury," in *Transactions of the Colonial Society of Massachusetts, 1930–1933*, vol. 28 (1932): 261–67.

Morton, Nathaniel. *New-England's Memorial* (Boston: S. Southwick, 1772).

Morton, Thomas. *New English Canaan* (London: Charles Greene, 1637).

Mulliner, John. *A Testimony against Periwigs and Periwig-Making* (Northampton: n.p., 1677).

Murdock, Kenneth B. *Increase Mather* (Cambridge, Mass: Harvard University Press, 1925).

Music in Colonial Massachusetts, 1630–1820, pt. 2: *Music in Homes and Churches*, ed. Barbara Lambert, Publications of the Colonial Society of Massachusetts, vol. 54 (1985).

Neal, Daniel. *The History of New England* (London: J. Clark, 1720).

Nichols, Roger L. *Indians in the United States and Canada* (Lincoln: University of Nebraska Press, 1998).

Nicholson, Adam. *God's Secretaries: The Making of the King James Bible* (London: HarperCollins, 2003).

Norton, Mary Beth. *In The Devil's Snare: The Salem Witchcraft Crisis of 1692* (New York: Alfred A. Knopf, 2002).

Noyes, Nicholas. *New-Englands Duty and Interest* (Boston: Bartholomew Green, 1698).

Palfrey, John Gorham. *History of New England*, 4 vols. (New York: AMS Press, 1966).

Parker, Thomas. *The Visions and Prophecies of Daniel Expounded* (London: E. Paxton, 1646).

Parris, Samuel. *The Sermon Notebook of Samuel Parris, 1689–1694*, eds. James F. Cooper and Kenneth P. Minkema, Publications of the Colonial Society of Massachusetts, vol. 66 (1993).

Penhallow, Samuel. *History of the Wars of New England* (Cincinnati: J. Harpel, 1859).

Perley, Sidney. *History of Salem, Mass.*, 3 vols. (Salem: Sidney Perley, 1928).

Poe, Edgar Allan. *Selected Writings* (Harmondsworth, Engl.: Penguin, 1967).

Pope, Robert G. *The Half-Way Covenant: Church Membership in Puritan New England* (Princeton, N.J.: Princeton University Press, 1969).

Prebble, John. *The Darien Disaster* (Harmondsworth, Engl.: Penguin, 1970).

Psalms [*The Psalms Hymns and Spiritual Songs of the Old* and *New Testament, Faithfully Translated* into *English Metre*] (Cambridge, Mass.: Samuel Green, 1651).

Quincy, Josiah. *The History of Harvard University*, 2 vols. (Cambridge, Mass.: John Owen, 1840).

Ranlet, Philip. "Another Look at the Causes of King Philip's War," *New England Quarterly* 61 (1988): 79–100.

Records *of the Court of Assistants of the Massachusetts Bay*, ed. John Noble, 3 vols. (Boston: Rockwell & Churchill, 1901–8).

Report *of the Record Commissioners of the City of Boston: Boston **Marriages**, 1700–1751* (Boston: Municipal Printing Office, 1898).

Ritchie, Robert C. *Captain Kidd and the War against the Pirates* (Cambridge, Mass.: Harvard University Press, 1986).

Rosenthal, Bernard. *Salem Story: Reading the Witch Trials of 1692* (Cambridge, Engl.: Cambridge University Press, 1993).

Rosenwald, Lawrence. "Sewall's *Diary* and the Margins of Puritan Literature," *American Literature* 58, no. 3 October 1986: 321–41.

Rowlandson, Mary. *Narrative of the Captivity and Restauration of Mrs. Mary Rowlandson* (Cambridge, Mass.: Samuel Green, 1682).

Saffin, John. *A Brief and Candid Answer to a Late Printed Sheet, Entituled, The Selling of Joseph* . . . (Boston: n.p., 1701).

Saffin, John. *His Book* (New York: Harbor Press, 1928).

Salem-Village Witchcraft: A Documentary Record of Local Conflict in Colonial New England, ed. Paul Boyer and Stephen Nissenbaum (Belmont, Calif.: Wadsworth, 1972).

Saltonstall Papers, 1607–1815, ed. Robert E. Moody, *Collections of the Massachusetts Historical Society*, vols. 80 and 81 (1972).

Scheiding, Oliver. "Samuel Sewall and the Americanization of the Millennium," in *Millennial Thought in America: Historical and Intellectual Contexts*, ed. Bernd Engler, Joerg O. Fichte, and Oliver Scheiding, 165–85 (Trier: WVT Wissenschaftlicher Verlag Trier, 2002).

Seasholes, Nancy S. *Gaining Ground: A History of Landmaking in Boston* (Cambridge, Mass.: MIT Press, 2003).

Seaver, Henry Latimer. "Hair and Holiness," *Proceedings of the Massachusetts Historical Society*, 3rd ser., vol. 68 (1946): 3–20.

Seventh Report of the Boston Record Commissioners (Boston: City of Boston, 1881).

Sewall, Samuel. "A **Letter** from Samuel Sewall to his Father," ed. David H. Watters, *New England Quarterly* 58, no. 4 (December 1985): 598–601.

Sewall, Samuel. "**Letters** to the Mathers," in *Collections of the Massachusetts Historical Society*, 4th ser., vol. 8 (1866): 516–17.

Sewall, Samuel. *A Memorial Relating to the Kennebeck Indians* (Boston: n.p., 1721), in Broadsides Collection, Massachusetts Historical Society.

Sewall, Samuel. "Mrs. Mehetabel **Holt**, A Person of Early Piety . . . ," poem (no place or date of publication), Broadsides Collection, Massachusetts Historical Society.

Sewall, Samuel. *Phaenomena quaedam Apocalyptica ad aspectum novi orbis configurata: Some Few Lines Towards a Description of the New Heaven as it Makes to Those Who Stand upon the New Earth* (Boston: Bartholomew Green, 1697).

Sewall, Samuel. *Proposals Touching the Accomplishment of Prophecies* (Boston: Bartholomew Green, 1713).

Sewall, Samuel. *The Selling of Joseph: A Memorial*, ed. with notes and commentary by Sidney Kaplan (Boston: University of Massachusetts Press, 1969).

Shepard, Thomas. *The Church: Membership of Children and Their Right to Baptism* (Cambridge, Mass.: Samuel Green, 1663).

Sibley, John Langdon. *Biographical Sketches of Graduates of Harvard University in Cambridge, Massachusetts*, 3 vols. (Cambridge, Mass.: Charles William Sever, 1873–85), continued by Shipton, Clifford Kenyon, vols. 4–18 (Cambridge, Mass.: Harvard University Press, 1933–75).

Silverman, Kenneth. *The Life and Times of Cotton Mather* (New York: Welcome Rain, 2002).

Slotkin, Richard, and James K. Folsom, eds. *So Dreadfull a Judgment: Puritan Responses to King Philip's War, 1676–1677* (Hanover, N.H.: Wesleyan University Press, 1978).

Smith, Carleton Sprague. "Broadsides and their Music in Colonial America," *Music in Colonial Massachusetts, 1630–1820*, pt. 1: *Music in Public Places*, Publications of the Colonial Society of Massachusetts, vol. 53 (1980): 157–368.

Stannard, David E. *The Puritan Way of Death: A Study in Religion, Culture and Social Change* (New York: Oxford University Press, 1977).

Taylor, Edward. *The Poems of Edward Taylor*, ed. Donald E. Stanford (New Haven, Conn.: Yale University Press, 1977).

Thorowgood, Thomas. *Iewes in America; or, Probabilities That the Americans Are of That Race* (London: H. Broome, 1650). Sewall's annotated copy is in the Boston Public Library, Rare Books and Manuscripts Collection.

Towner, Lawrence W. "The Sewall-Saffin Dialogue on Slavery," *William and Mary Quarterly* 21, 3rd ser. (1964): 40–52.

Twomby, Robert C., and Robert H. Moore. "Black Puritan: The Negro in Seventeenth-Century Massachusetts," *William and Mary Quarterly* 24, 3rd ser. (1967): 224–42.

Ulrich, Laurel Thatcher. *Good Wives: Image and Reality in the Lives of Women in Northern New England, 1650–1750* (New York: Alfred A. Knopf, 1982).

Upham, Charles W. *Salem Witchcraft*, 2 vols. (Boston: Wiggin & Lunt, 1867).

Von Frank, Albert J. "John Saffin: Slavery and Racism in Colonial Massachusetts," *Early American Literature* 29, no. 3 (1994): 254–72.

Ward, Edward. "A Trip to New-England" (1699), in *Five Travel Scripts*, ed. H. W. Troyer (New York: Columbia University Press, 1933).

Whitehill, Walter Muir. *Boston: A Topographical History* (Cambridge, Mass.: Belknap Press of Harvard University Press, 1968).

Whitman, Walt. *Leaves of Grass* (New York: Signet, 1960).

Wigglesworth, Michael [publ. anon.]. *The Day of Doom* (London: np 1666).

Wigglesworth, Michael. *The Diary of a Puritan, 1653–1657*, ed. Edmund S. Morgan (New York: Harper & Row, 1965).

Willard, Samuel. "A Brief Account of a Strange and Unusual **Providence** of God Befallen to Elizabeth Knapp of Groton," in *Remarkable Providences*, ed. John Demos, 358–71 (New York: G. Braziller, 1972).

Willard, Samuel. *The Fountain Open'd; or, The Admirable Blessings Plentifully to Be Dispensed at the National Conversion of the Jews*, 2nd ed. (Boston: B. Green, 1722).

Willard, Samuel. *The High Esteem which God Hath at the Death of His Saints* (Boston: printed by Samuel Green for Samuel Sewall, 1683).

Willard, Samuel. *Some Miscellany Observations on Our Present Debates Respecting Witchcrafts, in a Dialogue between S. and B. by P. and E.* (Boston: Congregational Quarterly, 1869).

Winship, George Parker. *The Cambridge Press, 1638–1692: A Reëxamination of the Evidence Concerning THE BAY PSALM BOOK and the ELIOT INDIAN BIBLE* (Philadelphia: University of Philadelphia Press, 1945).

Winslow, Ola Elizabeth. *Jonathan Edwards, 1703–1758* (New York: Collier Books, 1961).

Winslow, Ola Elizabeth. *Samuel Sewall of Boston* (New York: Macmillan, 1964).

Winsor, Justin. *Memorial History of Boston* (Boston: James Osgood, 1882).

Winthrop Papers. 5 vols. (Boston: Massachusetts Historical Society, 1929–47).

Yazawa, Mel. *The Diary and Life of Samuel Sewall* (Boston and New York: Bedford Books, 1998).

Index

"Both an account of a troubling historical episode and the portrait of a troubled, complex man." —*Wall Street Journal*

The Salem witch hunt has entered our vocabulary as the very essence of injustice. Judge Samuel Sewall presided at these trials, passing harsh judgment on the condemned. But five years later, he publicly recanted his guilty verdicts and begged for forgiveness. This extraordinary act was a turning point not only for Sewall but also for America's nascent values and mores.

In *Judge Sewall's Apology*, Richard Francis draws on the judge's own diaries, which enables us to see the early colonists not as grim ideologues, but as flesh-and-blood idealists, striving for a new society while coming to terms with the desires and imperfections of ordinary life. Through this unsung hero of the American conscience—a Puritan, an antislavery agitator, a defender of Native American rights, and a Utopian theorist—we are granted a fresh perspective on a familiar drama.

"An engrossing biography [that] gives readers insight into the character of colonial America. . . . The author's gifts as a writer are evident."
—ST. LOUIS POST-DISPATCH

"Before the eighteenth-century Founding Fathers came the seventeenth-century New England Puritans. They were a strange and wonderful tribe, bewitched or otherwise. In this superb study, Francis brings them back to life."
—JAMES GRANT, AUTHOR OF *JOHN ADAMS: PARTY OF ONE*

HARPER ● PERENNIAL
www.harperperennial.com

History
ISBN-13: 978-0-00-716363-2
ISBN-10: 0-00-716363-0

51595

9 780007 163632

EAN

USA $15.95 Canada $20.50

0806

Cover design by Mary Schuck
Cover paintings: top © Peabody Essex
Museum, Salem, Massachusetts / Bridgeman Art
Library; bottom © Massachusetts Historical Society,
Boston, Massachusetts / Bridgeman Art Library